D1072288

The New
CAMBRIDGE
English Course

TEACHER

3

INTERMEDIATE

MICHAEL SWAN
CATHERINE WALTER

CAMBRIDGE
UNIVERSITY PRESS

w/o

Published by the Press Syndicate of the University of Cambridge
The Pitt Building, Trumpington Street, Cambridge CB2 1RP
40 West 20th Street, New York, NY 10011–4211, USA
10 Stamford Road, Oakleigh, Victoria 3166, Australia

© Michael Swan and Catherine Walter 1992

First published 1992

Cover design by Michael Peters & Partners Limited, London
Typeset by Goodfellow & Egan Ltd, Cambridge
Printed in Great Britain by Redwood Press Limited, Melksham,
  Wiltshire

ISBN 0 521 37667 X Teacher's Book 3
ISBN 0 521 37639 4 Student's Book 3
ISBN 0 521 37651 3 Practice Book 3
ISBN 0 521 37663 7 Practice Book 3 with Key
ISBN 0 521 37671 8 Test Book 3
ISBN 0 521 37504 5 Class Cassette Set 3
ISBN 0 521 37508 8 Student's Cassette 3

Authors' acknowledgements

We are grateful to all the people who have helped us
with this book. Our thanks to:
- The many people whose ideas have influenced our
  work, including all the colleagues and students from
  whom we have learnt.
- Those institutions, teachers and students who were
  kind enough to comment on their use of The
  Cambridge English Course, and whose suggestions
  have done so much to shape this new version.
- The Cambridge University Press representatives and
  agents, for their valuable work in transmitting
  feedback from users of the original course.
- Diann Gruber, Tom Hinton, Clare Moore, Ramón
  Palencia and Lelio Pallini, who were kind enough to
  read and comment on the typescript; their perceptive
  suggestions and criticisms have resulted in substantial
  improvements.
- Desmond O'Sullivan, of ELT Publishing Services, for
  his most helpful advice and criticism at all stages of
  the project.
- The people who agreed to talk within range of our
  microphones: Janice Burton, Andrew and Tricia
  Carver, Class I at Chilton County Primary School,
  Elaine and Peter Hemsley, John Peake, Alexandra
  Phillips, Anthony Robinson, June Walmsley, Sue
  Ward, and Jane and Keith Woods.
- Steve Hall of Bell Voice Recordings, Jonathan Dykes
  and Robert Campbell, and all the singers and
  musicians: for doing a wonderful job on the songs.
- Peter Taylor of Taylor Riley Productions Limited,
  Peter and Diana Thompson, Andy Tayler and Leon
  Chambers of Studio AVP, and all the actors and
  actresses: they made recording sessions seem easy and
  created an excellent end product.
- Randell Harris for his exceptional skill, creativity and
  dedication in designing the book and in choosing and
  directing the illustrators; and to the illustrators
  themselves for their talent and their willingness to
  work to an exacting brief.
- Annie Cornford, for her professionalism and skill as
  our sub-editor.
- Barbara Hately Broad, for the thoughtfulness and
  accuracy of her invaluable secretarial assistance.
- Mark Walter Swan, Helen Walter Swan, Inge Bullock
  and June Walmsley for their readiness to be of help at
  all stages of the project.
- Colin Hayes and Peter Donovan of Cambridge
  University Press, whose confidence and support have
  made the author-publisher relationship so
  unproblematic.
- And finally Catherine Boyce and Nick Newton of
  Cambridge University Press, for their efficient, patient
  and unruffled management of a complicated editorial,
  design and production process.

Contents

v

Map of Book 3

	Grammar	**Phonology**
	Students learn or revise these grammar points	Students work on these aspects of pronunciation
Block A	Present and past tenses: terminology, formation and use; non-progressive verbs; infinitives and -ing forms after verbs; -ing forms after prepositions; -ing forms as subjects; verb + object + infinitive; modal auxiliaries; distancing use of past tenses; reported statements and questions.	Problems with sound/spelling relationships; perception and pronunciation of unstressed syllables; stress and rhythm; decoding rapid speech; /əʊ/ and /ɒ/.
Block B	Present Perfect for reporting 'news'; can with verbs of sensation; tenses of there is; use of -ing forms for activities; imperatives; comparative structures: worse and worst ; question tags; position of prepositions in questions and relative structures; leaving out object relative pronouns; building sentences with conjunctions and -ing forms; adverbials of degree; so do I, neither do I etc.	Stress and rhythm; /ə/ in unstressed syllables; vowel and consonant linking; intonation of question tags; /ð/ and /θ/.
Block C	Simple Past and Past Progressive; Simple Past tenses with as; Present Perfect Progressive; passives; hypothetical if-clauses with Simple Past and would; modal verbs, including will have to; should(n't) and must(n't); won't for refusals; infinitive of purpose; how to ...; imperative; by ...ing; two-word verbs.	Stress and rhythm; perception and pronunciation of unstressed syllables; stress for emphasis and contrast; weak and strong forms; initial consonant groups; final consonant groups; difficult pronunciation/spelling relationships.
Block D	Present Perfect Simple and Progressive; have to and modal verbs; modal verbs with perfect infinitives; past conditionals; reporting with infinitives; would you rather ...?; frequency adverbs; connecting adverbs and conjunctions; prepositions of movement.	Stress and rhythm; word stress; perception and pronunciation of unstressed syllables; assimilation of consonants and linking; vowel linking with /r/, /j/ and /w/; /ɪ/ and /iː/; /ɜː/ and /eə/; pronunciations of the letter o.
Block E	Past Progressive: use and pronunciation; will-future; it'll and there'll; passive infinitives after modal verbs; contractions; reported speech with would and had; position of frequency adverbs; use of noun, verb or adjective to express the same idea; word order: verb, object and adverb; verbs with two objects; punctuation.	Stress and rhythm; pronunciation of contractions; /h/; typical pronunciations of vowel letters; weak forms.

Functions and specific skills

Topics and notions

Students learn or revise ways of doing these things

Students learn to talk about

Requesting and giving personal information; making and replying to requests and offers; making corrections; reporting; asking to be reminded; asking about English; expressing degrees of formality; seeing a text as a whole; skimming; reading and listening for specific information; guessing unknown words; using dictionaries; managing discussion; predicting.

Physical appearance; food and drink; weather; animals; wishes, hopes and ambitions; language and language learning; sports, games and leisure; proportion (e.g. *three out of twelve*); various time relations.

Giving advice and instructions; giving news; asking for personal information; asking for confirmation and agreement; expressing opinions; indicating shared and divergent opinions; evaluating; agreeing and disagreeing; asking for things without knowing the exact words; defining, describing and identifying; comparing; greeting and welcoming; operating mealtime conventions; leave-taking; reporting; building up and shaping narratives; dividing text into paragraphs; listening for gist and for specific information.

Likes and dislikes; news; emergencies; parts of a car; honesty; manipulations of objects and materials; processes; condition; obligation; purpose; method; degree; time relations: simultaneous and successive events.

Discussing problems and giving advice; giving instructions; dealing with misunderstandings; making and accepting formal and emphatic apologies; expressing opinions; making complaints; studying text structure; constructing narrative; guessing unknown words; using dictionaries; listening and note-taking.

Work and time-structuring; electrical appliances; household tips; families; boy- and girlfriends; problems with relationships; politics and authority; rules and regulations; driving and traffic regulations; obligation; purpose; method; processes; changes; various time relations.

Speculating about the past; criticising past behaviour; reporting instructions and advice; asking for and giving directions; asking about and expressing preferences; persuading; discussing illness; extracting the main ideas from a text; reading and listening for detail; guessing meaning from context; writing simple reports; writing personal letters.

Places and landscape; buildings and rooms; families; family relationships; games-playing; illness; crime; rules and regulations; obligation; frequency; spatial relations; movement; various time relations; driving.

Making and replying to requests and offers; predicting; reporting; asking for things without knowing the exact words; inviting and replying to invitations; expressing degrees of formality; scanning; listening for detail.

Weather; everyday objects; uses of objects; horoscopes; clothes and accessories; parts of the body; wildlife and conservation; the future; simultaneous past actions.

Introduction

The nature and purpose of the course

This is Level 3 of *The New Cambridge English Course*, a four-level course designed for people who are learning English for general practical or cultural purposes. The course generally presupposes a European-type educational background, but with some adaptation it can be used successfully with learners from other cultural environments. The course teaches British English, but illustrates other varieties as well.

Level 3 is for intermediate students. In order to begin this level they should be able to understand and produce English well enough to handle a variety of everyday situations and topics (around the level of the Council of Europe's 'Threshold' level). Level 3 can be used to follow on from *The New Cambridge English Course 2* or any other elementary course. There is systematic revision work for students who still have problems with basic structures. Used as suggested, the book will take students up to a point where they have a good all-round working knowledge of English, and will be ready to start preparing for an examination such as the Cambridge First Certificate.

The approach in Level 3 is different from that of many intermediate courses. Features which may be new to your students include:
- multi-syllabus course organisation
- wide variety of presentation methodology
- mixture of factual and fictional topics
- opportunities for student choice
- emphasis on systematic vocabulary learning
- regular pronunciation and spelling work
- some use of authentic listening material
- deliberate inclusion of some 'too difficult' material (see *Basic principles*)
- active and varied 'communicative' practice.

These points are dealt with in more detail in the following sections.

Basic principles

The pedagogic design of Level 3 of *The New Cambridge English Course* reflects the following beliefs.

Intermediate learners

Intermediate language learners often have different backgrounds, problems, priorities and learning styles, so materials must be wide-ranging and flexible. Day-by-day improvement is not so obvious as at lower levels, and students need interesting short-term goals to maintain motivation. Many intermediate students prefer activities where progress or performance is easily measurable (e.g. grammar practice or tests). A course must however include other kinds of work where progress is less visible, and must help students to see the value of such activities. At this level, systematic skills practice is particularly important – intermediate students generally know much more English than they can use.

Respecting the learner

People generally learn languages best when their experience, knowledge of the world, interests and feelings are involved, and a course must allow students to 'be themselves' as fully as possible. But not everybody learns in the same way, and not everything can be taught in the same way. A course must provide fiction as well as fact; role play as well as real communication activities; personal as well as impersonal discussion topics; learner-centred as well as teacher-centred activities. Course material should not be childish and patronising, and it is worth remembering that the best classroom humour generally comes from the students, not from the textbook.

The language: multi-syllabus course design

A complete English language course will incorporate at least eight main syllabuses:
- **Vocabulary:** students must acquire a 'core' vocabulary of the most common and useful words in the language, as well as learning more words of their own choice.
- **Grammar:** basic structures must be learnt and revised.
- **Pronunciation** work is important for many students. Learners need to speak comprehensibly and to understand people with different accents speaking in natural conditions (not just actors speaking standard English in recording studios).
- **Notions:** students must know how to refer to common concepts such as *sequence*, *contrast* or *purpose*.
- **Functions:** learners must be able to do such things as *complaining*, *describing*, *suggesting* or *asking for permission* in English.
- **Situations:** a course must teach the stereotyped expressions associated with situations like *dinner parties*, *returning defective goods to shops*, *going to the doctor's* or *dealing with emergencies*.
- **Topics:** Students need to learn the language used to talk about subjects of general interest. The coursebook should include some controversial and emotionally engaging material, rather than sticking to bland, middle-of-the-road, 'safe' topics.
- **Skills:** learners need systematic practice in both receptive and productive skills. Reading and listening work will include some authentic interviews and texts, as well as specially written material.

How important is grammar?

Some students (for example examination candidates) may need a high level of grammatical correctness, and Level 3 provides systematic teaching and revision of all important structures. For many other intermediate students, however, skills development and vocabulary growth may be at least as important as grammar. (Vocabulary mistakes tend to outnumber grammar mistakes by more than three to one.) At this level, students have learnt most of the basic grammatical structures of English, and other aspects of language take on more importance. Students often feel that a lesson with no new grammar in 'doesn't teach anything'; they must learn not to judge their progress simply by the number of new structures taught.

'Learning' and 'acquisition'

Most people seem to learn a foreign language more effectively if it is 'tidied up' for them. This helps them to focus on high-priority language and to see the grammatical regularities.

However, learners also need to encounter a certain amount of 'untidy' natural language (even if this seems a bit too difficult for them). Without some unstructured input, people's unconscious mechanisms for acquiring language may not operate effectively.

A course should cater for both these ways of approaching a language (sometimes called 'learning' and 'acquisition' respectively). The occasional use of unsimplified authentic materials may require a change in learner expectations: many students and teachers are used only to texts in which every new word and structure has to be explained and learnt.

Methodology

– **Communicative practice:** where possible, language practice should resemble real-life communication, with genuine exchanges of information and opinions. Pair and group work can greatly increase the quantity and quality of practice.
– **Input and output; creativity:** students generally learn what they use and forget what they don't use. Lessons should lead up to genuine conversations, role play or writing activities in which students use creatively what they have learnt. If they can use their new language to entertain, inform or amuse each other, so much the better.
– **Error** is a natural part of learning, and over-correction can destroy confidence. Some learners will need a high level of accuracy, but very few will ever be perfect. Students' achievements should not be measured negatively (by how far away they are from perfection), but positively (by how successfully they can use the language for their own purposes).
– **Regularity and variety** need to be carefully balanced. If all the lessons are constructed in the same way, a course is easy but monotonous. Variety makes lessons more interesting, but too much variety can make material more difficult for teachers to prepare and for students to get used to.
– **Study and memorisation** are necessary, for most learners, for really thorough learning.
– **Learning and acquisition** should both be catered for.
– **The mother tongue**, if it can be used, can help to make explanations faster and more precise. The same is true of bilingual dictionaries, and students should practise their use.

Knowing where you are

Students can easily get lost in the complicated landscape of language study. A course must supply some kind of 'map' of their language-learning, so that they can understand the purpose of each kind of activity, and can see how the various lessons add up to a coherent whole. Regular revision should be provided, helping students to place the language items they are learning into the context of what they already know.

The organisation of the course

The material at each level includes a Student's Book, a Teacher's Book and a set of three Class Cassettes (for classwork); a Practice Book, with or without Key (for homework); an optional Student's Cassette containing selections from the Class Cassette Set (for home use); and an optional Test Book for teachers.

Student's Book 3 contains 70 to 100 hours' classwork (depending on the students' mother tongue, the way their classes are organised, where they are studying, whether they use the Practice Book, how strong their motivation is, their previous experience of English and various other factors). During this time students will revise basic material, learn new language forms and their uses, and practise receptive and productive skills.

Five blocks Level 3 of *The New Cambridge English Course* consists of five blocks. Each block is made up of eight numbered lessons, followed by a three-part consolidation section. A lesson generally provides enough work for an hour and a half upwards (depending on the learners' speed, motivation and previous knowledge).

General-purpose lessons The first, third, fifth and seventh lessons of a block are 'general-purpose' topic- or function-based lessons; work on grammar, pronunciation, vocabulary and skills leads up to communicative exchanges, discussions, dramatisations or writing exercises related to the theme of the lesson.

'Focus on Systems' lessons The second and sixth lessons in each block focus on language systems – points of grammar, vocabulary and pronunciation which have been selected for special attention. Teachers will choose exercises from these lessons according to the needs of their classes.

'Skills Focus' lessons The fourth and eighth lessons of each block provide training in particular aspects of listening, reading and writing skills.

Consolidation section After each block of eight lessons, there follow a **Summary** (which displays the language learnt in the block), a **Revision and Fluency Practice** section (with a wide choice of extra fluency activities), and a **Test**.

Sequence of lessons Each of the five blocks therefore contains the following sequence of lessons:

1. topic- or function-based lesson
2. focus on systems
3. topic- or function-based lesson
4. skills focus
5. topic- or function-based lesson
6. focus on systems
7. topic- or function-based lesson
8. skills focus
9. summary
10. revision and fluency activities
11. test

Grammar Revision Section At the end of the Student's Book, on pages 116–129, there is a Grammar Revision Section. This can be used to revise and reinforce points of basic grammar which should have been learnt at earlier stages, but which may have been forgotten or incompletely mastered. The exercises are designed for class use; the Teacher's Book gives guidance as to what revision activities may be appropriate for any given lesson.

Additional reference material Also at the back of the Student's Book there is an index of the vocabulary taught and revised in the course, with phonetic transcriptions; a guide to the phonetic symbols used; and a list of irregular verbs. At the back of the Practice Book there is a systematic 'Language Summary' which sets out all the structures taught at this level. The Teacher's Book also contains an index to the structures, functions and notions contained in the course.

Using the course

(Many teachers will of course know very well how to adapt the course to their students' needs. These suggestions are meant mainly for less experienced teachers who are unfamiliar with this approach.)

Preparation
You may need to prepare the first lessons very carefully in advance, until everybody is used to the approach. Later, less work should be needed – the teacher's notes will guide you through each lesson.

Choice
You don't have to do all the lessons in the book, or to do them in the 'right' order. (But if you drop a lesson, check that you don't 'lose' vital language material.)

Leave out exercises that cover points of language which your class don't need.

Don't do an exercise if you or your students really dislike it. (But don't leave out a strange-looking activity without giving it a try!)

Don't force a lesson on your students if it bores everybody; find another way to teach the material. But don't automatically drop a topic because it makes people angry – rage can get people talking!

The 'Focus on Systems' lessons are not meant to be worked through from beginning to end. Each of them deals with several separate points which can be taught as and when necessary.

The five 'Revision and Fluency Practice' lessons contain a wide choice of activities. These can be done at any time; it is probably best to spread selected activities out over the course, rather than working through them systematically when you come to the end of each block.

Timing
Motivated students should average an hour and a half or more per lesson. (Some lessons will of course go more quickly or more slowly than others.) The book should take a minimum of 70 hours to complete (plus any time spent on tests, homework correction etc.). If you don't have that much time, you will need to look through the book in advance and decide what to leave out. It is better to do part of the course thoroughly than to rush through all of it without giving students time to use and assimilate what they have learnt.

Learner expectations and learner resistance
Students have their own ideas about language learning. Up to a point, these must be respected – individuals have different learning strategies, and will not respond to methods which they distrust. However, learners sometimes resist important and useful activities which do not fit in with their preconceptions, and this can hinder progress. So you may have to spend time, early in the course, training students in new attitudes to language learning. Problems are especially likely to arise over questions of grammar and correction (students may want too much), over the use of authentic materials and over exercises involving group work.

Authentic recordings
The course contains some 'real life' recordings of conversations, interviews and other material. These teach vocabulary, stimulate discussion and train learners to understand natural speech (in a variety of accents). Students may not understand every word of what they hear. THIS DOES NOT MATTER! They need to experience some language which is beyond their present capacities – this happens in natural language learning all the time. (You can help by sometimes talking naturally in English about your interests, events in your life etc.)

Discourage students from asking for complete transcriptions and explanations of long recordings – this is not usually an efficient use of time.

Tapescripts and recording symbols
Tapescripts are provided in the Teacher's Book. Exercises using authentic recordings are marked ▣ᴬ. Exercises using scripted recordings are marked ▣ where the recording must be used, and ▣ where the exercise can be done without it.

Vocabulary learning
Words and expressions to learn or revise are listed at the end of each lesson. You may need to suggest techniques of learning new vocabulary. Some possible approaches are for students to:
- copy new words with their translations into a special notebook. Cover the words and try to recall them from the translation.
- note English-language explanations or examples of the use of new words. Write more examples.
- keep 'vocabulary diaries', listing new words under subject/grammatical headings (e.g 'verbs of movement'; 'professions'). Revise occasionally by trying to write from memory as many words as possible from the list.

Different people learn best in different ways – but for most students, some systematic vocabulary study is necessary.

Summaries and tests
You may need to show students how to use the Summary lessons. They should spent time, with you or on their own, looking at the material and studying the grammar, functional exponents and other language items. Encourage them to look back at the previous lessons to see exactly how the new items are used.

The Test lesson which finishes each block covers the language from the previous eight lessons. It is meant to give students and teacher an idea of how well the material has been assimilated. Only use those parts of the test that cover material important to your students. Don't worry if your students prepare the test in advance and get it all right – this is an extremely effective form of revision. If you wish to administer unseen tests as well, the Test Book provides a parallel test at the level of each Test in the Student's Book.

Practice Book
The Practice Book is an essential part of the course. It provides a choice of consolidation and revision exercises, together with regular work on reading and writing skills; it also includes activities using the Student's Cassette. Together with the fluency activities sections, the Practice Book ensures that students integrate current learning with areas previously covered and get additional opportunities for skills development. A 'with Key' version of the Practice Book contains answers to the exercises, where appropriate, if you wish your students to work on a self-study basis.

The Practice Book also includes a 'Language Summary': a concise summary of all the grammar points covered in Level 3 of the course.

Student's Cassette
The Student's Cassette consists of a selection of material from the Class Cassette Set, comprising all the recordings for the listening exercises in the Practice Book as well as the songs. Motivated learners who have the time can thus make active use of the Student's Cassette at home.

Supplementing the course
The course is relatively complete, and it should not need much supplementation if students are at the right level. Some extra work may be needed on problem points for speakers of particular languages. And of course, the more extra reading, listening and speaking students can do – in or out of class – the better. A circulating class library of supplementary readers can be useful.

Comments
The New Cambridge English Course, as a completely revised edition of a very successful course series, has had the benefit of the best sort of piloting programme – thousands of teachers have used the original edition over several years, and their feedback has helped us to shape the present version. But improvements are always possible, and we would be delighted to hear from users. Letters can be sent to us c/o Cambridge University Press (ELT), The Edinburgh Building, Shaftesbury Road, Cambridge CB2 2RU, Great Britain.

Michael Swan   Catherine Walter   December 1991

A1 Something in common

Requesting and giving personal information; asking for help; correcting misunderstandings; writing skills: description; listening skills: listening for gist; spelling and pronunciation.

1 Labels:

1. Write three words on a piece of paper that say something about you. Add a drawing if you want. Example:

engineer
skiing
cooking

2. Put the paper on yourself and look round you, reading labels and trying to find someone whose label has something in common with yours (if you can't, just find someone who looks nice!).
3. Interview the person, asking as many questions as you can – at least five questions about each word on the label. Make notes to help you remember the answers.

2 Find another pair of students, or report to a group. You and your partner should say everything you have learnt about each other from Exercise 1. You can ask your partner for help if you want. You can stop your partner if some of the information he or she gives is not correct. Useful expressions:

Asking for help:
I can't remember – what did you ...?
Can you remind me: why did you leave ...?
Where did you go ...?

Correcting your partner:
Er, that's not quite right.
Well, I didn't exactly ...
Excuse me, I didn't mean ...

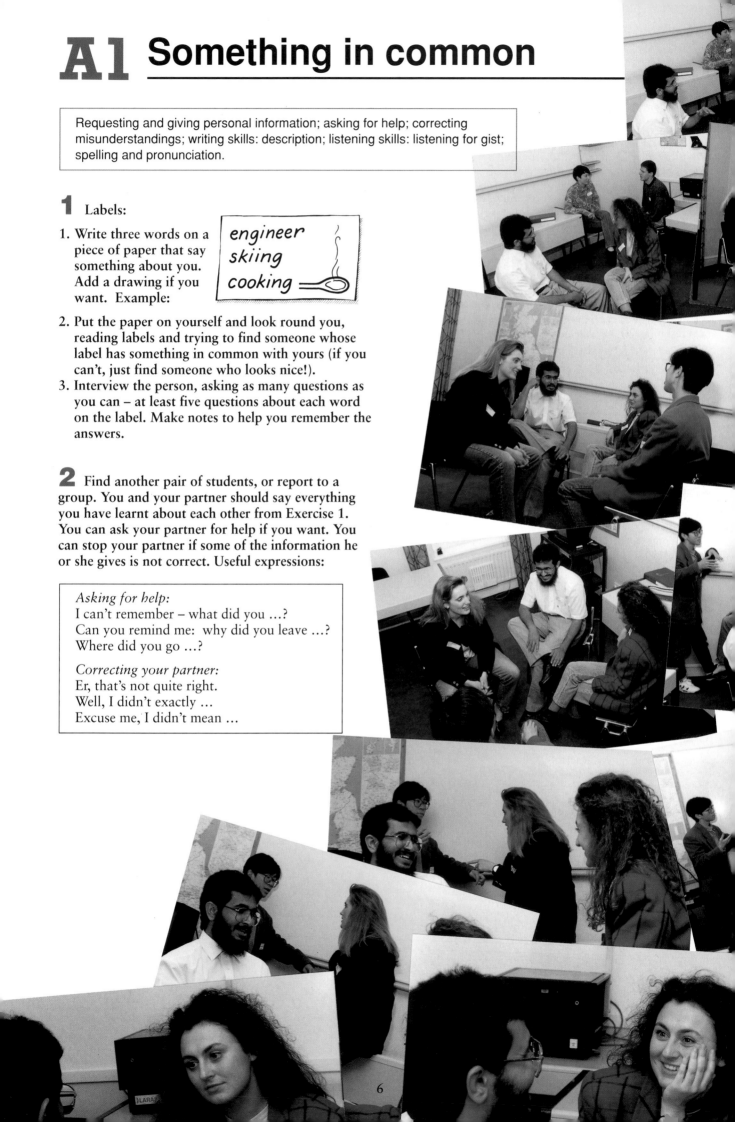

Lesson A1

Students practise requesting and giving personal information; they learn ways of asking for help and of interrupting to correct; they practise writing skills (descriptions) and listening skills (listening for gist).
Phonology: spelling/pronunciation correspondences.

Possible problems

Exercise types Some students may not be used to walking round the classroom talking to other students in English, with the teacher's role being that of informant and facilitator. If this is the case for some or all of your students and you do plan to have them walk round, you may want to explain briefly at the beginning of the lesson that this sort of exercise will give them opportunities to try and communicate in the English they have, and will help them outside the classroom. If you think that a class of adolescents may give you discipline problems until they are used to this sort of exercise, you may want to get them to do Exercise 1 without moving from their desks, and to do Exercise 2 in groups of six or more. If they know they will have to report before they do Exercise 1, there will be more pressure to find out information so they can be ready to report it to the group.

If you are short of time

Ask students to do Exercises 3 and 5, and/or Exercise 4, for homework. If they have the Student's Cassette, ask them to do Exercise 6 for homework.

Materials needed

You will need some small (about 10cm by 10cm) pieces of card or paper, one for each student and one for yourself, plus some means of attaching them to people's clothing: pins or tape.

Test Book recording

A recording for the Entry Test in the Test Book precedes this lesson on the Class Cassette.

1 Finding out about other students

• This exercise serves as an 'ice-breaker' for the class, and allows classes who do not know each other to begin to make acquaintance. It also helps you to get a general idea of the fluency and accuracy of the students.
• Distribute small pieces of card or paper and demonstrate to students what they are to do by making your own label or drawing one on the board. Your label should have three words or expressions, and some drawings if you wish, that say something about you as a person.
• Ask students to make their own labels. Walk round while they are doing this to give any help that is needed and to distribute tape or pins so that they can put their labels on themselves.
• Ask them to look round at the other students they can see without moving from their desks, or (ideally) to walk round the room. Each student should read the others' labels, trying to find someone whose label has something in common with theirs – or someone whom they like. Explain that when they have chosen partners they must ask each other as many questions as they can think of, at least five questions for each word or expression on the label. They should make notes to help them remember the answers. Give a time limit, say ten minutes, for this part of the exercise (you can always extend this if students seem to need more time).

• Walk round while they are working to note the levels of fluency and accuracy. You may wish to note any commonly recurring mistakes for later work.

2 Reporting, correcting, asking for verification

• Explain that students are going to report on what they have learnt about each other, and that the reporter can ask for help if he or she forgets something. Likewise the person who is being talked about can interrupt to correct wrong information.
• Go over the expressions in the box; make sure students understand them, and get them to practise saying them.
• Each pair of students from Exercise 1 should then choose another pair of students to report their findings to. So Student A from Pair 1 reports to Pair 2 what she has found out about Student B from Pair 1, and so on. (See *Possible problems* for potentially unruly classes.)

6

3 Vocabulary work

• Get the students to work in groups of three or four to try and add as many more words as they can to each list.
• Walk round while they are working to give any help that is needed.

Possible answers to Exercise 3
1. *Weight*: slim, overweight, plump
2. *Height*: short, of medium height
3. *Eyes*: blue, green, grey, small
4. *Hair*: long, brown, black, fair/blonde, grey, white, wavy, straight
5. *Other*: plain, handsome, good-looking, attractive

4 Spelling and pronunciation

• Let students work individually for a few minutes to decide which word in each group is pronounced with a different vowel sound from the others. Then let them compare their answers in pairs before you play the recording for them to check their answers.
• Let them practise saying the words, after you or the recording.

Answers to Exercise 4
1. *learnt* /lɜːnt/ is different (the others are pronounced with /eə/)
2. all words are pronounced with /ɜː/
3. *weight* /weɪt/ is different (the others are pronounced with /aɪ/)
4. all words are pronounced with /ɔː/
5. *said* /sed/ is different (the others are pronounced with /eɪ/)
6. *teach* /tiːtʃ/ is different (the others are pronounced with /ɪ/)
7. in most British dialects, all words are pronounced with /e/ (but Americans and people from the North of England tend to say /eɪt/ for *ate*)

5 Writing a description

• Tell students they are each to write a description of the person they interviewed in Exercise 1, as if describing her or him in a letter to a friend or family member.
• Tell them to start with a physical description using words and expressions from Exercise 3. Then they should go on and relate in an organised way all the information they found out in Exercise 1.
• Walk round while they are working to give any help that is needed.
• As students begin to finish, they can exchange papers to read. When everyone has finished you may wish to put the descriptions on the wall or notice board to give everyone a chance to read them.
• If you correct the papers, take care to say positive things about the content and overall organisation of the work as well as pointing out language mistakes.

6 Song: *Private Detective*

• Ask students to work in pairs or groups of three. They should look at the illustration for one minute; then each student should pick a different person in the illustration to describe to the others (without saying which person he or she is describing). The others should try to guess which person is being described.
• Then tell the students that they are going to hear a song in which two of the people in the picture are being described. Their task is to guess which two.
• Play the song once through. Let students compare notes in their groups. Walk round while they are doing this. If a few groups aren't sure, or there are a lot of wrong answers, play the recording again before discussing the answers with the students.

• When you do ask students to tell you which people are described, they should do so by telling you where the people are in regard to objects and other people in the picture, what they are doing, etc. – not just by pointing at them.
• Let the students turn to page 130 in their book and play the recording again, answering any questions the students may have about meaning.

Practice Book exercises
1. Word order in questions; giving true answers to some of the questions.
2. Vocabulary revision: 'odd word out'.
3. Reading a text and completing another one.
4. Student's Cassette exercise (Student's Book Lesson A1, Exercise 6). Students listen to the song and write down all the adjectives.
5. Recreational reading: a poem and a magazine article.
6. Extended writing: comparing oneself with someone else.

Pair and group work; walk-round exercises
Many of the exercises in the course suggest that students work together in pairs or groups, or move round the classroom talking to each other. Except in very small classes this is essential; it is the only way that students can get enough speaking practice to learn the language successfully. However, students may not be used to work of this kind, and you may need to introduce them to it gradually. With some classes (particularly with teenagers) it may be better to avoid full-scale walk-round exercises at the beginning. Instead, get students to talk to as many people as they can without moving from their seats.

In activities where more than one student is speaking at a time, teachers sometimes worry about the fact that they cannot listen to and correct everybody. This loss of control should not be seen as a problem. It is very important to do practice which bridges the gap between totally controlled exercises (where everything is checked) and real-life communication (where nothing is checked). In pair work and group work, you can supervise just as many people as you can in fully controlled exercises (i.e. one at a time); meanwhile, the people you are not supervising also get useful fluency practice. Even if some students take the opportunity to waste time or lapse into their own language, there will still be far more people practising English during this kind of work than when students answer questions one at a time.

3 Vocabulary: people's appearance. Add as many words to each category as you can.

1. *Weight*: thin, ...   4. *Hair*: short, red, curly, ...
2. *Height*: tall, ...   5. *Other*: pretty, ...
3. *Eyes*: big, brown, ...

4 📼 Look at these words. Many of them come in this lesson. In each group, do all four words have the same vowel sound or is one word different? Decide, check your answers with the recording, and practise saying the words.

1. hair   wear   learnt   where   5. said   weight   paper   say
2. curly   word   learnt   heard   6. big   pretty   thin   teach
3. eyes   height   right   weight   7. red   ate   went   said
4. tall   short   draw   talk

5 Write a short report about the person you interviewed in Exercise 1. Start with a physical description. Then give the information you learnt about the person. Pass your description to another student or let your teacher put it up for students to read.

6 📼 Song. Look at the picture. Which people are being described in the song?

Learn/revise: hair; eyes; height; weight; remember; remind; (hair:) grey, fair, red, black, brown, curly, wavy, straight, long, short; (eyes:) big, small, brown, blue, green, grey; short; tall; of medium height; thin; slim; overweight; pretty; plain; handsome; attractive; good-looking; general; I can't remember – what ...?; Can you remind me: why ...?; Er, that's not quite right; Well, I didn't exactly ...; Excuse me, I didn't mean ...

7

A2 Focus on systems

A choice of exercises: rules for the use of tenses; pronunciation of unstressed syllables; word-families.

GRAMMAR: USE OF TENSES

1 Do you know the names of the English present and past verb tenses? Try to match the examples with the names (there is more than one example of some tenses).

1. It *rains* nearly every day in winter.
2. When we were children, we usually *went* to the seaside for our summer holidays.
3. I *have* often *thought* of changing my job.
4. She was tired, because she *had been travelling* all day.
5. I *asked* her to come out for a drink, but she *was working*, so she couldn't.
6. Do you know that Phil *has written* a novel?
7. 'You look hot.' 'I*'ve been playing* tennis.'
8. It*'s raining* again.
9. I *live* in Manchester, but I*'m staying* with my sister in Glasgow at the moment.
10. When he *spoke* to me, I realised that I *had seen* him before.
11. He*'s been* to East Africa several times, so he speaks quite good Swahili.
12. Who *were* you *talking* to when I came in?
13. I*'m seeing* a lot of Mary these days.

A Simple Present
B Present Progressive
C Simple Past
D Past Progressive
E (Simple) Present Perfect
F Present Perfect Progressive
G (Simple) Past Perfect
H Past Perfect Progressive

... every day in winter.

2 Look at diagram A. It shows three different uses of the Simple Present Perfect tense. Which sentences from Exercise 1 are illustrated in the three parts of the diagram? Look at diagram B. Which tense does it illustrate? Can you make a similar diagram for one of the other tenses?

A

PAST – –×– –×– –×– –×– –×– –×– –×– –×– –×– –×– NOW
events repeated up to now

PAST – – –×– — RESULT → NOW
past events with a result now

PAST – – – – –×– — NEWS → NOW
past events that are still 'news'

B

PAST – –×– – – – – – – – – – –×– – – – NOW
'second', earlier past

8

Lesson A2

Grammar: rules for the use of present and past tenses.
Phonology: the perception of unstressed syllables.
Vocabulary: four lexical fields.

Note: 'Focus on systems' lessons
It is not necessary to work through 'Focus on systems' lessons continuously from beginning to end. The different sections of these lessons ('Grammar', 'Vocabulary' etc.) are generally separate and self-contained; teachers should choose the sections and exercises that are useful to their students and do them when it is convenient.

Language notes and possible problems
Use of tenses: revision   Students should by now be able to construct and use most English verb tenses without too much difficulty. This lesson concentrates on helping them to gain a conscious understanding of the rules for present and past tenses. Students who still make elementary mistakes in this area should do the appropriate exercises in the Grammar Revision Section at the back of the Student's Book.

---

1 Names of tenses
• It can be useful for students to know the names of the different English tenses. This makes it easier for them to get a mental picture of the tense system, and also simplifies discussion of grammar in class.
• Let students try the exercise individually at first before comparing notes in groups.
• Note that there exist different versions of the names of some tenses: for example 'Present Progressive' or 'Present Continuous', 'Simple Past' or 'Past Simple'.

Answers to Exercise 1
  1. Simple Present
  2. Simple Past
  3. (Simple) Present Perfect
  4. Past Perfect Progressive
  5. Simple Past; Past Progressive
  6. (Simple) Present Perfect
  7. Present Perfect Progressive
  8. Present Progressive
  9. Simple Present; Present Progressive
10. Simple Past; (Simple) Past Perfect
11. (Simple) Present Perfect
12. Past Progressive
13. Present Progressive

2 The uses of the tenses
• This is likely to be useful to some students, but not everybody is receptive to diagrams, and there will probably be some people who don't get much out of the exercise.
• Let students discuss the first and second parts of the question in groups. If they respond well to it, they could go on to try to produce their own tense diagrams for one or more of the other tenses.

Answers to Exercise 2
Diagram A illustrates sentences like numbers 3, 11 and 6 (in that order) in Exercise 1.
Diagram B illustrates the Simple Past Perfect.

3 The uses of the tenses (continued)

• This exercise can be done individually or by class discussion, as you prefer.

Answers to Exercise 3
1. Simple Present
2. Simple Past (or *used to*)
3. (Simple) Present Perfect
4. Past Progressive (or Simple Past to talk about a series of actions)
5. Present Perfect Progressive (... *because I've been playing football*)
6. Past Perfect Progressive
7. (Simple) Present Perfect; or Simple Past with time-reference

4 Exceptions

• Discuss the two exceptions round the class, asking different students for their views.
• See if students can think of any other non-progressive verbs. (Examples: *hear, remember, understand, like*.)

Answers to Exercise 4
Both *want* and *know* are non-progressive verbs – they are not normally used in progressive forms. Simple tenses are therefore used in situations where progressive forms of other verbs would be normal. (Compare *I want to go home* and *He's asking to go home*; *How long have you known Debbie* and *How long have you been seeing Debbie*.)

5 Test on the use of tenses

• This helps students to see whether there are still any gaps in their knowledge of tense use. It is probably best if they do the exercise individually in writing.
• You can use the Grammar Revision Section at the back of the book if students still have difficulty with any points.

Answers to Exercise 5
1. 'Cigarette?' 'No, thanks. I *don't smoke*.'
2. What *are you doing* in my room?
3. I've had a postcard from Ann. She says they *are having* a great time in Canada.
4. He told me *he's getting married* next year, but *I don't think* it's true.
5. '*Have you been* here before?' 'No, it's my first visit.'
6. I *have been waiting* for Jill to phone since six o'clock.
7. 'Why is your hair all wet?' 'I *have been swimming*.'
8. *Have you heard*? John *had* an accident yesterday.
9. He *was driving* down High Street when the car in front of him *suddenly stopped*.
10. When she came in I asked her where she *had been*, but she wouldn't tell me.

6 Hearing unstressed syllables: 'How many words?'

• Unstressed syllables in English are usually pronounced quickly and quietly. Vowels in these syllables are nearly always 'reduced': they are pronounced either /ə/ or /ɪ/, and not as they are written. Because of this, many students find the unstressed syllables of natural spoken English difficult to perceive and 'decode'. The problem is especially acute for students who speak languages (like Spanish) in which all syllables are normally pronounced clearly and with 'full' vowels. This exercise focuses students' attention on unstressed syllables.
• Play the recording, stopping after each sentence, and ask students just to say how many words they think they hear. Play the sentence again once or twice if necessary, and see if students can begin to tell you the words. Finally, get them to say the sentences with the same rhythm as the recording.
• This is a good kind of exercise to do regularly with students who have difficulty understanding spoken

English. You can easily make up your own sentences: they should contain only words that the students know, and include plenty of unstressed auxiliaries, prepositions and similar 'grammatical' words. It is important to say the sentences reasonably fast with a natural rhythm.

Tapescript and answers to Exercise 6
1. What sort of house do you live in? (8)
2. Can you tell me where there's a cheap hotel? (10)
3. I'd like to know what she was talking about when I came in. (14)
4. Could you give me one or two pieces of paper? (10)
5. This film's a lot better than the one we went to last week. (14)
6. Do you speak any other languages? (6)
7. Are you doing anything interesting at the weekend? (8)
8. Have you ever been up in a helicopter? (8)
9. I don't think any of them know what they're doing. (12)
10. I've got enough work to keep me busy for the next week or two. (15)

7 Lexical fields

• This is an easy introduction to systematic vocabulary study. It can be done individually or in groups, as you prefer. Let students/groups compare and discuss their solutions before you give them the answers.

Answers to Exercise 7
Animals: bear, camel, elephant, horse, mouse, rabbit, rat, squirrel
Food and drink: butter, carrot, chop, flour, lemon, lettuce, orange juice, pineapple
Parts of the body: cheek, chin, hip, moustache, stomach, thumb, toe, tongue
Weather: cloud, fog, hail, lightning, snow, sunshine, thunder, wind

8 Vocabulary extension

• Get students to do the exercise first of all without dictionaries, simply pooling their knowledge in groups.
• When they have done this, tell them to use their dictionaries to find out the English for a *few* more words that they really want to know, spending not more than five minutes. (There is no point in students writing long lists of words if they are not going to learn them.)

Practice Book exercises
1. Revision of vocabulary from the Student's Book lesson.
2. Revision of irregular verbs.
3. Putting in the correct tense (mixed tenses).
4. Writing questions for answers.
5. Recognising words from their dictionary definitions.
6. Recreational reading: *Strange but true!*
7. A choice of extended writing tasks: a description of Maria (see Exercise 4); a poem.

Practice Book work
Students' progress through the course will depend very much on the amount of work they do outside the class. However successful the lessons appear to be, most students will forget much of what they have learnt unless they do more practice, revision and reading in their own time. Make sure that your students do regular work from the Practice Book. Most of this can be self-corrected with the answer key (if your students have the *with Key* edition), so Practice Book work need not involve a very heavy correction load for the teacher.

The Practice Book provides a wide choice of work for different purposes, and few students will do all the exercises. You will probably suggest about two exercises per lesson, though some students may need more.

9

3 Which tenses would you choose for the following situations?

1. to talk about one of your habits
2. to talk about one of your childhood habits
3. to give news of a success in an examination
4. to answer a question about your movements at midday yesterday
5. to explain that you are tired because of a game of football
6. to explain that you were tired yesterday evening because of a game of football
7. to say that you can't go dancing because of an accident

4 Can you explain these two exceptions?

1. I **want** to go home.
   (~~I'm wanting to go home.~~)
2. How long **have** you **known** Debbie?
   (~~How long have you been knowing Debbie?~~)

When we were children …

5 Test yourself. Choose the right tenses for the following sentences. If you have problems, you may need to do some of the grammar revision exercises from pages 116–129.

1. 'Cigarette?' 'No, thanks. I *don't smoke / I'm not smoking*.'
2. What *do you do / are you doing* in my room?
3. I've had a postcard from Ann. She says they *have / are having* a great time in Canada.
4. He told me *he gets married / he's getting married* next year, but *I don't think / I'm not thinking* it's true.
5. '*Have you been / Were you* here before?' 'No, it's my first visit.'
6. I *am waiting / have been waiting* for Jill to phone since six o'clock.
7. 'Why is your hair all wet?' 'I *swam / have swum / have been swimming*.'
8. *Did you hear? / Have you heard?* John *had / has had* an accident yesterday.
9. He *drove / was driving* down High Street when the car in front of him *suddenly stopped / was suddenly stopping*.
10. When she came in I asked her where she *was / has been / had been*, but she wouldn't tell me.

PRONUNCIATION: HEARING UNSTRESSED SYLLABLES

6 📼 Listen to the recording. How many words do you hear in each sentence? (Contractions like *don't* count as two words.)

VOCABULARY: WORD-FAMILIES

7 Can you divide these words into four groups, and give each group a name?

bear	butter	camel	carrot	cheek
chin	chop	cloud	elephant	flour
fog	hail	hip	horse	lemon	lettuce
lightning	mouse	moustache		
orange juice	pineapple	rabbit	rat	
snow	squirrel	stomach	sunshine	
thumb	thunder	toe	tongue	wind

8 Choose one of the groups. Work with other students, and see how many words you can add. (Time limit five minutes.)

Learn/revise: *the vocabulary in Exercise 7.*

A3 Would you like to have ...?

Expressing wishes and hopes; spoken and written reports; verbs with infinitives and -ing forms; reported speech; pronunciation of /əʊ/ and /ɒ/; looking at vocabulary learning.

1 Work in small groups. Without using a dictionary, see how many names of jobs you can think of in English. Use a dictionary to add ten more useful words to your list. Exchange lists with another group. Do you know all their words?

2 📼 Read the text and try to guess what words might go in the blanks. Then listen to the recording and see if you were right.

Twenty five-year-old children from a British primary school class were asked what they wanted to be when they grew up. The answers were varied and interesting. Seven of the children had medical ambitions – there were four future ......1......, one ......2......, one ......3...... and one 'air force doctor'. Two children wanted to be ......4...... – not very surprising, as the school is in a small country village. Two of the children obviously liked school: they wanted to be ......5....... One child said he would like to be an ......6......, one hoped to be a ......7...... driver and one had decided to become a fisherman. Of the rest, two did not know what they wanted to be, and four gave rather unexpected answers.

3 What do/did you want to be or do in life? Write three or more sentences (using some of the following structures) and give them to the teacher. Then try to guess whose sentences the teacher is reading.

> I want(ed) to be ...
> I want(ed) to study ...
> I want(ed) to ...
> I hope to ...
> I would like/love/hate to ...
> I would like to start / stop / keep on ...ing
> I expect to ...
> My parents/teachers want(ed) me to ...
> and I still want to
> but I changed my mind
> My parents don't/didn't mind what I do/did.
> I think I have a good chance (of ...ing)
> I don't think I have much chance.
> When I leave school, I'll ...
> I think/hope I'll ...
> When I retire, I'm going to ...

10

Lesson A3

Students learn and revise ways of expressing wishes, hopes and intentions; practise elementary report-writing skills; discuss vocabulary-learning strategies.
Principal structures: verbs followed by infinitives and *-ing* forms; *want* + object + infinitive; elementary reporting.
Phonology: /əʊ/ and /ɒ/.

Language notes and possible problems

1. *Would like* and *want* Both of these occur in the lesson. You may need to point out that they have similar meanings, but that *would like* is less definite than *want* (and is often used in requests for that reason). Note that *would like* is not used to mean *wanted* (except in reported speech: see Exercises 2 and 6).

2. Infinitives and *-ing* forms Several common **verb + infinitive** structures are practised in this lesson; note also the use of *-ing* forms after *start, stop* and *keep on* (Exercise 3). Lesson A6 gives systematic work on infinitives and *-ing* forms.

3. Object + infinitive Structures like *My parents **wanted me to be** a doctor* or *I **would like my children to go** to university* are idiomatic to English: most languages do not have similar structures. Students are likely to find them difficult, and to make mistakes like * *My parents wanted that I ...* Lesson A6 has more work on this point.

4. Present tense with future reference Some students may want to use future verb forms in *when*-clauses referring to the future (e.g. * *When I will leave school, I will ...*). For practice on this point, see Grammar Revision Section page 123.

5. Reported speech You may want to point out the use of past tenses after past reporting verbs, even when referring to things that are still true (as in Exercise 2, and in the list of 'useful structures' in Exercise 6). Note that *would like* does not have a past form, and does not therefore change after past reporting verbs. Students who still have difficulty with elementary reporting structures should do the revision exercises on pages 124–125.

6. 'False friends' *Expect* (Exercise 3) is a false friend for speakers of some romance languages, and may be confused with *wait for/to*. There is a similar problem with *sensible* (Exercise 5) – some students may think it means the same as *sensitive*.

If you are short of time
Exercise 6 could be dropped.

1 Vocabulary expansion
• In this exercise, students pool their knowledge of vocabulary.
• After they have made and exchanged lists, you may like to combine everybody's contributions into one big list on the board.

2 Listening: what children want to be when they grow up
• Tell students that they are going to listen to a class of five-year-olds saying what they want to be when they grow up. Ask students to guess what the children will say. You may need to supply vocabulary.
• Get students to read the paragraph and discuss possible answers. If necessary, help them to see how the context gives clues to what is said (ask them what they expect to follow the reference to 'medical ambitions').

*An asterisk (*) marks an unacceptable or doubtfully acceptable utterance.

• Play the recording two or three times and explain any difficulties.

Tapescript for Exercise 2
'What do you want to be when you grow up?'
'A man.'   'A nurse.'   'A fisherman.'   'Somebody who works.'   'A dad.'   'An actor.'   'A car.' (!)   'A farmer.'
'I don't know.'   'Don't know.'   'A nurse.'   'A nurse.'
'A farmer.'   'An air force doctor.'   'A train driver.'
'Dentist.'   'A teacher.'   'A nurse.'   'A teacher.'
'A vet.'

Answers to Exercise 2
1. nurses   2. dentist   3. vet   4. farmers
5. teachers   6. actor   7. train

3 Students' ambitions
• Go over the structures, giving any explanations that are necessary (see *Language notes*).
• Ask students to write at least three sentences each on a sheet of paper, using some of the structures provided. They shouldn't write their names on the papers.
• Walk round while they are working to give any help that is needed.
• Collect the papers, shuffle and number them.
• Then either read them out yourself or pass them out for students to read aloud. (It doesn't matter if a student gets his/her own paper.)
• The number should be read, followed by the three sentences.
• Students write down the number followed by the name of the person they think wrote the sentences.
• When they have finished, call out the numbers and ask the writer of each paper to identify him/herself.

4 Pronunciation: /əʊ/ and /ɒ/

- Let students try this by themselves (individually or in groups) first of all. Then play the recording or say the words, giving them a chance to revise their answers if they want to.
- Go over the answers and practise pronouncing the words in the two groups. It may help students to pronounce /əʊ/ if they first practise the two separate parts of the vowel: the first part is pronounced like the end of *mother* and the second part like the end of *too*.
- There is more work on the pronunciation of /əʊ/ in Lesson A6.

Answers to Exercise 4

GROUP 1/əʊ/	GROUP 2/ɒ/
no	not
open	often
don't	gone
go	got
grow	job
hope	lost
know	on
most	stop
over	want
road	what
won't	

The word that doesn't belong is *one* /wʌn/.

Optional extra activity: mime

- Not all students are prepared to do mime exercises, but it is worth encouraging them to try. As well as being fun, mime is a useful way of setting up an 'information gap'.
- Tell students that they must think of something they would like to do, be or have, and act it for the class without using words. The other students must try to guess what it is that they want.
- Give them a minute or two to prepare, and then call for volunteers.
- As the class guess what is being mimed, they should begin their sentences with 'I think he/she wants / would like ...'.

5 Survey

- Look over the examples, and make sure students can manage the 'short answer' structures *Yes, I would, No, I wouldn't* and *I'd love/hate to.*
- Look through the expressions in the box and clear up any difficulties.
- Ask students to suggest some things that could be added to the lists in the box.
- Get them to prepare three questions (preferably one with *have*, one with *be* and one with another verb). Encourage them to include at least one idea that is not in the list.
- When students are ready, get them to talk to some of their neighbours asking each other their questions and noting the answers; or put them in groups of six or so to do the exercise. In more mature classes, this can be done as a 'walk-round' exercise with students talking to as many others as time allows.

6 Reports

- After students have finished their survey, look through the instructions for Exercise 6. Make sure students understand and can use the 'useful structures'. Point out the use of a singular verb form (e.g. *wants*) after *everybody, nobody* and *hardly anybody*, and the use of *they* to refer to *nobody*, even though *nobody* is

singular. You may also want to look through the grammar reference box on reported speech that is printed after the lesson material.
- Weaker students can simply write a few sentences. Encourage stronger students to give their paragraphs a bit of 'shape', using the one in Exercise 2 as a model if they wish.

7 Noting and learning vocabulary

- At this level, vocabulary expansion is a crucial priority for most students. Learners need efficient methods of noting down new vocabulary, and of learning what they have noted. It is important to spend time discussing this with the class.
- Get students' ideas, either by a general class discussion or by group discussion; this can be in the students' mother tongue if convenient. Add whatever comments and suggestions you have yourself.
- It is important for students to realise that not all words can be explained in the same way. Ways of noting information about vocabulary include:
  – writing the word with a translation
  – writing the word with a mother-tongue explanation
  – writing the word with an English explanation (useful formulae include *the same as ...; like ...; the opposite of ...; a kind of ...; the place where ...; the thing/stuff you use for ...ing; a person who ...*)
  – writing the word with examples of its use
  – writing the word with a drawing
  – writing the word with grammatical notes (e.g. *followed by infinitive*).
- You may like to discuss the relative value of bound notebooks, looseleaf notebooks and card-indexes (well-motivated students can carry cards around with them and learn vocabulary at odd moments).
- Although vocabulary is best learnt by using it appropriately, most students will need to back up their language exercises with some learning by heart. Here, too, it is worth discussing alternative approaches.

Practice Book exercises

1. Vocabulary revision: jobs.
2. Student's Cassette exercise (Student's Book Lesson A3, Exercise 4). Practising the pronunciation of /əʊ/ and /ɒ/.
3. Matching captions to cartoons.
4. Ordering the sentences in a text; paragraphing.
5. Writing a few sentences about personal wishes and hopes.
6. Writing a few sentences about how personal wishes and hopes have changed.
7. Extended writing: a letter to Father Christmas (Santa Claus).

4 🔲 Put the words into the two groups and practise pronouncing them. One word does not belong in either of the groups.

GROUP 1 /əʊ/   GROUP 2 /ɒ/

no   not
open   often
...   ...

don't	go	gone	got	grow	hope
job	know	lost	most	on	one
over	road	stop	want	what	won't

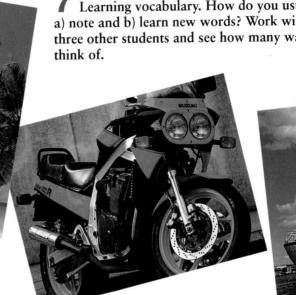

5 Survey. Choose three of the things in the box (or think of three other things) and ask some other students if they would like them. Examples:

'*Would you like to have a silver Rolls-Royce?*'
'*Yes, I would.*'

'*Would you like to be famous?*'
'*No, I certainly wouldn't.*'

'*Would you like to stay in bed all day?*'
'*I'd love/hate to.*'

to have:	more money a different job
	more free time a better love-life
	(more) children more patience
	your picture in a magazine
	political power a different house/flat
	more friends a private plane
	a silver Rolls-Royce a big motorbike
	two wives/husbands
to be:	famous an artist three years old
	more sensible
to:	stay in bed all day live to be 100
	speak a lot of languages travel a lot
	own a museum

6 Write a short report giving the results of your survey. Use some words and expressions from Exercise 2. Other useful structures:

Three people out of six want ...
One person would like ...
Everybody/Nobody would like / wants ...
(Almost) everybody
Hardly anybody
The only exception was ..., who would like ...
Most people said they would like / wanted ...
Nobody said they wanted ...
One person said he/she would like ...

When you have finished your report, show it to other people in the class.

7 Learning vocabulary. How do you usually like to a) note and b) learn new words? Work with two or three other students and see how many ways you can think of.

Reported speech. Compare:
– Three people **want** to be doctors.
  Three people **said** they **wanted** to be doctors.
  (~~... said they want to be doctors.~~)
– I **hope** to go to university.
  Annette **said** she **hoped** to go to university.
– What **do you want** to be?
  Twenty children **were asked what they wanted** to be. (~~... what did they want to be.~~)
– Phil **would like** to be a painter.
  Phil **said** he **would like** to be a painter.

Learn/revise: actor; artist; dentist; driver; farmer; husband; job; nurse; chance; country; exception; free time; magazine; motorbike; parents; patience; power; primary school; village; wife (wives); change one's mind; expect; grow up (grew, grown); keep on ...ing (kept, kept); leave school (left, left); (don't) mind; own; retire; famous; unexpected; varied; rather.

11

SKILLS FOCUS
SKILLS FOCUS
SKILLS FOCUS
SKILLS FOCUS
SKILLS FOCUS
SKILLS FOCUS

A4 Who should be paid most?

Reading and guessing unknown words; discussion.

1 Read the following text carefully, and try to get a general idea of what it says. Think about the meaning of the words and expressions that you don't know, but DO NOT use a dictionary or ask questions.

WORK AND PAY IN FANTASIA

I had a thought-provoking dream last night. In it, I was living in Fantasia – a place where people are paid according to their real value to society. There are some striking mismatches with what happens in other countries.

In Fantasia, doctors are paid for keeping people alive. A doctor is well rewarded as long as his or her patients stay healthy. But when a patient falls ill, the doctor's pay is reduced by half; and if a patient dies, the doctor has to pay massive compensation to the surviving spouse or relatives. Average life expectancy in Fantasia is 132, although doctors tend to die young.

Soldiers are paid on the same lines as doctors. In peacetime they get a reasonable wage, but as soon as war breaks out the government stops paying them. Officers earn far less than ordinary soldiers, and generals get least of all. This is because of the Fantasian principle that power is its own reward: people can have either money or power, but Fantasians avoid giving them both. Members of the House of Long Sentences (the Fantasian Parliament) get expenses payments, but no salary; the Prime Minister gets the least generous expenses.

Teachers' pay is worked out according to their teaching ability (pupils vote), their pupils' test results and the level at which they teach. On average, primary school teachers get double the pay of secondary school teachers, who in turn are wealthy by comparison with university teachers.

Housewives or househusbands receive a basic salary from the state, plus an extra 16,500 Fantasian Grotniks (about $4,500 US) annually for each small child in the family.

People who do dirty, strenuous, dull or distasteful work (e.g. rubbish collectors, coal miners, factory workers or sewage workers) are at the top of the Fantasian wages scale. Other highly-paid workers include gardeners (Fantasians like looking at flowers), hospital nurses and librarians. Among the poorest-paid workers are advertising agents, TV weather forecasters, traffic wardens and bank managers. Pop singers, who are all employed by the state, are paid starvation wages and allowed to give one concert a year (Fantasians don't like listening to loud noises).

The best-paid people in Fantasia are writers.

Guess what I do for a living.

Reading skills: guessing unknown vocabulary.
Speaking skills: discussion.

Language notes and possible problems
Guessing unknown words (Exercises 2 and 3)
Some students are thrown off balance when they meet words that they don't know (especially if they are used to the kind of language course in which everything is explained). Worrying about unknown vocabulary can distract students from paying attention to the overall meaning of what they are reading or listening to, and this makes their comprehension less efficient.

It can help to make anxious students more confident if they realise how easy it can be to guess the meaning of an unknown word. There are two kinds of clue.
1. The *context* often makes it clear what a word must mean. For instance, if a text says that doctors are *paid* for keeping people alive, and that a doctor is well *rewarded* as long as his or her patients stay healthy, it's not difficult to guess that *rewarded* means *paid* in this context.
2. The *form* of a word sometimes suggests its meaning. (For example, if students are trying to understand the expression *life expectancy* it helps if they notice the similarity between *expectancy* and *expect*.) Students who speak languages related to English (especially romance languages) should look out for similarities with mother-tongue words, though meanings are rarely exactly the same.

When students are working on Exercise 3, encourage them to look for clues of these kinds.

Note that the vocabulary itself is not very important in Exercises 2 and 3 – students must understand that they are learning a strategy, not words. Discourage them from spending a long time finding out the exact meanings of all the new vocabulary; the words which are likely to be useful at this stage are listed in the box at the end of the lesson, and the others are probably best ignored for the time being.

If you are short of time
Exercise 5 could be dropped.

---

1 Introductory reading
• Students have two tasks: to get a general idea of the meaning of the text, and to think about what the unknown words and expressions might mean. They should realise that the first will help with the second: if they pay attention to the overall meaning, they are more likely to make sensible guesses about particular items.
• When they have read through the text, get them to close their books and tell you anything they remember (not necessarily in logical sequence).

2 Introduction to guessing: choosing sensible alternatives

• Give students a few minutes to work alone, and then get them to compare notes with each other.
• When you go over the answers, ask students if they can say what clues help to show the meaning of each word or expression.

Answers to Exercise 2

1b: This is the only answer that really makes sense in the context; speakers of romance languages should also have noticed the similarity between *provoke* and a related mother-tongue word.
2c: This is the obvious answer: the whole text is about *differences* between Fantasian approaches to pay and those common in real countries.
3a: See note above in *Language notes*.
4b: The contrast with *But when a patient falls ill* strongly suggests that *healthy* must be the opposite of *ill*.

3 Guessing practice

• Make sure students understand what is meant by *the highlighted words or expressions*.
• Tell them that they are not expected to work out the exact meanings of the words and expressions, or even to get close to all of them – what is required is simply intelligent guesses, using the clues in the text.
• Give them plenty of time to choose items to guess, think about them and discuss them with other students.
• When they are ready, go through the expressions with the class and discuss the clues to the meaning of each one.
• Give students credit for wrong guesses, if these are sensible – somebody who thinks that *surviving* means *sad* or that *strenuous* means *dirty* may be making an intelligent guess after thinking hard about the words and looking at all the clues.
• You may like to finish by discussing the value of this kind of exercise. Help students to see how it will help their reading; make sure they see that the important thing is the *strategy* of guessing unknown words, not the meanings of the particular words that came up in the exercise.
• Get students to try guessing unknown words in other texts that they meet during their course.

4 Discussion

• The important thing here is the task – students have to work towards *an agreed group answer*, even if this does not reflect their own individual feelings. Having to do this will focus the discussion and give students a clear reason for talking.
• In a class with little experience of discussion, you may need to give some support. Put on the board some useful expressions like *What do you think?*, *I (don't) agree*, *Yes, but …* and so on.
• When all or most groups are ready, get them to tell the class about their lists.
• This exercise is adapted from *Discussions that Work* by Penny Ur (Cambridge University Press 1981).

5 Short talks

• Students will probably need a few minutes to prepare before giving their talks.
• Talks can be given either to the whole class or in smaller groups.
• When everybody has spoken, get the class (or groups) to vote for the most convincing speaker.

Practice Book exercises

1. Choosing between the infinitive and the -*ing* form.
2. Vocabulary and grammar: completing a text.
3. Deciding what is important in a job.
4. Revision of prepositions.
5. Recreational reading: sayings about money and work.
6. Reading skills (deducing meaning from context); writing a 'recipe for making millions'.

Correctness and correction
Fluency practice activities (like Exercises 4 and 5) work best if the students are allowed to talk without being corrected. Mistakes which seriously impede communication are worth dealing with on the spot, but anything else should be noted for attention later or ignored. Teachers sometimes feel (and students may encourage them to feel) that they are not doing their jobs unless they correct every mistake. This is quite unrealistic: casual correction has very little effect on students' accuracy, and too much correction can have a disastrous effect on their confidence. During fluency practice activities, it is much more constructive to pick out a limited number of high-priority errors to be dealt with by systematic work at another time.

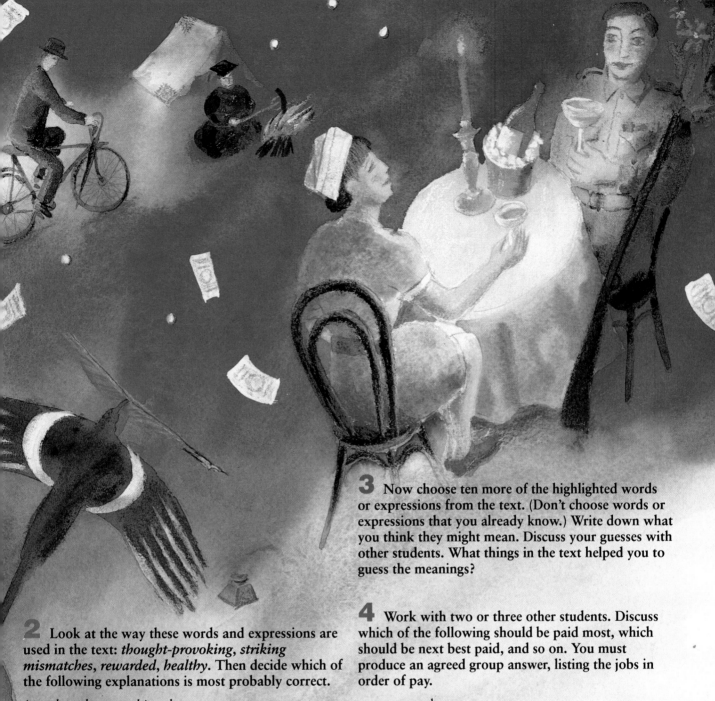

2 Look at the way these words and expressions are used in the text: *thought-provoking, striking mismatches, rewarded, healthy*. Then decide which of the following explanations is most probably correct.

1. *a thought-provoking dream*
   a. an intelligent dream
   b. a dream that made me think
   c. a frightening dream
   d. a dream that was full of thoughts

2. *there are some striking mismatches*
   a. people don't strike so often
   b. there are frequent contacts
   c. there are some very interesting differences
   d. there are some important things that are the same

3. *a doctor is well rewarded*
   a. doctors get plenty of money
   b. people think doctors are important
   c. plenty of people go to see doctors
   d. doctors are well trained

4. *healthy*
   a. satisfied with the way the doctor treats them
   b. well
   c. ill
   d. well paid

3 Now choose ten more of the highlighted words or expressions from the text. (Don't choose words or expressions that you already know.) Write down what you think they might mean. Discuss your guesses with other students. What things in the text helped you to guess the meanings?

4 Work with two or three other students. Discuss which of the following should be paid most, which should be next best paid, and so on. You must produce an agreed group answer, listing the jobs in order of pay.

army general
rubbish collector
government minister
head of large factory
hospital nurse
policeman/policewoman
primary school teacher

5 Choose a job, and talk for two minutes giving reasons why your job should be the best paid one in the country.

Learn/revise: ability; coal miner; concert; dream; expenses; factory; gardener; head (= boss); level; minister; nurse; peace; policeman (policemen); policewoman (policewomen); power; primary school; rubbish; salary; society; soldier; value; wage; war; work; earn; guess; tend; vote; average; extra; full; generous; healthy; reasonable; annually; double; according to; (far) less; least.

A5 Language: what matters most

Speaking and writing skills practice; thinking about language and language learning; asking about English.

1 Find out something new about English. Ask at least one question, using one of the following structures.

What does … mean?
What's this?
What are these?
What's this called in English?
Is this a pen or a pencil?
How do you say … in English?
What's the English for …?
What do you say when …?
Can you explain this word/expression/sentence?
How do you pronounce …?
How do you spell …?
Is this correct: …?

2 Language learning – what is important to you? Write your answers to the two following questions and give your answers to the teacher.

1. What is your main reason for learning English (in one sentence)?
2. How important is each of the following to you? Give each activity a number from 1 (unimportant) to 5 (extremely important).

speaking
understanding spoken English
writing
reading

Lesson A5

Students practise speaking and writing skills: they discuss their reasons for learning English, the aspects they want to concentrate on, and their views on methodology.
Principal structures: direct and reported questions.

Language notes and possible problems
1. Direct and reported questions As students interview each other in Exercise 3, they will need to convert the reported question structures on the questionnaire (e.g. *Find out how important each of the following is*) into direct questions (e.g. *How important is each of the following?*). This should help to remind them of the rules. If they have serious trouble with the word order, you may need to spend some time on the relevant exercises in the Grammar Revision Section at the back of the book.
2. Relevance This lesson may not have very much to say to secondary school students for whom English is a compulsory (and not necessarily very welcome) subject. If you feel it is likely to flop, drop it. (On the other hand, consulting students about their views on language teaching – see Exercise 5 – might be good for motivation.)
3. Mother tongue With weaker one-language classes, you might want to let students use their mother tongue for some of the discussion work in Exercises 5 and/or 6.

If you are short of time
Exercise 6 could be dropped.

1 Asking about English

• Students may not know how to ask in English about meaning, spelling, pronunciation etc.
• Give them a few minutes to think of a question (encourage them to ask about things they really want to know).
• Get them to ask their question, and answer them briefly. Look out for the common mistake *What means ...?*
• Encourage stronger students to ask more than one question.
• Tell them that if they have questions about English in future they should use these structures.

2 Students' priorities

• Give students a few minutes to answer the two questions. Encourage them to be honest – if they are totally uninterested in English, it's best if they say so. They should write their answers on a separate sheet of paper which they can hand in. Try to get them to distinguish between the importance of different skills, rather than just saying that everything is extremely important.
• When they are ready, get them to put their names on the papers and hand them to you. These will help you to get a reliable view of the class's priorities and attitude to English.

3 The questionnaire

- Look through the first two or three questions in the 'speaking' section with the class. Ask how they would express these questions in an interview, and make sure they can manage the change from reported to direct speech without serious grammatical mistakes.
- Tell students to look quickly through the rest of the questionnaire and to ask you if they have any problems.
- Then put them in pairs. Each student in turn should interview the other, asking questions from the section which corresponds to the interviewee's top priority, and noting the answers.

4 Writing reports

- Ask students to write short reports on what they have found out. Make it clear that this is not just a language exercise: they will be giving you information that will help you to plan your teaching effectively.
- When the reports are ready, collect them in.

5 Discussion: language teaching methods

- Students are likely to have their own opinions about how they can best learn languages. These may well not be very well-informed or realistic, but it is probably a good thing to bring everything out into the open, so that you and the students can get a better understanding of each other's point of view.
- In each group, one of the students will need to be the 'secretary', making notes on what is said. The discussion should end up with a list of suggestions which can either be handed to you or read out.
- When you have listened to or read the students' suggestions, tell them what you feel yourself (if possible, without dismissing the students' views as 'wrong').
- It is probably a good thing to come back to these questions from time to time during the course, explaining the reasons for your choice of methods, activities and materials, and getting reactions and suggestions from the students.

6 Students' lessons

- If you have suitable students who are prepared to volunteer to try a language lesson, this can be an extremely interesting and instructive activity. Students are likely to end up with a better understanding of the difficulty of language teaching, and an increased respect for their teacher. (On the other hand, even an experienced teacher can often learn something from his/her students' attempts to teach a language.)
- Volunteer teachers will need to prepare their lessons at home, and perhaps to discuss them with you before they start. However, it's best if they make their own decisions about methods rather than adopting yours.
- If you have a lot of 'teachers', do the activity in groups.

Practice Book exercises

1. Making questions.
2. Reporting questions and answers.
3. Revision of articles.
4. Ways of describing things: *a 30p stamp*.
5. Ways of describing things: *a stamp that costs 30p*.
6. Recognising and distinguishing sentence rhythm.
7. Recreational reading: Goldwynisms; English obsessions with the weather; *Strange but true!* (languages).

Supplementation

For most students, the course should need little supplementation (though specific nationalities may need some extra work on particular grammar or pronunciation problems). However, no coursebook can give students enough exposure to the spoken or written language, and students will only learn English successfully if they do supplementary reading and listening.

A good way to give a class extra listening practice is to chat to them casually, for a couple of minutes in every lesson or so, about anything that comes into your head – your childhood, your family and friends, your education, what you did yesterday, or anything else you feel like talking about. There is no need to make this an 'exercise' with comprehension questions; what you say will be interesting enough in itself to make students concentrate.

As regards reading, a good approach is to provide a circulating class library of supplementary readers at the right level. You will need one copy each of as many different titles as you have students, with one or two extras. The books should preferably be chosen mainly for their interest rather than for their cultural value. Again, this activity should be as undemanding as possible, with little or no school-type work attached. You could perhaps require, for example, that a student simply write a very short comment after reading a book, saying what it was about and what he/she enjoyed (or did not enjoy) about it. In less motivated classes you may want to give a guideline time for students to finish each book.

3 Read quickly through the questionnaire. Then do section A, B, C or D.

LANGUAGE PRIORITIES QUESTIONNAIRE

A SPEAKING

Interview a student for whom speaking is important. Find out:
1. How important (1–5) each of the following is: a) natural speed b) a correct accent c) good grammar d) a wide vocabulary.
2. In which countries he/she expects to speak English, and with what kinds of people.
3. If he/she expects to speak English mostly with native speakers (e.g. British, Australian or American people) or mostly with non-native speakers.
4. If he/she expects to use English mostly for business or professional purposes, for travel, for social contacts, or for other reasons (what?).
5. If he/she expects to use English: a) in ordinary conversation b) on the telephone c) in meetings d) to give lectures or demonstrations.
6. What subjects he/she wants to be able to talk about in English.
7. If he/she needs to know the specialist vocabulary of any subjects (which?).
8. If he/she finds it especially difficult to speak English (and if so, why).
9. If he/she has any other information to give you.

B UNDERSTANDING SPOKEN ENGLISH

Interview a student for whom understanding spoken English is important. Find out:
1. How important (1–5) it is to understand each of the following: a) conversations b) phone calls c) TV/radio d) songs e) lectures f) other things (what?).
2. What accents he/she needs to understand.
3. If he/she needs to know the specialist vocabulary of any subjects (which?).
4. If he/she finds it especially difficult to understand spoken English (and if so, why).
5. If he/she has any other information to give you.

C WRITING

Interview a student for whom writing is important. Find out:
1. How important (1–5) each of the following is: a) correct spelling b) correct grammar c) a wide vocabulary.
2. What he/she wants to be able to write in English (business letters, personal letters, examination answers, academic essays, professional papers/reports, ...?).
3. What subjects he/she wants to be able to write about.
4. If he/she needs to know the specialist vocabulary of any subjects (which?).
5. If he/she finds it especially difficult to write English (and if so, why).
6. If he/she has any other information to give you.

D READING

Interview a student for whom reading is important. Find out:
1. How important (1–5) each of the following is: a) fast reading b) exact understanding of every word c) a wide vocabulary.
2. What kind of things he/she expects to read in English (newspapers, novels, letters, reports, technical manuals, ...?).
3. What subjects he/she expects to read about.
4. If he/she finds it especially difficult to read English (and if so, why).
5. If he/she needs to know the specialist vocabulary of any subjects (which?).
6. If he/she has any other information to give you.

4 Write a short report about the student you interviewed, and give it to the teacher. This will help him/her to plan a suitable English course for the class.

5 Work in groups of three or four. In each group, choose one of the activities (speaking, understanding spoken English, writing or reading). Discuss good ways of learning to do this activity better, and write some suggestions for the teacher. Ask for help if necessary.

6 If you speak a language that the other students don't know, prepare and give a short lesson to the class. Discuss the lesson afterwards: did you find out anything about language learning and teaching?

Learn/revise: accent; business; contact; conversation; demonstration; essay; examination; grammar; information; lecture; meeting; novel; purpose; reason (for sth); report; sentence; song; speed; spelling; subject; suggestion; technical manual; travel; vocabulary; choose (chose, chosen); discuss; plan; correct; difficult; exact; important; main; natural; professional; social; specialist; suitable; wide; especially; extremely; mostly; for ... reason; *the questions in Exercise 1.*

A6 Focus on systems

A choice of exercises: word-families; infinitives and *-ing* forms; pronunciation of /əʊ/.

VOCABULARY: SPORTS, GAMES AND LEISURE

1 Do you know the names of these sports, games and leisure activities? How many more can you think of?

GRAMMAR: INFINITIVES AND *-ING* FORMS

2 Some of the sentences in the box have infinitives and the others have *-ing* forms. Look at the rules, and decide which one gives the best explanation.

> I would love **to learn** judo.
> We expect **to win** the basketball championship.
> If you want **to camp** here, you have to register at the office.
> I like **dancing**.
> When did you start **playing** the piano?
> I'm going to stop **boxing** – I'm getting too old.

Rules
1. We use infinitives to say what people do, and *-ing* forms to say what happens to people.
2. We use *-ing* forms to talk about the present and past, and infinitives to talk about the future.
3. We use *-ing* forms after most verbs.
4. We use infinitives after most verbs.
5. We use infinitives after some verbs and *-ing* forms after others.

3 Do we normally use infinitives or *-ing* forms after these verbs?

be able   enjoy   expect   hope   keep on   learn   need   would like

4 Do we normally use infinitives or *-ing* forms as subjects of sentences? Which of the following sentences seem most natural?

1. Skiing is my favourite sport.
   To ski is my favourite sport.
2. Learning a language is a lot of work.
   To learn a language is a lot of work.
3. Running makes me tired.
   To run makes me tired.

Give examples of: your favourite activities; things that are hard work; things that make you happy or tired.

Lesson A6

Vocabulary: lexical fields (sports, games and leisure).
Grammar: rules for the use of infinitives and *-ing* forms.
Phonology: /əʊ/.

Note: 'Focus on systems' lessons

It is not necessary to work through 'Focus on systems' lessons continuously from beginning to end. The different sections of these lessons ('Grammar', 'Vocabulary' etc.) are generally separate and self-contained; teachers should choose the sections and exercises that are useful to their students and do them when it is convenient.

Language notes and possible problems

Infinitives and *-ing* forms   Students have met a large number of different uses of infinitives and *-ing* forms, but they may be confused about the exact differences between the two structures. This lesson covers some of the more common uses, and should help students to get a clearer idea of the grammar involved. The exercises are mostly rather short, and should not take up a lot of time. With a good class, you may also wish to run over other uses of infinitives and *-ing* forms, including:
– infinitives without *to*
– infinitives of purpose (e.g. *I went to America to learn English*)
– adverbial uses of *-ing* forms (e.g. *Walk round the room, reading everyone else's label and asking questions*)
– preparatory *it* with infinitive subjects (e.g. *It's important to eat properly*).

1 Vocabulary building: lexical fields

• This can be done in groups, with students pooling their knowledge. If they want to, let them use dictionaries to find out some of the words they don't know, but discourage them from listing more words than they can learn.

Answers to Exercise 1
(Alternative answers are possible in some cases.)
1. climbing   2. swimming   3. water-skiing   4. painting
5. basketball   6. sailing   7. skiing   8. parachuting
9. horse riding   10. singing   11. fishing   12. judo
13. rugby football   14. stamp collecting
15. rally driving   16. cycling   17. tennis
18. badminton   19. boxing   20. running
21. listening to music   22. chess   23. camping
24. dancing   25. football   26. playing the piano

2 Choosing between rules

• Get students to read the sentences and rules, and explain anything that is not clear.
• Let them discuss the rules in groups for a few minutes (in their mother tongue if necessary), and then find out what they think.
• Help them to see that only rule 5 really corresponds to the facts (as exemplified in the six sentences). Students need to realise that different verbs are used in different structures, and that there are not many general rules: for each verb, one has to learn what kinds of word can follow it.

3 More verbs: checking on students' knowledge

• This exercise helps students to check on whether they have noticed what structures are used with some common verbs that they have met in the last few lessons. It can be done by class or group discussion.

Answers to Exercise 3
be able + infinitive
enjoy + *-ing*
expect + infinitive
hope + infinitive
keep on + *-ing*
learn + infinitive (usually)
need + infinitive (usually)
would like + infinitive

4 *-ing* forms as subjects

• In some languages, infinitives are commonly used as subjects. Students may not realise that this is unusual in English – we either use *-ing* forms or (in some cases) construct the sentence with preparatory *it* and a postponed infinitive.
• Get students to discuss the sentences. They will probably agree that *-ing* forms are more natural.
• Then get them to continue the exercise with examples of their own, using *-ing* forms for the activities.

5 -ing forms after prepositions

• This can also be done by class or group discussion. Most students should be able to see that all the sentences contain prepositions followed by -ing forms, and they may decide (correctly) that all prepositions are followed by -ing forms, not infinitives.

• When they have finished discussing this, get them to continue the exercise by making examples of their own.

6 Verb + object + infinitive

• This structure is not found in most other languages, and students may find it difficult. Look out for mistakes like *My parents want that I become a doctor.

• Get students to decide which picture goes with the sentence in the book.

• Then let them work in groups to make sentences appropriate to the other seven pictures.

• This could be followed up with a group mime exercise: pairs or groups mime situations in which one or more people want the other(s) to do something; the rest of the class have to decide what.

Answers to Exercise 6

A woman wants some people to sign a paper goes with picture 6. Possible sentences for the other pictures:

1. She wants him to take the dog for a walk.
2. He wants his father to lend him his car.
3. He wants his mother to cut his hair.
4. He wants her to post some letters.
5. He wants somebody to take him to Manchester.
7. She wants her mother to mend her bicycle.
8. She wants them to wash/clean the car.

7 Pronunciation: /əʊ/

• Let students try the words by themselves first of all. Then play the recording or say the words and get them to try to improve their pronunciation. It may help students to pronounce /əʊ/ if they first break it into its two parts: the vowel at the end of *mother* and the vowel at the end of *too*.

8 /əʊ/ (continued)

• Continue with the recording (or read out the definitions below). Students will hear definitions of the words they have just been practising: they must say the words corresponding to the definitions.

Tapescript for Exercise 8

1. the past of *speak*
2. the opposite of *open*
3. *do not*
4. the opposite of *come*
5. the capital of Italy
6. the past of *break*
7. the opposite of *yes*
8. the opposite of *closed*
9. the opposite of *under*
10. *will not*

9 /əʊ/ (continued)

• Get students to practise the sentences in the box.

• Ask some or all of the following questions (or make up others of your own which can be answered in the same way). Pick out students to answer – they must use the sentences in the box.

Will you live to be 100 years old?
Will you get married next year?
Is it going to rain tomorrow?
Do you ever dream in English?
What's my mother's/father's/husband's/wife's/brother's/ sister's name?
Are you ever going to be rich?
Is your English getting better?
Can you run 1km in five minutes?
Will you be here this time next year?
Will you sleep well tonight?
Will you ever travel round the world?
Did you lock your door before you came to school?
Do you know how old I am?
Do you like coffee with salt in?
Do you ever read Shakespeare in English?
How much money have I got in my pocket/bag?
Are you a good singer?
Do you think you will ever go to prison?
Will you fall in love next weekend?
Are you happy?

Practice Book exercises

1. Verb + object + infinitive; requests.
2. Choosing between the infinitive and the -ing form.
3. Translation of material from Lessons A1 to A6.
4. Word stress.
5. Recreational reading: prose fiction.
6. Writing a poem using verbs in the -ing form.

Use of the mother tongue
Some time ago, language teaching theorists believed that it was quite wrong to use the mother tongue in the classroom. Fortunately, this dogma is now dying out, and most teachers realise that foreign language learning cannot completely bypass the learners' first language, especially in the early stages. Sensible use of the mother tongue, where possible, can speed up class management, and can help to make grammar and vocabulary explanations clearer and more complete. On the other hand, translation-based exercises are generally less effective than English-only exercises, and are probably best used only as quick tests or comprehension checks.

5 Look at the following sentences. Can you make a rule?

In Fantasia, doctors are paid **for keeping** people
   alive.
He is thinking **of taking up** water-skiing.
What's your main reason **for learning** English?
I've got a good chance **of getting** into university.
Thank you **for helping** me.
I'm not very good **at swimming**.
It's difficult to make money **without working**.

Now complete these sentences:

1. I'm (not) very interested in ...ing.
2. I'm thinking of ...ing next weekend / next week /
   next year.
3. Do you think I've got a good chance of ...ing ...?
4 I'm (not) very good at ...ing.
5. I couldn't live without ...ing.

6 Look at the pictures. In one of them, a woman wants some people to sign a
paper. (NOT ~~A woman wants that some people sign a paper.~~) Which picture is it?
Can you make sentences yourself for the other pictures?

PRONUNCIATION: /əʊ/

7 📟 Listen to the words and try to pronounce them correctly.

no   go   so   hope   know   broke   spoke   over   don't   won't
open   closed   Rome   phone

8 📟 Now listen to the definitions and say which words the speaker is talking
about.

9 Practise the sentences. Then answer the teacher's
questions, and make up similar questions for other
students.

I think so.   I don't think so.   I hope so.
I hope not.   I don't know.   No.
No, I don't.   No, I won't.

Learn/revise: *some of the vocabulary from*
Exercise 1.

17

A7 Could you do me a favour?

Conversation skills (requests, offers and replies; formal and informal language); listening skills (stress and rhythm); modal auxiliary verbs.

1 📼 Complete the conversation with the words and expressions in the box. Then listen to the recording and check your answers.

PAUL: Hey, John.
JOHN: Yeah?
PAUL: .... ?
JOHN: Sure. What is it?
PAUL: Well, ..., I'm .... until Friday. ...., do you think?
JOHN: Yes, OK.
PAUL: ...., John. Thanks ....
JOHN: ....

> the thing is   a lot
> Could you do me a favour
> That's all right
> That's very nice of you
> short of money
> Could you lend me £10

2 📼 Read the following conversation. Which words or parts of words do you think are stressed? Mark the stresses, listen to the recording and check your answers. Then practise the conversation in pairs.

ANNIE: Excuse me. I'm sorry to trouble you. We've got a problem.
MR OLIVER: Oh, yes? What's the matter?
ANNIE: Well, you see, it's like this. We're cycling, and we haven't got anywhere to sleep tonight.
MR OLIVER: I see. Have you tried the Crown Hotel?
ANNIE: Yes, but it's much too expensive. So we wondered if we could sleep in your barn.
MR OLIVER: Yes, all right. I don't mind. You don't smoke, do you?
ANNIE: Oh, no. Neither of us do. Well, thank you very much.
MR OLIVER: Not at all. Would you like to come into the house for a wash?
ANNIE: Oh, that's very kind of you.
MR OLIVER: This way.

Lesson A7

Students learn conversation skills (ways of making and replying to offers and requests; handling formal and informal language); they practise listening skills (stress and rhythm).
Principal structures: modal auxiliary verbs.
Phonology: stress; decoding rapid speech.

Language notes and possible problems

1. Softeners   Note the use of *well, the thing is, it's like this* and *you see* in the dialogues to introduce and ease the way for a difficult explanation which the speaker might find embarrassing.

2. Modals   Modal auxiliary verbs are common in interpersonal transactions such as offers and requests. Several typical uses of modals occur in this lesson; most of them should already be familiar to the students. Note the frequent use of *could* and *would*; also *shall* in interrogative offers (typical of British English) and *I'll* in declarative offers (e.g. *I'll open it for you*).

3. 'Distancing' use of past tenses   Past tenses are sometimes used in requests and questions: they sound less direct, and therefore more polite. Examples in this lesson are **Could** you ..., **Would** you like ..., we **wondered** if we **could** sleep ...

4. Stress   Exercise 2 is particularly useful for students who speak 'syllable-timed' languages, in which there is not a great difference in speed, loudness or clarity between one syllable and another. Students who speak 'stress-timed' languages such as German, Dutch, or Scandinavian languages may not need to spend so much time on this exercise.

5. Formality   In Exercises 4 and 5, students work on levels of formality. They should realise that the formality of an expression can depend on the situation – a formula like *Could you ...?* might seem quite formal in a casual conversational request, but not formal enough when asking an important favour from a stranger.

1 Dialogue completion

• This is an easy prediction exercise. Its purpose is to help students concentrate on some of the new expressions that they will be using later.
• Run over the pronunciation and stress of the expressions in the box; explain anything that is not clear.
• Get students to work individually or in groups, deciding how to fill in the gaps.
• Play the dialogue and let them check their answers.

Answer to Exercise 1
PAUL: Hey, John.
JOHN: Yeah?
PAUL: *Could you do me a favour?*
JOHN: Sure. What is it?
PAUL: Well, *the thing is,* I'm *short of money* until Friday. *Could you lend me £10,* do you think?
JOHN: Yes, OK.
PAUL: *That's very nice of you,* John. Thanks *a lot.*
JOHN: *That's all right.*

2 Stress and speaking practice

• Make sure students are clear about what is meant by stress, and understand what they have to do.
• If they are not used to this kind of work, you may like to take the dialogue a sentence or two at a time.
• Most of the sentences can be stressed in more than one way. The important thing is that the students grasp the general principle: that some English words (and syllables of longer words) sound much more prominent than others, because they are pronounced more slowly,

louder, with 'full' vowels, and often on a higher pitch.
• When students are ready, let them practise the conversation in pairs, paying special attention to stress.

Answers to Exercise 2
(Alternative answers are possible.)
ANNIE: Excuse me. I'm **sorry** to **trouble** you. **We've** got a **problem.**
MR OLIVER: Oh, **yes**? **What's** the **matter**?
ANNIE: Well, you **see**, it's like **this.** We're cycling, and we haven't got anywhere to **sleep tonight.**
MR OLIVER: I **see.** Have you **tried** the **Crown Hotel**?
ANNIE: **Yes,** but it's **much** too expensive. So we wondered if we could **sleep** in your **barn.**
MR OLIVER: Yes, all **right.** I don't **mind.** You **don't smoke, do** you?
ANNIE: Oh, **no.** Neither of us **do.** Well, **thank** you very **much.**
MR OLIVER: Not at **all.** Would you **like** to **come** into the **house** for a **wash**?
ANNIE: Oh, that's very **kind** of you.
MR OLIVER: **This way.**

18

3 Decoding rapid speech

• The recording contains a number of expressions from the dialogues in Exercises 1 and 2. They are spoken at fast colloquial speed, with all the contractions and alterations in pronunciation that this implies.
• Although students should by now be very familiar with the expressions, they may have to work hard to catch them all.
• Play each one and then pause so that students can write it down or say it.

Tapescript and answers to Exercise 3
Excuse me.
Thanks a lot.
What's the matter?
Could you do me a favour?
That's very nice of you.
All right.
I see.
It's like this.
Not at all.
Would you like to come into the house?
I'm sorry to trouble you.
I don't mind.

4 Informal and formal language

• Students probably already realise that there are differences in the language people use to talk to strangers and to friends when they are, for example, greeting or making requests.
• Explain what is meant by *informal* and *formal*, if necessary.
• Then see if students can add to the two lists.

Answers to Exercise 4
Students should find some of the following:

INFORMAL	FORMAL
OK	all right
Thanks a lot	Thank you very much
That's all right	Not at all
Could you	We wondered if you could
nice	kind

5 Informal and formal language (continued)

• This can be done in groups or by class discussion. Obviously various alternatives are possible in most cases.

Possible answers to Exercise 5
1. 'Would you like some coffee?'   'I'd love some.'
2. 'I wonder if I could use your phone?'   'Of course.'
3. 'Would you like to dance?'   'I'd love to.'
4. 'Would you mind passing the salt?'   'Here you are.'
5. 'Shall I open it for you?'   'That's very kind of you.'
6. 'Would you like some more bread?'   'No, thank you.'
7. 'Would you like a drink?'   'I'd love one.'
8. 'Would you like orange juice?'   'I'd prefer water, thanks.'

Optional activity: follow-up to Exercise 5
• If you feel that students need more practice in the use of these conversational formulae, tell them that they are going to hear some questions, and that they should give reasonably polite, formal answers, using the expressions they have practised during the lesson.
• Ask the following questions (or make up similar ones yourself), and pick out students to answer. Various answers are possible to each question.
Can I take your coat?
Shall I make you a cup of tea/coffee?
Would you like some toast / fried eggs / champagne ...?
Would you like to go and see a film this evening?
Shall I put the TV on?
Would you like a drink?
Would you like to have a rest?
Would you like to see my family photos?
Shall I telephone the station for you?
Would you like to wash your hands?
Would you like to dance?
Would you like something to eat?
Could I possibly use your phone?
Could I look at your dictionary?
Would you like to use my car?

6 Students' dialogues

• The first option is more suitable for weaker students; the other requires more fluency and confidence. In a mixed-ability class you may wish to invite students to choose which they are going to do. Note, however, that the second option needs more preparation time than the first.
• Walk round while students are preparing, and give whatever help is needed.
• Get them to practise once or twice before performing for the class.
• You may wish to tape- or video-record the performances. If so, warn students in advance: this will encourage them to aim for a high standard.
• If time is short, you may need to postpone this exercise to the next lesson. Try not to leave it out, however: activities like this, in which students use creatively what they have learnt, are extremely important for effective learning.

Practice Book exercises
1. Situational language: matching pairs of sentences.
2. Vocabulary and grammar: completing a telephone dialogue.
3. Simple Past of regular verbs: spelling.
4. Student's Cassette exercise (Student's Book Lesson A7, Exercise 1). Students mark and practise sentence stress.
5. Recreational reading: a choice of two articles.
6. Reading (advertisements) and writing (a letter in answer to one of them).

3 🔲 Close your books, listen to the recording and write the words and expressions that you hear.

4 Can you find some examples of informal and formal language in the two conversations?

INFORMAL	FORMAL
Hey	Excuse me
Yeah?	Oh, yes?
...	...

5 Can you make these conversations more formal? The expressions in the box will help. Example:

INFORMAL: '*Give me your coat.*' '*Here.*'
FORMAL: '*Shall I take your coat?*'
        '*Oh, thank you. Here you are.*'

1. 'Have some coffee.' 'Yeah, thanks.'
2. 'Can I use your phone?' 'Sure.'
3. 'Do you want to dance?' 'OK.'
4. 'Pass the salt.' 'Here.'
5. 'I'll open it for you.' 'Thanks.'
6. 'More bread?' 'No.'
7. 'Want a drink?' 'Yes, OK.'
8. 'Orange juice?' 'No, water.'

> Shall I ...?
> Would you like ...?
> Could I/you (possibly) ...?
> I wonder(ed) if I/you could ...?
> Would you mind ...ing?
> I'd love one/some.
> I'd love to.
> I'd prefer ...
> That would be very nice.
> Of course.
> Here you are.

6 Do one of the following activities.

EITHER: Prepare a conversation with another student. One of you offers something or asks for something, and the other answers. First act out the conversation *without speaking*. The other students will try to decide what the words are. Then act your conversation again with the words.

OR: Prepare a conversation with one or two other students. The conversation must begin '*I'm/We're sorry to trouble you*' or '*Could you do me/us a favour?*'. Use plenty of words and expressions from the lesson. You must also bring into your conversation at least two of the things in the pictures, and at least two of the sentences in the box.

> We've got a problem.
> It makes too much noise.
> We need at least six.
> It's a funny green colour.
> You are so beautiful.
> I don't like children.
> You see, it's Thursday.

> **Learn/revise:** barn; favour; problem; wash (*noun*); cycle; lend (lent, lent); offer; prepare; wonder; expensive; *expressions from Exercises 1, 2 and 5.*

> Reading skills: reading for gist, for main ideas, predicting, dictionary skills; listening for gist; oral fluency.

1 Read the article. Don't take more than five minutes. You can use a dictionary or ask the teacher for help (but try to guess the meaning of a word first).

Parachutist, 81, wins place of honour at jump

Even experts were a little surprised when a man of 62 turned up at a parachute training school and said he was interested in learning to become a parachutist.

They agreed to put him through the course, but only after giving him a series of tests to prove that he was fit enough.

Mr Archie Macfarlane completed the course successfully, surprising everyone with his agility and toughness.

A few weeks later, when he was ready for his first jump, he confessed to the chief instructor: "I told you a bit of a lie. I'm really 75."

That was six years ago and yesterday Archie Macfarlane made his 18th jump. He was given the place of honour – first out of the plane – at a weekend meeting for parachutists over 40 years old.

Archie's interest in parachuting is just one of the hobbies that his wife has to worry about. He also enjoys motorcycling and mountaineering.

Last year he fell while climbing on Snowdon, and had to be rescued by helicopter.

His daughter said: "Sometimes I think he ought to give it all up. But as my mother says, so long as he's happy, it's better than being miserable. He tried hang-gliding once and said he thought it was a bit too easy."

Now Archie is thinking of taking up water-skiing.

(adapted from a press report)

2 Here are some dictionary definitions of words from the article. Each word has more than one definition. Choose the definition that fits each of the words in the article best. Do you know what the abbreviations in the definitions mean?

fit /fɪt/ **1** *v* to be the right size or shape (for): *This dress doesn't fit me.* **2** *n* the way in which something fits: *This coat's a beautiful fit.* **3** *n* a short attack (of a slight illness or violent feeling): *a fit of coughing | She hit him in a fit of anger.* **4** *adj* in good health or bodily condition: *She runs three miles every morning; that's why she's so fit.*

take sbdy./sthg. **up** /ˈteɪk ˈʌp/ *v adv* [T] **1** to begin to do; interest oneself in: *John took up writing poetry while at school.* **2** to fill; use: *The work took up the whole of Sunday.* **3** to continue: *I'll take up the story where I left off.*

tough /tʌf/ *adj* **1** strong; not easily weakened: *These mountain sheep are very tough.* **2** difficult to cut or eat: *tough meat –* opposite **tender 3** difficult to do; demanding effort: *a tough job*

4 rough; hard: *The government will get tough with people who avoid paying taxes.* **5** *infml* too bad; unfortunate: *Tough luck!* **– toughly** *adv* **– toughness** *n* (U)

turn up /ˈtɜːn ˈʌp/ *v adv* **1** [T] (**turn sthg. up**) to find: *to turn up new information* **2** [I] to be found: *The missing bag turned up, completely empty, in the river.* **3** [T] (**turn sthg. up**) to shorten (a piece of clothing) – compare TURN-UP **4** [I] to arrive: *He turns up late for everything. | Don't worry, something will turn up.* (= happen) **5** [T] (**turn sthg. up**) to increase the force, strength, loudness, *etc.*, of (a radio, heating system, *etc.*) by using controls

(adapted from *Longman Active Study Dictionary of English*)

20

Lesson A8

Reading skills: skimming; reading for main ideas; seeing the text as a whole; dictionary skills; prediction.
Listening skills: predicting; listening for gist.
Speaking skills: discussing; reporting.

Language notes and possible problems

1. Extensive reading In this lesson you will help students to practise some of the skills that go towards proficiency in reading. But if students are to become fluent readers of English, they must also do taskless extensive reading, and this will almost certainly have to take place outside the classroom, given the time constraints of most learning situations. The extensive reading will not only help students with their reading skills; it will also reinforce vocabulary they have learnt, and there is very solid evidence that it will make them better writers. So it is a good idea from the beginning of the course to set up a system to ensure that students read regularly. For detailed suggestions, see the note on 'supplementation' in the Teacher's notes to Lesson A5.

2. Dictionaries Students should preferably have both bilingual and English-English dictionaries. Good English-English dictionaries are: *Longman Active Study Dictionary of English*; *Oxford Student's Dictionary of Current English*; *Longman Dictionary of Contemporary English* (more advanced); *Oxford Advanced Learner's Dictionary of Current English* (more advanced). Translating dictionaries vary greatly in quality; encourage students to buy good-sized up-to-date dictionaries.

It is important to make sure students can use their dictionaries effectively. They need to understand how a dictionary entry is organised, and what kind of information they can get from each part. When looking up a new word, they must also be able to find the part of the entry which corresponds to the way the word is used in the context in which it appears. (For instance, it may be important to note whether a word is a noun, verb or adjective before looking it up.)

Students should realise that dictionaries are only really helpful in one direction. They are good at giving the meanings of words, but they are not generally very useful if one doesn't know what word to use for a particular meaning. English-only dictionaries cannot help at all with this, of course, and translating dictionaries often give several alternatives without making it clear which one is correct in a particular case.

Exercises 1 and 2 provide a good opportunity to check whether students are using their dictionaries effectively.

3. -ing forms for activities In the text in Exercise 1, students will see several *-ing* forms used to talk about activities. You may want to point out that this is a common usage in English; and that we even use *-ing* forms in some cases where there are no corresponding verbs (for example, *mountaineering* and *hang-gliding*, but not *I mountaineered* or *she hang-glided*).

Optional extra materials

If you plan for your students to do the first optional activity, you will need something to use as blindfolds for half the students in your class.

If you are short of time

Ask students to prepare Exercises 3 and 4 for homework and then discuss them briefly in class. Ask students to do Exercise 7 as a written homework exercise.

1 Reading for gist

• This encourages students to read the text for overall meaning.
• Tell students that they have five minutes to read the text and get a general idea of the meaning. Let them ask questions or use dictionaries while reading, but encourage intelligent guessing.
• If students work with their dictionaries, check that they understand how to use them effectively.
• After five minutes, ask for a few volunteers each to say one important thing about what they have read.
• Then go straight on to the next exercise.

2 Dictionary skills

• This is a good point to talk about dictionaries to the students and to encourage them all to have both a good English learner's dictionary and a good bilingual dictionary.
• Ask them to tell you as many things as possible that they can find out from a dictionary.
• Then ask them to look at the dictionary entries in Exercise 2 and to ask you and the other students the meanings of any abbreviations that they don't understand.
• Talk about the fact that one word can have several meanings, and that when you use a dictionary you must choose the right meaning for the context.
• Let them work individually choosing the right meanings for the words that appear in the article in Exercise 1; then let them compare answers in pairs or small groups before checking with you.

Answers to Exercise 2
1. fit – meaning 4
2. take up – meaning 1
3. tough – meaning 1
4. turn up – meaning 4

3 Careful reading: summaries

• Ask students to re-read the article, using a dictionary where necessary or asking you for help. When they have finished they should read the three rival summaries to try and decide which is the best.
• They should compare answers in pairs, saying in each case why each summary was chosen or eliminated and trying to come to a common view.
• Then check the answers with the whole class and discuss what makes one summary better than the others. It is best not to ask students to give reasons for their choices if they do not volunteer them: some students may have trouble being articulate about *why* they chose one summary rather than another. Do, however, give them reasons when you discuss the answers.

Answer to Exercise 3
Students will probably choose one of the first two summaries. The second is rather more satisfactory than the first, which has a lot of detail from the first part of the text but very little from the last four paragraphs. The third summary is inaccurate (the text does not say either that Archie Macfarlane is too old for outdoor sport, or that his wife wishes he would stop).

4 Choosing vocabulary to learn

• Ask students to look over the article again; each student should choose seven or more words to learn.
• When they have chosen their words individually, look at the 'useful expressions' with them. Put them into groups of four or five, and ask each person to tell the group two of his/her words and why they were chosen.

5 Interview: prediction and warmup

• Let students look at the picture and read the beginning of the article.
• Get them to use their dictionaries or ask you about any words they have trouble with. Make sure they understand what *blind* means – but let them try and guess what *dressage* means.
• Put them in groups of three or four to decide what other information they will find in the article.
• Let groups compare answers before going on to Exercise 6.

6 Listening for gist: what are the questions?

• Students will hear an interview with Janice Burton, first without the questions and then with the questions.
• Get them to look over the words in the box and use their dictionaries to look up the ones they don't know.
• Go over the questions with them, making sure they understand them.
• Play the recording once through, pausing after each answer for students to write down the letter of the question they think is being answered.
• Put students into pairs to compare the order of questions each has written down.
• You may want to play the recording without questions through once more and let students consult again.
• Then play the complete recording so that students can check their answers.
• It is not worth going over the recording word for word so that students can understand it in detail; the purpose of the recording is to practise listening for gist, and class time can be better spent than by going over it in detail.
• A few notes on the recording:
1. It is Olympia in Greece, the site of the ancient Olympic Games, where Mrs Burton had her most exciting moment in dressage.

2. Mrs Burton uses *me* instead of *my* as a possessive determiner; this is very common in many British dialects.
3. Though Mrs Burton uses the term *the disabled*, many people feel that *people with disabilities* is less discriminatory: it puts the people first and the disabilities second.

Answers to Exercise 6
f; d; h; b; e; c; g; a

Tapescript for Exercise 6: see page 147

7 Oral fluency practice

• This exercise has two options in the Student's Book. Additional options are given below for teachers who have the time/resources/class to make them work.
• For the options in the Student's Book: make sure the students understand the instructions. Put them in pairs and give them three minutes for each pair to choose which option they are taking.
• Let them know how much time they have before the reporting phase of the exercise.
• Walk round while they are working to give any help that is needed.
• Warn them a couple of minutes before reporting time, and then when the time is up each pair should report to one or more other pairs.

Optional activity: 'How does it feel to be blind?'
• This option is possible for a small class, when it will not disrupt other classes for your students to be walking round the building.
• Students should work in pairs. One member of each pair should be blindfolded, and the other should help him or her to go for a five-minute walk, preferably going outside. If there is time, students should then switch roles so that the other student has a chance to be blindfolded too. Then they should come back to the classroom and report to another pair, or to a group, about how it felt. Some questions to consider:
1. What was the hardest thing?
2. Did anything surprise you?
3. If there were blind people in your school, what could be done to make things easier for them?

Optional activity: simulated interview
• If you have enough cassette recorders to give one to each group of four to six students, get the groups each to prepare and record a simulated radio programme interviewing Archie Macfarlane (plus possibly his wife, his daughter, and his parachuting instructor).
• They can use the information in the lesson as a basis, and either script the interviews, or, preferably, talk them over and then record them spontaneously. Remind students that they can always have a second try if they are not satisfied with any part of the interview. They can invent any details they choose.

Practice Book exercises
1. Completing sentences with the past participles of irregular verbs.
2. Choosing between the infinitive and the -*ing* form.
3. Student's Cassette exercise (Student's Book Lesson A8, Exercise 6). Students complete a report of the interview with Janice Burton.
4. Reading skills: deducing meaning from context.
5. Extended writing: someone who has overcome a great challenge.
6. Crossword.

3 Re-read the article, using a dictionary where necessary. Then read these three summaries of the article. Which one is the best summary? Why are the other two not so good?

1. Archie Macfarlane started parachuting when he was 75 (although he said he was younger), and he has done 18 parachute jumps over the last six years. Recently he was given the place of honour at a parachutists' meeting. His wife and daughter are worried about him.
2. Archie Macfarlane is an unusual person. Although he is an old man, he is interested in very tough sporting activities like parachuting, mountaineering and water-skiing. His wife and daughter are worried, but think it's best for him to do things that make him happy.
3. When Archie Macfarlane first learnt parachute jumping, he pretended that he was only 62. In fact, he is much older than that, and he is really becoming too old to take part in outdoor sporting activities. His wife and daughter wish that he would stop motorcycling, mountaineering and hang-gliding.

4 Choose at least seven words and expressions to learn from the article in Exercise 1. Work with another student and compare your lists. Talk about the reasons for your choices. Useful expressions:

I think this word is important.
This is a useful expression.
This is a very common word.
I like the sound of this word.
I'm interested in parachuting.

5 Look at this picture, and read the beginning of the article about Janice Burton. How do you think the report will continue?

Blind swimming champion to ride dressage in Greece

Janice Burton, former Special Olympic swimming champion, has been training hard for another sport.

6 🔲 Make sure you know the meanings of the words in the box. Then read the questions below and listen to the interview with Janice Burton. You will only hear her answers, not the interviewer's questions. Match the questions to the answers and write down the correct order for the questions. Then listen to the complete interview to check.

analyse	attract	compete	competent
competition	competitive	cross country	
disabled	feel	hips	precise	skating

a. How did you learn that?
b. How often do you work with your horse?
c. What do you enjoy most about the dressage?
d. What first attracted you to this sport?
e. What has been your most exciting moment in dressage?
f. What is dressage exactly?
g. What's the most difficult thing about dressage for you?
h. You've been in quite a few competitions?

7 Work in pairs. Do one of the following tasks. Report to the class if there is time.

1. What sorts of sports (besides swimming and dressage!) could blind people participate in? Choose a sport that you both know about, and discuss how you could help a blind person take part in it. If the sport has rules, would you have to change any of them? Report what you decide to another pair.
2. Think of a shopping area in the town or city where you are studying. What could be done to make it easier for blind people to shop there? Talk with one another, trying to think of as many things as you can. Then report to another pair.

Learn/revise: area; article; champion; city; competition; expert; hips; hobby; lie; rescue; rule; town; training; skating; agree (to do sth); attract; compete; enjoy; feel (felt, felt); ride (rode, ridden); switch; take part in (took, taken); take (sth) up; turn up; blind; competent; competitive; disabled; fit; precise; tough; unusual; worried; outside; preferably; successfully.

21

Summary **A**

Rules for the use of present and past tenses

(See also diagrams in Lesson A2)

Simple Present

> repeated or permanent events: past, present and future

It **rains** nearly every day in winter.
I **live** in Manchester, but I'm staying with my sister in Glasgow at the moment.

Present Progressive

> temporary events happening just now, or just around now

It's **raining** again.
I'm **seeing** a lot of Mary these days.

(Simple) Present Perfect

> events repeated up to now

I have often thought of changing my job.

> past events with a result now

He's **been** to East Africa several times, so he speaks quite good Swahili.

> past events that are still 'news'

Do you know that Phil **has written** a novel?

Present Perfect Progressive

> events repeated or continuing up to now, or up to a few moments ago

'You look hot.' 'I've **been playing** tennis.'

Simple Past

> events that happened one or more times in the past; no connection with now

I **asked** her to come out for a drink.
When we were children, we usually **went** to the seaside for our summer holidays.

Past Progressive

> events continuing around a particular time in the past

What **were** you **doing** this time yesterday?

> events already happening when something else happened

I asked her to come out for a drink, but she **was working**, so she couldn't.
The phone rang while I **was having** a bath.

(Simple) Past Perfect

> 'second', earlier past

When he spoke to me, I realised that I **had seen** him before.

Past Perfect Progressive

> events repeated or continuing 'up to then'

She was tired, because she **had been travelling** all day.

Non-progressive verbs

I **want** to go home. (~~I'm wanting to go home.~~)
How long **have you known** Debbie?
    (~~How long have you been knowing Debbie?~~)

> Some other common non-progressive verbs: *like, see, love, hate, prefer, mean, remember, understand, hear, smell, sound, taste, seem*; some uses of *think* and *feel*.

Infinitives and *-ing* forms after verbs

> We use infinitives after some verbs and *-ing* forms after others.

> Examples of verbs usually followed by infinitives: *agree, be able, expect, have, hope, learn, need, want, would like, would love.*

She **agreed to help** me.
I **expect to do** badly in the exams.
I **would love to learn** Japanese.
If you **want to go** to China you **have to get** a visa.

> Examples of verbs usually followed by *-ing* forms: *enjoy, keep on, like, start, stop.*

I **like being** with you.
When did you **start playing** the piano?
When will you **stop smoking**?

Verb + object + infinitive

My parents **wanted me to study** medicine.
    (~~My parents wanted that I study medicine.~~)
She **wants him to help** her.
    (~~She wants that he helps her.~~)

-ing forms as subjects

Skiing is my favourite sport. (~~To ski is ...~~)
Learning a language is a lot of work.
Running makes me tired.

Summary of language taught in Lessons A1–A8.

This section displays most of the more important systematic language points that students should have learnt or revised in the last eight lessons. Spend a short time going over the material with the students, answering questions and clearing up any difficulties. Get them also to look over the vocabulary from Lessons A1–A8 (in the *Learn/revise* panels at the end of each lesson), making sure they know at least the more important new words and expressions. They may need to spend time at home consolidating their learning before moving on.

Study and memorisation

Even when lessons are motivating, communicative and apparently successful, very few students will remember everything they have learnt unless they do further work. Besides doing the Practice Book exercises, most students will also need to spend some time on formal study of the new language material. They should look over the summaries and back over the lessons, making sure they know the new words and structures and remember how they are used.

For many students, memorisation of vocabulary is useful or necessary. It is worth discussing different possible ways of recording meanings (translation, mother-tongue explanation, English explanation, example in context …) and ways of memorising vocabulary. Learning by heart has become unfashionable, but it can be a very useful element in language study.

-ing forms after prepositions

We use *-ing* forms after all prepositions.

In Fantasia, doctors are paid **for keeping** people alive.
He is thinking **of taking up** water-skiing.
I'm not very good **at swimming**.
It's difficult to make money **without working**.

Reported statements and questions

- Three people **want** to be doctors.
  Three people said they **wanted** to be doctors.
  (~~... said they want to be doctors.~~)
- What **do you want** to be?
  Twenty children were asked **what they wanted** to be. (~~... what did they want to be.~~)
- How important **is** each of the following?
  Find out how important each of the following **is**. (~~... how important is each of the following.~~)

Modal auxiliary verbs

Can I **use** your phone? (~~Can I to use ...?~~)
Could you **lend** me £10? (~~Could you lending ...?~~)
Could you do me a favour?
Shall I take your coat?
I'll open it for you.
Would you like ...?

Irregular verbs in Lessons A1–A8

INFINITIVE	PAST	PAST PARTICIPLE
choose	chose	chosen
feel	felt	felt
grow	grew	grown
keep	kept	kept
leave	left	left
lose	lost	lost
mean	meant	meant
say	said	said
spell	spelt	spelt
wear	wore	worn

Asking about English

What does ... mean?
What's this?
What are these?
What's this called in English?
Is this a pen or a pencil?
How do you say ... in English?
What's the English for ...?
What do you say when ...?
Can you explain this word/expression/sentence?
How do you pronounce ...?
How do you spell ...?
Is this correct: ...?

Asking for help

I can't remember. What ...?
Can you remind me? Why ...?

Correcting

Er, that's not quite right.
Well, I didn't exactly say ...
Excuse me, I didn't mean ...

Reporting surveys

Three people out of twelve ...
Most people want ...
Everybody wants ... (~~Everybody want ...~~)
Nobody wants ... (~~Nobody want ...~~)
almost everybody
hardly anybody
The only exception was ...

Requests, offers and replies

Formal
'Shall I take your coat?' 'Oh, thank you.'
'Would you like ...?' 'I'd love one/some.'
                        'I'd love to.'
                        'I'd prefer ...'
                        'That would be very nice.'
'Excuse me. I'm sorry to trouble you.'
'Could I/you (possibly) ...?' 'Of course.'
                               'Here you are.'
'I wonder(ed) if I/you could ...?' 'Yes, all right. I don't mind.'
'Would you mind ...ing?' 'Not at all.'
'That's very kind of you.' 'Not at all.'
'Well, thank you very much.' 'Not at all.'

Informal
'Have some coffee.' 'Yeah, thanks.'
'Can I use your phone?' 'Sure.'
'Do you want to dance?' 'OK.'
'Pass the salt.' 'Here.'
'More bread?' 'No.'
'Want a drink?' 'Yes, OK.'
'Orange juice?' 'No, water.'
'I'll open it for you.' 'Thanks.'
'Could you do me a favour?'

Vocabulary

Look through the 'Learn/revise' boxes at the ends of Lessons A1–A8.

Revision and fluency practice A

A choice of activities.

1 📼 Story in sound. Listen to the recorded sounds. Then try to write down everything you heard in the correct order.

2 Half-dictation. The teacher will dictate the first half of each sentence; you decide how to continue and write the rest.

3 Exchanging photos. Work in groups; show the other students photos of your family and friends. Talk about your own photos and ask questions about the others.

4 Follow-up questions. Prepare questions using *Are you ...?*, *Can you ...?* and *Have you got ...?* Talk to at least two students and ask your questions. After each question has been answered, ask two or more 'follow-up questions'. Examples:

'Have you got a car?' *'Yes, I have.'*
'What sort of car? What colour is it?'

5 Which one is different? Can you find a reason why each one of the words in the box is different from all the others? Examples:

'A cow is the only one that has horns.'
'A lion is the only one that is dangerous to people.'

horse	cat	mouse	camel	lion	cow

Now do the same for one of these boxes.

India	China	the USA	France	Egypt	Israel

apple	orange	strawberry	banana
grape	peach		

fridge	piano	armchair	car	bus	table

nose	ear	arm	hand	mouth	foot

London	Paris	Copenhagen	Beijing	Rio

6 Look at the advertisements. Do you believe what they say? Possible answers:

'I'm sure it's true.'   *'It might be true.'*
'It's probably true.'   *'It's probably not true.'*
'It may be true.'   *'It can't be true.'*

Make up similar advertisements yourselves in groups.

225652.

WHITE MAGIC MAKES IT HAPPEN! For help with love, money etc, send date of birth, lock of hair, £10 and stamped addressed envelope

Your hands hold the key to your future!

To know about your love life, call
071-276-45__

SPEAK A NEW LANGUAGE IN ONLY THREE WEEKS
Have you ever wished you could

MAKE $1,000,000 FAST!
For details, send $8 to

BUCKETS OF MONEY

FROM MR GLO'S SLOT MACHINES

IT'S TRUE - you will collect your slot machine takings in strong buckets! 'Mr Glo' puts slot machines in your own town ... **For you to collect cash!**
Start P/time - 2-3 hrs/wk gives a remarkable income. Add machines gradually to become Full-time (10 hrs will be enough)
NO OVERHEADS, NO PREMISES, NO WORRIES.
MIN INVEST £7,000 AV INVEST £10,000
Phone for brochure
(0742) 723666 24 HOURS
GLO-LEISURE LTD
Glo-Leisure Ltd., Glomel House, 58-64 Penistone Road, Sheffield S6 3AE

Mr. GLO

The lazy way to a great body!
Would you like to make your body beautiful with no exercise or dieting?

College degrees by mail!
Legal, fast, inexpensive.
Bachelors, Masters, Doctorates. Free brochure from The University of

24

┌──────────────────────────────────┐
│ **Revision and fluency** │
│ **practice A** │
│ **Students and teacher choose** from a range of │
│ practice activities. │
└──────────────────────────────────┘

Teaching notes
Detailed teaching notes are not provided for all exercises in this section, since most of the activities are self-explanatory.

---

1 Story in sound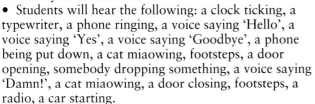
• Students will hear the following: a clock ticking, a typewriter, a phone ringing, a voice saying 'Hello', a voice saying 'Yes', a voice saying 'Goodbye', a phone being put down, a cat miaowing, footsteps, a door opening, somebody dropping something, a voice saying 'Damn!', a cat miaowing, a door closing, footsteps, a radio, a car starting.

2 Half-dictation
• Dictate the following sentence-beginnings (or any others you feel like). Students should write the half-sentences and then make up their own continuations.
1. As soon as she walked into the room, ...
2. I'm having a lot of trouble deciding what to ...
3. One Saturday morning in late summer, ...
4. If you want to lose all your friends, ...
5. All through history, people have ...
6. Nobody knows who really ...
7. If you climb to the top of a high mountain, ...
8. I believe that everybody should ...
9. Everybody started laughing because ...

5 Which one is different?
• This exercise is taken from *Discussions that Work*, by Penny Ur, Cambridge University Press 1981, by kind permission of the author and publisher. (This book is a gold-mine of fluency activities.)
• If students like the exercise, they can go on to make up their own lists for each other.

7 Are you a good detective?

Answers to Exercise 7

1. The pistol is Ann's. (From what John says, it can't be his, and from what Ann says, it can't be Mary's.)
2. The coat doesn't belong to the businessman or the film star, so it belongs to the doctor. So the painting can't belong to the doctor; nor can it belong to the businessman (because it belongs to a woman). So the painting must belong to the film star.

8 Question box

- Encourage students to write questions which will lead to discussion.
- Before students put their questions in the box, check them for serious mistakes.
- When students have drawn out their questions and answered them, make sure they don't put them back in the box.
- A student can reject a question, saying 'I'd rather not answer' (put this on the board) – but only once.
- In a large class, you may want to make two or more subgroups.

11 Sketches

- If students are not used to this kind of activity, you may need to give them fairly detailed instructions.
- Get them to begin by choosing a situation (quickly) and deciding on their roles.
- As they prepare their conversations, be ready to help with vocabulary (and ideas as well, if necessary).
- Discourage students from writing long ambitious conversations full of difficult language or 'translationese' – they should stick mainly to the English that they know, and that the rest of the class will understand.
- When each group is ready, make any essential corrections and then get them to practise a few times (with movements if possible). Unless they are going to learn the script by heart, everybody should have a copy of the complete dialogue.
- Finally, get each group to perform their sketch in front of the class. Try to avoid starting either with the best group (this could discourage the others) or with the worst (panic is infectious).
- Some groups may need to be pressurised to finish the exercise and perform their sketches, but they will be pleased when they have actually done it. (But look out for students who are genuinely so shy that they should not be forced to perform.)
- If you tape- or video-record the sketches, this can give students an incentive to aim for a high standard.

7 Are you a good detective?

1. The police stop a car. There are three people in the car: John, Ann and Mary. On the back seat there is a pistol. John says 'It's mine.' Ann says 'It's hers.' Mary says 'It's his.' Nobody is telling the truth. Whose is the pistol?
2. In the car, the police find a diamond necklace, a valuable painting and a fur coat. The police find out that they belong to a film star, a businessman and a doctor. The diamonds don't belong to the doctor. The coat doesn't belong to the businessman. The painting belongs to a woman. The film star never wears fur coats. Who does the painting belong to?

8 Question box. Each student writes three questions on separate pieces of paper. One of the questions must begin *Have you ever ...*, and one must begin *Do you ...* The questions are folded up and put in a box. Students take turns to draw out questions and answer them.

9 Discussion. Look at the following statements. Try to find two with which you agree strongly, and two with which you disagree strongly. Find somebody who has a different opinion from you about one of your four statements, and spend five minutes trying to change his/her view.

Everybody should know how to cook.
The speed limit should be lower.
Education should be more practical.
Everybody in the world should learn English.
Children over 14 should be free to do what they like.
It is always wrong to tell lies.
Smoking should be banned in all public places.
Censorship is always wrong.
Divorce should be easier.
It is always wrong to smack a child.
You should fight for your country if you are asked to.

10 Mime. Work in groups of three. Each group must prepare and act out (without words) a scene in which they are having trouble with a large object. The others must decide what the object is.

11 Sketches. Work in small groups. Prepare and practise a conversation which takes place in one of the following situations: at an airport, in a clothes shop, at dinner, at a hotel reception desk, in a garage. The conversation must include the following: a problem, a misunderstanding, an interruption. When you are ready, act out your conversation for the rest of the class.

12 Look at the cartoons. Tell other students what you think about them. Find out which are the most and least popular cartoons. Useful expressions:

I don't see the joke.
What do you think of this one?
This one's really funny.
It isn't funny at all.
I think it's wonderful/stupid.
It makes / doesn't make me laugh.

"Now if the passengers on the left hand side will put their left arms through the windows and do this – while those on the right hand side ..."

"Your bath's ready, dear."

25

Test A

LISTENING

1 📼 Make sure you know what the words and expressions in this box mean. Then listen to the recording. Who does each speaker think should be paid most?

> army general   rubbish collector
> government minister   head of large factory
> hospital nurse   policeman/policewoman
> primary school teacher

Now make sure you know what these expressions mean. Listen to the recording again. Which jobs are they used to talk about? Can you write down at least two other things that the speakers say about the jobs?

a. demanding job
b. long hours
c. not be paid at all if …
d. one of the most important jobs
e. paid a very good wage
f. taken very seriously
g. thankless job
h. very poorly paid

GRAMMAR

2 Choose the right tense for each verb.

Last night I (1) *have seen / saw* an interesting programme on television. It (2) *has been / was* about a new way of teaching science subjects to schoolchildren. For three years now a school in London (3) *has been teaching / is teaching* science in this way to some of its students, and these students (4) *have done / did* significantly better in examinations than the students in ordinary classes. It (5) *is working / works* like this: students (6) *are not only learning / not only learn* about science, but are taught to think about their own way of thinking. One of the teachers on the programme said, 'Older good teaching methods (7) *have made / made* people think, but it (8) *has been / was* in a sense unconscious. When a child (9) *is having / has* to explain to somebody else how they have solved a problem, that really makes them think about their own thinking.'

   Researchers (10) *are not fully understanding / do not fully understand* how the methods (11) *are working / work*. But marks in examinations (12) *have increased / increased* dramatically. Unfortunately, nothing (13) *is being done / is done* at the moment to train other teachers in the new methods.

3 Infinitive or *-ing* form?

1. I would like (*travel*) all over the world.
2. I think Mary has a good chance of (*win*) the election on Sunday.
3. We expect (*arrive*) at the station at 4.30 on Saturday.
4. Do you think Ann will agree (*have*) the meeting in her office?
5. If the phone doesn't stop (*ring*), I am going to throw it out of the window.
6. When did you start (*learn*) Chinese?
7. They hope (*go*) to the meeting in Helsinki next year.
8. Doesn't your brother want (*learn*) (*drive*)?
9. My sister likes (*swim*), but she doesn't like swimming pools.
10. My cousin doesn't really need (*work*), but he enjoys (*be*) around people and (*do*) something useful.
11. (*Eat*) fatty foods, (*drink*) alcohol and (*smoke*) are all bad for your heart.
12. After (*work*) all day, I don't really feel like going out again in the evening.

LANGUAGE IN USE

4 In this dialogue, A is speaking formally and B is speaking informally. Change the dialogue to make it *either* all formal *or* all informal.

A: Excuse me, Barbara. I'm sorry to trouble you, but I'm afraid I have a problem.
B: Yeah?
A: The thing is, I need to go to the doctor's and my car won't start. I wonder if I could possibly borrow yours?
B: Yeah, OK.
A: Thank you very much. That's really very kind of you.
B: Or do you want me to drive you?
A: Oh, yes, please. That would be very nice. Thank you so much.
B: OK. Want to leave now?
A: Well, yes, if it's not too much trouble. My appointment's at ten.
B: OK, give me my keys off that shelf and we can go.
A: Thank you so much, Barbara. Here you are.

5 Write one sentence or question for each situation.

1. Say something about what you want(ed) to do or be in life.
2. Say something about your parents' hopes for you.
3. What do you say to someone if you forget what they've told you?
4. What can you say to correct someone politely if they report something you haven't said?

26

Test A

This test covers work done in Lessons A1–A8.

Administration of the test

1. General procedure Give students a few minutes to look over the test and make sure they understand what they are to do in each part. Don't worry if you think students have looked at the test beforehand – this is just as good a way as any of revising the material. If it is important for any reason that students do unseen tests, a set of parallel tests for photocopying are available in a separate Test Book.

2. Listening (Exercise 1) Make sure that students understand the words and expressions in the first box; they should hear you pronounce them, so they will know how they sound.

Students should write the numbers 1 to 3 on their papers, and be prepared to note what each speaker says about who should be paid most.

Play the recording, pausing after each speaker for students to note their answers.

Then go over the expressions in the list. Play the recording again while students note down which expressions are used to talk about which job. You will probably want to play the recording a second time so students can check their answers.

3. Speaking (Exercise 10) You will have to take students aside in pairs for the Speaking part of the test. If you have a large class and a short class period, you may have to drop this part of the test.

Explain to students what they will be doing in Exercise 10 after they finish the Listening exercise. Each student should think of the relative he or she is going to describe before beginning the rest of the test.

Call each pair of students out of the class, for example to your desk or to the back of the classroom, while the others work on the written part of the test.

Try to make the students feel comfortable. Get them to tell each other about the relatives they have chosen. The 'listener' can ask questions for clarification. Each student should talk for about two minutes and then swap roles.

Remember that what you are looking for in this Speaking test is fluency, not perfect grammar or pronunciation. What counts is whether the students can make themselves understood.

LISTENING

1

1. primary school teacher
2. hospital nurse
3. hospital nurse
hospital nurse: a, b, g, h
primary school teacher: d, e, f
army general: c

Tapescript for Exercise 1

1. I think a primary school teacher should be paid the most. I think it is one of the most important jobs there is. Your first few years at school are the most formative, and a really good teacher should be taken very, very seriously and paid a very good wage.

2. I think a hospital nurse should be paid the most because it is such a, a thankless job. It's not appreciated nearly as much as it, as it should be. Erm, nurses really do get a raw deal: they're very poorly paid at the moment; they work very, very long hours; they're constantly on their feet, they're on call, and, I just think they really should be appreciated.

3. I think a hospital nurse should be paid the most of, of, this, er, of the list that we, we have in front of us erm, for, for much the same reasons that have been said before: it is a very, very demanding job. You're dealing with people that you've never met before, and often, often in rather intimate ways, and it's, it's, it's a very very difficult job. Erm, I think an army general should, should, should not be paid at all if they go to war. Er, so it would be a very good incentive for stopping wars, maybe.

GRAMMAR

2

1. saw	8. was
2. was	9. has
3. has been teaching	10. do not fully understand
4. have done	11. work
5. works	12. have increased
6. not only learn	13. is being done
7. made	

3

1. to travel	7. to go
2. winning	8. to learn to drive
3. to arrive	9. swimming / to swim
4. to have	10. to work; being; doing
5. ringing	11. Eating; drinking; smoking
6. learning	12. working

LANGUAGE IN USE

4

(Many possible answers. Two possibilities are given here.)

A Hey, Barbara, I've got a problem.
B Yeah?
A I need to go to the doctor's and my car won't start. Could I borrow yours?
B Yeah, OK.
A Thanks.
B Or do you want me to drive you?
A Oh, all right. Yeah, why not?
B OK. Want to leave now?
A Well, yeah, my appointment's at ten.
B OK, give me my keys off that shelf and we can go.
A Here.

* * *

A Excuse me, Barbara. I'm sorry to trouble you, but I'm afraid I have a problem.
B What's the matter, Anne?
A The thing is, I need to go to the doctor's and my car won't start. I wonder if I could possibly borrow yours?
B Oh, of course you can.
A Thank you very much. That's really very kind of you.
B Or if you prefer, I would be happy to drive you. Would you like that?
A Oh, yes, please. That would be very nice. Thank you so much.
B Not at all. Shall we leave now?
A Well, yes, if it's not too much trouble. My appointment's at ten.
B All right. I wonder if you could give me my keys off that shelf, and we can go.
A Thank you so much, Barbara. Here you are.

5

1. (Many possible answers; possibly in the form 'I want(ed) to …')
2. (Many possible answers; possibly in the form 'My parents want(ed) me to …')
3. (For example) I can't remember – what … / Can you remind me – why …
4. (For example) Er, that's not quite right … / Well, I didn't exactly … / Excuse me, I didn't mean …

PRONUNCIATION

2. S (/ɜː/)
3. weight (/eɪ/) (the others have /aɪ/)
4. S (/ɔː/)
5. red (/e/) (the others have /eɪ/)
6. one (/ʌ/) (the others have /əʊ/)
7. S (/əʊ/)
8. most (/əʊ/) (the others have /ɒ/)
9. S (/ɒ/)

VOCABULARY

grammar – sentence
hair – wavy
height – tall
horse – riding
pronounce – accent
minister – vote
music – sing
soldier – war
wage – earn

WRITING

8 (Many possible answers; look for a fair degree of fluency, accuracy and appropriateness.)

READING

9

1. False
2. a New York rubbish collector
3. £1000 a month
4. university teachers
5. (b) Not many people want to be New York rubbish collectors.
6. in Britain

SPEAKING

10 (Remember that fluency is what counts here.)

Test Book recording
A recording for Test 1 in the Test Book follows this lesson on the Class Cassette.

PRONUNCIATION

6 In each group, have all the words got the same vowel sound or has one got a different sound? Write *S* for 'the same' or write the word that is different.

1. fair   where   wear   earn   *earn*
2. nurse   shirt   learn   word
3. eyes   weight   mind   height
4. tall   course   talk   draw
5. grey   red   plain   steak
6. don't   grow   hope   one
7. road   over   know   won't
8. want   lost   most   stop
9. not   what   often   gone

VOCABULARY

7 Match each word in column A with one or more words in column B.

A	B
artist	accent
grammar	earn
hair	painting
height	riding
horse	sentence
pronounce	sing
minister	tall
music	vote
soldier	war
wage	wavy

WRITING

8 Choose one of these tasks; write 100 words or more.

1. Describe a real or imaginary friend (what they look like, what kind of a person they are, what they do, what they enjoy doing, …).
2. Write about some things that you really wanted to do when you were younger, and some things that you would really like to do sometime in the next ten years.
3. What should be the best paid job(s) in your country? Why?

READING

9 Read the text and answer the questions.

An intriguing book, *World paychecks: who makes what, where and why*, makes some interesting international comparisons. In Japan, for example, teachers earn far less than factory workers, but in Denmark they are near the top of the wages scale. A New York rubbish collector makes three times as much as an Indian army general. A German bus driver gets double the pay packet of a British bus driver. In China some university teachers earn as much as government ministers, but Chinese newspaper and television journalists are the most poorly paid ones in the world. And so on.

In part, says the writer, this is because of the law of supply and demand. New York rubbish collectors are well paid because it is hard to find enough people who want to do the job, and in India generals do badly because everyone (well, almost everyone) wants to be a general. But other facts – whether having a certain job makes you famous, for example – also make a difference.

It may interest you to know that the President of the United States earns three times what the Prime Minister of Britain does, but that the Prime Ministers of India and China get only about £40 a week. I leave you to draw your own conclusions.

One of the other interesting bits of information in the book is that Britain pays its civil servants (the people who are paid to help the government run things like the tax system and the post office) more than America and most of Europe. Don't ask me who decides these things; no one asked for my opinion.

(from an article by William Davis in *Punch*)

1. True or false: in Denmark, factory workers earn more than teachers.
2. Who earns more, an Indian army general or a New York rubbish collector?
3. If a British bus driver earns £500 a month, how much does a German bus driver earn?
4. Who earns more in China, university teachers or journalists?
5. Which is true:
   a. A lot of people want to be New York rubbish collectors.
   b. Not many people want to be New York rubbish collectors.
6. Do civil servants earn more in America or in Britain?

SPEAKING

10 Work with another student. Each of you must tell the other about someone in your family. Speak for about two minutes while your partner listens carefully. Then the partner must tell the teacher as much as she or he remembers.

B1 Emergency

Reporting and responding to emergencies; giving advice; Present Perfect for reporting 'news'; *can* with verbs of sensation; *there has been*; imperatives; /ð/ and /θ/; listening for gist; listening for specific information.

1 📼 Listen to the recording, and match the sentences with the pictures. Then turn to page 130 and fill in the missing words in the sentences.

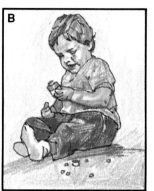

2 Look at these pictures. Imagine you are in these situations, and make sentences like the ones in Exercise 1.

28

Lesson B1

Students learn to report and respond to emergencies and practise giving advice; they practise listening for gist and for specific information.
Principal structures: Present Perfect for announcing that events have just happened; *can* with verbs of sensation; *there has been*; imperatives.
Phonology: pronouncing /ð/ and /θ/.

Language notes and possible problems

1. The Present Perfect tense   Remind students that the Present Perfect is often used to report recent events which are 'news' (emergencies, for example). It is not used in narratives about the less recent past. Nor is it used with finished-time adverbials, even when reporting 'news'.

It may be necessary to remind students that this use of the Present Perfect is not only confined to emergencies. There is more work on the Present Perfect in the Grammar Revision exercises at the end of the book.

2. *Can* with verbs of sensation   You will want to point out to students that when *see, hear, feel, smell,* and *taste* have their basic meaning of 'receiving information through the senses', they are not usually used in progressive tenses; *can* is used instead for the present (and *could* for the past).

3. *There has been*   Students are likely to have difficulty with some of the tenses of *there is*; make sure they use this form in their practice. Lesson B2 has more systematic work on the tenses of *there is*.

4. Imperatives are revised in this lesson. Make sure students know how to form them.

If you are short of time

If pronunciation is not a high priority for your students, drop Exercise 4. Do Exercise 5 by listening to the recording directly, without asking the students to try to fill in the blanks first.

1 Listening for gist and matching

- Ask students to look at the pictures in their books for one minute. Tell them to write the numbers 1 to 7 on a piece of paper.
- Play the recording or read the sentences yourself. When the students hear a sentence, they should write down the letter of the corresponding illustration next to the number of the sentence. You will probably want to play the recording or read the sentences more than once.
- Go over the answers with the class (only in the form 1B, 2E, and so on).
- Ask students to turn to page 130 in their books and try to write down the complete sentences. They will probably want you to play the recording once again.
- Check the answers with them and answer any questions about meaning and pronunciation. You will probably want students to practise pronouncing some of the words.
- Point out the use of the Present Perfect for announcing 'news' (as in sentences 1, 4 and 6). You may want to revise the form of the Present Perfect. Some students may not have met *there's been* before.
- Point out the use of *can* in *I can hear terrible screaming ...* and *I can smell gas in my flat.*

Answers and tapescript for Exercise 1
1B. *My baby's just eaten* some aspirins.
2E. *There's a fire in the* corridor, *and I'm on the fifth* floor.
3F. *I can't turn the water* off in the bathroom. *The floor's* covered with water.
4G. *There's been an* accident. *A woman is* hurt. She's bleeding.

5A. *I can hear terrible* screaming *from the flat* upstairs.
6C. *There's been* a burglary.
7D. *I can smell* gas *in my flat.*

2 Reporting emergencies

- Ask students to work in pairs. They should look at the pictures for Exercise 2 and try and write a sentence as if they were reporting each picture. Point out that there can be more than one correct sentence for each picture.
- Walk round while they are working to give any help that is needed.
- When they have finished, go over the sentences. Accept any reasonable answers, but make sure that they use the Present Perfect and *can* with verbs of sensation where these are appropriate.

Possible answers to Exercise 2
(Other answers are possible in some cases.)
1. Smoke is coming out of my neighbour's window.
2. There's been an accident. A man is hurt. He's unconscious.
3. There's a fire in my kitchen.
4. Somebody has stolen my motorbike.
5. I think my neighbour has fallen down the stairs. I can hear her calling for help.

28

3 Advice in emergencies

- Get students to work in small groups of three or four. They are to imagine what they might say if a friend phoned them with each of the emergencies in Exercises 1 and 2.
- Tell them they can ask you for help with new English words they want to use, and walk round while they are working to give any help that is needed.
- You may want to put a time limit on this exercise so students don't go on too long, or to tell them to write answers for as many of the problems as they can in, say, ten minutes.
- Go over the answers with the whole class or with each group as you walk round.

4 Pronunciation practice: /ð/ and /θ/

- Students practise /ð/ and /θ/ in sentences from the lesson.
- Get the students to repeat after you or the recording, chorally and individually.
- You may want to remind students that when they make these sounds their tongues should be touching the bottom of their top front teeth.

5 Predicting and listening

- Explain that the illustration is from a British phone box, and give the students a few minutes to read it.
- Ask students to work individually at first to try and predict what goes in the blanks in the conversation. Point out that for some blanks it is possible to have more than one suitable answer. The students should not worry if they cannot fill in all the blanks. Then get them to compare their answers in small groups.
- Play the recording while students listen and check their answers. You will probably want to play the recording more than once.
- Discuss the students' predictions. Recognise and approve suitable answers that are different from the recording.

Tapescript and answers for Exercise 5

OPERATOR: Emergency. *Which* service, please?
FATHER: Ambulance.
OPERATOR: *What number are you ringing from?*
FATHER: 744-6972.
OPERATOR: *Hold on.* I'll put you through.
OFFICER: Ambulance Service. *Can I help you?*
FATHER: *My son has fallen off a* wall, and *I think his leg is* broken.
OFFICER: *Your name and address, please?*
FATHER: Colin Jackson, 7 Latton Close.
OFFICER: *All right,* Mr Jackson, we'll be right there. *You can cover your son to keep him* warm, but don't move him.
FATHER: *Thank you.*

6 Role play

- Ask for six volunteers to play the roles of the fire, ambulance and police services in a telephone role play. Put these six students into pairs, with one pair for each service. Each pair should think about what sort of emergencies they will be faced with, what sort of questions they will want to ask (for example, *Is she unconscious?*), and what sort of advice they will want to give about what to do until help arrives.
- Divide the rest of the class into small groups of three to five students. Ask each group to make a list of five emergencies to report to the emergency services on 999. Don't worry if some students decide to do silly emergencies – this may be a means of defusing the

discomfort that thinking about real emergencies induces.
- Walk round while the students are working to give any help that is needed.
- Call the six 'emergency services' volunteers up to the front of the room. Get them to sit with their backs to the rest of the class (to help simulate telephone conversations). Find out who has taken which role. Remind them that as well as asking any necessary questions about the emergency and giving advice, they must ask for an address in each case. They should write the address down.
- You will play the part of the operator. Ask the other groups to 'phone' you with their emergencies. Using the model in the book, ask them what service they want and what number they are ringing from (remind them that telephone numbers in English are said one number at a time, and make sure you can understand the numbers they give you). Then 'put them through' to an appropriate person on the panel at the front of the room, perhaps by tapping that person on the shoulder.

Practice Book exercises

1. Distinguishing between *is* and *has*.
2. Writing what someone should/shouldn't do in an emergency.
3. Choosing the right tense (Present Perfect and Simple Past).
4. Reply questions; keeping the conversation going.
5. Student's Cassette exercise (Student's Book Lesson B1, Exercise 5). Students mark and practise sentence stress.
6. Extended writing: an emergency.
7. Recreational reading: warning notices; newspaper articles.

Sense of progress

As students learn more, it becomes more difficult for them to get a sense of progress. This is natural: beginners who learn twenty more words have doubled their knowledge, but for intermediate students another twenty words may only represent an improvement of one per cent. It is very important at this level to think about short-term goals. Students need plenty of interesting speaking and writing tasks so that they can do something with their English. Success in such tasks will give them a sense of achievement, and this will counteract the feeling that they have reached a 'plateau' and are not getting anywhere. For this reason, even if time is short, it is important not to drop the longer, more creative speaking and writing exercises in the course. (It is better to leave out some lessons than to rush through everything too fast.)

---

3 Work in small groups. Suppose friends phone you to announce the emergencies in Exercises 1 and 2. What do you say to them? You can ask your teacher for help with words. Examples:

'My baby has just eaten some aspirins.' *'Take her to hospital immediately.'*
'I can't turn the water off in the bathroom.' *'Turn it off at the mains.'*

4 📼 Practise saying these after your teacher or the recording.

There's a   There's a fire   There's a fire in my kitchen.

There's been   There's been an accident.   There's been a burglary.

there   right there   We'll be right there.

through   put you through   I'll put you through.

think   I think   I think his leg is broken.

5 📼 Phoning about an emergency. Here are some instructions from a British phone box.

Fill in the blanks in the conversation; then listen to the recording. Have you thought of some good words and expressions that are not on the recording?

OPERATOR: Emergency. .... service, please?
FATHER: Ambulance.
OPERATOR: ....?
FATHER: 744-6972.
OPERATOR: .... I'll put you through.
OFFICER: Ambulance Service. ....?
FATHER: .... wall, and .... broken.
OFFICER: ....?
FATHER: Colin Jackson, 7 Latton Close.
OFFICER: ...., Mr Jackson, we'll be right there. .... warm, but don't move him.
FATHER: ....

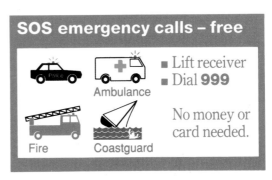

SOS emergency calls – free

■ Lift receiver
■ Dial **999**

No money or card needed.

Ambulance

Fire   Coastguard

(reproduced by kind permission of BT)

6 Role play: work in groups.
Emergency service workers (fire, police and ambulance): you are going to answer the telephone. First spend some time thinking of what sort of emergencies people may ring about, and what you will say to the people who ring.
People with emergencies: you are going to phone the emergency services. First make a list of five emergencies to phone about.

Present Perfect for announcing 'news'
There's been an accident.
   (~~There was an accident.~~)
My baby has just eaten some aspirins.

Can with ***see, hear, smell, feel***
I can smell gas.   (~~I am smelling gas.~~)
I can hear terrible screaming.   (~~I am hearing ...~~)

Imperatives
Keep him warm, but **don't move** him.

Learn/revise: accident; ambulance; aspirin; burglary; corridor; emergency; fire; flat; gas; help; hospital; leg; officer; operator; service; smoke; bleed (bled, bled); break (broke, broken); drive (drove, driven); fall (fell, fallen); move; scream; steal (stole, stolen); turn off; terrible; warm; immediately; upstairs; (We'll be) right there.

B2 Focus on systems

A choice of exercises: pronunciation of /ð/ and /θ/; tenses of *there is*; building sentences with conjunctions and *-ing* forms; vocabulary expansion.

PRONUNCIATION

1 🔲 The same or different? You will hear twelve pairs of words. If the two words in a pair are the same, write *S*. If they are different, write *D*.

2 🔲 Can you hear a *th*? Write the numbers of the pairs; then listen to the recording, and write ✔ if you hear *th* and ✗ if you hear something else.

/ð/ or /d/	/ð/ or /z/	/θ/ or /s/	/θ/ or /t/
1. there / dare	6. then / Zen	11. think / sink	16. three / tree
2. than / Dan	7. with / whizz	12. thought / sort	17. through / true
3. they / day	8. writhe / rise	13. thing / sing	18. thank / tank
4. other / udder	9. bathe / bays	14. youthful / useful	19. path / part
5. those / doze	10. thee / zee	15. path / pass	20. fourth / fought

GRAMMAR: *THERE IS*

3 Can you use the different forms of *there is*? Look at the expressions in the box and then complete the sentences. You will need to use questions or negative forms in some of them.

there is/are	there was/were
there has/have been	there had been
there will be	there would be

1. .... an accident! Come at once!
2. I don't think .... another world war.
3. Do you think .... people like us on other planets?
4. She came screaming out of the bathroom because .... a spider in the bath.
5. When I got to the hotel she told me .... a mistake, and they had given my room to somebody else.
6. If people drove more slowly, ... fewer accidents.
7. .... many people who speak three languages perfectly.
8. .... anybody at home if I come round to your place tomorrow?
9. .... any letters for me, have there?
10. .... policemen in the 18th century?

4 Think of three things that were different when you were a small child, or when your parents were children. Begin *There was(n't)* ... or *There were(n't)* ... Think of three things that will be different in 100 years. Begin *There will/won't be* ...

GRAMMAR: BUILDING SENTENCES

5 Look at the examples.

*Walk round the room **reading** everybody else's label.*
*Interview the person, **asking** as many questions as you can.*
*Mr Archie Macfarlane completed the course successfully, **surprising** everyone.*
*I sat in the garden **wondering** what to do next.*

Now rewrite these sentences using *-ing* forms.

1. She sat in the corner and cried.
2. Walk round the room and ask people questions.
3. She played cards all night, and lost a lot of money.
4. I lived in France for a year, and worked as an English teacher.
5. He drove round the corner on the wrong side of the road, and nearly killed an old lady.
6. We had a nice evening together; we talked and listened to music.
7. Two metres of snow fell; it completely blocked the road.
8. He slept peacefully, and dreamt that he was back at home.
9. He ran out of the house; he was screaming.
10. I took Lucy's car; I knew that she would understand.

Lesson B2

Phonology: /ð/ and /θ/.
Grammar: tenses of *there is*; building complex sentences with adverbial subordinate clauses and participle clauses.
Vocabulary: lexical fields (parts of a car / everyday objects).

Note: 'Focus on systems' lessons
It is not necessary to work through 'Focus on systems' lessons continuously from beginning to end. The different sections of these lessons ('Grammar', 'Vocabulary' etc.) are generally separate and self-contained; teachers should choose the sections and exercises that are useful to their students and do them when it is convenient.

Language notes and possible problems

1. Pronunciation Most students are likely to have difficulty with /ð/ and /θ/, since these sounds do not occur in many languages. (Note, however, that they are both found in European Spanish – /ð/ as a variety of /d/ between vowels, and /θ/ as a separate phoneme, written c or z.) Speakers of most other languages are likely to confuse /ð/ with /d/ or /z/, and /θ/ with /t/ or /s/, depending on the position of the sound and the student's mother tongue. Regular ear-training of the kind given in Exercises 1 and 2 may help.

Some students may be worried by the fact that Exercises 1 and 2 involve some unusual words. Try to discourage them from asking about the meanings of all of the words, and explain that it is not the words themselves that are important, but the practice that they provide in distinguishing sounds.

2. There is Students should be able to handle simple forms of *there is*, but they may not yet be at ease with forms like *there has been* or *there will be*. Exercises 3 and 4 will help with this. Note also that in many languages the equivalent of *there is/are* is an invariable form with no singular/plural difference; this can lead to mistakes in English.

3. Complex sentences Students are now beginning to work systematically on sentences containing various kinds of subordinate clause. People who speak non-European languages are especially likely to have difficulty with some structures – for instance sentences beginning with conjunctions (e.g. *After he left school he joined the army*).

---

1 Pronunciation: /ð/ and /θ/: ear-training

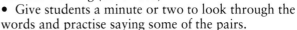

• Here students listen for the differences between /ð/ and /z/, /ð/ and /d/, /θ/ and /s/ and /θ/ and /t/.
• Tell them to write the numbers 1–12; then play the recording or say the words. (Do give each of the words in a pair the same intonation; otherwise students will hear them as different even if they are the same.)
• Students write 'S' after each number if the two words they hear are the same, and 'D' if they are different.
• If students have difficulty in hearing the distinctions, repeat the exercise (or the part of it that they had trouble with).

Tapescript and answers to Exercise 1
1. those, doze   (*D*)
2. they, they   (*S*)
3. there, dare   (*D*)
4. then, Zen   (*D*)
5. bathe, bathe   (*S*)
6. with, with   (*S*)
7. think, sink   (*D*)
8. thing, thing   (*S*)
9. path, pass   (*D*)
10. three, tree   (*D*)
11. path, part   (*D*)
12. thank, thank   (*S*)

2 Ear-training (continued)

• Give students a minute or two to look through the words and practise saying some of the pairs.
• Make sure they understand that, whatever the spelling, there is only *one* difference in pronunciation between the words in each pair: they simply have to decide whether they hear *th* or something else.
• Play the recording or say the words, while students write their answers.
• Go over the answers; repeat the exercise if necessary.

Tapescript for Exercise 2
1. there   6. Zen   11. think   16. tree
2. Dan   7. with   12. sort   17. true
3. they   8. rise   13. sing   18. thank
4. udder   9. bays   14. youthful 19. path
5. those   10. thee   15. pass   20. fought

3 Tenses of *there is*

• This is probably best done individually in writing, so that you can see if any students are having difficulty.
• Get students to be careful with the pronunciation of *there* (it is unstressed, pronounced /ðə/, not /ðeə/), when they are giving their answers.

Answers to Exercise 3
1. There has been   6. there would be
2. there will be   7. There aren't/not
3. there are   8. Will there be
4. there was   9. There haven't been
5. there had been   10. Were there

4 Past and future of *there is*

• This can be done as a whole-class exercise, with students volunteering examples or taking it in turns to speak.
• You may like to give them a couple of minutes to think of examples before they start talking.
• Again, pay attention to the pronunciation of *there*.

5 Using *-ing* forms to build complex sentences

• Students have not yet worked on the use of *-ing* forms to introduce 'participle clauses' in complex sentences, though they are probably reasonably familiar with the construction. This exercise gives them simple practice in making sentences of this kind.
• Look through the examples clearing up any problems. Get students to suggest other ways of constructing the sentences (e.g. *Walk round the room and read ...*).
• You may want to point out that conjunctions are not usually needed before *-ing* form structures of this kind, and that they either follow the main clause directly or are separated by a comma (but not by a semi-colon).
• Then get students to do the exercise individually or by class discussion, as you prefer.

Answers to Exercise 5
1. She sat in the corner *crying*.
2. Walk round the room *asking* people questions.
3. She played cards all night, *losing* a lot of money.
4. I lived in France for a year, *working* as an English teacher.
5. He drove round the corner on the wrong side of the road, *nearly killing* an old lady.
6. We had a nice evening together, *talking and listening* to music.
7. Two metres of snow fell, *completely blocking* the road.
8. He slept peacefully, *dreaming* that he was back at home.
9. He ran out of the house *screaming*.
10. I took Lucy's car, *knowing* that she would understand.

6 Using conjunctions to build complex sentences

• Look through the examples with the students and clear up any difficulties. They should see that a clause introduced by one of these conjunctions (except *so*) can generally come either before or after the other clause. (Which clause actually comes first depends on what is emphasized – the more important information in a sentence tends to come last.)

• Point out, too, that a comma is generally used when the subordinate clause (the one with the conjunction) begins the sentence, though this does not always happen if both clauses are short.

• Note that *when* can be used either to talk about simultaneous events (like *while*) or to talk about successive events (like *after*). Compare the use of simple and progressive verb forms in the two pairs of examples.

• When students are ready, get them to combine sentences from the list (orally or in writing, as you prefer). Ask for at least three complex sentences; more ambitious students could try to make one with each of the eight conjunctions. There is no reason why they should not produce silly combinations provided they use the conjunctions appropriately.

• This can also be done as an oral chain activity: Student A reads out a half-sentence, and Student B has to complete it by adding one of the other half-sentences (justifying his/her answer if necessary). Then Student B reads out a half-sentence, and Student C has to complete it; and so on.

7 Vocabulary expansion: the parts of a car / everyday objects

• An alternative way of doing the first option is to present it as a challenge. Give students a time limit (e.g. ten minutes) to learn as much vocabulary as they can; then go and look at a car and let them see how many of the words they can recall without opening their books. If they are sufficiently interested in the subject matter, they could also learn some of the vocabulary of driving (e.g. *start, change gear, accelerate, overtake, slow down, park*).

• Another useful vocabulary expansion activity is to get students to empty their pockets or handbags (within reason), and let them work in groups pooling their knowledge or using dictionaries to learn the names of all the objects they have turned out.

Answers to Exercise 7 (picture B)
1. calculator   2. paper-clip   3. (pair of) scissors
4. (ball of) string   5. envelope   6. stamp   7. diary
8. penknife / pocket knife   9. bunch of keys / key-ring with keys   10. pocket torch / flashlight   11. postcard
12. audio cassette   13. screwdriver   14. light bulb
15. door-handle.

Practice Book exercises
1. Tenses of *there is/are*.
2. Writing sentences beginning with *There would/ wouldn't be*.
3. Completing sentences with *although*, *because* or *so*.
4. Word stress.
5. Revision of compound nouns from the Student's Book lesson.
6. Recreational reading: two poems.
7. Creative writing: a short story.

6 Look at the examples of how to use conjunctions. Do you know all the conjunctions?

The phone always rings **when** I'm cooking supper. / **When** I'm cooking supper, the phone always rings.

I didn't say anything **when** he asked my name. / **When** he asked my name, I didn't say anything.

He joined the army **after** he left school. / **After** he left school, he joined the army.

My bicycle was stolen **while** I was shopping. / **While** I was shopping, my bicycle was stolen.

Come and see us **before** you go to America. / **Before** you go to America, come and see us.

I'll give you a ring **as soon as** I arrive. / **As soon as** I arrive, I'll give you a ring.

I never travelled abroad **until** I was 18. / **Until** I was 18, I never travelled abroad.

She passed her exams **because** she worked hard. / **Because** she worked hard, she passed her exams.

She passed her exams **although** she had a bad teacher. / **Although** she had a bad teacher, she passed her exams.

There wasn't any beer, **so** I had a glass of fruit juice.

Now use the conjunctions to join some of these sentences together.

They fell in love.
She got very angry.
The train arrived.
Nobody spoke.
It was raining.
Mary failed all her exams.
She hated her teacher.
He ate too much.
She got up.
He started work.
The police were looking for him.
This job is finished.
Ann walked out of the house.
Jake fell off his bicycle.
He went to Scotland.
He wasn't very good-looking.
I'll stay here.
She telephoned the police.
There was nothing in the fridge.
I walked and walked.
I was really tired.
There was nothing to do.
We danced all night.
You answer my question.
The cat ran away.
He couldn't drive.
It was a warm day.
There was water all over the floor.
We went to a restaurant.
He lost his job.
I'll be very happy.

TWO VOCABULARY AREAS

7 Choose one of these exercises.
1. Study picture A and learn as many of the words as you want to. Then go and look at a car. See how many of the words you can remember without looking at your book.
2. Study picture B. How many of the objects do you know the names of? Use your dictionary to find out the names of the others. Close your book and try to write down the names of all the objects in the picture from memory. Test yourself tomorrow – how many of the words do you still know?

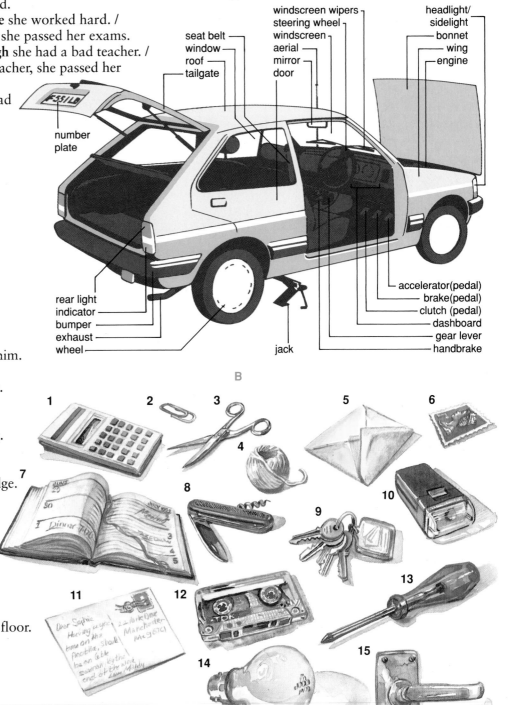

A

windscreen wipers
steering wheel
windscreen
aerial
mirror
door

seat belt
window
roof
tailgate

headlight/ sidelight
bonnet
wing
engine

number plate

rear light
indicator
bumper
exhaust
wheel

jack

accelerator(pedal)
brake(pedal)
clutch (pedal)
dashboard
gear lever
handbrake

B

1 2 3 4 5 6 7 8 9 10 11 12 13 14 15

Learn/revise: *vocabulary from Exercise 7.*

B3 How honest are you?

Vocabulary expansion; revision of comparatives; linking vowels and consonants; general skills practice.

1 Read the questions and note your answers.

1 You find a wallet containing £1,000. There are no papers inside to show who it belongs to. Do you hand it to the police or keep it?
   a Hand it to the police.
   b Keep it.
   c Not sure.

2 You have an expensive meal in a restaurant. When you check the bill, you see that the waiter has forgotten to charge you for the drinks. Do you tell him or keep quiet?
   a Tell him.
   b Keep quiet.
   c Not sure.

3 Do you think it is all right to hide some of your earnings from the tax inspector?
   a Yes.
   b No.
   c Not sure.

4 Have you ever pretended to be ill to get off work or school?
   a Often.
   b Once or twice / occasionally.
   c Never.

5 You are staying in a hotel, and you see that they have very nice towels. Do you take any home with you?
   a All of them.
   b Just one.
   c None.
   d Not sure.

6 You advertise your house for sale. Somebody offers you a good price, and you agree to sell to her. Before you sign the contract, somebody else offers you another £5,000. Do you stay with the first buyer or sell to the second?
   a Stay with the first.
   b Sell to the second.
   c Go back to the first and ask for £5,000 more.
   d Not sure.

7 One of your family (mother, father, wife, husband, child) has some very strange friends. One day you find a letter from one of these people lying around the house. Do you read it?
   a Yes.
   b Certainly not.
   c Perhaps.

8 In your opinion, how serious is shoplifting?
   a Not at all serious – most people do it at one time or another.
   b You might do it if you really needed something and hadn't got enough money.
   c You would never do it.

9 You are playing cards (not for money) and you see that somebody is cheating. What do you think about it?
   a It doesn't matter.
   b It's annoying, but not too serious.
   c You refuse to go on playing unless they stop.
   d You stop the game, because you won't play with people who cheat.

10 Travelling in a taxi, you find a torch lying on the seat – it must have been dropped by the last passenger. What do you do?
   a Put it in your pocket.
   b Give it to the taxi driver.
   c Just leave it.
   d Not sure.

11 Have you ever cheated in an exam?
   a Often.
   b More than once.
   c Once.
   d Never.

12 What do you think about travelling without a ticket on public transport?
   a OK.
   b Not really OK, but you might do it.
   c Completely wrong – you would never do it.

13 Is it ever right to tell lies about yourself to impress other people?
   a It can be.
   b Never.
   c Not sure.

14 Is it all right to take stationery from the place where you work?
   a Yes.
   b No.
   c Not sure.

15 Have you answered all the questions completely honestly?
   a Yes.
   b No.
   c Well, nearly.

Check your score at the bottom of the next page.

─── Lesson B3 ───

Students practise reading, speaking and writing skills; they discuss approaches to vocabulary learning.
Principal structures: comparative structures (*worse than; not as bad as; the worst*).
Phonology: linking.

Language notes and possible problems

1. Linking (Exercise 4) In spoken English, words tend to 'run into each other'. Students may need to practise linking words together naturally. Note the following points:

– Some learners (e.g. many German-speakers) tend to separate a word beginning with a vowel from the word that comes before it, by making a slight hesitation or 'glottal stop'. The first group of expressions in Exercise 4 gives practice in *consonant + vowel* linking. Note also that final *r* needs to be pronounced before a following vowel (second group). The third group gives practice in *vowel + vowel* linking. If students find this difficult, get them to pronounce a small *w* between the two vowels (e.g. *'towimpress'*).
– When two consonants come together, the first is often 'assimilated' to the second – it changes its pronunciation so as to make for an easier transition to the second consonant. So, for example, the /t/ in *wallet* changes to an incomplete /k/ before the *c* in *wallet containing*; the /t/ in *it* changes to an incomplete /p/ before the *b* in *it belongs*. Many students tend to pronounce consonants unnaturally clearly and separately in these cases. The fourth group of expressions gives practice in *consonant + consonant* linking.
– Some students have trouble pronouncing /h/, and they may find it particularly hard after a vowel. The last group of expressions give practice in pronouncing *vowel + h*.

Note that poor linking does not usually make students more difficult to understand. However, it prevents them from pronouncing English fluently and naturally, and is therefore worth working on if students have the time and motivation.

2. Timing This is a long lesson, and you may need to devote a separate session to Exercise 5 (Students' questionnaires).

If you are short of time
Drop Exercise 4.

---

1 Questionnaire

• This can be done by class discussion. Go through the questions explaining any problems, and getting students to note their answers.
• Encourage discussion whenever students have things they want to say.
• At the end of the exercise, get students to check their scores. (The 'results' have, of course, no scientific value, and students shouldn't take them seriously.) Students may disagree with the scoring: if so, encourage them to say why.
• Finally, see how much of the vocabulary from the questionnaire students can remember with their books closed.

2 Students choose vocabulary to learn

- It is important that students should be able to make some of the decisions about their learning.
- Give them a few minutes to choose words that they particularly want to learn. Help them to establish the exact meanings, guiding them in efficient dictionary use if necessary.
- Get them to compare notes with other students about their choice of vocabulary, and to tell you what made them choose the words they did. (This can be done in the mother tongue if convenient.)
- This may also be a good opportunity to talk again about different ways of noting and learning new vocabulary (see teaching notes for Lesson A3, Exercise 7).

3 Comparisons

- This gives students some brief revision of comparative structures. If more is needed, there are exercises on comparatives in the Grammar Revision Section on page 129.
- Check that students are clear about the difference between *worse* and *worst*.
- This exercise, again, may lead to discussion.

4 Pronunciation: linking

- Choose the group(s) of expressions that correspond to your students' pronunciation problems (see *Language notes*).
- Make sure students understand what they are supposed to be doing, and then demonstrate the correct pronunciation (using the recording as a model if you wish).
- Get students to practise the expressions until they are fluent.

5 Students' questionnaires

- Give students plenty of time to choose a subject and write out a questionnaire of ten or more questions.
- You will probably need to help with vocabulary, but discourage students from trying to write complicated questions in difficult English that the others won't be able to understand.
- When they are ready, let them answer each other's questionnaires.

Practice Book exercises

1. Revision of vocabulary from the Student's Book lesson.
2. Distinguishing between /ð/ and /θ/.
3. Students read and write about when people lie.
4. A puzzle: revision of comparatives and superlatives.
5. Students read and write about whether women are more truthful than men.
6. Recreational reading: a choice of three texts about honesty and dishonesty.

2 Vocabulary. Choose some words and expressions to learn from the questionnaire. Compare notes with another student and talk about the reasons for your choices.

3 You probably feel that some of these things are worse than others. Make sentences. Examples:

'I think shoplifting is worse than cheating at cards.'
'I don't think reading other people's letters is as bad as cheating in exams.'
'I think telling lies is the worst thing.'

shoplifting
reading other people's letters
cheating at cards
cheating in exams
travelling without a ticket
avoiding income tax
stealing towels from a hotel
telling lies about yourself

4 📼 Pronunciation: joining words together. Choose the group(s) that you find difficult and practise saying the expressions.

consonant + vowel
you find a wallet
hand it to the police
some of your earnings
tax inspector
one of your family
lying around
not at all serious
put it in your pocket

r + vowel
in your opinion
at one time or another
your earnings

joining two vowels
to impress other people
who it belongs to
somebody else offers you another £5,000
you agree

joining two consonants
a wallet containing £1,000
who it belongs to
hand it to the police
when you get the bill
you see that the waiter has forgotten
lying around the house
it doesn't matter

vowel + h
in a hotel
do you take any home?
you have an expensive meal
to hide some of your earnings
you advertise your house for sale
lying around the house

5 Work with two or three other students. Make up a questionnaire for the class (you choose the subject). Some ideas: 'How sociable are you?' 'How generous are you?' 'How hard-working are you?'

"Don't lie to me—you've been to the pub again."

Learn/revise: bill; meal; pocket; price; public transport; score; shoplifting; tax; ticket; torch; towel; wallet; advertise; avoid; belong (to); cheat; check; contain; drop; find (found, found); hide (hid, hidden); impress; keep (kept, kept); leave (left, left); lie (lying, lay, lain); lose (lost, lost); need; offer; play cards; sign; steal (stole, stolen); tell lies (told, told); expensive; generous; hard-working; honest; quiet; serious; sociable; strange; sure; valuable; wrong; all right; for sale; keep quiet; it doesn't matter; nearly.

terrible!
60: You even give dishonest answers to questionnaires – that's
you're kind to children and animals.
46–59: You seem to be a rather dishonest person. But perhaps
others.
31–45: You're honest about some things and dishonest about
23–30: You're more honest than average.
16–22: You're a very honest person.
15: Are you sure you answered Question 15 honestly?
RESULTS

12: a4, b3, c1   13: a3, b1, c2   14: a3, b1, c2   15: a1, b3, c2
9: a3, b3, c2, d1   10: a3, b1, d2   11: a4, b3, c2, d1
5: a6, b4, c1, d3   6: a1, b4, c3, d2   7: a4, b1, c3   8: a5, b3, c1
1: a1, b6, c3   2: a1, b4, c3   3: a4, b1, c3   4: a4, b2, c1
CHECK YOUR SCORE

33

B4 No trousers

SKILLS FOCUS
SKILLS FOCUS
SKILLS FOCUS
SKILLS FOCUS
SKILLS FOCUS
SKILLS FOCUS
SKILLS FOCUS

Writing skills: predicting a story line, shaping narratives, connecting sentences, dividing texts into paragraphs, expanding stories; speaking skills: storytelling.

1 Your teacher will read or play you a story sentence by sentence. Try and guess how the story continues.

2 Now turn to page 130 and look at the story. Then work in pairs to answer the following questions.

1. What are the words or expressions in the story that tell you about time? For example, *Last week* or *While he was putting the first pair of trousers on*.
2. The word *and* is used to join ideas in the story, as in *He chose two suits to try on **and** went to the changing rooms*. How many other ways can you find of joining ideas?
3. Why do you think the paragraph divisions come where they do?

3 Here is the first sentence of the story with two new pieces of information added in different ways. Which ways do you think are most successful?

1. Last week my next-door neighbour Steve went to a department store to buy a new suit. *The department store is in the middle of town. Steve needed the suit for a job interview.*
2. Last week my next-door neighbour Steve went to a department store *which is in the middle of town* to buy a new suit, *which he needed for a job interview*.
3. Last week my next-door neighbour Steve went to a department store *in the middle of town* to buy a new suit, *which he needed for a job interview*.
4. Last week my next-door neighbour Steve went to a department store *which is in the middle of town* to buy a new suit *for a job interview*.
5. Last week my next-door neighbour Steve went to a department store *in the middle of town* to buy a new suit *for a job interview*.
6. Last week my next-door neighbour Steve went to a department store *in the middle of town* to buy a new suit, *because he had a job interview*.
7. Last week my next-door neighbour Steve, *needing a new suit for a job interview*, went to a department store *in the middle of town*.
8. Last week my next-door neighbour Steve needed a new suit *for a job interview*, so he went to a department store *in the middle of town*.

34

Lesson B4

Writing skills: predicting a story line; writing and expanding narratives; connecting sentences; dividing texts into paragraphs.
Speaking skills: storytelling.

Language notes and possible problems

1. Content and form in writing   Good writers (both native writers and second-language writers) think about content first, often leaving questions of form for a later draft. This is why in Exercises 1 to 3 students are asked first to concentrate on what is happening in the story, and only then to look at formal techniques. Students should be encouraged to do the same in their own writing; make sure students write on every other line in Exercise 5 and encourage them to feel free to make modifications to their first draft.

2. Writing and audience   Writing in the classroom can be somewhat artificial – when we write in 'real life' we are writing for an audience of one person or more, and we have an aim in mind; the people who read what we have written read for content, not form. So in Exercise 5 when students are writing a story we have asked them to imagine an audience, in order to give themselves an idea of the tone they will adopt; and they are then asked to read each other's stories for content, as a real reader would.

3. Several meanings of _get_ are exemplified in the story for Exercises 1 to 4. Students can practise using _get_ in Exercise 3 in the Practice Book.

If you are short of time

Get students to do Exercise 5 for homework and bring the results back to class, to exchange stories with each other.

1 Predicting a story line

• This preliminary exercise aims to sensitise students to the shape of a story and emphasizes the importance of concentrating on content before looking at form.

• Ask the students to close their books. Read the story on page 130 sentence by sentence, or play the recording if you prefer, pausing after each sentence. After each sentence, ask students what they think will happen in the rest of the story.

• Accept any suggestions the students put forth, without judgment.

2 Narrative structuring

• Ask students to turn to page 130 and give them a few minutes to look over the story you have just read. Answer any questions they have about meaning.

• Put them into pairs or threes. Go over the questions in Exercise 2 and make sure they understand what they are to do before they begin.

• Walk round while they are working to give any help that is needed.

Possible answers to Exercise 2
(Students may have different, acceptable answers to Questions 2 and 3; the main point is for them to look closely at how the narrative is structured.)
1. (Last week)
   (While he was putting the first pair of trousers on)
   Now
   Later that afternoon
   after we managed to get a new house key made for him
   When we got to the store
   When we got there

2. **Paragraph 1:** Sentence 4: _but_ joins verb phrases
   Sentence 6: _So_ is used to indicate consequence
   (Students may also note the infinitive structures in Sentences 1, 2 and 3.)
   Paragraph 2: last sentence: _So_ indicates consequence
   Paragraph 3: second sentence: _Wondering_ used to show simultaneity
   (In the last sentence, students may also note the infinitive structures after _used_.)

3. Students may say that each paragraph signals a change of place; or they may say that there is a gap in time between each paragraph. Both answers are acceptable.

3 Expanding the story: analysis

• Ask students to work individually reading the sentences and deciding which are the most successful.

• Then put them into groups of three or four and ask each group to try and come up with a joint list of the three most successful solutions.

• Go over the answers with the students. It is best not to ask students to give reasons for their choices if they do not volunteer them: some students may have trouble being articulate about _why_ they chose one summary rather than another. Do, however, give them reasons when you discuss the answers.

Answers to Exercise 3
Solutions 3, 5 and 8 are probably the best ways of stating the information; they are economical and they vary the rhythm of the sentences.
Solutions 6 and 7 are also good.
Solution 1 lacks connecting devices and so sounds rather monotonous.
Solution 2 repeats _which_, leading to a rather heavy sentence; Solution 4 is also heavy, using a relative clause with _which_ for a small piece of information.

34

4 Expanding the story: practice

• Put the students into groups of three or four. Make sure that they understand the instructions.
• If you think your students need more help than Exercise 3 has given them, you may want to do the first sentence with the whole class as an example.
• Each group must then choose two or more of the pieces of information. They should then decide where each goes in the story and how they are going to structure it to make it fit in. They may also want in some cases to make changes to nearby sentences when they insert the new information.
• Each group should write out the part of the story that has the new information.
• Walk round while they are working to give any help that is needed.
• Discuss the answers with the students, or get the groups to exchange papers and see how other groups have approached the problem.

5 Writing a picture story

• Start by asking students to look at the pictures and decide what the relationships between the people are.
• If you feel that some students will get stuck trying to imagine what happens in the blank frames, you can either elicit possibilities with the whole class or put the students in pairs or small groups for two or three minutes to discuss this.
• Otherwise just point out that some of the frames are blank, and that students must invent what happens in those frames: for instance, whatever happens in the first blank frame makes the mother and father angry with the daughter and her with them.
• The writing part of the exercise should be done individually. Ask students to write on every other line of their papers so that they can go back and change things if they want to. Tell them that they can just write the story out quickly the first time and then go back and make changes to make better connections in the story. If you think your students may tend to write too little or too much, you may want to give them a time limit, or say, for instance, that they should write about two sentences per frame.
• Walk round while students are working to give any help that is needed.
• As students finish, get them to exchange their stories to read. They can comment on or ask questions about the stories (concentrating on content, not form). Another approach is to put the stories up on the walls of the room as they are finished, for students to walk round and read.
• If you take the stories up to comment on, make sure that you too comment on the content as well as the form of the stories, perhaps using two different colours of ink.

6 Storytelling

• Put students into groups of three to five. Give them a few moments to think of a story (true or not) about someone being tricked (as in the first story in the lesson).
• Students tell their stories to the group in turn.
• If there is time, the group can vote on its best story to be re-told to the class as a whole.

Practice Book exercises
1. Revision of indefinite pronouns (*anybody, everything*, etc.).
2. Student's Cassette exercise (Student's Book Lesson B4, Exercise 1). Students listen to the story and try to write down as much of the first seven sentences as they can.
3. Different meanings of *get*.
4. Revision of vocabulary from the Student's Book lesson.
5. Reading skills (deducing meaning from context).
6. Writing skills: putting a story into order; using linking words; paragraphing.

4 Now choose two or more of these pieces of information, and add them to the story. Make any other changes that are necessary, and write out the part of the story that has the new information.

1. I was at my office when Steve phoned.
2. The man who phoned Steve said that Steve's driving licence was in the wallet (but no money).
3. The store is about half an hour's drive from Steve's home.
4. When we got to the store we went straight to the security department.
5. The security department phoned several other departments. Nobody knew who had called Steve.

5 Work on your own. Look at the pictures. Your task is to write the story. Imagine you are one of the characters – the mother, the father, the daughter or the son. Then decide who you will write to – a friend, a relative … Imagine what happens in the blank frames; add any other imaginative details you want to. When you have finished, exchange stories with another student and read each other's stories.

6 Have you ever been tricked (like Steve in the first story)? Or has someone you know been tricked? Or do you know a good story about this kind of trick? Work in groups of three to five, and tell each other your stories. If there is time, each group should choose one of the stories to tell to the whole class.

Learn/revise: credit card; department; department store; driving licence; hand; key; middle; money; neighbour; pair; phone call; security; story; suit; thief (thieves); town; trick (*noun and verb*); trousers; wallet; catch (caught, caught); choose (chose, chosen); drive (drove, driven); find (found, found); get (got, got); happen; leave (left, left); manage (to); phone; rescue; reach; run after (ran, run); shout; wonder; try on; nobody; stuck; as well; last (week, *etc.*); later that (afternoon, day, *etc.*); next door.

B5 Small talk (1)

Greeting and welcoming; asking for confirmation; asking for personal information; mealtime conventions; question tags; intonation; listening skills: listening for specific information.

1 📼 Listen to the dialogue, and write the numbers and letters of the expressions you hear.

1. a. I go.
   b. I'm going.
   c. I'll go.

2. a. Nice to see you.
   b. It's nice to see you.
   c. Nice seeing you.

3. a. Are we late?
   b. We're late.
   c. Aren't we late?

4. a. You're first.
   b. You're the first.
   c. You're not first.

5. a. Who is coming?
   b. Who ever's coming?
   c. Who else is coming?

6. a. Can I take your coat?
   b. Let me take your coat.
   c. Shall I take your coat?

7. a. You know Lucy, do you?
   b. You know Lucy, don't you?
   c. You don't know Lucy, do you?

8. a. I think we've met her once.
   b. I think we met her once.
   c. I think we'll meet her one day.

9. a. What can I get you to drink?
   b. What can I give you to drink?
   c. What would you like to drink?

10. a. The room doesn't look nice, John.
    b. Does the room look nice, John?
    c. Doesn't the room look nice, John?

11. a. You've changed it about.
    b. You've changed it round.
    c. You've changed it over.

2 📼 Listen again.
Which of these do you hear?

a. don't you?
b. do you?
c. isn't it?
d. wasn't it?
e. aren't we?
f. haven't you?

3 📼 Real questions or not? Listen to the sentences. Does the voice go up or down at the end? Examples:

The piano was over by the window, wasn't it?

You know Lucy, don't you?

1. It's a lovely day, isn't it?
2. You're French, aren't you?
3. She's got fatter, hasn't she?
4. The train leaves at 4.13, doesn't it?
5. Children always like cartoon films, don't they?
6. It's your birthday next week, isn't it?
7. Hotels are expensive here, aren't they?
8. Ann said she'd phone, didn't she?

4 Work with two or three other students. Act out a 'greeting' scene like the one in Exercise 1.

36

Lesson B5

NOTE: Organisation and timing

This lesson and Lesson B7 are based on a series of five dialogues which portray different stages in a dinner-party. Each dialogue generates a good deal of work, and students are led up to the point where they can improvise their own 'social' conversations in groups. The two lessons really consist of five mini-lessons, and should be handled as such. The Teacher's Book instructions are organised accordingly.

These lessons will probably take longer than usual to work through, particularly if you have time to make a detailed study of the language of the dialogues. This is not, however, essential; much of the new language is 'preview' material which will come up again.

The texts of the three dialogues in Lesson B5 are at the end of the Student's Book, on pages 130 to 131. Ideally, students should not look at these until they are asked to do so in Exercise 10. But some students are very uncomfortable if they cannot see the written word fairly soon. If it is necessary, let them look at the text of each dialogue after work on it is finished – but try and get them to mask the following dialogues while they read. It is important to do each set of exercises before reading the dialogue.

— Dialogue 1

Students learn some conventional 'social' language used in greeting and welcoming people and asking for confirmation; they practise the skill of listening for specific information.

Principal structures: question tags with affirmative sentences.

Phonology: intonation of question tags.

Language notes and possible problems

Question tags The meaning of the question-tag structure will probably be easy for students to grasp. Many languages have an expression which is added to a sentence in order to invite the hearer's agreement. But students will probably find the structure difficult to learn, and the intonation will certainly cause problems. Students need to learn:

– that the tag is negative if the sentence is affirmative.
– that *be* or an auxiliary is repeated from the main sentence; or if the main sentence has neither *be* nor an auxiliary, the tag contains *do/does/did*.
– that the intonation of the tag depends on the speaker's intention: a rising intonation means that the speaker wants information (it is a real question); a falling intonation means that the speaker is sure of the hearer's agreement.

Note that thorough work on question tags will be done in Lesson B6.

If you are short of time

You can leave out Exercise 2.

1 Listening comprehension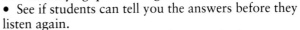

• Ask students to look at the picture and tell you as much as they can about it.
• Play the dialogue once while students just listen.
• Tell them to write down the numbers 1 to 11 on a piece of paper and play the dialogue again.
• Students should listen for the numbered expressions and try to write the correct letter each time.
• You may need to play the dialogue once more.
• Let them compare notes; then give them the answers.

Answers to Exercise 1
1c; 2a; 3a; 4b; 5c; 6b; 7b; 8a; 9a; 10c; 11b

2 Identifying question tags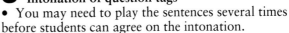

• See if students can tell you the answers before they listen again.
• Then play the dialogue so they can check.

Answers to Exercise 2
The tags they hear are *don't you?*, *haven't you?* and *wasn't it?*

3 Intonation of question tags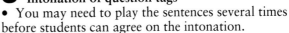

• You may need to play the sentences several times before students can agree on the intonation.
• Check the answers with them.
• Elicit or explain the meaning of the two intonation patterns (see *Language notes*), and get students to imitate them.
• Point out how these question tags are constructed.

Answers to Exercise 3
1, 3, 5 and 7 go down; 2, 4, 6 and 8 go up.

4 Improvisation

• Ask for three or four volunteers.
• Get them to improvise a scene similar to the one in the dialogue. (Start by getting two of the students to go out of the room and knock on the door.)
• Then get the class to do it in groups. Walk round listening, and help if necessary.

Dialogues and improvisations: fluency and accuracy

In activities like Exercise 11, the emphasis is on fluency. It is very important for students to practise talking at reasonable speed without stopping to think everything out. In exercises of this kind, it is best not to interrupt students with corrections unless there is a real breakdown in communication. Any serious mistakes can be noted and dealt with in another lesson.

'What are we learning?'

Some students will be used to courses with a central structural syllabus, where the main purpose of each lesson is to teach a new point of grammar. They may feel quite uneasy at lessons like this one, where the grammar work is less important than other things such as vocabulary or skills practice. And in lessons which teach no grammar at all they may complain that they are learning nothing useful.

You may need to explain that this is a complete English course, not just a grammar course; and that grammar is only one of several things which students must work at if they want to learn English successfully. Point out that they cannot judge their progress simply by the number of new structures learnt. (Vocabulary mistakes tend to outnumber grammar mistakes by more than three to one.)

While some of the lessons in this course concentrate on grammar, others focus on vocabulary, speaking practice, listening practice, reading skills or other things. If students are helped to understand the exact purpose of each lesson, and the importance of each different part of the syllabus, they will be less uneasy about lessons which do not give priority to grammar.

— Dialogue 2 —

Students learn ways of giving and eliciting personal information and asking for repetition; they practise the skill of listening for specific information.
Phonology: more practice on the intonation of question tags.

Possible problems
Handling the dialogue The main purpose of the dialogue is to provide listening practice. Do not go through the text in detail unless students particularly want to. If you do decide to study the text, the best time to do it is after Exercise 10.

If you are short of time
You can spend a minimum of time on Exercise 6.

5 Listening comprehension 🔲
- Play the dialogue; then ask students to read the sentences and note their answers.
- Play the dialogue again while they check answers.
- Let them compare notes; then give them the answers.

Answers to Exercise 5
1T; 2T; 3F; 4F; 5F; 6T; 7F; 8F; 9DK; 10T; 11T

6 Recall 🔲
- Play the dialogue once again.
- Ask students to work individually, writing down any sentences they can remember.
- You may like to try to rebuild the dialogue on the board, or let students do it in groups.

7 Real questions: rising intonation 🔲
- Get students to repeat the sentences.
- Make sure everyone can manage the intonation reasonably well.
- Remind students that a rising intonation on a question tag indicates a real question.

8 Asking for agreement: falling intonation 🔲
- Get students to repeat the sentences.
- Make sure they understand the meaning of a falling intonation here – the speaker expects agreement.

— Dialogue 3 —

Students learn polite formulae for mealtimes; they practise the skill of listening for specific information.
Principal structures: more work on the structure of question tags.

If you are short of time
You can leave out or shorten Exercise 11. But note that students will get a great deal of fluency practice from this exercise, and their enjoyment of it will serve to help them retain the language they use.

9 Listening for specific information 🔲
- Students may not be familiar with all the words for food and drink in this dialogue.
- Play it once through while they listen, and then once again (perhaps pausing once or twice) while they try to note the words they recognise.
- Give them a few moments to finish writing, let them compare notes, and give them the answers.
- Explain the meanings of the new words and practise their pronunciation.

Answers to Exercise 9
salt   mustard   beef   potato   meat   beans
carrot   bread   wine

10 Choosing vocabulary to learn
- Ask students to look over the tapescripts of the dialogues; each student should choose seven or more words or expressions to learn.
- When they have chosen their words individually, put them into pairs. Ask each person to tell the group two of her/his words and why they were chosen.

11 Improvisation
- Make a 'compartment' at the front of the class, with two rows of four chairs opposite each other.
- Ask for six volunteers to 'get onto the train'.
- Tell them that they're on a long train journey, they're bored, so they should start a conversation.
- Every few minutes, stop the train at a station and let a few people get off and a few new ones get on.
- If things are going well, establish a second compartment; appoint ticket collectors, immigration officers to check passports; tea vendors, etc.

Optional variant for Exercise 11
- When the six volunteers go onto the train, give them each an envelope with a sentence in it. Each person has to try and steer the conversation around so their sentence can be inserted naturally. Some possible sentences:
1. My goldfish died last week, and I have no idea why.
2. There were a lot of old cars parked in a circle.
3. She was carrying a typewriter case full of bananas.
4. My grandfather smoked forty cigarettes a day.
5. We can't do it if the weather's not nice.
6. He only worked on Tuesdays and Fridays.

Practice Book exercises
1. Vocabulary and grammar: completing a conversation based on dialogues in the Student's Book lesson.
2. Writing short forms of first names.
3. Student's Cassette exercise (Student's Book Lesson B5, Exercise 5). Students mark and practise sentence stress.
4. Revision of prepositions.
5. Question tags.
6. Reading skills: deducing meaning from context.

5 🔊 Listen to the dialogue. Then look at the following sentences. Are they true or false? Write T (true), F (false), or DK (don't know).

1. Lucy works in a pub.
2. She likes her work.
3. She doesn't meet many interesting people.
4. Lucy's job is always hard work.
5. There is only one barman in her pub.
6. John works in a bank.
7. He likes his job very much.
8. He has just been made manager.
9. He's going to move to another town soon.
10. Lucy wouldn't like to move to another town.
11. John has lived in the same place for six years.

6 🔊 Listen again. Can you write down some sentences from the dialogue?

7 🔊 Real questions. Listen and repeat.

1. That's hard work, isn't it?
2. You're an accountant, aren't you?
3. You have to move round, don't you?
4. It'll be in another town, won't it?

8 🔊 Asking for agreement. Listen and repeat.

1. It's a nice day, isn't it?
2. She's very pretty, isn't she?
3. Good clothes are expensive, aren't they?
4. You're tired, aren't you?

9 🔊 Listen to the dialogue. Write down all the words you hear for things that you can eat or drink.

10 Turn to pages 130 and 131 and look over the tapescripts of the dialogues. Choose seven to ten words or expressions to learn. Show your list to another student and say why you have chosen two of the words/expressions.

11 Work with four or five other students. You are all in the same compartment on a long train journey. Act out a conversation in which you get to know one another.

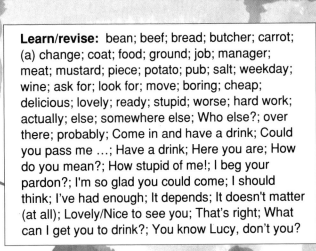

> **Learn/revise:** bean; beef; bread; butcher; carrot; (a) change; coat; food; ground; job; manager; meat; mustard; piece; potato; pub; salt; weekday; wine; ask for; look for; move; boring; cheap; delicious; lovely; ready; stupid; worse; hard work; actually; else; somewhere else; Who else?; over there; probably; Come in and have a drink; Could you pass me ...; Have a drink; Here you are; How do you mean?; How stupid of me!; I beg your pardon?; I'm so glad you could come; I should think; I've had enough; It depends; It doesn't matter (at all); Lovely/Nice to see you; That's right; What can I get you to drink?; You know Lucy, don't you?

B6 Focus on systems

> A choice of exercises: question tags; position of prepositions in questions; /ə/ in unstressed syllables; verbs for everyday actions involving objects and materials.

GRAMMAR: POSITION OF PREPOSITIONS IN QUESTIONS

1 Can you complete these questions?

What are you looking ....?
What are John and Lucy talking ....?

Now read the following answers and write the questions.

1. They're talking about politics.
2. I went with Henry.
3. I'm looking for Alice.
4. I bought it for you.
5. I'm thinking about holidays.
6. I'm listening to Radio 2.
7. I'm looking at your ear-rings.
8. The letter was from Andy.
9. She's in love with me.
10. She comes from Iceland.

GRAMMAR: QUESTION TAGS

2 Study the examples and then complete the sentences.

Your father **is** a doctor, **isn't** he?
The film **was** pretty boring, **wasn't** it?
We **were** right, **weren't** we?
The Lewises **have** gone on holiday, **haven't** they?
Ann **will** be pleased to see us, **won't** she?
Peter **would** like to be a doctor, **wouldn't** he?
Rita **can** speak seven languages, **can't** she?

There **are** tigers in Siberia, **aren't** there?

I'm late, **aren't** I? (~~...amn't I?~~)

You **drink** coffee, **don't** you?
She **arrived** late, **didn't** she?

1. It's cold, ...?
2. Anne was ill last week, ...?
3. You've met Sally, ...?
4. Your children were all at the same school, ...?
5. You'll be home before midnight, ...?
6. Maurice looks very like his father, ...?
7. It would be nice to go and see Chris, ...
8. Your father came from Canada, ...?
9. These cars use a lot of petrol, ...?
10. You're working next weekend, ...?
11. There's somebody at the door, ...?
12. I'm cooking supper tonight, ...?

3 Study the examples and then complete the sentences.

She **isn't** happy, **is** she?
You **haven't** seen my brother anywhere, **have** you?
The film **wasn't** much good, **was** it?
You **can't** swim, **can** you?
Your mother **wouldn't** like to come, **would** she?
Cats **don't** eat cornflakes, **do** they?
The postman **didn't** come this morning, **did** he?
There **isn't** any milk in the fridge, **is** there?

1. It isn't raining, ...?
2. You weren't there this morning, ...?
3. Kate can't speak Spanish, ...?
4. The meat doesn't look very nice, ...?
5. You wouldn't like to help me, ...?
6. Penny hasn't phoned, ...?
7. You won't get married before you leave school, ...?
8. They didn't tell you to work at the weekend, ...?
9. John wasn't happy in his last job, ...?
10. There weren't any messages for me, ...?
11. You don't mind if I open the window, ...?
12. This isn't your coat, ...?

4 🔲 Asking for agreement. Listen and say the question tags. Example:

'It's a nice day,...' '...isn't it?'

PRONUNCIATION: /ə/ IN UNSTRESSED SYLLABLES

5 🔲 The vowel /ə/ comes one or more times in each of the following words (the number of times is shown in brackets). Decide which vowels are pronounced /ə/. Listen to the recording and check your answers; then practise the words.

barman (1)   autumn (1)   breakfast (1)
compare (1)   continue (1)   concert (1)
Britain (1)   England (1)   foreign (1)
London (1)   tomato (1)   usually (1)
photograph (1) excellent (2)   America (2)
accountant (2) agreement (2)   dangerous (2)
policeman (2)   photographer (3)

6 🔲 Listen to the recording and decide how many words there are in each sentence. (Contractions like *don't* count as two words.)

Lesson B6

Grammar: question tags; clause-final prepositions in questions.
Phonology: /ə/ in unstressed syllables; hearing unstressed syllables.
Vocabulary: verbs for everyday actions involving objects and materials.

Language notes and possible problems

1. Question tags   Students have already done some work on question tags. In Exercises 2–4 they make a more systematic study of the topic, covering negative and non-negative tags. Note that the rules for constructing tags also apply to other abbreviated verb forms, like those in 'short answers' (e.g. *Yes, I did*), in 'reply questions' (e.g. *Oh, did you?*) and in *So/Neither do I* etc. (see Lesson B7).

2. Clause-final prepositions   This is a difficult structure for most students. One way of explaining it is to tell them that an expression like *look at* or *listen to* is almost one word – we like to keep the two parts together, even if this means separating a preposition from its object. More advanced students could be told that this also happens, for example, in relative clauses (e.g. *There's the girl **I was talking about**)* and in some infinitive structures (e.g. *It's a nice place **to live in**)*.

3. The vowel /ə/   Students do not generally realise that this is the commonest vowel in English, replacing the 'written' vowel in most unstressed syllables. Exercise 5 may help to make them more conscious of this.

---

1 Clause-final prepositions

• Look at the two examples. When students have done them, give any necessary grammatical explanations.
• Get students to write questions for the answers. This exercise is probably best done individually in writing.

Answers to Exercise 1
What are you looking *at*?
What are John and Lucy talking *about*?
1. What are they talking about?
2. Who did you go with?
3. Who are you looking for?
4. Who did you buy it for?
5. What are you thinking about?
6. What are you listening to?
7. What are you looking at?
8. Who was the letter from?
9. Who's she in love with?
10. Where does she come from?

2 Question tags after affirmative sentences

• Look through the examples with the students. Make sure they understand that *be* and auxiliaries are repeated in tags, but that other verbs (e.g. *drink, arrive*) are replaced by forms of *do*. They should also note that the *there* of *there is* is treated like a subject pronoun in tags, and that *aren't I?* is used instead of **amn't I?*
• The exercise can be done individually in writing or by class/group discussion, as you prefer.

Answers to Exercise 2
1. isn't it?	5. won't you?	9. don't they?
2. wasn't she?	6. doesn't he?	10. aren't you?
3. haven't you?	7. wouldn't it?	11. isn't there?
4. weren't they?	8. didn't he?	12. aren't I?

3 Question tags after negative sentences

• This can be done in the same way as Exercise 2.

Answers to Exercise 3
1. is it?	5. would you?	9. was he?
2. were you?	6. has she?	10. were there?
3. can she?	7. will you?	11. do you?
4. does it?	8. did they?	12. is it?

4 Mixed tags

• Students will hear sentences twice. First, with the tag left out: they have to supply it. Then they will hear the whole sentence including the tag; they should repeat it.
• In this exercise, only falling intonations ('asking for agreement') are used in the tags.
• Students can take turns to speak or answer in chorus.

Tapescript and answers to Exercise 4
– It's a nice day   It's a nice day, isn't it?
– She's French   She's French, isn't she?
– They've got a new car
   They've got a new car, haven't they?
– You're not working tomorrow
   You're not working tomorrow, are you?
– Peter lives in London   Peter lives in London, doesn't he?
– The shop doesn't open on Saturdays
   The shop doesn't open on Saturdays, does it?
– He'll be here tomorrow
   He'll be here tomorrow, won't he?
– There's a post office round the corner
   There's a post office round the corner, isn't there?
– The potatoes weren't very nice
   The potatoes weren't very nice, were they?
– He didn't say thank you
   He didn't say thank you, did he?
– I'm early   I'm early, aren't I?
– Mary can't swim   Mary can't swim, can she?

5 /ə/ in unstressed syllables

• Get students to discuss and work out each answer.
• Say the word or play the recording, and get students to decide whether or not their answers were correct.
• Practise saying the word.
• Students should note how a change of stress can completely change the pronunciation of a vowel (compare *photograph* and *photographer*).

Answers to Exercise 5
barman /ˈbaːmən/	tomato /təˈmaːtəʊ/
autumn /ˈɔːtəm/	usually /ˈjuːʒəli/
breakfast /ˈbrekfəst/	photograph /ˈfəʊtəgraːf/
compare /kəmˈpeə(r)/	excellent /ˈeksələnt/
continue /kənˈtɪnjuː/	America /əˈmerɪkə/
concert /ˈkɒnsət/	accountant /əˈkaʊntənt/
Britain /ˈbrɪtən/	agreement /əˈgriːmənt/
England /ˈɪŋglənd/	dangerous /ˈdeɪndʒərəs/
foreign /ˈfɒrən/	policeman /pəˈliːsmən/
London /ˈlʌndən/	photographer /fəˈtɒgrəfə(r)/

6 Perceiving unstressed syllables: 'how many words?'

• Play each sentence, more than once if necessary, and get students to decide how many words they hear.
• See if they can work out what most of the words are.
• Give them the answer, and then get them to practise the sentence with a natural rhythm.

Tapescript and answers to Exercise 6
1. There was somebody at the door, wasn't there? (9)
2. You couldn't help me for a few minutes, could you? (11)
3. She'll be fourteen at the end of the month, won't she? (13)
4. I've forgotten the names of some of the children. (10)
5. What were you and your brother talking about? (8)
6. What do you want me to look at? (8)
7. I'm looking for a sweater that doesn't cost too much. (12)
8. Where did you get those ear-rings? (6 or 7)
9. I bought them from one of the people that I work with. (12)
10. You won't forget to write to the people that we met on holiday, will you? (16)

38

7 Verbs for everyday actions involving objects and materials

- Let students work on this in groups, pooling their knowledge.
- When they are ready, go over the answers with them and give any additional explanations that are needed.
- For extra practice, mime or do the actions and get the students to tell you what you are doing.
- Let them do the same thing in groups.

Answers to Exercise 7
1. bend 2. touch 3. hit 4. polish 5. catch 6. pull
7. drop 8. pick up 9. cut 10. break 11. pour
12. push 13. tear 14. throw 15. slice 16. switch off
17. switch on 18. swing 19. mend 20. sharpen
21. scratch 22. put down 23. roll 24. kick 25. lift
26. tie 27. turn

8 Irregular verbs

- This can be done individually in writing or by class discussion, as you prefer.
- If students do badly on this exercise, you may need to do regular revision of common irregular verbs. (This is one of the few areas of English grammar where learning by heart is really useful.)

Answers to Exercise 8
Irregular verbs (infinitive, past tense and past participle):
bend – bent – bent
break – broke – broken
catch – caught – caught
cut – cut – cut
hit – hit – hit
put (down) – put – put
swing – swung – swung
tear – tore – torn
throw – threw – thrown

9 Finding things

- Students should be able to find things for most of the verbs, if not all.

Practice Book exercises

1. Student's Cassette exercise (Student's Book Lesson B6, Exercise 4 – the last six questions only). Students listen and write down the questions, and then practise saying them with the correct intonation.
2. Question tags.
3. Writing questions for answers.
4. Word order in questions; giving true answers to some of the questions.
5. Translation of material from Lessons A7 to B6.
6. Recreational reading: a humorous story.

Rhythm, stress and comprehension
English is 'stress-timed'. Stressed syllables are slower and clearer than unstressed syllables; they come at roughly equal intervals. Unstressed syllables tend to be fitted in quickly so as not to interrupt the rhythm. (*There was a man in the garden*, with eight syllables and two stresses, doesn't take much longer to say than *back door*, with two syllables and two stresses.)

Speakers of 'syllable-timed' languages need a lot of practice in this area if they are to speak naturally enough to be easily understood. And they may have great difficulty in understanding English speech because they don't perceive unstressed syllables. (*There was a man in the garden* may simply be heard as *Bzzz man bzzz garden*.) Activities like Exercise 6 in this lesson are particularly important for such students; you can easily make up your own to supplement the ones in the book.

VOCABULARY: DOING THINGS TO THINGS

7 Match the verbs and the pictures.

bend	break	catch	cut	drop	hit	kick	lift	mend
pick up	polish	pour	pull	push	put down	roll	scratch	
sharpen	slice	swing	switch off	switch on	tear	throw		
tie	touch	turn						

8 Which of the verbs in Exercise 7 are irregular? Do you know the past tenses and past participles?

9 Can you find things in the classroom that can be bent, broken, cut, dropped *etc.*? Try to find one thing for each verb.

Learn/revise: *the verbs in Exercise 7.*

39

B7 Small talk (2)

Expressing opinions; agreeing and disagreeing; *So/Neither (do) I*; leave-taking;
listening skills: listening for gist and for specific information; speaking;
pronunciation: fluency practice.

1 📼 Listen to the dialogue. What do you think they were talking about? Can you remember any of the things they said?

2 📼 Which of these words and expressions come in the dialogue? Write down your answers; then listen again and see if you were right.

> I liked it all   lovely   nonsense
> I didn't think much of it   I cried
> I couldn't help it   It made him laugh
> It didn't say anything to me
> I may be very old-fashioned   So am I
> I like violence   Why did you like it?
> It was really really boring   three old men
> Who wrote it?   I've never heard of him

3 Write down the names of a food, a sport, an animal and a person (singer, actor, writer, ...) that you like. Tell another student, and listen to his or her answers.

> I like ...
> I quite like ...
> I really like ...
> I like ... very much.
> I love ...

> So do I.
> I don't.
> I quite like him/her/it/them.
> I've never heard of
> him/her/it/them.

Write down the names of a food, a sport, an animal and a person (singer, actor, writer, ...) that you don't like. Tell another student, and listen to his or her answers.

> I don't like ...
> I don't much like ...
> I really don't like ...
> I don't like ... at all.

> Neither/Nor do I.
> I do.
> I don't mind him/her/it/them.
> I've never heard of
> him/her/it/them.

Lesson B7

NOTE
This lesson follows on from Lesson B5: the two lessons are based on a series of five dialogues which portray different stages in a dinner-party. So it is necessary to have done Lesson B5 before doing Lesson B7.
The texts of the two dialogues in Lesson B7 are at the end of the Student's Book, on page 134. Ideally, students should not look at these until they are asked to do so in Exercise 7. But some students are very uncomfortable if they cannot see the written word fairly soon. If it is necessary, let them look at the text of each dialogue after work on it is finished – but try and get them to mask Dialogue 5 while they read Dialogue 4. It is important to do each set of exercises before reading the dialogue.

Dialogue 4

Students learn more ways of expressing opinions, and of agreeing and disagreeing with other people's opinions; they practise listening for gist and for specific information.
Principal structures: *so/neither/nor do I.*

Language notes and possible problems
So do I etc.   Most students will have already met *So do I* (and *So am I, So have I,* etc.). They may not yet have met the negative equivalent *Neither am I* etc. (Note that *neither* is most often pronounced /ˈnaɪðe(r)/ in standard British English, but that many British people say /ˈniːðə(r)/; the standard American pronunciation is /ˈniːðə(r)n/.) The alternative form *Nor do I* is common in British English.
   The abbreviated verb structures used in *So am I, Neither am I* etc. are similar to those used in question tags (see Lesson B6) and in 'short answers'. As in these, *be* or an auxiliary is repeated from the main sentence; if the main sentence has neither *be* nor an auxiliary, *So do I* etc. is used.

If you are short of time
You can leave out Exercise 4.

1 Listening comprehension

• Play the dialogue once while students listen, and see if they have an idea of what the conversation is about.
• Ask if they can remember any words or expressions.

2 Recall

• Get students to write the words and expressions which they think come in the dialogue.
• Then get them to compare notes in groups.
• Play the dialogue again, more than once if they want, and let them check.
• Then discuss the answers with them, explaining any difficulties.

Answers to Exercise 2
The expressions which occur in the dialogue are:
lovely   nonsense   I didn't think much of it   I cried
I couldn't help it   It didn't say anything to me
It was really really boring   Who wrote it?

3 Expressing and reacting to opinions
• Go over the instructions for the first part of the exercise and make sure students understand *So do I* and the other expressions illustrated.
• Then get them to write down their four words.
• Call on one or two students to tell their neighbours what they like. The neighbours should answer truthfully, using the expressions illustrated.

• When you are satisfied that everybody understands what to do, divide the class into pairs and let them go ahead.
• To get additional practice, you can tell students to change partners once or twice.
• Go on to do the second part of the exercise in the same way.

4 Books, films, plays, etc.

• This can be done in groups, or as a whole-class exercise.
• Go over the expressions first, and make sure there are no problems.
• Opinions can be expressed in the same ways as in the previous exercise. There is a wider choice of expressions for conveying reactions.
• It is best if students talk about things which the others are likely to have read or seen – for example, recent films or TV programmes.

5 Discussion

• If the class is sufficiently confident and fluent, they may be able to say more things about some of the books, films etc. that they mention.
• Encourage them to talk as freely as possible.
• Don't correct mistakes unless they are a serious obstacle to communication (though you may wish to note points for attention at another time).

— Dialogue 5

Students learn expressions used in leave-taking. They practise the skill of listening for specific information, and finish with a large-scale improvisation.
Principal structures: *ought to* and *had better* are previewed.
Phonology: fluency practice.

Language notes and possible problems

1. *Ought to*   This is previewed here. You may like to explain that *ought* means practically the same as *should,* but that it is used with a *to*-infinitive.
2. *Had better*   You will need to explain that the *'d* in *We'd better* is a contraction of *had,* not *would* or *should,* and that *better* does not really mean 'better' (the expression simply means the same as *should* or *ought to*). You will probably want to point out that *had better* is followed by an infinitive without *to*.
3. *Enjoy oneself*   You will probably want to point out the use of the reflexive pronoun here.
4. *Thank you* so *much*   This *so* is stressed; point out that it is a conversational equivalent of *very,* and especially common in women's speech.

If you are short of time

You can leave out Exercise 9.

6 Detecting differences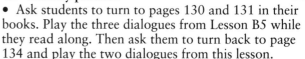

• Look at the sentences in the list first of all. Explain any difficulties.
• Then play the recording, and ask students to write the versions of the expressions that actually occur in the dialogue. Point out that none of the expressions in the list are incorrect.
• Play the dialogue once more, and give students time to finish writing.
• Then let them compare notes in groups, before discussing the answers (see *Language notes*).

Answers to Exercise 6

It's getting late.
We've got a long way to go.
Yes, we'd better be going, too.
Thank you *so* much, Ann.
We really enjoyed ourselves.
Thank you for coming.
You must come over to us soon.
I'll give you a ring.

That's not mine. (*or:* This is mine.)
Well, whose is this, then?
Is it old and dirty?

7 Choosing vocabulary to learn

• Ask students to look over the tapescripts of the dialogues; each student should choose seven or more words or expressions to learn.
• When they have chosen their words individually, put them into pairs. Ask each person to tell the group two of her/his words and why they were chosen.

8 Fluency practice

• Ask students to turn to pages 130 and 131 in their books. Play the three dialogues from Lesson B5 while they read along. Then ask them to turn back to page 134 and play the two dialogues from this lesson.
• Each student should choose at least one sentence whose pronunciation he or she wants to check.
• Students should say their sentences to you, trying to get a good intonation and rhythm.
• You should simply say the sentences after the students without making any comments or corrections.
• Tell students to try the sentences again, making any changes they want to and comparing their pronunciation with yours until they are satisfied.

9 Improvisation

• This can be done either with one group at a time 'performing' for the others, or with several groups working simultaneously.
• The first approach is more demanding, but will probably achieve greater concentration, especially if you tape- or video-record the performances.
• Get students to help you put on the board a list of what was happening in each of the five dialogues. The list should look something like this:
– Greeting and introducing
– Asking for and giving personal information
– Talking about the food and drink
– Talking about films/books etc.
– Saying goodbye
• Divide the class into groups of six to eight, trying to make sure there are some confident students in each group.
• Tell the class that each group will have to play out a dinner-party scene, but will not have time to prepare it in detail beforehand. Make it clear that they should act out their scenes properly, with appropriate movements.
• Give each group a minute or two to divide up the roles, but don't allow them time to prepare what they are going to say.
• If you have students who tend to go on and on, you may want to impose a time-limit on each sketch, say five minutes.

Practice Book exercises

1. Expressing personal opinions of books, films, etc.
2. *So am I, Neither do I,* etc.
3. Disagreeing.
4. Revision of irregular verbs.
5. Student's Cassette exercise (Student's Book Lesson B7, Exercise 6). Students try to complete sentences from the recording.
6. Recreational reading: a poem.
7. Reading (a thank-you letter) and writing (a thank-you letter).

4 Write down the names of three books / films / television programmes / plays *etc.* that you liked and three that you didn't. Tell another student, and listen to his or her answers.

I liked ...
I really liked ...
etc.

So did I.
I didn't.
I didn't think much of it.
I haven't seen it.
I've never heard of it.
etc.

I didn't like ...
I didn't much like ...
etc.

Neither/Nor did I.
I did.
I quite liked it.
I haven't read it.
etc.

5 Talk some more about books / films / television programmes / plays *etc.* that you have read or seen.

6 🔲 Look at these sentences. They are like sentences in Dialogue 5, but they are not quite the same. Listen to the dialogue and write the exact sentences.

It's late.
We've got to go a long way.
We'd better go, too.
Thank you very much, Ann.
I really enjoyed myself.
Thanks for coming.
You must come and see us soon.
I'll phone you.
This isn't mine.
Well, whose is that, then?
It's old and dirty.

7 Turn to page 134 and look over the tapescripts of Dialogues 4 and 5. Choose seven to ten words or expressions to learn. Show your list to another student and say why you have chosen two of the words/expressions.

8 🔲 Turn to pages 130 and 131, and then to page 134. Listen again to Dialogues 1 to 5 as you read the tapescripts. Then choose a sentence and try to say it with a good pronunciation. The teacher will say it for you correctly.

9 Improvisation. Work in groups of six to eight. Act out a dinner party. See how long you can go on for.

> **Learn/revise:** beginning; coffee; end; middle; nonsense; ring (telephone); rubbish; sex; violence; enjoy (yourself); hear of (heard, heard); move (house); awful; boring; dirty; lovely; old; old-fashioned; quite (= rather); whose; mine; I couldn't help it; I didn't think much of it; It didn't say anything to me; Thank you for coming; We ought to be on our way; We'd better be going.

B8 What's a hamburger?

Listening for overall meaning; giving spoken descriptions and definitions;
asking for things when you don't know the exact words; reading and interpreting;
guessing unknown words; summarising.

1 📼 Listen to the descriptions.
Can you do better?

2 How quickly can you match the words and the
descriptions? (There is one word too many.)

bill	boat	bus	crash	cup	cupboard
dancing	envelope	hairbrush	hotel		
ice cream	microphone	office	perfume		
rabbit	salt	sing	sleep	soap	
station	suitcase	trees	window	wrist	

1. Something that makes you cool in hot weather.
2. The thing that joins your hand to your arm.
3. A thing that is useful when you travel.
4. A liquid that makes you smell nice.
5. Stuff (that) you put on food.
6. A thing (that) you tidy your hair with.
7. Something (that) you put a letter in.
8. A thing (that) you speak into.
9. Stuff for washing with.
10. A thing for drinking out of.
11. A place where you can stay overnight.
12. A place where you go to catch a train.
13. A room that has a desk, typewriter, telephone *etc*.
14. A big vehicle with seats.
15. A way of moving to music.
16. A kind of box on the wall: you keep things in it.
17. You can travel across water in it.
18. Very big plants; birds and animals live in them.
19. You have to pay it.
20. When you do this, it may sound nice.
21. It can happen if you drive too fast.
22. You do it at night when you are tired.
23. You can see through it.

3 Now describe one of the things in the pictures.
You must not use its name (if you know it), and you
must not use your hands to help you explain. The
other students will try to decide which thing you are
talking about. Useful structures:

something (that) ...
a thing (that) ...
something / a thing that you wear when ...
something / a thing that you use to ... / for ...ing
a thing for ...ing
a thing with ...
a thing that has ...
stuff that ...
stuff for ...
liquid that/for ...
you use it to ... / for ...ing
you use it when you ...
you can ... it
a kind/sort of ...
it happens when you ...
you do it ...

Lesson B8

Speaking skills: describing, defining and other paraphrase strategies.
Listening for overall meaning.
Reading skills: interpreting author's intention; guessing unknown words; summarising.

Language notes and possible problems
1. Relative structures   Exercises 1–3 involve various structures relevant to the skills of defining and describing, including relative pronouns. Some students may have difficulty with the 'contact clause' structure, in which an object relative pronoun is dropped.
2. End-position of prepositions   These exercises also include examples of structures (relative clauses and -*ing* clauses) ending in prepositions. This, too, is likely to cause difficulty.
3. With   Note how *have* and *with* can be used to express identical meanings. Compare (Exercise 2): *a room that has a desk* and *a big vehicle with seats.*
4. Pronunciation   The word *thing* comes up very often in this lesson. Encourage the correct pronunciation of /θ/ and /ɪ/.
5. Vocabulary   Students will probably want to note and learn the names of some of the objects that come up in the various exercises. Discourage them from spending too much time on this – the purpose of this lesson is not to teach vocabulary, but to teach strategies that can be used to compensate for lack of vocabulary.

Extra materials
Some of the activities in this lesson may need extra materials. See the instructions for Exercise 3 and the optional activity that follows.

1 Listening: definitions
● This is an authentic recording of people giving spontaneous unprepared definitions. (The questions have been re-recorded.)
● Play each definition and ask students if they can improve on it – for example by making it clearer and shorter.

Tapescript for Exercise 1
'What's a frying-pan?'   'A frying-pan is a utensil used to cook on a stove. It's a type of a pot, made out of sometimes cast iron, and it's usually about an inch and a half in depth, and about eight to twelve inches in diameter, and has a long handle, that usually doesn't get hot, so that you can hold onto it, and you use it to put some oil in, and fry different types of foods and vegetables and meats.'
   'What's a bus?'   'A bus is a form of motorised transport. You probably see a lot of them, a lot of cars, lorries and buses around, they're big metal things with wheels on that make a rumbling noise, and a bus is a rather big one full of lots of people.'
   'What's a suitcase?'   'It's something you use to carry clothes, and other personal items in, when you go on a trip.'
   'What's air?'   'Air is something that is all around us, that we can't see, but which we need to live in, and consists of a lot of different things in it, hydrogen, oxygen, lots of different things depending on where you are!'
   'What's flu?'   'The flu is something that you get that gives you symptoms of fever, headache, sometimes nausea, which is a sick feeling in your stomach, and it usually incapacitates you for a few days.'
   'What are pyjamas?'   'Pyjamas are most uncomfortable forms of clothing that some people wear, but I haven't worn them for years, consisting of trousers and a shirt, for going to sleep in. Unfortunately they usually twist around and get very uncomfortable, and a lot of people don't need them these days.'

2 Matching words and descriptions
● This exercise introduces the structures that are used for defining and describing. It can be done in small groups, with students sharing their knowledge of vocabulary.
● After students have discussed the answers to the questions, you may want to go over the use of relative pronouns, the position of prepositions and other points of grammar with them (see *Language notes*).
● When discussing relatives, get them to look at the sentences in which *that* can be left out (4–8). See if they can work out for themselves why *that* can be left out in these sentences but not in the others.

Answers to Exercise 2
1. ice cream	9. soap	17. boat
2. wrist	10. cup	18. trees
3. suitcase	11. hotel	19. bill
4. perfume	12. station	20. sing
5. salt	13. office	21. crash
6. hairbrush	14. bus	22. sleep
7. envelope	15. dancing	23. window
8. microphone	16. cupboard	

3 Paraphrase strategies
● In a foreign language, it is often necessary to talk about something, or ask for something, without knowing the right words. It is usually possible to do this successfully by describing, defining, or using some other type of paraphrase. This exercise gives students practice in this valuable skill.
● Go over the list of 'useful structures' and deal with any problems. Get students to look at how these structures are used in Exercise 2. Encourage them to use these structures in the activity that follows.
● Each student should come out in front of the class and describe one of the objects illustrated, without saying its name or using his/her hands. (Tell students to put their hands in their pockets or behind their backs.) The class should note the number of the object they think the student is talking about.
● When the student has finished, ask the class what number they have noted. Find out if they were right.
● In a large class, you may prefer to demonstrate the exercise and then get students to do it in groups.
● The objects are:

1. a windscreen wiper	17. a flower pot
2. a rake	18. a birdcage
3. scales	19. a comb
4. a compass	20. a can of paint
5. a lampshade	21. a harmonica
6. a ball of string	22. an eclipse
7. a screwdriver	23. clothes pegs
8. washing up liquid	24. a frying pan
9. garden shears	25. a magnifying glass
10. a bicycle saddle	26. a brick
11. binoculars	27. a wheelbrace
12. a crutch	28. a hammer
13. an axe	29. pliers
14. insecticide	30. roller skates
15. a shoelace	31. a volcanic eruption
16. a mousetrap	

Alternatives/options for Exercise 3: see next page.

Alternative/optional extension to Exercise 3

• The exercise can also be done with pictures cut out of magazines and/or real objects, which can be used instead of or as well as the pictures in the book.
• Give each student in turn a picture or object, without letting the rest of the class see it, and tell him/her to describe it to the class.
• The class should draw the object the student is describing, or write the name in their own language.
• When the student has finished, he/she should show the picture or the object.
• Objects that could be used include: clothes-brush, corkscrew, tin-opener, knife, fork, spoon, alarm clock, torch, map, credit card, key.

Optional extra activity

• Get a volunteer to come out in front of the class (preferably somebody with a good vocabulary).
• The student's hands should be behind his or her back, and he or she should face the class.
• Put a small object into the student's hands without letting anybody see it.
• The class have to ask questions to find out what it is.
• The person holding the object can give any information asked for except the name of the object (if he or she knows what it is).
• When the class have identified the object, put its name on the board if necessary.
• Ask for another volunteer and do the same thing again.
• Suggestions for objects: key, paper clip, diary, comb, ring, piece of soap, sweet, egg, light bulb, battery, paper handkerchief, grape, tie, credit card, pocket knife, stamp, toy car.

4 Reading practice

• Make sure students realise that they do not have to understand every word of the text.
• Give them five minutes or so to read the text without dictionaries or vocabulary explanations.
• Then get them to answer the questions. Question 3 will need to be done in writing; the others can be done by group or class discussion.

Answers to Exercise 4

2. Snack seems most likely to have said the first sentence, Pilcer the second and Wilson the third.
4b.

5 Song: *Do you know*

• Explain to students that they are going to hear a 'riddle song'. Make sure they understand the seven alternatives.
• You may like to pre-teach some key words such as *twist, flick, pin, grip, lever, tone*. But don't explain *snap*, or other words which would give away the exact nature of the objects.
• Play the recording right through once while students listen with books closed. See if anybody has understood enough to make any guesses.
• Play the song again, while students follow with books open or closed as you prefer. Pause after each verse and chorus and discuss students' guesses.

Answers to Exercise 5

1. A camera
2. A motorbike
3. A fire extinguisher
4. A telephone

Practice Book exercises

1. Vocabulary and grammar: writing job definitions.
2. Relative clauses: leaving out *that*.
3. End-position of prepositions.
4. Student's Cassette exercise (Student's Book Lesson B8, Exercise 5). Students try to fill gaps in the song from memory before checking with the recording.
5. Recreational reading: a poem.
6. Creative writing: extending the poem in Exercise 5.
7. Crossword: writing the clues.

Selective and global reading and listening

Not all spoken and written texts are meant to be studied in detail. Some texts are used just to present certain language points; the students' task is to extract particular pieces of information from the text, but not to study and understand every word. In other cases, students are required to grasp the main points of a text without worrying about details.

Students may have followed other courses in which nothing is presented without being immediately explained. So they may be uncomfortable if they leave a text without having studied every word in every line. It is important for them to realise that there are different ways of listening and reading for different purposes, and that it is not always necessary to understand everything in order to 'get the message'. Indeed, they must get used to coping with speech and writing in which not everything is clear – they will have to do this all the time in real-life use of English.

So if students ask you to spend an extra half hour or so 'going through' a text which is not meant to be studied in this way, it is probably best to refuse (telling the students why), unless you are very sure that the time could not be used more profitably for other purposes.

---

4 Read the text carefully, but without using a dictionary. Then answer the questions.

ELEPHANTS ARE DIFFERENT TO DIFFERENT PEOPLE

Wilson and Pilcer and Snack stood before the zoo elephant.

Wilson said 'What is its name? Is it from Asia or Africa? Who feeds it? Is it a he or a she? How old is it? Do they have twins? How much does it cost to feed? If it dies, how much will another one cost? If it dies, what will they use the bones, the fat and the hide for? What use is it besides to look at?'

Pilcer didn't have any questions; he was murmuring to himself, 'It's a house by itself, walls and windows, the ears came from tall cornfields, by God; the architect of those legs was a workman, by God; he stands like a bridge out across deep water; the face is sad and the eyes are kind; I know elephants are good to babies.'

Snack looked up and down and at last said to himself, 'He's a tough son-of-a-gun outside and I'll bet he's got a strong heart, I'll bet he's strong as a copper-riveted boiler inside.'

They didn't put up any arguments.
They didn't throw anything in each other's faces.
The three men saw the elephant three ways.
And let it go at that.
They didn't spoil a sunny Sunday afternoon.
'Sunday comes only once a week,' they told each other.

from *Home Front Memo* by Carl Sandburg

1. Whose way of looking at the elephant do you like best – Wilson's, Pilcer's or Snack's?
2. Find out what *tusk* means. Then decide which of the three men might have said each of these sentences.
   a. Those tusks could break down a house.
   b. Those tusks are curved like the sky.
   c. How much do those tusks weigh?
3. Look at how these words are used in the text: *feed, twins, hide, murmuring, arguments, spoil.* Write down what you think each one might mean (in English or in your own language). Then check in a dictionary and see if you were right.
4. Here are three summaries of the text. Which do you think is the best?
   a. Elephants are complicated animals and you can see them in different ways.
   b. Different people see the world in different ways; that is no reason to fight.
   c. People should agree with each other on Sundays.

5 📼 Listen to the song. Each of the four verses describes one of the following things: a TV, a motorbike, a telephone, a car, a fire extinguisher, a washing machine, a camera. Can you decide which? (The text is on page 131.)

Leaving out object relative pronouns
a liquid (that) people put on
a thing (that) you tidy your hair with
stuff (that) you put on food

End-position of prepositions
a thing you tidy your hair with
something you put a letter in
a thing you speak into
stuff for washing with
a thing for drinking out of

Learn/revise: argument; arm; bill; boat; bone; box; bridge; desk; envelope; hairbrush; hand; hotel; ice cream; kind (*noun*); microphone; office; perfume; rabbit; sort; stuff; suitcase; thing; twins; typewriter; window; wrist; bet (bet, bet); cost (cost, cost); describe; die; feed (fed, fed); join; keep (kept, kept); put on (put, put); smell (smelt, smelt); spoil; taste; tidy; travel (travelled); use; alive; cool; deep; kind (*adjective*); tired; tough; besides; I'll bet.

Summary B

Present Perfect for giving 'news'

My baby **has** just **eaten** some aspirins.
There **has been** an accident. (~~There was an accident.~~)

can with verbs of sensation

I **can** smell gas. (~~I am smelling gas.~~)
I **can** hear terrible screaming.

Tenses of *there is*

Do you think **there are** people on other planets?
There has been an accident.
She screamed because **there was** a spider in the bath.
The hotel receptionist told me **there had been** a
    mistake: they had given my room to somebody
    else.
I don't think **there will be** another world war.
If people drove more slowly **there would be** fewer
    accidents.

Irregular verbs in Lessons B1–B8

INFINITIVE	PAST	PAST PARTICIPLE
bend	bent	bent
bet	bet	bet
bleed	bled	bled
break	broke	broken
catch	caught	caught
choose	chose	chosen
cost	cost	cost
cut	cut	cut
drive	drove	driven
fall	fell	fallen
feed	fed	fed
feel	felt	felt
find	found	found
hear	heard	heard
hide	hid	hidden
hit	hit	hit
keep	kept	kept
leave	left	left
lie	lay	lain
lose	lost	lost
put	put	put
read /riːd/	read /red/	read /red/
run	ran	run
see	saw	seen
smell	smelt	smelt
steal	stole	stolen
swing	swung	swung
take	took	taken
tear	tore	torn
tell	told	told
throw	threw	thrown

-ing forms for activities

reading other people's letters   **telling** lies
shoplifting   **cheating** at cards   **stealing** towels

Giving advice and instructions: imperatives

Take her to hospital immediately.
Keep him warm, but **don't move** him.

Comparative structures; *worse* and *worst*

Travelling without a ticket isn't **as bad as** shoplifting.
I think shoplifting is **worse than** cheating at cards.
I think telling lies is **the worst** thing.

Question tags after affirmative sentences

Your father **is** a doctor, **isn't** he?
The Lewises **have** gone on holiday, **haven't** they?
Ann **will** be pleased to see us, **won't** she?
Peter **would** like to be a doctor, **wouldn't** he?
Rita **can** speak seven languages, **can't** she?
There are tigers in Siberia, **aren't there?**
    (~~... aren't they?~~)
I'm late, **aren't** I? (~~... amn't I?~~)
You **drink** coffee, **don't** you?
She **arrived** late, **didn't** she?

Question tags after negative sentences

She **isn't** happy, **is** she?
You **haven't** seen my brother anywhere, **have** you?
The film **wasn't** much good, **was** it?
You **can't** swim, **can** you?
Ann **wouldn't** like to help us, **would** she?
Cats **don't** eat cornflakes, **do** they?
The postman **didn't** come this morning, **did** he?
There isn't any milk in the fridge, **is there?**

Intonation of question tags

> *Real questions*

Your father **is** a doctor, **isn't** he?
You **haven't** seen my brother anywhere, **have** you?

> *Asking for agreement*

The film **was** pretty boring, **wasn't** it?
She **isn't** happy, **is** she?

Position of prepositions in questions

What are you looking **at?**
What are John and Lucy talking **about?**
Who did you go **with?**

44

Summary B

Summary of language taught in Lessons B1–B8.

This section displays most of the more important systematic language points that students should have learnt or revised in the last eight lessons. Spend a short time going over the material with the students, answering questions and clearing up any difficulties. Get them also to look over the vocabulary from Lessons B1–B8 (in the *Learn/revise* panels at the end of each lesson), making sure they know at least the more important new words and expressions. They may need to spend time at home consolidating their learning before moving on.

Position of prepositions in relative structures

a thing you tidy your hair **with**
something you put a letter **in**

Building sentences with conjunctions

The phone always rings **when** I'm cooking supper.
When I'm cooking supper, the phone always rings.
He joined the army **after** he left school.
While I was shopping my bicycle was stolen.
Come and see us **before** you go to America.
As soon as I arrive, I'll give you a ring.
I never travelled abroad **until** I was 18.
Because she worked hard, she passed her exams.
She passed her exams **although** she had a bad teacher.
There wasn't any beer, **so** I had a glass of fruit juice.
… a new suit, **which** he needed for a job interview.

Leaving out object relative pronouns

a thing (that) you tidy your hair with
stuff (that) you put on food

Building sentences with *-ing* forms

Walk round the room **reading** everybody else's label.
Interview them, **asking** as many questions as you can.
Mr Archie Macfarlane completed the course
    successfully, **surprising** everyone.
I sat in the garden **wondering** what to do next.

Indicating time in stories

Last week Steve went to a department store.
While he was putting the trousers on, he saw …
Now he was stuck in the department store.
Later that afternoon he got a phone call.
When we got to the store nobody knew …

Uses of *get*

He **got** the new trousers on.
He **got** a phone call.
We think we have **got** your keys as well.
Would you like to come and **get** them?
When we **got** to the store …
They had used Steve's keys to **get** into his house.
What can I **get** you to drink?

Expressing opinions; adverbials of degree

I like …	I don't like …
I quite like …	I don't much like …
I really like …	I really don't like …
I like … very much	I don't like … at all
I love …	
I don't mind …	

Sharing and not sharing opinions

'I like …'	'So do I.' / 'I don't.'
'I liked …'	'So did I.' / 'I didn't.'
'I don't like …'	'Neither/Nor do I.' / 'I do.'
'I didn't like …'	'Neither/Nor did I.' / 'I did.'

I quite liked it.   I didn't think much of it.
I've never heard of it.   I haven't read/seen it.

Greeting and welcoming

Nice to see you.
Let me take your coat.
You know Lucy, don't you?
I think we've met her once.
Lovely to see you.
I'm so glad you could come.
What can I get you to drink?

Mealtimes

'Could you pass me …?' 'Here you are.'
This is delicious.
Would you like some more?
Have another potato.
No, thanks. That was lovely, but I've had enough.
'I *am* sorry.' 'That's all right. It doesn't matter at all.'

Time to go

We'd better be going.
We ought to be on our way.
Thank you so much.
We really enjoyed ourselves.
Thank you for coming.
You must come and see us soon.
I'll give you a ring.

Describing

something / a thing (that) …
something / a thing that you wear when …
something / a thing that you use to … / for …ing
a thing for …ing / with … / that has …
stuff / liquid that … / for …
you use it to … / for …ing / when you …
you can … it
a kind / sort of …
it happens when you …
you do it when … / to …

Vocabulary

Look through the 'Learn/revise' boxes at the ends
of Lessons B1–B8.

Revision and fluency practice B

A choice of activities.

1 📼 Listen to the story about the lift, and see if you can answer the question at the end.

2 Reading report. Talk to the class about what you have been reading recently in English.

3 Three wishes. Imagine that your fairy godmother appears and gives you three wishes. You can wish for anything you like (except for more wishes). Write your wishes. Now work with someone else. Write down what you think he/she has wished for. Then exchange wishes and see if you were right. Useful structures:

I want ...
I would like ...
I wish I was/had/could ...
I thought you would wish for ...
I'm surprised you want ...

4 Happy memories. Work in groups of three or four. Tell each other about a happy memory that you have.

5 Make up a class story. One person starts, the next person continues, and so on in turn. Here is a possible beginning:

'Mary was walking home late at night ...'

6 Work with another student and complete the following dialogue. Practise it and act it out to the class.

Hello.
....
Yes, speaking. Who's that?
....
Oh, hello. Didn't recognise your voice.
....
No, I haven't seen her for a long time.
....
No, she hasn't. Not for two or three months.
....
Yes, she probably is.
....
No, I'm afraid I don't.
....
My God! Really? What are you going to do?
....
....
....

Well, let me know if I can help at all. That's terrible. I *am* sorry.
....
I'd love to, but I'm not free on Tuesday. How about Thursday?
....
OK. What time?
....
Right. See you then. Bye.

7 Here are some typical English children's jokes. Read them and say what you think about them. Do you know any better jokes? Useful expressions:

I don't see the joke.
What do you think of this one?
This one's really funny.
It isn't funny at all.
I think it's wonderful/stupid.
It makes / doesn't make me laugh.
I think number 4 is the best/worst.

1. LUCY: How did you get that cut on your forehead?
   MIKE: I bit myself.
   LUCY: But how could you bite yourself on the forehead?
   MIKE: I stood on a chair.

2. A little man asked for a job cutting down trees. 'You don't look very strong,' said the manager. 'What experience have you got?' 'I cut down thousands of trees in the Sahara desert,' said the man. 'But there aren't any trees in the Sahara,' said the manager. 'No,' said the man. 'Not now.'

3. GIRL: You remind me of the sea.
   BOY: You mean I'm wild, restless, romantic?
   GIRL: No, you make me sick.

4. WOMAN: I'm having trouble with my husband. Every morning he washes the car.
   FRIEND: You should be pleased. Most wives wish their husbands would wash the car more often.
   WOMAN: In the bath?

5. A girl took her dog with her to the film of *Alice in Wonderland*. The usherette saw the dog, and was about to throw it out. But then she saw that the dog seemed to be enjoying the film, so she let it stay. After the film she said to the girl 'It certainly surprised me to see your dog enjoying the show.' 'Me too,' said the girl. 'He didn't like the book at all.'

Revision and fluency practice B

Students and teacher choose from a range of practice activities.

Teaching notes
Detailed teaching notes are not provided for all exercises in this section, since most of the activities are self-explanatory.

---

1 The liftboy
• Tell students they are going to hear a story about a liftboy (pre-teach this word).
• Explain that they must do their best to remember everything they hear. (Most of the details in the story are irrelevant, but don't tell students this.)
• The question at the end is 'What is the name of the liftboy?' Unless students remember the first sentence ('Imagine you're a liftboy') and realise that the name is their own, they will probably insist that they have not been told the answer.
• The tapescript of this exercise is not provided, as detailed study of the text is unnecessary.

2 Reading report
• It is important, if at all possible, to make sure that students read regularly in English – this makes an enormous difference to their progress. Regular reporting exercises can help to encourage them.

5 Class story
• It might be fun to record the story and play it back to the class after they have finished.

9 The zoo problem

(We are grateful to Penny Ur and Cambridge University Press for permission to reproduce this exercise from *Discussions that Work*.)

- Give students a few minutes to study the plan and look up any unknown animal names in their dictionaries. Make sure they can pronounce the names of the animals.
- Go through the information and make sure students understand what problems the zoo is faced with.
- Then get students to work in groups of three or four. Tell them that each group is a committee responsible for reorganising the zoo so as to solve as many of the problems as possible.
- Give them 15 or 20 minutes to work out their solutions; then let groups compare notes.
- If time allows, you can have a general class discussion about the various solutions. (There is of course no one right answer.)

8 Improvisation. Work in groups of four, and act out the following situation.

Mrs Smith is annoyed because her neighbours play loud music late at night. She goes next door to complain, but they won't turn the music down. So she calls the police, and a three-sided argument develops.

9 Are you good at organising? Study the plan and the information. Then work in groups and find a good way of reorganising the zoo.

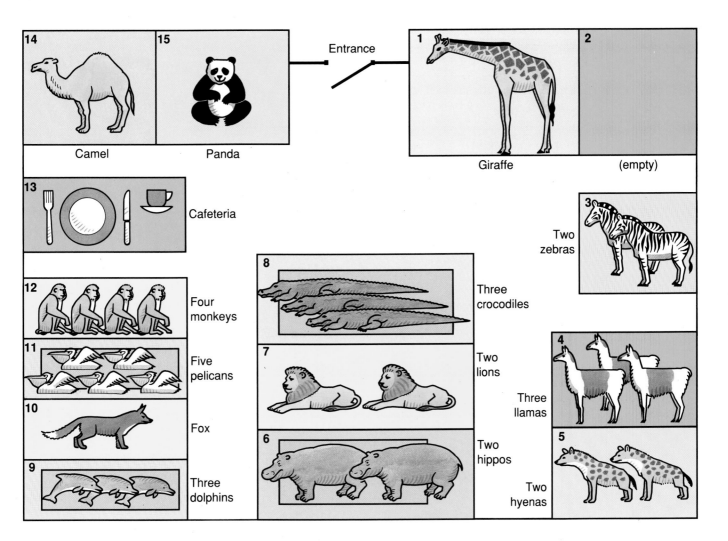

INFORMATION
1. The giraffe is going to have a baby soon, so it must be put somewhere quiet.
2. One of the lions has died; the other should move to a smaller enclosure.
3. Small children are frightened by seeing the crocodiles as they come in.
4. The zoo has been given a new panda.
5. The monkeys are very noisy.
6. The camel is rather smelly.
7. All the enclosures should be filled.
8. Harmless animals should not be put next to predators (animals which are their natural enemies and might frighten them).
9. The zoo has enough money to buy two wolves or four flamingoes or a pair of small deer.

(from *Discussions that Work*, Penny Ur)

Test B _____

1 [cassette icon] **Which of these expressions come in the dialogue? Write *S* (the same) or *D* (different).**

1. We'd better be going
2. So have we
3. Thank you so much
4. We've had a wonderful time
5. Will you be in tomorrow
6. That would be lovely
7. Have you left them in your coat
8. They don't seem to be here
9. Those are yours, aren't they
10. Thank you for a lovely evening

2 [cassette icon] **Listen to the dialogue again and answer the questions.**

1. Why were the people together?
2. What time of the day was it?
3. What did David lose? Where did he think he had put them? Who found them?

PRONUNCIATION

3 [cassette icon] **Real question or not? You will hear seven questions. Listen to each one, and write *R* if the end of the question goes up and *N* if the end of the question goes down. The first two questions are done for you as examples.**

1. You're from Jersey, aren't you? .....*R*.....

2. Hilary didn't come, did she? .....*N*.....
3. Your sister's a journalist, isn't she?
4. Helen's had measles, hasn't she?
5. Jeremy hasn't left, has he?
6. You've finished your work, haven't you?
7. You'll be here for a while, won't you?

4 **Circle the vowels which are pronounced /ə/. The first word is done for you as an example.**

adv(e)rtise   bumper   burglary   delicious
department   generous   microphone   mustard
officer   potato

GRAMMAR

5 **Choose the right verb forms.**

1. .... there .... any teachers at the meeting tomorrow? (*be*)
2. There .... a major accident on the M4 near Reading, and motorists are asked to drive very carefully. (*be*)
3. I .... over the bridge yesterday when I .... my pen and it .... into the river. (*walk; drop; fall*)
4. Gloria .... last night while I .... a shower. (*phone; have*)
5. I .... to phone her back, but there .... no answer. (*try; be*)
6. You work in Barcelona, ... you?
7. You haven't got a pen I could borrow, ... you?
8. Carolyn won't be here before nine, ... she?
9. 'My sister ran in the Boston Marathon last year.' 'Really? So .... I!'
10. He ran out of the room, ... his briefcase open on the desk. (*leave*)

6 **Join each pair of sentences using one of the words from the box (add or take away any other words you need to).**

after	although	as soon as	because
before	so	until	when

1. She'll arrive. I'll phone you immediately.

   I'll phone you as soon as she arrives.
2. She was only twelve. She was very strong.
3. My father died. Then we stopped going to the mountains.
4. I like coffee, but we didn't have any. I drank tea.
5. I wore a coat. I thought it was going to be cold.
6. He used to travel a lot more. Then his children were born.
7. I can't leave for the moment. I can leave at ten.
8. I was watching television. There was a knock at the door.

7 **Write these questions in the right order.**

1. are at looking what you ?
2. about are talking they who ?
3. buy did for it she who ?

8 **Describe these.**

1. a boat (Begin *A boat is …*)
2. salt
3. an artist

Test B

This test covers work done in Lessons B1–B8.

Administration of the test

1. General procedure Give students a few minutes to look over the test and make sure they understand what they are to do in each part.

2. Listening (Exercise 1) Give students a few minutes to look over the sentences in the box.

Students should write the numbers 1 to 10 on their papers, and be prepared to note whether each expression comes in the dialogue or not.

Play the recording, twice or three times, pausing after each speaker for students to note their answers.

3. Listening (Exercise 2) Give students a few minutes to read the questions. They may want to write some answers down now – they can probably write at least the answer to the first question.

Play the recording once more and then give students time to check their answers before going on to the Pronunciation exercises.

4. Pronunciation (Exercise 3) Make sure students understand the instructions, and know how they are to mark their answers. Play the first two sentences for them as examples.

Play the rest of the recording twice, pausing after each item.

5. Speaking (Exercise 15) You will have to take students aside in threes for the Speaking part of the test. If you have a large class and a short class period, you may have to drop this part of the test.

Explain to students what they will be doing in the speaking exercise after they finish Exercise 3.

Call each group of three students out of the class, for example to your desk or to the back of the classroom, while the others work on the written part of the test.

Try to make the students feel comfortable. Give them a few moments to decide on who will play which role, and then let them begin by you and the other 'guests' pretending to knock on the door. Let them go on for a few minutes, until you consider that you have a fair idea of their ability to communicate.

Remember that what you are looking for in this Speaking test is fluency, not perfect grammar or pronunciation. What counts is whether the students can make themselves understood.

LISTENING

1

1D; 2S; 3D; 4D; 5S; 6S; 7D; 8S; 9D; 10S

Tapescript for Exercise 1

DEBORAH: Well, we'd better go. It's late, and we've got a long way to go.

STEVE: So have we. We should be on our way as well.

JEREMY: Yes, we'd better go, too. Thank you very much, Anne. We've had a lovely time. And the food was wonderful.

ANNE: Well, thank you for coming.

KARIMA: You must come over to us soon. Will you be in tomorrow if I ring to fix a date?

ANNE: Yes, I think so … yes, until half past three, at least. That would be lovely, Karima.

DAVID: Oh, what have I done with my car keys?

DEBORAH: Did you leave them in your coat?

DAVID: (goes through pockets of coat) Well, I thought I had, but they don't seem to be here.

ANNE: These are yours, aren't they, David? They were over here on the floor.

DAVID: Oh, yes, thanks, Anne. And thank you for a lovely evening.

KARIMA: Yes, thanks so much, Anne. Bye now.

EVERYBODY: Bye.

2 (In these or other words):
1. They had just finished dinner together (at Anne's).
2. Late evening / night.
3. His keys; in his coat; Anne

PRONUNCIATION

3 Tapescript and answers
3. Your sister's a journalist, isn't she? N
4. Helen's had measles, hasn't she? N
5. Jeremy hasn't left, has he? R
6. You've finished your work, haven't you? R
7. You'll be here for a while, won't you? N

4 bumper burglary delicious department
generous microphone mustard officer potato

GRAMMAR

5
1. Will (there) be
2. has been
3. was walking; dropped; fell
4. phoned; was having
5. tried; was
6. don't
7. have
8. will
9. did
10. leaving

6
2. Although she was only twelve, she was very strong.
3. After my father died, we stopped going to the mountains.
OR: We stopped going to the mountains after my father died.
4. I like coffee, but we didn't have any, so I drank tea.
5. I wore a coat because I thought it was going to be cold.
6. He used to travel a lot more before his children were born.
7. I can't leave until ten.
8. I was watching television when there was a knock at the door.
OR: When I was watching television there was a knock at the door.

7
1. What are you looking at?
2. Who are they talking about?
3. Who did she buy it for?

8 (Many possible answers, for example:)
1. A boat is a thing that carries people on water.
2. Salt is stuff you put on your food to make it taste better.
3. An artist is a person who makes beautiful things for people to see.

READING AND WRITING

9 (Students may notice the North American usage in the omission of a preposition before *Saturday* in lines 7 and 20.)
1. stable
2. collapsed
3. piled
4. devised
5. heading
6. gave way
7. precarious
8. encountered

10 (Many possible answers; look for a fair degree of fluency, accuracy and appropriateness.)

LANGUAGE IN USE

11 (Many possible answers, for example:)
1. Yes. I think my daughter has broken her leg.
2. Yes, please, it's lovely. / No, thank you, it's lovely but I have to drive.
3. That's all right. It doesn't matter.
4. Orange juice, if there is some, thanks.
5. I thought it was terrible.

VOCABULARY

12 (Fifteen or more of these verbs:)
bend, bent, bent
bleed, bled, bled
break, broke, broken
catch, caught, caught
choose, chose, chosen
cut, cut, cut
drive, drove, driven
fall, fell, fallen
feel, felt, felt
find, found, found
get, got, got
hide, hid, hidden
keep, kept, kept
leave, left, left
lie, lay, lain
(*or* lie, lied, lied)
lose, lost, lost
put, put, put
run, ran, run
smell, smelt, smelt
steal, stole, stolen
take, took, taken
tear, tore, torn
tell, told, told
throw, threw, thrown

13
2. soft *or* easy
3. light
4. switch off
5. end
6. break
7. put down *or* drop
8. lose
9. cheap

14
2. card
3. store
4. service *or* driver
5. pedal
6. seat
7. wheel

SPEAKING

15 (Remember that fluency is what counts here.)

Test Book recording
A recording for Test 2 in the Test Book follows this lesson on the Class Cassette.

READING AND WRITING

9 Read the newspaper article and answer the questions.

Buried Sisters

TWO ELDERLY SISTERS whose collection of newspapers almost filled their small home are in stable condition in hospital after a tunnel
5 through the papers collapsed, trapping them for several hours Saturday.

Police said Eva Collins, 82, and her sister, Margaret Wentworth, 79, had
10 thousands of papers dating back to the 1960s in the semi-detached home they shared on Roderland Road.

"They were piled nearly to the ceiling," according to Sergeant Alex
15 Dungannon, who said the sisters had apparently devised a series of tunnels through which they could move on hands and knees to various rooms. The women were heading from their living
20 room to the kitchen Saturday when the passage they were using gave way, he said.

The collapse "sounded like an avalanche, like the whole house was
25 coming down," said neighbor Tim Francis, who occupies the other side of the house. Francis rushed next door, but was unable to reach the women. It took fire department and police officials
30 several hours to rescue them, working through precarious piles of newspapers.

"There were tons of them," said Dungannon. "It may sound funny now, but it was a dangerous situation."
35 Neighbors said the sisters seemed friendly and normal when they encountered them outdoors, but they knew of no one who had been invited inside the home.
40 A hospital official said the women suffered a variety of injuries, none of them life-threatening. "They're both pretty tough, I guess," she said.

(from *Family News*, by Joan Barfoot
© copyright Joan Barfoot 1989)

Find words or expressions that mean:

1. ill, but not getting worse (*lines 1–7*)
2. fell down (*lines 1–7*)
3. put on top of one another (*lines 8–15*)
4. invented (*lines 13–22*)
5. going (*lines 13–22*)
6. fell down (*lines 13–22*)
7. unsafe, likely to fall down (*lines 23–31*)
8. met (*lines 35–43*)

10 Choose one of these tasks. Write 150 words or more.

1. Imagine you are Tim Francis, the neighbour in the story. Write a letter to a close friend telling the story from your point of view.
2. Write a story about something that surprised you, or surprised other people. The story does not have to be true.

LANGUAGE IN USE

11 Write appropriate replies to these.

1. Ambulance service. May I help you?
2. Would you like some more wine?
3. Oh, I am sorry. How stupid of me!
4. What can I get you to drink?
5. What did you think of the film?

VOCABULARY

12 Write the past tense and past participle forms of fifteen or more of these verbs.

bend   bleed   break   catch   choose   cut
drive   fall   feel   find   get   hide   keep
leave   lie   lose   put   run   smell   steal
take   tear   tell   throw

13 Write the opposites of these words and expressions.

1. pull   push
2. hard
3. heavy
4. switch on
5. beginning
6. mend
7. pick up
8. find
9. expensive

14 Two-word expressions. Complete these.

1. driving   licence
2. credit ....
3. department ....
4. ambulance ....
5. brake ....
6. .... belt
7. steering ....

SPEAKING

15 Work with two other students. Imagine one of you has invited the other two, and your teacher, to your home for a dinner party. Say hello, have drinks, and begin dinner.

49

Listening and reading skills; discussion; vocabulary; stress and rhythm.

1 🔲 Close your books and listen to the recording. What are Tony's two jobs? Can you remember anything about how he spends his day?

2 Read the transcript of Tony's interview, and then see if you can put the pictures in the right order.

INTERVIEWER: How do you organise your work?

TONY: Well, I'm married, so to be alone in the mornings, the first thing is to get rid of my wife, who fortunately has a job, so she gets up in the morning, makes a cup of tea, rouses me, I come downstairs, wander round the kitchen, have my cup of tea, iron her clothes for her that she's put out for me on the first floor landing on top of the ironing board, so I do her ironing – by that stage she's in the bath, so I'm – by that stage it's half past eight, quarter to nine, I'm only half an hour from being on my own – come down and make sure she's got all the lunch in a bag, by that stage I've finished my tea, I've finished the ironing, she's out of the bath, I'm in the bath, she goes upstairs and gets dressed; by the time – if this is all synchronised properly – by the time I get out of the bath and go upstairs she's fully dressed; and then by the time I'm dressed and come downstairs she's just about to hop on her bicycle and go off to work, which makes it about nine o'clock or nine fifteen.

And then I'm on my own. And I fluffle around for half an hour, putting off sitting down, make myself another cup of tea; but I'm usually working by ten o'clock. Then I work till twelve o'clock, half past twelve, then reward myself with some lunch, have a cup of tea, waste another ten minutes, start working about one o'clock again, and work till two o'clock, half past two.

Thereafter I become a househusband, and get the house organised for the evening when my wife comes home, at anywhere between six and seven o'clock, and the house has got to be tidy or I get into trouble. And doing it all myself involves doing most of the housework, most of the ironing, all the washing, a good part of the cooking ...

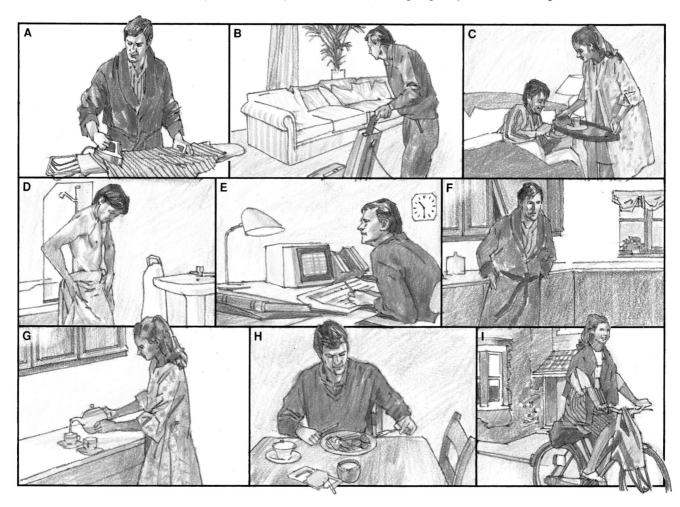

3 Tony is a writer and 'househusband'. He works alone all day. Would you like his kind of life? Why (not)?

Lesson C1

Students expand their vocabulary through activities related to the topic of work, including listening for specific information, reading for overall meaning, and discussion.
Phonology: stress and rhythm.

Language notes and possible problems
1. Level   This is a relatively hard, text-heavy lesson, a bit more demanding than usual. Most students should by now be able to cope with work at this level, but if your class are likely to find it hard going you may prefer to break the lesson up and spread it over two sessions.
2. *By* (time)   Exercise 1 contains several examples of the use of *by* to mean 'at or before; during the time up to'. This needs careful explanation; otherwise students are likely to misuse *by* and *by the time* to mean 'when'.
3. *-ing* forms   Note the examples of *-ing* forms used after verbs and prepositions in Exercises 2 and 4. The Practice Book has a revision exercise on the various uses of the *-ing* form.

If you are short of time
Give Exercise 4 for homework.

---

1 Listening for specific information
- Do this exercise with books closed.
- Tell students that they will hear an interview with somebody who has two jobs.
- They don't need to understand every word. They just have to decide what the two jobs are, and to get a general idea of how Tony spends his day.
- Play the recording once or twice, getting students to tell you what they have understood.
- Note that Tony has an Australian accent.

2 Reading comprehension
- Tell students to read through the text without using dictionaries or asking for explanations.
- Then ask them to look at the pictures.
- If you want some extra practice of the Present Progressive, ask what is happening in each picture.
- Then tell students to write the numbers of the pictures in the correct order.
- Let them compare notes in pairs or small groups before discussing the answer.
- You may like to comment on *by* in *by that stage*, *by ten o'clock* and *by the time* (see *Language notes* above). Explain other important words if necessary, but don't spend too much time going through the text: Exercises 4 and 5 pick up key language points. Note that '*fluffle*' is a word invented by Tony.

Answer to Exercise 2
G; C; F; A; D; I; E; H; B

3 Personalisation
- This exercise gives students a chance to react to what they have heard and read.
- One approach is to start by asking everybody for a simple 'Yes' or 'No' answer. Then put the 'Yeses' and 'Noes' into separate groups, and ask each group to list reasons for their answers. Finally, get each group to tell the others what they feel.

4 Vocabulary consolidation

- Give students time to study the list of words and expressions, looking back to see how they are used.
- Encourage students to ask for help (in English) if they can't remember meanings or pronunciations.
- When students are ready, get them to try to complete the text. You may like to do this partly as an individual activity, partly in small groups, and partly as a whole-class exercise.

Answers to Exercise 4
1. job   2. relationships   3. trade union   4. organise
5. chance   6. on business   7. on her own
8. housework   9. all day   10-12. washing/ironing/shopping
(*any order*)   13. anywhere between   14. waste
15. cooking   16. outdoors   17. salary   18. careful
19. get rid of   20. put off   21. able   22. extremely
23. grows up

5 Student-directed vocabulary learning

- It is important for students to share responsibility for choosing what they learn.
- Give them a few minutes to pick out words and expressions that they particularly want to learn and remember from the texts in Exercises 2 and 4.
- Then ask students to show their lists to each other and explain why they chose particular items.
- Run over the different ways of noting the meanings of words: by translations, by English explanations, or by examples of their use. Different approaches may suit different students; and not all words can best be explained in the same way.
- Students' lists shouldn't be too long: discuss how many new items they can really expect to learn, and ask what they are going to do in order to fix the words in their minds.

6 Rhythm and stress

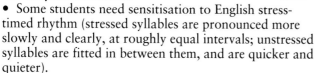

- Some students need sensitisation to English stress-timed rhythm (stressed syllables are pronounced more slowly and clearly, at roughly equal intervals; unstressed syllables are fitted in between them, and are quicker and quieter).
- Make sure that students understand 'stressed syllable', and that they remember what kind of words generally carry stress. ('Content' words like nouns, verbs, adjectives usually have at least one stress; 'form' words like articles, prepositions, auxiliaries and pronouns are often unstressed.)
- Ask students, working in groups, to copy the text and mark the stresses. Then play the recording and discuss their answers.
- There will be some disagreement – stress is a question of 'more or less' rather than 'either/or'. This doesn't matter: the main point is for students to develop sensitivity to English stress and rhythm patterns, so that they can understand speech more easily and improve their own pronunciation.

Answer to Exercise 6 (some variations possible)
Well, I'm **mar**ried, **so** to be a**lone** in the **mor**nings, the **first thing** is to **get rid** of my **wife**, who **for**tunately **has** a **job**, so she **gets up** in the **mor**ning, **makes** a **cup** of **tea**, **rous**es me, I **come** downstairs, **wan**der **round** the **kitch**en, **have** my **cup** of **tea** ...

7 Students' ideal working routines

- Tell students that they have to plan a routine involving some sort of work – lying in bed all day drinking wine doesn't count.
- Give them ten minutes or so to work out what they are going to do. Remind them that they must use new vocabulary from Exercises 2 and 4.
- Then get them to report in groups or to the class.

Practice Book exercises
1. Choosing between the *-ing* form and the infinitive.
2. Choosing between *at* and *by*.
3. Spelling: single and double letters.
4. Student's Cassette exercise (Student's Book Lesson C1, Exercise 1 – last two paragraphs only). Students listen for differences between the recording and the transcript.
5. Vocabulary revision: office equipment.
6. Recreational reading: a choice of three texts.
7. A choice of extended writing tasks about living and working, using language from the Student's Book lesson.

4 Complete the text with the words and expressions in the box. You may need to make small changes. You can use a dictionary or ask somebody for help if you like.

> able   all day   anywhere   between   careful
> chance   cooking   extremely   get rid of
> grow up   housework   ironing   job
> on business   on one's own   organise
> outdoors   put off   relationships   salary
> shopping   trade union   washing
> waste (time or money)

Bill Radford has a ......1...... in a small factory. He doesn't much like the work, but he enjoys the ......2...... with the other workers, and he gets on well with the boss. He belongs to a ......3...... and helps to ......4...... the work of the local branch. Sometimes he has a ......5...... to travel ......6......, which he enjoys very much.

His wife, Ann, has been unemployed for the last two years. She stays at home and looks after the house. After getting their six-year-old daughter Sally ready and driving her to school, she starts on the housework. Although she likes being ......7......, she finds ......8...... boring, and doesn't like to stay at home ......9....... So she tries to get through the washing up, the ......10...., the ......11...., the ......12...... and so on as quickly as possible. This takes her ......13...... two and three hours; after that she usually has lunch. She doesn't like to ......14...... time, so after lunch she goes off to the public library and reads books on politics or history until it's time to fetch Sally from school. In the evenings Bill and Ann share the ......15.......

At weekends they try to spend some time ......16......: they often go walking in the country, or take Sally on trips to places like the zoo or the seaside.

Money is a big problem. Bill doesn't earn a very good ......17......, and their income is hardly enough for three people to live on, so they have to be very ......18...... about what they spend. They can't really afford to keep the car, and will have to ......19...... it soon, but they have decided to ......20...... selling it until Sally is old enough to go to school by bus. They are just not ......21...... to save money, and they're ......22...... worried about their old age. Sally wants to be a teacher or a nurse when she ......23......, but Ann and Bill hope she will do something where she can earn enough money to live a better life than her parents.

5 Choose words and expressions to learn from Exercises 2 and 4. Compare notes with other students, and talk about the reasons for your choices. Do you choose words because they are common, because they are important, because they are useful, because you are interested in the subject, because you like the sound of them, because they are easy to learn ...?

6 🎧 Pronunciation. The first five stressed syllables are marked. Which other syllables do you think are stressed? Listen to the recording and see if you were right.

Well, I'm married, so to be alone in the mornings, the first thing is to get rid of my wife, who fortunately has a job, so she gets up in the morning, makes a cup of tea, rouses me, I come downstairs, wander round the kitchen, have my cup of tea ...

7 Imagine that you can do exactly what work you like. Think about the job, and plan your daily routine. When you are ready, tell the class. You must use at least five of the new words and expressions that you have learnt from this lesson.

'I get up at ten o'clock ...'

Learn/revise: bag; branch; chance; cooking; factory; first floor; housework; income; ironing; job; relationship; salary; shopping; TV; washing; fetch; get dressed; get up; grow up (grew, grown); iron; organise; put off ...ing (put, put); share; waste (time/money); alone; boring; careful; married; tidy; unemployed; extremely; outdoors; upstairs; by (= not later than); all day; as ... as possible; be able to; get into trouble; get on with sbdy; get rid of sbdy/sth; make (a cup of) tea; on business; on my own; on top of.

C2 Focus on systems

A choice of exercises: the names of common electrical appliances; two-word verbs; *should(n't)* and *must(n't)*; pronunciation of final consonant groups; hearing unstressed syllables.

VOCABULARY: ELECTRICAL APPLIANCES

1 Work in groups of three or four and make a list of all the electrical appliances (e.g. *fridge, CD player, iron*) you can think of. Try to find at least twenty.

2 If you could have just five of the things in your list (plus leads, plugs and sockets), which would you choose? Which five are the least important?

3 Look at the picture below and listen to the recording. Which thing is described in each sentence? Example:

'It's plugged in and switched on. It's black and white.'
'The radio.'

GRAMMAR: TWO-WORD VERBS

4 Look at the examples. Can you make a rule?

Please switch the light off.
Please switch off the light.
Please switch it off.
BUT NOT ~~Please switch off it.~~

Could you pick those papers up?
Could you pick up those papers?
Could you pick them up?
BUT NOT ~~Could you pick up them?~~

5 Look at the sentences and say what you should do. Use these verbs.

switch on	switch off	turn up
turn down	plug in	unplug

Example:
What should you do if you've finished using your calculator? *'Switch it off.'*

What should you do if:
1. the radio isn't loud enough?
2. the CD player's too loud?
3. you see in the newspaper that there's an interesting TV programme just starting?
4. you don't want to watch TV any more?
5. the TV's on fire?
6. the cooker's too hot?
7. you want to use your calculator?
8. the iron isn't getting the creases out of your clothes?
9. the iron's burning your clothes?
10. you've finished with the iron?
11. you've just taken the hoover out of the cupboard and you want to start using it?

GRAMMAR: *SHOULD, SHOULDN'T, MUST* AND *MUSTN'T*

6 Look at the examples. What do you think is the difference between *should* and *must*?

You should switch the light off before you change a bulb.
You must use the right kind of batteries in a calculator.
You shouldn't drive too fast on wet roads.
You mustn't drive at over 30mph in towns.

Lesson C2

Vocabulary: electrical appliances.
Grammar: verbs with adverb particles; *should(n't)* and *must(n't)*.
Phonology: final consonant groups; hearing unstressed syllables.

Language notes and possible problems

1. *Must* and *must not* Students practise the use of *must* to talk about actions which are considered very important or necessary. Note that *must not* expresses negative obligation, not the absence of obligation. German speakers, among others, may find this confusing (the German expression *ich muss nicht* means *I don't need to*, not *I mustn't*).

2. *Must* and *should* *Must* expresses a stronger degree of obligation than *should*. Instructions or advice expressed with *must* leave the reader/hearer little or no freedom; *should* implies that the reader/hearer can choose whether or not to comply. In many cases, of course, both are possible, with the choice of verb depending on the speaker's/writer's attitude rather than the objective facts.

3. Phrasal verbs with adverb particles Note that with verbs like *switch on/off* or *turn up/down*, the particle (*on/off* etc.) can come before or after a noun object, but can only come after a pronoun object (see examples in Student's Book).

Not all two-word verbs are combinations of **verb + particle**. Some (like *listen to*, *look for* or *look after*) consist of **verb + preposition**, and with these the rules for word order are not the same. It is probably best not to go into the details of this for the moment.

1 Vocabulary expansion: pooling information

• Students should work in groups sharing their knowledge.
• If they do not know a word they should use a dictionary, ask other students, or ask you.
• Put on the board:
  Excuse me, what's this called?
  What do you call a thing for drying hair?
  How do you say ... in English?
  How do you pronounce ...?
  How do you spell ...?
• When students have done as much as they can, discuss their lists and practise the pronunciation of the words. (Note especially iron (/aɪən/).)

2 Priorities

• Give students a few minutes to make their choices and compare notes among themselves.
• Then ask them to explain their decisions.

3 Listening: identifying items

• Get students to look at the picture for a moment.
• Explain *plugged in* and *switched on/off*.
• Then play the recording, pausing after each sentence while students write their answers.
• Let them compare notes, then play the recording again and discuss the answers.

Tapescript and answers to Exercise 3
1. It's plugged in and switched on. It's black and white. (*radio*)
2. It's not plugged in. It's got a three-pin plug. (*electric kettle*)
3. It's plugged in but it's switched off. It's white. (*TV*)
4. It's plugged in and switched on. It's white. (*food mixer*)
5. It's plugged in but it's switched off. It's black. (*iron*)
6. It's not plugged in. It's got a two-pin plug. (*hair-dryer*)
7. It's plugged in and switched on. It's black. (*vacuum cleaner*)

4 Two-word verbs: working out the rules

• Give students a few minutes to think about the problem and discuss it among themselves.
• Then go over the rules with them (see *Language notes* above).

5 Practice: *What should you do if ...?*

• Go over the six boxed expressions.
• Explain the meanings of any expressions which are not clear.
• Go through the exercise orally, and then consolidate by asking students to write the answers to one or two of the questions.
• Note that more than one answer is often possible.

Optional activity: memory test

• Do a series of ten or a dozen actions which illustrate the expressions which have just been learnt.
• For example: switch on the light; switch on the cassette player; switch off the light; turn up the cassette player; unplug a heater; turn down the cassette player; switch on the light; plug in the heater; unplug the cassette player.
• Ask students what you did; see if anybody can remember the exact sequence.
• Get a student to do the same thing.

6 *Should(n't)* and *must(n't)*: working out the rules

• This, too, can be done by group discussion.
• Students should be able to see that the difference is related to the strength or importance of the obligation (see *Language notes* above).
• Make sure students understand the meaning of *mustn't* (see *Language notes*).

7 Practice

• Go through the exercise asking students which word they think is the best in each case.

• Note that in many of the sentences two answers are possible, depending on how strongly people feel.

8 Road signs

• This can be done individually or by class discussion, as you wish.

• Explain any problems of vocabulary as you go through.

Answers to Exercise 8

1. must   2. must   3. must   4. must not
5. must not   6. must not   7. should   8. must not
9. must not   10. should

9 Students make up regulations and advice

• This can be done individually or in groups, as students prefer. Help with vocabulary if necessary.

• In Option 1, get them to see who can make up the craziest regulations.

• When students are ready, let groups tell each other their regulations/advice.

10 Final consonant clusters

• Some languages contain no final consonant clusters at all, and speakers of these languages will have difficulty with this aspect of English pronunciation. (If your students do not have this kind of problem, drop the exercise.)

• Ask students to repeat the words and sentences after you or the recording.

• Then go round the room letting each student say one line in turn until you think they have had sufficient practice.

• This exercise will not be enough to help students with real problems in this area, but will serve as sensitisation so that you can work on clusters as they come up in future lessons.

11 'How many words?'

• Play the recording, stopping after each sentence while students try to decide how many words there are and what they are. You may need to play the sentences more than once.

• When students have worked out the sentences, get them to practise saying them with a natural rhythm.

Tapescript and answers to Exercise 11

1. Can I help you?   (4)
2. I've got a problem with a radio.   (8)
3. How long have you had it?   (6)
4. Where did you buy it?   (5)
5. What colour is it?   (4)
6. I don't remember how much it cost.   (8)
7. Can I bring it into the shop?   (7)
8. What's your address?   (4)

Practice Book exercises

1. Writing definitions.
2. Two-word verbs: position of the particle.
3. Modal verbs in traffic regulations.
4. Student's Cassette exercise (Student's Book Lesson C2, Exercise 10). Students listen and repeat the words, paying special attention to final consonant groups.
5. Capital letters and punctuation.
6. Recreational reading: a poem; facts about power and technology.
7. Students write about their three favourite electrical appliances, explaining their choices.

7 Which word do you feel is best – *should, shouldn't, must* or *mustn't*?

1. You .... always switch electrical appliances off when you are not using them.
2. Small children .... watch violent programmes on TV.
3. In Britain, before you start using a new electrical appliance, you .... put the right kind of plug on.
4. When you put a plug on, you .... be careful to put the wires in the right places.
5. You .... touch electrical appliances when you are in the bath.
6. When you move into a new house or flat, you .... check the electrical wiring.
7. You .... plug too many things into the same socket.
8. You .... wash white and coloured clothes separately.
9. You .... clean out the fridge from time to time.
10. You .... let the iron get too hot if you are ironing silk.
11. You .... turn your radio up loud at night.
12. In Britain, you .... buy a licence every year if you have a TV.

8 Look at the road signs and complete the descriptions. Use *must, should* or *must not*.

1. You .... go.
2. You .... stop.
3. You .... stop if the road in front of you is not clear.
4. You .... drive into this street.
5. You .... turn right.
6. People .... walk here.
7. You .... drive carefully – the road is slippery.
8. You .... park here.
9. You .... overtake.
10. You .... look out for fallen rocks.

9 Do one of these tasks.
1. Make up some traffic regulations for Fantasia (a strange country where everything is different). Example:
   '*You must not drive at over 30 mph on Sundays.*'
2. Give some advice to somebody who wants to go on a safari in East Africa. Example:
   '*You must have injections. You should take binoculars.*'
3. Give some advice to a foreigner who is planning to visit your country.

PRONUNCIATION: FINAL CONSONANT GROUPS; UNSTRESSED SYLLABLES

10 [cassette] Say these words and expressions. Be careful to pronounce the ends of the words clearly.

lamps   bulbs   lamps and bulbs
plugs   sockets   plugs and sockets

plugged   plugged in   It's not plugged in.
finished   finished it   I finished it.
switched   switched on   It's not switched on.
thanked   thanked him   I thanked him.
asked   asked for   She asked for help.

fridges   They've got two fridges.
switches   Where are the switches?
torches   The torches were in the car.

isn't   She isn't in.
doesn't   It doesn't open.
wasn't   It wasn't switched on.
hasn't   She hasn't arrived yet.
hadn't   She said she hadn't forgotten me.
wouldn't   I wouldn't use it.
couldn't   I couldn't understand him.
shouldn't   You shouldn't ask questions like that.

11 [cassette] Listen to the recording. How many words do you hear in each sentence? What are they? (Contractions like *that's* count as two words.)

> **Learn/revise:** plug in; unplug; pick up; switch on/off; turn up/down; electric(al); *the names of the electrical appliances in Exercise 1.*

C3 How to do it

Advice and instructions; giving opinions; giving a prepared talk; modal verbs;
infinitive of purpose; *by ...ing*; pronunciation (words beginning with 2 or 3 consonants).

1 Here are some useful practical tips for everyday life.
Unfortunately, the beginnings and ends have got mixed up.
Can you sort them out?

To make tomatoes easier to peel,	rub them with lemon first and then wash them.
If you want to pick up a rabbit,	you should rub it with liquid brass cleaner.
To get cigarette stains off your fingers,	cover them with very hot water for a minute or two.
If you catch German measles,	put cold water in one and stand the other in hot water.
You can clean dirty saucepans	by packing them with wet newspaper and leaving them overnight.
To get dust out of a guitar,	don't hold its ears.
If two glasses are stuck together,	don't visit anyone who is pregnant unless you're sure she's already had them.
To get small scratches off your watch glass,	you should put rice inside it, shake it and empty it.
You can make tight shoes more comfortable	by filling them with cold water and vinegar and letting them boil for five minutes.

Lesson C3

Students practise giving advice and instructions; discuss choice of vocabulary to learn; give prepared talks.
Principal structures: imperatives; modal verbs; infinitive of purpose; *by ...ing*.
Phonology: initial consonant clusters.

Language notes and possible problems
1. Modal verbs *Can, should* and *must* occur in this lesson.
2. Infinitive of purpose Students may need to be reminded about this structure, which comes four times in Exercise 1. Look out for mistakes like **For to make ...* or **For make ...*
3. *By ...ing* If students have difficulty with this structure, there is an exercise on it in the Practice Book.
4. Pronunciation Initial consonant clusters (Exercise 4) are difficult for many learners. Look out for extra vowels in clusters beginning with *s-* (e.g. *'estand'* or *'setand'*). Italians tend to voice the initial *s* before other voiced consonants such as *m* (*'zmile'*). In clusters beginning *ex-*, look out for *es-* (*'Escuse me'*). Students who speak Northern or Eastern European languages are unlikely to need Exercise 4.

If you are short of time
Exercise 7 could be dropped.

1 Mixed-up tips
• This can be done in groups. If your students are competitive, ask them to see which group can write out the correct versions of the tips first.
• They will need to use dictionaries for some words.

Alternative to Exercise 1: split halves
• If you prepare slips of paper with the half-sentences from Exercise 1 on them, it can be done as a walk-round activity.
• Hand out the slips and tell students to learn by heart what is written on them.
• They should then walk round saying their half-sentences and trying to find their 'other halves'.
• Finally, get pairs to read out their tips to the class.

Answers to Exercise 1
To make tomatoes easier to peel, cover them with very hot water for a minute or two.
If you want to pick up a rabbit, don't hold its ears.
To get cigarette stains off your fingers, rub them with lemon first and then wash them.
If you catch German measles, don't visit anyone who is pregnant unless you're sure she's already had them.
You can clean dirty saucepans by filling them with cold water and vinegar and letting them boil for five minutes.
To get dust out of a guitar, you should put rice inside it, shake it and empty it.
If two glasses are stuck together, put cold water in one and stand the other in hot water.
To get small scratches off your watch glass, you should rub it with liquid brass cleaner.
You can make tight shoes more comfortable by packing them with wet newspaper and leaving them overnight.

2 Structures: beginnings and ends
• Give students a minute or two to study the examples in Exercise 1 and work out how they are constructed.
• They should be able to see that *You can ...* and *by ...ing* go together, and that the other beginnings and ends can be freely combined.
• Then get the students to rewrite tips as shown. You may need to remind them of the difference in strength between *shouldn't* and *mustn't*.

3 Completing tips
• Ask around the class to see if anybody can suggest answers; or get students to work in groups to see how many they can complete.

Possible answers to Exercise 3
The night before an examination, do something relaxing and then get a good night's sleep.
To find out how far away a thunderstorm is, count the time between the flash and the bang. Five seconds = one mile; three seconds = one kilometre.
You can get a tight ring off by putting soapy water on your finger.
You can keep a mirror from misting up by rubbing it with a cut potato or apple.
If you're going on a long flight, wear loose comfortable clothing and don't drink alcohol.
To keep wasps away from a picnic, put a glass of sugar water or beer a few metres away.
To get chewing gum off a piece of clothing, hold the back over the steam from a kettle.

4 Pronunciation: initial clusters
• Give students as much practice as they need to get the clusters right. You may want to play the recording or say the words for them to imitate.
• If they have serious difficulty with the first group, get them to start by making the *s* too long and gradually shortening it.
• Note that the first syllable of *examination* is generally pronounced /ɪgz/, not /ɪks/.

5 Choosing vocabulary
• This will help you to see what kind of vocabulary students feel is most useful for them.
• When they have compared notes, you may like to give your own opinion about what sort of words and expressions are particularly worth learning.

6 Students make up exercises
• Give groups ten minutes or so to work out their tips and mix them up.
• Then let them exchange lists and put each other's tips in order.
• Invite groups to read out any particularly interesting tips to the whole class.

7 Prepared talks
• This will work best if students speak from notes, rather than writing out the whole of what they are going to say.
• If class time is short, you may prefer them to prepare their talks at home and give them in the next lesson.
• When they are giving their talks, it's best not to interrupt with corrections unless communication has completely broken down. Serious mistakes can be noted for attention on another occasion.
• Encourage the class to ask as many questions as possible after each talk.
• In a large class, get students to do the exercise in groups; ask each group to choose a particularly interesting talk to be repeated for the whole class.

Alternative to Exercise 7
Another way of doing this exercise is to say that you are a Martian, and to ask students to tell you how to do various everyday things (e.g. work a cooker, drive a car, boil an egg, comb your hair, make a train journey, ...).

Practice Book exercises
1. *You can ... by ...ing ...*
2. Writing sentences about ways of saving money.
3. Distinguishing between countable and uncountable nouns.
4. Completing sentences with *some* and *any*.
5. Making vocabulary networks (*food*; *drinks*).
6. Reading skills (deducing meaning from context); labelling a picture with words from the text.
7. Recreational reading: prose fiction.

Letting students make up exercises
Activities like Exercise 6, in which students make up exercises for others to do, can be very good for morale. It is good if students can take some of the responsibility for the choice and design of their learning activities, so that they are not always obviously in a subordinate role. And it is nice if, at least sometimes, it is the students who do the clever things in the class, rather than the teacher, the book and the cassette player.

2 Look at the different beginnings and ends from Exercise 1. Which of the following beginnings can go with which ends?

BEGINNINGS: ENDS:
To ...   imperative (e.g. *rub*)
If ...   negative imperative (e.g. *don't hold*)
You can ...   *you should ...*
                by ...ing

Rewrite two of the tips using different beginnings and/or ends. Rewrite one of the tips using *you shouldn't* or *you mustn't*.

3 Can you complete these tips?

The night before an examination, ...
To find out how far away a thunderstorm is, ...
You can get a tight ring off ...
You can keep a mirror from misting up ...
If you're going on a long flight, ...
To keep wasps away from a picnic, ...
To get chewing gum off a piece of clothing, ...

4 📼 Pronunciation: practise these words. Can you think of any other words that begin with *s* + consonant?

school   scratches   small   smell   smoke
specialist   speed   spelling   sport   stains
stand   stop   stuck   stuff

Now practise these. Can you think of any other words that begin with *ex*?

examination   excuse   explain   extremely

5 Choose the five most useful new words to learn from Exercises 1 and 3. Compare notes with other students – have you chosen the same words?

6 Work in groups. Each group writes four tips (serious or funny). Then copy the tips, with the beginnings and ends out of order, and give them to another group to put in order. Ideas:

How to mend things.
How to clean things.
How to cook things.
How to keep things safe/clean.
How to make cats/dogs/people/children do what you
    want them to.
How to stop cats/dogs/people/children doing things
    that you don't want them to do.
How to attract men/women.

7 Prepare a talk about how to do something. (For example, how to make ...; how to mend ...; how to cook ...; how to use ...) When you are ready, give your talk to the other students.

'... then you put the other one on top of the first one and glue them together.'

Infinitive of purpose
To get dust out of a guitar, ...
    (~~For to get dust out of a guitar ...~~)
    (~~For get dust out of a guitar ...~~)

Modal verbs
You **can** clean dirty saucepans ...
    (~~You can to clean ...~~)
You **should** put rice inside it ...
    (~~You should to put ...~~)
You **mustn't** visit anyone ...
    (~~You mustn't to visit ...~~)

Imperative
Rub them with lemon.
Don't hold its ears.

Learn/revise: brass; chewing gum; dust; examination; flight; (German) measles; guitar; lemon; liquid; mirror; newspaper; picnic; rabbit; rice; ring; stain; saucepan; thunderstorm; tip; vinegar; wasp; attract; boil; clean; cover; empty (*verb and adjective*); fill; mend; mix up; pack; peel; rub; shake (shook, shaken); sort out; comfortable; dirty; everyday; practical; pregnant; safe; tight; useful; overnight; unfortunately.

SKILLS FOCUS
SKILLS FOCUS
SKILLS FOCUS
SKILLS FOCUS
SKILLS FOCUS
SKILLS FOCUS

C4 Quick thinkers

1 Here are four reports from British newspapers. The sentences have been mixed up. Work in groups of four. Each student should choose a different report and try to put it together, with the sentences in the right order. See if you can do it without looking up any words in the dictionary. When you are ready, read your report to the others in your group.

Policeman saves boy on motorway

Quick-thinking van driver

Firemen catch a man in mid-air

Helicopter pilot saves swimmers

A quick-thinking helicopter pilot saved 3 swimmers from shark attacks yesterday.

A quick-thinking van driver saved 11 people trapped in a blazing house in Birkenhead early today.

After a few minutes they were frightened away, and the swimmers were able to get back safely to the beach.

After shouting for help, the man jumped from a top-floor window with his clothes on fire.

But a policeman had seen him fall.

Firemen who were fighting the fire on a balcony below heard his shouts and realised what was happening.

Four adults and seven children were trapped in the bedroom above.

He brought his helicopter down until he was just over the water, and hovered above the sharks.

He dashed across the motorway and grabbed the five-year-old to safety from under the wheels of a vehicle that was almost upon them.

He was seriously injured and lay helpless in the fast lane with traffic hurtling towards him.

Last night 22-year-old Mr Luke Savage, of Moreton Grove, Chester, was recovering in hospital.

Little John Parker faced death when he fell from a car as it sped down a busy motorway.

Mrs Anne Redman of Newbury was driving past a house in Beaufort Road when she saw the ground floor on fire.

Mrs Redman backed her van across the pavement, smashed through the front fence, and drove up to the front of the house.

Police Constable Peter O'Donnell, careless of his own life, leapt from a moving patrol car.

Swimmer Marion Jacobs said afterwards, 'He saved our lives. If he hadn't come when he did, the sharks would have had us.'

The trapped occupants were able to jump to safety via the roof of the van.

They leaned out and grabbed him by the legs as he hurtled past.

Three firemen caught a man in mid-air yesterday as he leapt from a blazing house.

While he was flying off the Australian coast near Sydney, the pilot saw sharks approaching the swimmers.

Yesterday John, of The Close, Newleigh, Herts, was in hospital with head and leg injuries, but was described as 'satisfactory'.

Lesson C4

Reading and writing skills: studying text structure; guessing unknown words; narrative.
Principal structures: Simple Past and Past Progressive tenses in narrative.

Language notes and possible problems
1. Past Progressive   Clever students may notice that the Past Progressive is not always used with *as* (*as he **leapt** ...; as it **sped** ...*): in this case the conjunction is enough to make the time relations clear.
2. Guessing unknown words   See *Language notes* to Lesson A4.

---

1 Sorting out texts
• As far as possible, put students in groups of four, with each student in a group working on a different text.
• Try to get them not to use dictionaries or ask you about words at this stage unless it is absolutely essential; this will encourage them to think about the overall meaning of the texts without worrying too much about particular vocabulary problems.
• The exercise is easier than it looks, and students should finish it quite quickly. They should end up with each student writing out a complete version of their text.
• When students are ready, get them to read their texts to their groups.
• Then get them to check their answers (see below).
• Don't explain vocabulary at this stage if you intend to do Exercise 2.
• Note that all four texts are adapted from genuine news reports.

Answers to Exercise 1
The reconstituted texts are printed on pages 131 and 132 of the Student's Book, so that students can use them to check their answers, and for reference in Exercises 2–5.

2 Vocabulary: guessing unknown words
- This exercise helps students to see how easy it can be to understand a new word by looking at the way it is used.
- Ask students to find the words, and to say roughly what they think they mean. Tell them whether they are right.
- See how quickly students can find the words that mean the same as *blazing* (*on fire*), *grabbed* (*caught*), *above* (*over*) and *leapt* (*jumped*).
- Ask if students have noticed any words and expressions that are repeated in the reports (*quick-thinking, save, jump, on fire, trapped, grabbed, hurtling, leapt, blazing*).

3 Students choose vocabulary to learn
- It is important that students should be able to make some of the decisions about their learning.
- Give them a few minutes to choose words that they particularly want to learn. Help them to establish the exact meanings, guiding them in efficient dictionary use if necessary.
- You may like to ask them to compare notes with other students about their choice of vocabulary, and to tell you what made them choose the words they did.
- This may also be a good opportunity to talk again about different ways of noting and learning new vocabulary (see teaching notes on Lesson A3, Exercise 7).

4 Use of tenses
- This gives you a chance to do some quick revision of the rules for the use of the Past Progressive. If students are still unclear about this, you may wish to spend time on the revision exercises on page 117.

5 Students complete a report
- This is probably best done in groups. Give students 15 minutes or so to work out how the girl saved the cyclist, and to write the missing part of the report.
- As they work, walk round giving whatever help is needed. Encourage them to use one or two Past Progressives, as well as words and expressions from the lesson.
- When everybody is ready, let groups exchange reports or read them out to the whole class.

Optional extra activity: students design exercises for each other
- If time allows, and students have not run out of energy, you could get them to design their own versions of the task in Exercise 5, for other students to complete.
- Put them in pairs or small groups and tell them to write the beginning and end of a news report.
- When they have done this, they pass it to another group, who have to fill in the middle.

Practice Book exercises
1. Reading for speed and accuracy; following instructions.
2. Completing sentences with *when* or *if*.
3. Putting in the correct tense (mixed tenses).
4. Vocabulary revision: family relations.
5. Writing down words from memory.
6. Logic test.
7. Extended writing: a time when getting out of trouble required some quick thinking.

2 Find the words *blazing, grabbed, above, leapt, hurtling* and *sped* in the reports in Exercise 1. Look at how they are used. Can you see what they mean without using a dictionary? Can you find other words in the reports that mean the same as *blazing, grabbed, above* and *leapt*?

3 Choose some more words to learn from the reports. Ask the teacher, or use a dictionary, to help you find out the exact meanings.

4 Look at the way the Past Progressive tense is used in the example. Can you find more examples of the Past Progressive in the reports?

Mrs Anne Redman of Newbury *was driving* past a house in Beaufort Road when she *saw* the ground floor on fire.

5 Here are the beginning and end of another news report. Can you write the middle? Try to use some vocabulary and structures from Exercises 1–4.

Quick-thinking five-year-old saves cyclist

Cyclist Norman Pratt went out of control as he was coming down a steep cliffside road yesterday, and ended up hanging by his hands from a small bush, with a 200-foot drop below his feet.

23-year-old Pratt, from Harlow, Essex, said 'She was wonderful. I couldn't have held on much longer. If she hadn't come when she did, I would have fallen to my death.'

Simple Past and Past Progressive tenses
Mrs Anne Redman of Newbury *was driving* past a house in Beaufort Road when she *saw* the ground floor on fire.

Learn/revise: adult; death; ground floor; helicopter; motorway; neighbour; pilot; safety; traffic; vehicle; approach; dash; frighten; jump; pull; recover; save; trap; busy; helpless; injured; quick; above; afterwards; almost; away; on fire; over; seriously; via.

C5 It doesn't work

Making and accepting apologies; correcting misunderstandings; making complaints; listening skills: predicting, listening for specific information; reading skills: guessing words from context; pronunciation: stress for emphasis and contrast.

1 📼 Here is a dialogue with most of the words missing. Some blanks need one word; some need several words. See if you can guess what is missing, and listen to the recording to check your guesses.

ASSISTANT: ...., madam. .... help ....?
CUSTOMER: .... manager, ...
A: Furniture, madam? Second floor.
C: .... <u>Ma-na-ger</u>.
A: .... furniture.
C: .... But .... manager, ...?
A: Well, ... busy .... appointment?
C: No, ... complaint.
A: A complaint. .... Well, I'll just see if she's free.

2 Work with a partner, and make up a short conversation which includes a misunderstanding and an apology. You can use one of these sentences if you like.

I thought you said Thursday.
I thought you said goodbye.
I thought you said five pence.
I thought you said five o'clock.
I thought you said steak.
I thought you were talking to me.

3 📼 Close your book, and listen to the second dialogue. How much can you remember?

4 Now read the second dialogue and do the tasks.

MANAGER: Good afternoon, madam. I understand you have a complaint.
C: Yes, I've got a problem with this hair-dryer.
M: I'm sorry to hear that. What's the trouble?
C: Well, first of all, I ordered it two months ago and it only arrived yesterday.
M: Oh, dear. That's very strange.
C: Well, it's probably because you addressed it to Mr Paul Jones at 29 Cannon Street. I'm *Mrs Paula* Jones, and my address is *39* Cannon Street.
M: Well, I'm really sorry about that, madam. We do …
C: And secondly, I'm afraid it's useless. It doesn't work.
M: Doesn't work?
C: No. It doesn't work. It doesn't dry my hair. When I switch it on, it just goes 'bzzzzz', but it doesn't get hot at all.
M: Well, I really am very sorry about this, madam. I do apologise. We'll be happy to replace the dryer for you. Or we'll give you a refund instead, if you prefer.
C: And thirdly, …

1. **Thinking about meaning: match each word or expression in *italics* in the first column with the closest meaning in the second column.**

1. I *ordered it* two months ago …	a. wrote on it the name and address of
2. *That's very strange.*	b. take this and give you money
3. … *addressed it to* …	c. take this and give you another
4. I'm afraid *it's useless.*	d. no one can use it
5. It doesn't *work*.	e. in place of my other suggestion
6. … to *replace the dryer* …	f. I'm surprised
7. … we'll *give you a refund* …	g. do what it should do
8. … give you a refund *instead*, …	h. asked you to send it

2. **Find these expressions in the second dialogue.**

   1. Find an expression to use before you say something unpleasant: for example, ... *I've crashed your car.*
   2. Find four ways of saying *I'm sorry* and write them down from weakest to strongest.
   3. Find a verb to fit in this sentence: *When I touched it, it* .... '*whirr*'.
   4. Find a verb to fit in this sentence: *It was warm this morning, but now it has* .... *cooler.*

3. **Listen to the second dialogue again.**

58

Lesson C5

Students learn ways of making and accepting emphatic apologies and correcting misunderstandings, and of making complaints; they practise listening skills (prediction, listening for specific information) and reading skills (guessing words from context).
Phonology: stress for emphasis and contrast.

Language notes and possible problems
1. Stress for emphasis   Students' own languages may not use stress for emphasis as English does (for example, the sentence in the dialogue *He's **very** busy just now*). You may need to reassure students that they will not seem overly dramatic if they emphasize in this way.
2. Stress for contrast   Students learn to correct misunderstandings by stressing the right word or expression. Again, this may not come easily to some nationalities.
3. Emphatic apologies   Two similar ways of adding emphasis occur in the apologies in the dialogues:
1. The assistant in the first dialogue says *I **am** sorry*, and the manager says *I really **am** very sorry* in the second dialogue. The normally unstressed auxiliary is stressed, and in the manager's apology put in an unusual place, after *really*.
2. The manager says *I **do** apologise*. You will want to point out to students that *do*, *does*, and *did* can be used for emphasis with affirmative verbs in appropriate cases, and are stressed.
4. Got   Note the omission of *got* in *Have you an appointment?* (formal style).
5. Won't   Note that *won't* is used not only for people but also for things which 'refuse' to do what we want (see Exercise 6).

---

1 Predicting a dialogue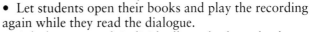
• Let students work individually for five minutes reading the dialogue and trying to predict what goes in the blanks. Answer any questions about meaning that the students may have.
• Then get them to compare answers in small groups.
• Play the recording, more than once if necessary, so that students can check their answers.

Tapescript and answers to Exercise 1
ASSISTANT: *Good afternoon*, madam. *Can I help you?*
CUSTOMER: *Yes, I'd like to see the* manager, *please.*
ASSISTANT: Furniture, madam? Second floor.
CUSTOMER: *No, the <u>manager</u>. Ma-na-ger.*
ASSISTANT: Oh, I *am* sorry. I *thought you said* furniture.
CUSTOMER: *That's all right.* But *can I see the* manager, *please?*
ASSISTANT: Well, *I'm afraid she's <u>very</u>* busy *just now. Have you an* appointment?
CUSTOMER: No, *I haven't. I want to make a* complaint.
ASSISTANT: A complaint. *Oh, I see.* Well, I'll just see if she's free.

2 Misunderstandings and apologies
• Get students to look at the complete dialogue on page 132 of their books. Point out:
1. The use of stress for contrast in *No, the <u>manager</u>. <u>Ma-na-ger</u>.*
2. The emphatic apology *I <u>am</u> sorry* (use of *am* instead of contraction and use of stress for emphasis).
3. The way the woman accepts the apology: *That's all right*.
• Ask students to work in pairs to make up very short exchanges.
• Each exchange must contain a sentence beginning *I thought you said …*, an apology and an acceptance.
• As an example of what is wanted, you could give them something like this:
   A: I'm thirsty.
   B: No, it's Friday.
   A: No, *thirsty*. I'd like a drink.
   B: Oh, I *am* sorry. I thought you said Thursday.
   A: That's all right.
• You might need to point out that the misunderstood words should sound like the originals – as in *thirsty* and *Thursday*.

3 Listening and remembering
• Get students to listen to the dialogue, books closed.
• Ask them to tell you any words they remember. You may want to put the correct words on the board in the approximate place they are found in the dialogue.
• Play the recording again and see if students can fill in any other words.
• If your students are still interested, play the recording a third time; otherwise go on to Exercise 4.

4 Focus on vocabulary
• Let students open their books and play the recording again while they read the dialogue.
• Ask them to work individually to do the tasks that follow the dialogue. Then they can compare answers in pairs or small groups.
• Go over the answers with them, and answer any other questions they have about the dialogue.
• Point out the use of *am* in *I really am very sorry* and of *do* in *I do apologise*.
• Finally, play the dialogue again.

Answers to Exercise 4
Part 1
1h; 2f; 3a; 4d; 5g; 6c; 7b; 8e
Part 2
1. I'm afraid
2. I'm sorry to hear that.
   I'm really sorry about that, madam.
   I really am very sorry about this, madam.
   I do apologise.
3. went
4. got

5 Contrastive stress

• This exercise shows students how a change in stress can alter the meaning of a sentence.
• Go slowly over the examples, making sure that students can hear the difference in stress and understand what it implies.
• Get them to imitate the two example sentences (saying the stressed words on a higher pitch); this will help them to hear the difference.
• Play the rest of the sentences.
• Discuss the answer to each one before going on.

Tapescript and answers to Exercise 5
1. You've got *two* sisters, haven't you?
2. You've got two *sisters,* haven't you?
3. You *work* in London, don't you? (Possible answer: No, I live there – I work outside London.)
4. Is that *Mary's* father? (No, it's Ann's father.)
5. Did you say you had a new *red* Lancia? (No, a white one.)
6. Do you need *English* for your work? (No, French.)
7. a. Would you like *me* to telephone Peter and Anne? (No, not you.)
   b. Would you like me to *telephone* Peter and Anne? (No, write.)
   c. Would you like me to telephone Peter *and* Anne? (No, just Peter.)

6 Problems

• Go over the examples with the students and make sure they understand what to do. Make sure they realise what *'s* means in Sentence a, and point out what *won't* means.
• They should realise that each object can have several things wrong with it, and that some problems can apply to more than one object.
• Let students work individually. Help them when necessary, but encourage them to rely on their dictionaries so as to practise reference skills.
• When about half the students have finished, divide the class into groups of three or four and let them compare answers.
• Then go over the answers with the whole class, practising the pronunciation of the sentences.

Answers to Exercise 6
c. 1, 2, 3, 4, 5
d. 1, 3, 4 (and arguably 2 and 5 as well)
e. 1, 3, 4, 5
f. 1, 4, 5
g. 2, 4
h. 1, 4, 5

7 Complaints: fluency practice

• Divide the class in half: one side of the class are to be customers and the other side shop managers.
• To begin with, let them work with people who have the same role as themselves. They should look over the lesson again to remind themselves of vocabulary.
• Go over the instructions for each group and make sure they understand what they are to do.
• Then tell the students what their time limit will be for the exercise, and let the shop managers stand around the room at their desks, while the customers approach them to complain. When a pair has finished their conversation, the customer can try again at another shop.
• Walk round while they are working to give help if communication breaks down entirely, but try not to interrupt if the students are managing to make themselves understood to one another.

Practice Book exercises
1. Recreational reading: practical advice presented in a humorous way.
2. Student's Cassette exercise (Student's Book Lesson C5, Exercise 1). Students mark and practise sentence stress.
3. Completing sentences with an infinitive or an *-ing* form.
4. Students write a few sentences saying when they started and stopped doing things.
5. Reading skills: separating three mixed-up stories and writing one of them out in full.
6. A choice of writing tasks: a story about something that didn't work; a letter of complaint.

59

5 🔲 **Stress. Listen carefully to these questions, and then write answers to them (beginning *No, …*). When you have done that, practise saying the questions and answers.**

1. You've got *two* sisters, haven't you?
   No, just one.

2. You've got two *sisters*, haven't you?
   No, two brothers.

3. You work in London, don't you?
4. Is that Mary's father?
5. Did you say you had a new red Lancia?
6. Do you need English for your work?
7. Would you like me to telephone Peter and Anne?
   (*three times, with different answers*)

6 **Match the objects with the problems. You can use a dictionary. The first two answers are done for you.**

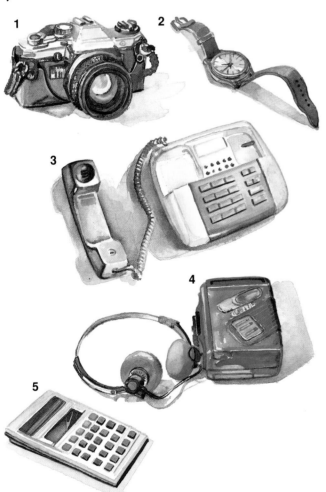

1
2
3
4
5

a. It's started going very fast. *2, 4*
b. It won't start. *4*
c. It doesn't work.
d. It makes a funny noise.
e. One of the buttons is stuck.
f. It won't turn off.
g. It's stopped.
h. It won't switch on.

7 **Your teacher will tell you to be a customer or a shop manager. Follow the appropriate instructions.**

Customers
There is something wrong with your camera/watch/ telephone *etc*. Decide what is wrong. Decide whether you want it repaired or replaced, or whether you want a refund. Decide whether you are going to be friendly to the shop manager. You can look back at the dialogues for vocabulary. Then go and complain.

Shop managers
You are the manager of a shop. Decide whether you are feeling friendly or not today. Decide whether your shop gives refunds, or only offers to repair or replace. Decide how long repairs take. You can look back at the dialogues for vocabulary. Then get ready for some complaints.

> **Learn/revise:** appointment; complaint; conversation; customer; furniture (*uncountable*); hair-dryer; manager; problem; refund; complain; dry; get (for changes) (got, got); go (for sounds) (went, gone); order; repair; replace; busy; free (= not busy); funny (= strange); stuck; useless; first of all; instead; probably; secondly; thirdly; whether; I do apologise; I really am very sorry; I thought you said …; if you prefer; It doesn't work; It won't start; That's all right; That's very strange; What's the trouble?

C6 Focus on systems

A choice of exercises: passives; situational language; contrastive stress; weak and strong forms.

GRAMMAR: PASSIVES

1 Choose the correct caption for the cartoon.

'They die if they | don't put / aren't put / haven't put | the right way up.'

2 Look at the sentences. Do you remember how to make passive verbs? Try to match the tense names with the sentences (there is one name too many).

1. Britain *is governed* from London.
2. Where's the TV? *Is it being repaired*?
3. Some very good comedy films *were made* in Britain in the 1950s.
4. The President started feeling ill while he *was being interviewed*.
5. He *has been taken* into hospital.
6. When do you think the first restaurant *will be opened* on the moon?

> Past Progressive
> Future
> Simple Present
> Simple Present Perfect
> Present Progressive
> Present Perfect Progressive
> Simple Past

3 Active or passive? Choose the best continuation. Can you see why it is best?

1. She lives in a charming old house.
   a. Somebody built it in the 15th century.
   b. It was built in the 15th century.
2. Spanish is a very useful language to learn.
   a. People speak it in a lot of different countries.
   b. It is spoken in a lot of different countries.
3. She bought a new dress, but she didn't like it.
   a. So she gave it to her sister.
   b. So it was given to her sister.
4. My aunt is a very successful writer.
   a. She has just written a new novel.
   b. A new novel has just been written by her.
5. The novel is about a woman who becomes a dictator.
   a. They are publishing it next month.
   b. It is being published next month.
6. I'll tell you what made me so cross.
   a. The way Mary told everybody what to do annoyed me.
   b. I was annoyed by the way Mary told everybody what to do.

4 Imagine that you are in a busy station restaurant at about 10.30 in the morning. Can you think of ten or more things that *are being done*? Examples:

Coffee is being served.
Sandwiches are being made.

> **Useful vocabulary:** bake   boil   clean
> cook   cut up   defrost   fry   make
> prepare   pay   roast   serve   wash

5 Imagine that you return to your old school after 20 years. A lot of things *have been done*, and the place looks very different. Can you think of six or more changes? Examples:

A new library has been built.
My old classroom has been turned into a museum.

> **Useful vocabulary:** build   close down
> extend   modernise   open   pull down
> rebuild   renovate   repair   turn into

Lesson C6

Grammar: passives.
Vocabulary: situational language.
Phonology: contrastive stress; weak and strong forms.

Language notes and possible problems

1. Passives   This lesson deals with some less easy points: terminology, choice between active and passive, and two of the more difficult tenses. Some students may still not be very sure of how to construct basic passive verb forms. See page 128 for some elementary practice material.

2. Contrastive stress   Note that not all languages use higher pitch for contrastive emphasis; some students may find it very difficult to perceive and produce this use of stress in English.

3. Weak and strong forms   Students have already done a little work on the weak and strong forms of some words. When they do Exercise 8 you may like to tell them a little more about weak and strong forms. There are quite a number of words – about fifty – which have two different pronunciations, depending on whether they are stressed or not. They are 'grammatical words': pronouns, prepositions, auxiliary verbs and conjunctions. Most often they are unstressed, and so the weak form is much more common than the strong form. Most students tend to overuse the strong form, which is pronounced with the written vowel. (Weak forms usually have /ə/ or no vowel at all.) Examples of words with weak and strong forms:

must (/məst, ms/; /mʌst/)
can (/kən, kn/; /kæn/)
have (/həv, əv/; /hæv/)
was (/wəz, wz/; /wɒz/)
that (/ðət/; /ðæt/)
than (/ðən, ðn/; /ðæn/)
and (/ənd, ən, n/; /ænd/)
but (/bət/; /bʌt/)
am (/əm, m/; /æm/)
are (/ə(r)/; /ɑː(r)/)
us (/əs/; /ʌs/)
them (/ðəm, ðm/; /ðem/)
from (/frəm, frm/; /frɒm/)
for (/fə(r)/; /fɔː(r)/)

1 Passives: cartoon caption

• This will help you to see whether any students still have difficulty in forming basic passive structures. It can be done by discussion round the class. Make sure everybody realises that *don't put* and *haven't put* are impossible because they are active, not passive.

2 Passives: structure and terminology

• Get students to match the sentences with the tense names.
• Then ask them if they can make a rule about how to construct passive verb forms.
• They should come up with something like 'Put the verb *be* in the tense you want, and follow it with the past participle of the verb you want' (though they are unlikely to put it in quite these words).

Answers to Exercise 2
1. Simple Present
2. Present Progressive
3. Simple Past
4. Past Progressive
5. Simple Present Perfect
6. Future

3 Choice between active and passive

• Students should find it easy to choose the most appropriate continuations in most cases, but they may have more difficulty in deciding why.
• Let them discuss the question in groups and try to come up with a rule. They should come to see that it is often a question of who or what one is already talking about. In the first question, the topic is the house, not the builders, and so it is most natural to make *it* (= 'the house') the subject of the second sentence. In questions 2–5, the same kind of thing happens in slightly different ways: the subject of the second sentence is chosen so as to give continuity of topic, and this determines whether the verb will be active or passive. In question 6, the principle of 'end-weight' operates: we prefer to avoid having very long and heavy subjects followed by short verb phrases, and the passive structure makes it possible to get *the way Mary told everybody what to do* to the end of the sentence.

Answers to Exercise 3
1b; 2b; 3a; 4a; 5b; 6b

4 and 5 Two difficult passive structures

• These exercises can be done individually, in groups or by class discussion, as you wish. Students will need to ask you for vocabulary.
• As an alternative situation for the Present Perfect Passive, students can imagine that they come back to their home town after 20 years.

6 Vocabulary: situational language

• This gives students a chance to revise and expand their knowledge of the stereotyped expressions that are typical of particular everyday situations.
• The first part of the exercise can be done by discussion round the class.
• After that, you may like to divide the class into pairs or small groups, with each group working on a different situation, building up a list of typical expressions.
• Let them get information from each other, from reference books, from students in other groups and of course from you. Make sure they ask for help in correct English (e.g. *How do you say ...?*).
• Finally, you can get groups to teach each other the language that they have listed.

Answers to Exercise 6

(Alternative answers are possible in some cases.)
Could I have the bill, please? *restaurant*
I want to send this airmail to Russia. *post office*
It's a nice colour, but it's a bit too small. *clothes shop*
How many nights? *hotel*
What time does it leave? *enquiry office at railway station, bus station* etc.
Could you check the oil? *garage / petrol station*
Three pounds of the big ones and two of those, please. *greengrocer's*
I'm sorry. You've got the wrong number. *on the phone*

7 Contrastive stress

• Go over the example. Make sure students remember how to give special stress to words.
• Play the recording, stopping after each sentence and getting the answer first from volunteers, then from the whole class in chorus or individually.
• You can give further practice by saying untrue things about the class and the students, or about current events, and getting students to correct you. Students can also make up untrue sentences for others to correct.

Tapescript and possible answers to Exercise 7

1. She's got two children.
   ('No, she hasn't. She's got *three* children.')
2. He came by car.
   ('No, he didn't. He came by *bus*.')
3. He's eating too much.
   ('No, he isn't. He's *drinking* too much.')
4. There's a dog sitting on the wall.
   ('No, there isn't. It's a *cat*.')
5. She's reading a newspaper.
   ('No, she isn't. She's *buying* a newspaper.')
6. The post office is on fire.
   ('No, it isn't. The *bank*'s on fire.')
7. One person's singing.
   ('No, *a lot* of people are singing.')
8. She's wearing white gloves.
   ('No, she's *carrying/holding* white gloves.')

8 Weak and strong forms

• Go over the examples and practise the weak and strong pronunciations.
• Ask students about the first sentence.
• Play the recording and let students check their answers.
• Do the same with the second sentence.
• Ask students why they think *must* is weak in the first sentence and strong in the second. (In the first sentence, *must* is next to *go*, which takes the stress; in the second, *must* is the only verb, so it takes the stress.)
• Get them to practise the sentences.
• Do the rest of the exercise in the same way.

Answers to Exercise 8

1. weak
2. strong
3. strong (emphasized)
4. strong (the only verb)
5. weak (*get* is stressed)
6. weak (*swim* is stressed)
7. strong (the only verb)
8. weak (*understand* is stressed)
9. weak (*been* is stressed)
10. strong (not an auxiliary verb here)
11. weak
12. strong
13. weak
14. strong
15. weak
16. strong

Practice Book exercises

1. Grammar and vocabulary revision: passives; items in a kitchen and what they are made of.
2. Word stress.
3. Vocabulary revision: completing sentences with words from Exercise 2.
4. Passives (mixed tenses).
5. Revision of irregular verbs; spelling of past tenses and part participles of regular verbs.
6. Advising: *should*.
7. Reading skills: deducing meaning from context.

VOCABULARY: SITUATIONAL LANGUAGE

6 What situations do you think the following expressions might be used in? Choose one of the situations and see how many more typical expressions you can think of.

Could I have the bill, please?
I want to send this airmail to Russia.
It's a nice colour, but it's a bit too small.
How many nights?

What time does it leave?
Could you check the oil?
Three pounds of the big ones and two of those, please.
I'm sorry. You've got the wrong number.

PRONUNCIATION:
CONTRASTIVE STRESS; WEAK AND STRONG FORMS

7 📟 Contrastive stress. Look at the pictures and listen to the sentences. There are some mistakes in the sentences. Can you correct them? Make sure you use the right stress. Example:

'It's ten past two.'
'No, *it isn't. It's ten past* three.'

8 📟 Weak and strong forms. Some words have two pronunciations: a 'weak form' and a 'strong form'. Examples:

	WEAK FORM	STRONG FORM
must	/ms, məst/	/mʌst/
can	/kn, kən/	/kæn/
have	/(h)əv/	/hæv/
was	/w(ə)z/	/wɒz/

Which pronunciation do you think *must, can, have* and *was* have in these sentences? Listen and check your answers.

1. I must go soon.
2. Oh, must you?
3. I really *must* stop smoking soon.
4. Yes, you must.
5. We must get some more milk.
6. I can swim, but not very well.
7. Yes, I can.
8. Nobody can understand what he says.
9. Where have you been?
10. What time do you have breakfast?
11. We've been talking about you.
12. Oh, have you?
13. I was late for work this morning.
14. That *was* nice – thank you very much.
15. Sally was here this afternoon.
16. Oh, was she?

Learn/revise: airmail; bill; wrong number; bake; boil; build (built, built); check; clean; close down; cook; cut up (cut, cut); discover; fry; govern; interview; invent; modernise; pay (paid, paid); prepare; publish; pull down; record; repair; rebuild; roast; send (sent, sent); serve; speak (spoke, spoken); turn into; wash.

C7 Love and other problems

Discussion, reading and writing; *should*; Present Perfect Progressive; conditionals.

1 The following texts are typical of letters and replies which are published in British teenagers' magazines. Read them carefully, but don't use your dictionary unless it is absolutely necessary. Are you surprised by anything in the letters or the answers? Do you agree or disagree strongly with anything that is said? Which reply do you agree with more? Why?

Should I lie to my parents?

Can you help me? I've fallen in love with a really nice boy I know at College. I'm 16, but I don't have a lot of freedom – I'm Asian, and my family have very strict attitudes because of their religion. So I'm not allowed to go out in the evenings, and even if I did go out with this boy during College hours I couldn't tell my parents, because they'd be really upset if they knew I was going out with a white boy. I feel bad about the situation, because I love my parents and they trust me, but this relationship is really important to me. What do you advise?

■ I understand your problem, but I really don't think you should go out with him. It's all right for the two of you to be friends, but you mustn't get yourself into a situation where you have to lie to your parents. Their religious beliefs are an important part of your family life, and it would be a mistake to go against the rules that they have made for you. If you did go out with the boy you would eventually get found out, and then the trust between you and your parents would be destroyed.

If you need to talk it over, you could get in touch with ASHA – a group that gives advice to young Asian women like yourself who are caught between two cultures. Their help is free and confidential. You can phone them on 071 274 8854.

SHOULD I ASK HER OUT?

I'm 16, and I really fancy a girl at my school. For the last few weeks I've been getting more and more attracted to her, and it's turning into a very serious relationship. The trouble is that she's Asian, and I know my parents would object if I asked her out. They are Catholics, and they would be shocked and angry if I got involved with a Muslim girl. I respect their beliefs, and I don't want to go behind their backs, but I have to think of myself. What should I do?

The first thing is to make absolutely sure of your own feelings. You haven't been seeing this girl for very long, and there's no point in upsetting your whole family for a relationship that might not last.

But if you're convinced that this is the real thing, then you must make sure what your parents' attitude is. Do you really know they wouldn't let you go out with the girl? Maybe they will. Talk the situation over with them, calmly and openly – that way you can be certain what they feel instead of just guessing.

If they really do object, you will have to make a decision. You can either respect their beliefs and live the way they want, or you can do what *you* think is right. If you tell your parents firmly that you're going to go out with the girl, then you won't be going behind their backs, and you will be showing them that you have a right to follow your own opinions, even if these are very different from theirs.

2 Which of the following sentences is closest to the answer to the first letter, and which is closest to the answer to the second letter?

1. Your parents may let you go out with your friend, but if they don't you will have to decide between your beliefs and your parents' beliefs.
2. If you talk carefully to your parents they will almost certainly let you go out with your friend.
3. You shouldn't go out with your friend because it is bad to go against your family's religion and culture.
4. You shouldn't go out with your friend because it would make your parents unhappy.

Lesson C7

Students practise reading, writing and discussion.
Principal structures: *should*; Present Perfect Progressive; conditionals.

Language notes and possible problems

1. Present Perfect Progressive   The letters in the lesson contain several examples of the Present Perfect Progressive, and Exercise 3 gives students a chance to recapitulate its use. There is further work on the point in Lesson D6.

2. Conditionals   The letters in Exercise 1 contain a number of sentences with *if*, including several constructed with past tenses and *would.* This is a good opportunity for students to look again at this structure. If students need further work on *if*-structures, there are some revision exercises on pages 126–127.

3. *Should* and *would*   Some students may confuse *should* (used to give advice or instructions) with conditional *would* (especially if they know that *should* can also be a first-person alternative to *would*).

4. *Do* in affirmative clauses   Note the contrastive use of *do* in *if*-clauses to talk about the possibility of unlikely or uncertain things happening (e.g. *if you did go out with the boy*).

5. *Eventually* (Exercise 1, reply to first letter)   This word is a 'false friend' for speakers of many European languages. Make sure students realise it means 'in the end' and not 'possibly'.

6. *Advice*   Students may need to be told that this word is uncountable in English. Look out for mistakes like ** an advice* or ** advices.*

7. Cultural background   If students are not familiar with the cultural background to the situation described in the letters in Exercise 1, you may need to explain that Britain has a number of Indian, Pakistani and Bangladeshi immigrants, and that their traditional attitudes to boy-girl relationships often differ sharply from modern British attitudes.

Optional extra materials
List of more suitable questions for Exercise 5, if you feel the questions in the book won't interest your class.

If you are short of time
Drop either Exercise 5 or Exercise 6.

---

1 Two letters
• A prediction exercise is a good way of starting. Tell students to keep their books closed, and explain that they are going to hear the beginning of a letter written to the advice column of a teenagers' magazine. Read the first two sentences of the first letter and ask them how they think it continues.
• When students have given their ideas, read them the letter and then ask if they can guess what the answer will be.
• Let them open their books and read through the two letters. Encourage them to read reasonably carefully, but without using their dictionaries unless they really need to.
• Ask for reactions to the letters – surprise, agreement, disagreement, or anything else they wish to express. If a discussion starts up at this stage, let it run.

2 Choosing between summaries
• Give students a minute or two to make up their minds, and then let them compare notes with each other before giving them the answers.
• Sentence 3 is closest to the first answer, and sentence 1 to the second.

3 Present Perfect Progressive

• Give students a minute or two to think about the question and discuss it among themselves.
• You may need to remind them of the rule: that we use this tense to talk about events (or series of events) continuing up to the present, especially when we are saying how long the events have gone on.

4 Language for discussion

• This should help to prepare students for Exercises 5 and 6.
• Go over the list of expressions with them, explaining any difficulties.
• Give students a few minutes to find or think of any other expressions that they wish to add.

5 Discussion

• In each group, the three students should choose different questions. If you don't feel that these questions correspond to the class's concerns and interests, suggest some more suitable alternatives.
• Tell students that each of them is responsible for finding out what the others think about the question that he or she has chosen.
• When discussion begins to dry up, each student should report briefly to the class, saying what the group's views were on his/her question.

6 Writing practice: problem letters and replies

• Decide – in consultation with the class if you wish – which of the activities you wish them to do. The first activity is more suitable for a weaker class. Good classes with plenty of time could do more than one.

First activity

• Let students choose a letter to answer. Put students who have chosen the same letter into small groups, and give them ten minutes or so to write their answers. Go round helping where necessary.
• When they are ready, get each group to read out their answer to the class, or let them put their answers on the class notice board for the others to read.

Second activity

• If students do this, discourage them from writing complicated letters in over-ambitious English that the others won't understand.
• Groups will probably need 10–15 minutes to think of a problem and write a letter.
• When they are ready, they should give copies of their problem letters to two other groups.
• Their next task is to write answers to the letters they have received, and pass these back to the original writers.
• Students should find it interesting to compare the two different pieces of advice they have been given. Particularly interesting or amusing exchanges can be read to the class.

Third activity

• If there are lively people on the panel this can be a lot of fun.
• In a strong class, you could change the panel for each letter.

Practice Book exercises

1. Past and conditional verbs in *if*-sentences (hypothetical, 'second' conditionals).
2. Completing sentences with verbs in the Present Perfect Progressive.
3. Completing sentences ending in relative clauses.
4. Spelling: *ie* or *ei*.
5. Recreational reading: a choice of two poems and two newspaper articles.
6. Matching problems and advice; writing a letter of advice.

3 Look at these two examples of the Present Perfect Progressive.

For the last few weeks I've been getting more and more attracted to her.
You haven't been seeing this girl for very long.

Why is the Present Perfect Progressive used here? Look out for more examples in the lesson.

4 Here are some expressions that are useful when discussing problems or giving advice. Can you find any others in the letters in Exercise 1? Can you think of any more useful expressions for discussion that you would like to know in English? Ask your teacher if necessary.

I (don't) think you should …
There's nothing wrong in …ing
I would(n't) advise you to …
I (don't) think it's a good idea to …
It's not worth it
It's (not) worth …ing
I'd be surprised if …
You can either … or …
It is important to …
If I were you, I'd …
Why don't you …?
Try …ing

5 Work in groups of three. Choose one of the following questions; say what you think, and find out what the others in the group think. Talk about your own experience, or about people you know, if possible. Use a dictionary or ask for help if necessary. Finish by giving a brief report of your discussion (two or three sentences) to the class.

1. Should children be free to choose their own boy/girlfriends at age 13? At age 16?
2. At what age should children be free to go out with their friends in the evenings?
3. Should there be different rules for boys and girls?
4. What advice would you give to a friend who wanted to marry somebody of a different race?
5. How much should children respect their parents' religious and cultural beliefs?

6 The class should work in groups of three or four, and do one of these three activities.
EITHER: Each group chooses one of the following letters and writes an answer.
OR: Each group writes a problem letter, makes two copies, exchanges problems with two other groups, and writes answers to the problem letters it gets.
OR: Each group writes a problem letter. Four or five students (the 'experts') then come and sit at the front of the class. The others read out their problem letters; the 'experts' give their advice.

CHOCOLATE ADDICT

I'm a chocolate addict. My friends and family cannot believe how much I can eat. I often choose to eat chocolate rather than a proper meal, partly because it's quicker, but also because I prefer it. It seems to give me more energy, though I feel sick if I eat too much.
I've put on a lot of weight, and I hate that, but if I'm feeling fed up about being fat, I just eat some chocolate to cheer myself up.
The people at work treat it as a joke – they don't often buy me presents of chocolate. I really do think I'm addicted to chocolate. What can I do?

EXTRA LESSONS

I'm 17, and I've fallen in love with my maths teacher. He's in his first teaching job since he left university, and there's only about ten years' difference in our ages. Recently he's been giving me extra maths lessons after school and yesterday he asked me out for a drink. What should I do?

MUM'S A SLAVE

I have just been spending a week with my parents, who are a happily-married couple in their fifties. What worries me is that my father has a very old-fashioned attitude to housework. He really treats my poor mother like a servant. She has a bad heart, and it makes me angry to see her carrying in heavy loads of shopping, doing all the cooking, cleaning and washing, and so on. Should I speak to my father?

STILL A PRISONER

I'm 25 and have just come out of prison after two years inside. My problem is that I feel very insecure and lonely and I don't know what to do with myself. I have no friends, as in the past I've behaved very badly to people. I'm worried that I won't ever be able to live a normal life again. Can you help?

Learn/revise: advice; attitude; belief; culture; decision; magazine; opinion; parents; problem; race; religion; reply; rule; the right to do sth; advise; agree (with sbdy); allow; ask sbdy out; destroy; disagree; fall in love with (fell, fallen); fancy; find out (found, found); go out with sbdy; guess; lie (lied, lied); object; respect; talk sth over; trust (*verb*); Asian; attracted (to sbdy); confidential; cultural; religious; surprised; worried; eventually; behind sbdy's back; *the 'useful expressions' in Exercise 4.*

C8 Government

Listening skills: predicting, note-taking; reading skills: dictionary skills, reading for detail; vocabulary of politics; choice between speaking and writing activities.

1 How much do you know about these governments?
Can you fill in any of the blanks?

	Britain	The USA	Your country or another country
consists of	.... countries; each is divided into counties	50 states; each is divided into counties	....
is governed from	London	....	....
Laws are made by	....	....	....
which consists of	House of Commons and House of Lords	....	....
Members are called	...............s of .... ('MPs') (Commons)	....	....
They are elected	every five years or less (Commons)	....	....
Head of government is called	.... Minister ('PM')	....	....
Is head of government separately elected?	No; leader of majority party in House of Commons becomes PM	....	....
Real power is held by	PM and his/her ministers ('cabinet')	....	....
Do local or regional government bodies have any power?	partly responsible for education, health care, police, roads	....	....
How many large political parties are there?	three; Labour (...............-wing), ... (right-wing) and Liberal Democrats (centre)	....	....
Ceremonial head of state?	King or	....	....

64

Lesson C8

Listening skills: predicting; listening and note-taking.
Reading skills: reading for specific information; dictionary skills.
Speaking and writing skills: choice between prepared speeches, interview with note-taking and reporting, and letter-writing.
Vocabulary: politics.

Language notes and possible problems

1. **The vocabulary** in this lesson may be quite easy for some students, whose languages have cognates for most of the words. Where this is not the case, you will want to do the optional activity before Exercise 1.

2. **Note-taking** is a skill that some students may need for study or exam purposes. Even for students who do not fall into these categories, it is a useful way to practise listening comprehension, encouraging students to focus on the most important ideas in a spoken passage.

3. **Dictionary use** Students should now be losing their dependence on their mother tongues as they become more able to learn English through English. A good bilingual dictionary will continue to be an essential tool, but students should also have a good English-English dictionary. The *Oxford Advanced Learner's Dictionary of Current English* and the *Longman Dictionary of Contemporary English* are both excellent, though rather advanced. An extremely good lower-level dictionary is *Longman Active Study Dictionary of English.* Not all learners are used to finding their way through dictionary entries. If your students have difficulty here, Exercise 2 provides an opportunity to give some useful information and advice.

4. **Passives** Some students may still have difficulty with basic passive structures; the revision exercises on page 128 may help.

If you are short of time

Get students to prepare Exercise 7 individually for homework, and give their reports/speeches in another class period.

Optional extra materials and equipment

If you are doing the optional exercise before Exercise 1, prepare photocopies, an overhead transparency, or the board before the lesson.

For Exercise 1, it will make students' work easier if you make one photocopy of the table for each student to work with.

Optional exercise to precede Exercise 1: learning new words

• Prepare photocopies of the following list or put it on the board or overhead projector.
• The students should choose words they do not know from the list, each student choosing three or four words. Make sure all the words that will be new for students are chosen.
• They should find out the pronunciation and meaning of the words, using their dictionaries and asking for help from you.
• Each student should then walk round telling everyone else what his/her words are and what they mean.

Congress	minority	govern
Conservatives	member	centre
country	minister	left-wing
Queen	parliament	local
county	political party	regional
government	power	responsible
head of state	state	right-wing
King	consist of	partly
law	divide (into)	separately
majority	elect	

1 Using vocabulary

• Put students into groups of three or four. If your students come from different countries, group any people from the same country together.
• Distribute photocopies of the table, if you have made them beforehand, or ask students to copy the table. They must work to see how many of the blanks in the table they can fill. Tell students not to worry if they leave some blanks empty.
• Walk round while they are working to help them with the meanings and pronunciation of the words in the table, but do not give them any factual information.
• When groups begin to finish, they can compare answers with each other.
• Do not correct the answers now; explain that students will get another opportunity to work on the table in Exercise 6.

2 Dictionary skills

- If students are not used to English-English dictionaries they may find these dictionary entries initially baffling.
- Look through the first entry with the class, explaining the main conventions used if necessary.
- At this stage, students need only realise that numbers are used to distinguish different meanings/uses, and that each meaning is demonstrated by an explanation, sometimes followed by examples.
- When the structure of the entry is reasonably clear, ask students to look at the three dictionary entries and decide as quickly as they can which definition of each word gives the meaning that the word has in Exercise 1, and to compare answers among themselves. Students should not have much trouble deciding which are the correct definitions.
- If students are interested, you may like to ask them what they think is meant by the various abbreviations *n(oun)*, *v(erb)*, *sing(ular)*, *pl(ural)*, *cap(ital)*, C(ountable), U(ncountable) and S(ingular, no plural form).
- Students may also like to try to decipher the phonetic transcriptions, if they are not yet used to these. (Note that alternative pronunciations are sometimes given.)

Answers to Exercise 2
cabinet 2; country 1; house 3

3 Introduction to note-taking 📼

- In this and the next two exercises, students will hear a simple lecture (in three parts) on the United States' system of government.
- Look over the notes and ask students what they think they mean.
- Explain *federation* if necessary.
- Teach the word *abbreviation*.
- Ask if students can think of ways of abbreviating the notes.
- Play the recording of the first part of the talk (up to *near the east coast*).

4 Completing notes 📼

- Look over the incomplete notes and explain any difficulties.
- Get students to abbreviate the notes.
- Play the recording of the second part of the talk, up to *road-building and many other things* (more than once if necessary), and ask students to complete the notes, using abbreviations as much as possible.
- Let them compare notes with each other and then discuss the answers.

5 Taking notes 📼

- Look at the seven words listed in the exercise instructions; demonstrate the pronunciation (so that students will recognise them when they hear them), and ask students to decide on abbreviations for them (so that they can make quick notes). It is not necessary to discuss their meanings; if students do not know them already, the text will give them clear explanations.
- Play the first sentence of the third part of the talk and tell students to make a note. Write some of their notes on the board and discuss the different approaches, suggesting improvements if necessary.
- Then continue, either playing the whole of the rest of the recording while students take notes (if they are fluent), or breaking it into sections and stopping after each (if they are less good at note-taking).
- They will not of course understand everything they hear; their job is simply to note what they do

understand. Don't help them out by explaining things or saying the sentences more slowly for them – this would destroy the purpose of the exercise.
- Go over the notes with the students; make sure that they understand that there is not just one form for correct answers, but that several different ways of noting the material are possible.
- Alternatively, just collect the notes; give them back to their authors a few days later, and see how much of the information they can reproduce just from their notes.

Tapescript for Exercises 3–5: see page 148

6 Review of Exercise 1

- Now give students a chance to look back at the table in Exercise 1 and see if they can fill in some more blanks, based on the information gained in Exercises 2–5.
- Let students compare answers with one another before checking with you.

Answers to Exercises 1 and 6: see page 148

7 Oral/written fluency practice

- Give students a few minutes to look over the options in Exercise 7. Answer any questions they have about meaning.
- Different students / groups of students can choose different activities; though if there are speeches, it is more enjoyable if the class has at least three speeches of each sort to listen to. You can get them to vote for the best speech.
- If some students choose the third option, remind them of the form of a letter in English.
- Walk round while students are working to give any help that is needed.

Optional activity
- Students in multicultural classes may enjoy giving expository speeches about the political systems in their own countries to each other, based on their notes in Exercise 1.

Practice Book exercises
1. Grammar and vocabulary revision: completing a text.
2. Student's Cassette exercise (Student's Book Lesson C8, Exercises 3 to 5 – the first two paragraphs only). Students listen and write down as much as they can.
3. Completing *if*-sentences (hypothetical, 'second' conditionals).
4. Translation of material from Lessons B7 to C8.
5. Recreational reading: *Murphy's Law*, etc.
6. Extended writing: a system of government.
7. Crossword.

2 Dictionary skills: these three words come in Exercise 1. There are two or more definitions for each word. Which definition gives the meaning that the word has in Exercise 1?

cab•i•net /ˈkæbɪnɪt, ˈkæbənət, ˈkæbnɪt, ˈkæbnət/ *n* **1** a piece of furniture, with shelves and doors, or drawers, used for showing or storing things: *a* FILING CABINET | *I put my collection of old glasses in the cabinet.* **2** [+ *sing./pl. v*](in various countries) the most important ministers of the government, who meet as a group to make decisions or to advise the head of the government

coun•try /ˈkʌntri/ *n* -tries **1** [C] a nation or state with its land or population: *Some parts of this country are much warmer than others.* **2** [C] the people of a nation or state: *The country is opposed to war.* **3** [*the* S] the land outside cities or towns; land used for farming or left unused: *We're going to have a day in the country tomorrow.* **4** [U] land with a special nature or character: *good farming country.*

house /haʊs/ *n* houses /ˈhaʊzɪz, ˈhaʊzəz/ **1 a** a building for people to live or work in **b** the people in such a building. **2** a building for a stated purpose: *a hen house* | *a storehouse.* **3** a law-making body, or the building where it meets | *the* **Houses of Parliament** (= both Britain's law-making bodies) | *the* **House of Commons** (= the lower but more powerful law-making body, whose members are elected by the people) | *the* **House of Lords** (= the higher law-making body whose members are not elected). **4** (*cap. in names*) an important family, especially noble or royal: *The House of Windsor is the British royal family.*

(adapted from *Longman Active Study Dictionary of English*)

3 📼 **You will hear part of a talk on the government of the United States. Before you listen, look at these notes.**

US federation 50 states
48 between Canada, Mexico; + Alaska, Hawaii
fed cap Washington, S of N Y, near E coast

4 📼 **Now listen to the next part of the talk and try to complete these notes.**

Washington centre federal govt, but each state has
   own ....
State govts make own laws, responsible for ....

5 📼 **Now listen to the rest of the talk and try to make notes yourself. (You will need abbreviations for these words: *Congress, Representatives, Senate/ Senators, Democrats, Republicans, President.*)**

6 **Look back at Exercise 1. Can you fill in any more of the blanks now?**

7 **Do one of these activities.**

1. Work with one or two other students, or work alone. Write a political speech – serious or funny – to try and get yourself elected president of your English class. Students and teacher each have one vote. You, or one of you, should give your speech to the class. Practise your speech beforehand so that you can look at the class for at least part of the time instead of just reading the speech.

2. Work with one or two other students, or work alone. Write and give a political speech for a serious national political party or a funny one (for example: the anti-television party; the cats for Congress party; the anti-shoe party). Practise your speech beforehand so that you can look at the class for at least part of the time instead of just reading the speech.

3. Is there something you would like to change in another country – the killing of certain animals, or the making or testing of certain types of weapons or chemicals, for example? Work alone or with another student to write a letter to the head of that country in English. Find out where to send the letter by asking the consulate or embassy of that country. Send the letter. Report any answers to the class orally.

4. If you are in a class with students from other countries, choose one student to interview about how her/his country is governed. Make notes and report to a group or the whole class.

Learn/revise some of these: appointment; body; cabinet; capital; Congress; Conservatives; country; county; Democrats; federation; government; head (= person); head of state; health care; House of Commons; House of Lords; King; Labour; law; Liberal Democrats; majority; member; Member of Parliament (MP); minister; minority; parliament; police (*plural*); (political) party; power; President; Prime Minister (PM); Queen; Representative; Republicans; road; Senate; Senator; state; approve; become (became, become); consist (of); divide (into); elect; govern; hold (held, held); centre; federal; left-wing; local; national; political; real; regional; responsible; right-wing; each; every (five years); own (*determiner*); partly; separately; slightly.

Summary C

Simple Past and Past Progressive tenses

Mrs Anne Redman of Newbury **was driving** past a house in Beaufort Road when she **saw** the ground floor on fire.

Simple tenses with *as*

They leaned out and grabbed him by the legs **as** he **hurtled** past.

Three firemen caught a man in mid-air yesterday **as** he **leapt** from a blazing house.

Present Perfect Progressive

For the last few weeks I'**ve been getting** more and more attracted to her.

You **haven't been seeing** this girl for very long.

Recently he'**s been giving** me extra maths lessons after school.

I **have** just **been spending** a week with my parents.

Passives

Simple Present
Britain **is governed** from London.
Paper **is made** from wood.

Present Progressive
Where's the TV? **Is** it **being repaired**?
Be careful what you say – this conversation **is being recorded**.

Simple Past
Some very good comedy films **were made** in Britain in the 1950s.
Our house **was built** in the 15th century.

Past Progressive
The President started feeling ill while he **was being interviewed**.
They knew that they **were being watched**.

Present Perfect
He **has been taken** into hospital.
Oil **has been discovered** under the White House.

Future
When do you think the first restaurant **will be opened** on the moon?
Her new book **will be published** next month.

if with Simple Past and *would*

My parents **would** object if I **asked** her out.
If you **did go** out with the boy you **would** eventually get found out.

Modal verbs

You **can clean** dirty saucepans … (~~You can to clean …~~)
You **should put** rice inside it … (~~You should to put …~~)
You **mustn't visit** anyone … (~~You mustn't to visit …~~)
Should I lie?
Should I go out with him?

will have to

If they really do object you **will have to** make a decision.

should and *must*

You **should** switch the light off before you change a bulb.
You **must** use the right kind of batteries in a calculator.
You **shouldn't** drive too fast on wet roads.
You **mustn't** drive at over 30mph in towns.

Infinitive of purpose

To get dust out of a guitar, put rice inside it, shake it and empty it.
(~~For to get dust out of a guitar …~~)
(~~For get dust out of a guitar …~~)

how to …

how to mend things
how to clean things
Do you know **how to** get to Dover?

Imperative

Rub them with lemon.
Don't hold its ears.

by …ing

You can make tight shoes more comfortable **by packing** them with wet newspaper and **leaving** them overnight.

Two-word verbs

Please **switch** the light **off**.
Please **switch off** the light.
Please **switch** it **off**.
BUT NOT ~~Please switch off it.~~

Could you **pick** those papers **up**?
Could you **pick up** those papers?
Could you **pick** them **up**?
BUT NOT ~~Could you pick up them?~~

Summary C

Summary of language taught in Lessons C1–C8

This section displays most of the more important systematic language points that students should have learnt or revised in the last eight lessons. Spend a short time going over the material with the students, answering questions and clearing up any difficulties. Get them also to look over the vocabulary from Lessons C1–C8 (in the *Learn/revise* panels at the end of each lesson), making sure they know at least the more important new words and expressions. They may need to spend time at home consolidating their learning before moving on.

Irregular verbs in Lessons C1–C8

INFINITIVE	PAST	PAST PARTICIPLE
become	became	become
build	built	built
cut	cut	cut
fall	fell	fallen
find	found	found
grow	grew	grown
hold	held	held
pay	paid	paid
put	put	put
send	sent	sent
speak	spoke	spoken

by (= not later than)

I'm usually working **by** ten o'clock.
By that stage she's in the bath.
By the time (that) I get out of the bath she's fully
    dressed.
By the time (that) I come downstairs she's just about
    to go off to work.

Discussing problems and giving advice

I (don't) think you should …
There's nothing wrong in …ing
I would(n't) advise you to …
I (don't) think it's a good idea to …
It's not worth it
It's (not) worth …ing
I'd be surprised if …
You can either … or …
It is important to …
If I were you, I'd …
Why don't you …?
Try …ing

Misunderstandings

I thought you said Thursday.

Formal apologies

I'm really sorry about that.
I really am very sorry.
I do apologise.

Stress

In a sentence, we usually stress (pronounce more
loudly and clearly) the words with most meaning –
nouns, ordinary verbs, adjectives and adverbs.
Other words (pronouns, auxiliary verbs,
prepositions, conjunctions and articles) are more
often unstressed – they are pronounced more
quickly and quietly.

Well, I'm married, so to be alone in the mornings, the
first thing is to get rid of my wife, who fortunately
has a job, so she gets up in the morning, makes a cup
of tea, rouses me, I come downstairs, wander round
the kitchen, have my cup of tea …

Longer words are not stressed on all syllables: one
syllable usually carries the stress, and the others are
pronounced more quickly and quietly.

married   alone   fortunately

Vocabulary

Look through the 'Learn/revise' boxes at the ends
of Lessons C1–C8.

Revision and fluency practice C

A choice of activities.

1 🔲 Listen and say how the people sound. You can use some of the adjectives in the box. Example:

'She sounds surprised.'

afraid	amused	angry	cross	pleased
relaxed	unhappy	surprised	upset	
worried				

2 🔲 Finding differences. Read the text and then listen to the recording. There are eleven significant differences between the two reports. Can you find all of them?

AN UNEMPLOYED man killing time before a date decided to turn to crime to ease his money problems. He wrote out a note reading 'I've got a gun in my pocket and I'll shoot it off unless you hand over the money'.

But David Smith, aged 21, failed to get any cash in spite of going into three shops in London Road, West Croydon.

At a chemist's a girl assistant refused to accept the note, believing that it contained an obscene suggestion. Next door, in a hardware shop, the Asian assistant said that he could not read English.

In desperation Smith, of High Road, Whitelea, Kent, went to a takeaway food shop, but the assistant could not read the note because he did not have his glasses.

Smith told police 'I've been a fool. When the judge hears about this he won't believe anyone could be so stupid. I only pretended to have a gun'.

3 Logic problems.

1. You are trying to win money at roulette, by betting on red or black. Red has come up the last ten times. How do you think you should bet?
   a. Red is obviously 'hot' tonight, so you should bet on red.
   b. It's obviously time for black to come up again, so you should bet on black.
   c. Red and black are equally likely, so it doesn't matter how you bet.
2. A couple have four children. What are the chances that they have two boys and two girls?
   a. 50–50.
   b. More than 50–50.
   c. Less than 50–50.

4 Mystery man. You are detectives working for the missing persons office in a big city police headquarters in Scotland. A man has been found wandering in the streets, suffering from loss of memory. Look at the following pieces of evidence, and then try to make up a theory about the man – what he does, where he comes from, *etc.*

1. The man looks European; he has a dark complexion and black hair. He is about 40, tall and athletic, but rather overweight.
2. He is dressed in pink silk pyjamas, made in Bangkok.
3. When questioned, he only says 'I can't remember', in English but with a strong French accent.
4. His hands are covered with engine oil.
5. He has a bag containing the following:
   – $60,000 in US currency
   – photographs of three beautiful women: two European-looking, one Oriental
   – a photograph of the British Minister of Defence
   – a receipt from a car-hire firm
   – two love letters: one in English, beginning 'My Darling Freddy', and the other in French, beginning 'Serge, mon amour'
   – a gun with the number removed
   – a screwdriver
   – a silver spoon
   – one more thing (you choose)

5 Here are some words from a dialogue. Can you complete it?

ANDY: going/shops/Mike
MIKE: Yes/get/something/you
ANDY: If/mind   haven't/toothpaste/left
        Could/me/some
MIKE: OK
ANDY: like/Sanident/if/got
MIKE: OK
ANDY: Oh/run out/soap
MIKE: OK/get/you
ANDY: And/mind/posting/same/time
MIKE: Not at all
ANDY: give/you/money
MIKE: No/wait/come back/simpler
ANDY: All right   Thanks/indeed
MIKE: welcome

Revision and fluency practice C

Students and teacher choose from a range of practice activities.

Teaching notes
Detailed teaching notes are not provided for all exercises in this section, since many of the activities are self-explanatory.

Materials needed
If you do Exercise 8 you may want to prepare cards in advance; alternatively, students can prepare them as part of the exercise.

1 How do the people sound?
- Make sure the students remember the meanings of all the adjectives in the box.
- Ask them to write the numbers 1 to 8 on a piece of paper.
- Tell them that they will hear eight people, and must decide how each one is feeling.
- Play the recording through once, pausing briefly after each item.
- Then play it straight through again.
- Students may want to listen a third time if they are not sure of all the answers.

Tapescript and answers to Exercise 1
1. Oh, my goodness! I wasn't expecting you! (*surprised*)
2. Ah, this is nice. (*relaxed/pleased*)
3. That was a stupid thing for her to do. (*cross/angry*)
4. (Laughter) (*amused*)
5. You stupid idiot! (*angry/cross*)
6. It's dreadful – I don't know what to do. (*unhappy/upset*)
7. It's coming closer! (*afraid*)
8. Where can he be? He should be here by now. (*worried*)

2 Finding differences
- Give students a few minutes to look through the text and clear up any problems.
- Then play the recording (more than once if necessary).
- Make sure they understand that they are after differences of substance, not just changes of wording.

Tapescript and answers to Exercise 2
(The differences are italicised.)
This is a true story that was reported in the papers a few years ago. There was this guy, *aged about 30 or so*, who was out of work, and so of course he had money problems. Well, one evening he was going out to *visit his old mother*, and he had a bit of time to spare, so he thought he'd try crime as a way of solving his problems. So he wrote out this note, saying 'I've got a gun *in my bag*, and I'll shoot it off unless you hand over the money'. Then he went into *four* shops, one after the other, and you know he didn't get a penny. In the first shop, that was a chemist's, there was *a middle-aged woman* serving, and she wouldn't accept the note because she thought it said something dirty. So he went next door to a *grocer's*, where he found an Asian assistant who couldn't *speak* English. Then he tried a *Chinese* takeaway food shop, but the *manager* couldn't read the note because *he had eye trouble*. In the end, of course, the guy got himself arrested. He was really upset, and kept saying how stupid he was, and how *he wouldn't have fired the gun anyway*.

3 Logic problems
Answers to Exercise 3
1. C. The roulette table has no memory.
2. C. There are eight chances out of sixteen that they have three of one sex and one of the other; six chances out of sixteen that they have two of each; and two chances out of sixteen that they have four boys or four girls. The sixteen possible combinations are as follows:

First child: b b b B b B B b g G G g G g g g
Second child: b b b B g G G g b B B b G g g g
Third child: b b g G b B G g b B G g B b g g
Fourth child: b g b G b G B g b G B g B g b g

Creative activities: discussion, role play etc.
Creative activities are very important both pedagogically and psychologically. Students probably do not assimilate new material very effectively until they are given a chance to use it themselves to express their own ideas. So it is at the 'free use' stage of a lesson that most of the learning is likely to take place. (It is therefore a false economy, even if time is very short, to drop the longer and more creative output activities.) And it is of course very motivating for students if they can use their English from time to time to say interesting or amusing things – if they can inform, entertain, surprise or move each other by their use of language.

Some students enjoy role play, and may indeed be more articulate when acting a part than when expressing their own views and feelings. (Shy people are sometimes 'liberated' by being given a role to play.) Other students prefer to be themselves, and do best in exercises where they can say what they really think. It is important to provide exercises that are suitable for both kinds of personality, and to remember that there is not necessarily something wrong if some of one's students are unenthusiastic about role play or if others don't want to talk about themselves.

Correction is generally out of place in creative speaking exercises, and should only be used sparingly in creative writing exercises.

8 Mime: verbs and adverbs

• Prepare a lot of cards with verbs referring to activities, and another lot with adverbs of manner. (If you like, students can suggest ideas for the cards; or they can make the cards themselves.)

• Suggestions:

Verbs: sit, walk, read, talk, sing, run, write, play the piano, teach, sleep, drive, cook, eat, drink, paint, travel, play football.

Adverbs: happily, unhappily, fast, slowly, noisily, beautifully, politely, lazily, intelligently, lovingly, badly, well, sexily, crazily, quietly, energetically, aggressively.

• Put the cards in two piles face down. Students should draw one verb card and one adverb card, and then try to show the class what they have got by doing or miming the action in the appropriate way. The class must try to guess what is on the two cards.

6 Now practise the dialogue in Exercise 5 with a partner, but imagine that one of you is hard of hearing, tired, very old or bad-tempered. Make whatever changes you like.

7 Improvisation (groups of four). Two of you come home and find two strangers in your house/flat. Act out the scene.

8 Mime: verbs and adverbs. The teacher will give you two cards – one with a verb and one with an adverb. Act out the combination; the class will try to decide what you are doing. Example:

'You're reading unhappily.'

9 What makes a good teacher? Here are four of the qualities needed by a good teacher: *knowledge of the subject, patience, humour, intelligence.* List them in order of importance, and add any others that you think are missing. Then work with two other students and try to draw up an agreed group list, running from most to least important.

10 Look at the cartoons and talk about your reactions. Which ones do you find funny? Which ones don't make you laugh? Are there any that you don't understand? Discuss your reactions with other students.

'Nobody calls me stupid. Meet me outside when the big hand and the little hand are on the 12'

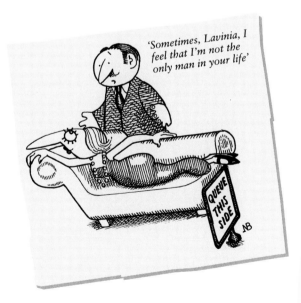

'Sometimes, Lavinia, I feel that I'm not the only man in your life'

'Cheesebur...'

Test C

LISTENING

1 ⊡ Listen and take notes. The words in the box may help you.

Dublin	Éire	Fianna Fáil	Fine Gael
local authorities		national language	
official	Progressive Democrats		province

PRONUNCIATION

2 ⊡ **Stress.** Listen carefully to these questions, and write answers beginning *No,...* Examples:

Your sister lives in *Spain*, doesn't she?
No, she lives in Italy.

Your *sister* lives in Spain, doesn't she?
No, my brother does.

1. Has Anne got a red car?
2. Is Mike's aunt a dentist?
3. Did you say that your brother was coming this evening?
4. Didn't the President study mathematics at university?
5. Would you like some wine before dinner?

3 Remember that some words have two pronunciations: a 'weak form' and a 'strong form'. Examples:

	MUST	CAN	HAVE	WAS
WEAK:	/ms, məst/	/kn, kən/	/(h)əv/	/w(ə)z/
STRONG:	/mʌst/	/kæn/	/hæv/	/wɒz/

Which pronunciation do *must, can, have* and *was* have in these sentences? Write *W* (weak) or *S* (strong). Don't worry about negatives – they're always strong.

1. Of course she must.
2. I think I must phone my mother today.
3. I can't come today, but I can tomorrow.
4. When can we leave?
5. I wonder where the twins have gone.
6. We haven't lost Ted, have we?
7. I think I'll have a shower.
8. That *was* a nice dinner. Thank you so much.
9. Yes, she was.

4 Look at these words. In each group, the underlined sounds are the same except in one word. Which word is different?

1. <u>ou</u>t kn<u>ow</u> h<u>ow</u> f<u>ou</u>nd
2. t<u>au</u>ght w<u>a</u>lk p<u>a</u>ss t<u>a</u>ll
3. d<u>e</u>stroy <u>e</u>ventually r<u>e</u>spect h<u>e</u>licopter
4. <u>a</u>fterwards <u>a</u>dvise <u>a</u>gree <u>a</u>llow

GRAMMAR

5 Put the verb in the right form.

1. .... red wine out of clothes, ... white wine on the stain. (*get, pour*)
2. You can .... sunglasses by .... them with washing-up liquid. (*clean, wash*)
3. If you want .... a musical instrument well, you must .... every day. (*play, practise*)
4. Do you know how .... this? (*mend*)
5. Ms Abbott .... home from work when she .... the child fall off the bridge. (*walk, see*)
6. After .... for help, she .... off her shoes and .... in .... him. (*shout, take, jump, save*)
7. A lot of modern medicines .... from plants. (*make*)
8. The music for 'The Marriage of Figaro' .... by Mozart. (*write*)
9. The results .... tomorrow morning at nine o'clock. (*announce*)
10. All the beautiful buildings in our cities .... by exhaust gases from cars – we must .... something to stop this. (*destroy, do*)
11. The statue .... while it .... to another room in the museum. (*break, move*)
12. I don't think it's a good idea .... the children about it. (*tell*)
13. Do you think people should have the right .... what's on their medical records? (*know*)
14. For the last few weeks, I .... extra lessons after school. (*have*)

6 Choose the best word: *should* or *must*.

1. If you are American, you .... have a passport to get into Britain.
2. If you go to Hawaii, you .... take sunglasses.
3. You .... pay tax on most things that you buy in Britain.
4. If you want to become an Irish citizen, you .... learn some Irish – it's the law.
5. If you want to enjoy a holiday in Greece, you .... learn some Greek.

LANGUAGE IN USE

7 Write appropriate replies to these.

1. Oh, I *am* sorry.
2. I'm afraid this personal stereo I bought from you doesn't work.
3. I've got a problem.
4. Hello. Is Kevin there, please?
5. My wallet's just been stolen.

Test C

This test covers work done in Lessons C1–C8.

Administration of the test

1. General procedure Give students a few minutes to look over the test and make sure they understand what they are to do in each part.

2. Listening (Exercise 1) Give students a few minutes to look over the words in the box. You will have to pronounce *Éire* (/ˈeərə/), *Fianna Fáil* (/ˈfiːnə ˈfɔɪl/) and *Fine Gael* (/ˈfiːnə ˈɡeɪl/) for them, and make sure they know how the other words sound. Remind the students about the note-taking they did on the American government. They should work in the same way here, making brief notes of the main points. Encourage them to use abbreviations: elicit abbreviations for *Fianna Fáil, Fine Gael, Progressive Democrats, national* and *language*.

Play the recording, twice or three times, pausing where obliques (/) are marked in the tapescript for students to take notes.

3. Pronunciation (Exercise 2) Make sure students understand the instructions, and know how they are to mark their answers. Point out that they are to work only with the affirmative forms of the verbs. Play the first two sentences for them as examples.

Play the rest of the recording twice, pausing after each item for students to write their answers.

4. Pronunciation (Exercise 3) Remind students about weak and strong forms, and go over the pronunciations of the words in the list. Then students must decide whether each sentence contains a weak or strong form of the modal auxiliaries listed.

5. Speaking (Exercise 15) You will have to take students aside in pairs for the Speaking part of the test. If you have a large class and a short class period, you may have to drop this part of the test.

Explain to students what they will be doing in the speaking exercise after they finish Exercise 2.

Call each pair of students out of the class, for example to your desk or to the back of the classroom, while the others work on the written part of the test.

Try to make the students feel comfortable. Give them a few moments to decide on who will play which role and what the situation is, and then let them begin. Let them go on for a few minutes, until you consider that you have a fair idea of their ability to communicate.

Remember that what you are looking for in this Speaking test is fluency, not perfect grammar or pronunciation. What counts is whether the students can make themselves understood.

LISTENING

1 (Many acceptable answers. Students should cover the main points. A sample set of notes:)
Rep. of Ireland (Éire) = 4 prov., each ÷ counties
in Atlantic O., w of GB
nat'l lg Irish, Eng. 2nd offic. lg
central govt Dublin powerful; local auth. some power

Laws made Parliam't
2 houses: H of Reps & Senate
Reps elec. 5 yrs; Sens elec/apptd
PM elec by H of R
Pres ceremonial, elec every 7 yrs
PM real power, chooses cabinet

4 main parties: FF, FG, ProgDems and Labour
FF and FG big but need help for majority
FF and FG rt-wing
FF religious, country; FG not religious, city

Tapescript for Exercise 1: see page 149

PRONUNCIATION

2 Tapescript and possible answers
(Many possible answers, for example:)
1. Has Anne got a *red* car? (*No, a green one.*)
2. Is *Mike's* aunt a dentist? (*No, but Susan's aunt is.*)
3. Did you say that your brother was coming *this* evening? (*No, darling, I said tomorrow evening.*)
4. Didn't the *President* study mathematics at university? (*No, actually, I think it was the Prime Minister.*)
5. Would you like some wine *before* dinner? (*No, thank you, I'll just have some with my dinner.*)

3
1. strong (short answer – no main verb)
2. weak (used with the main verb)
3. strong (used without main verb)
4. weak (used with the main verb)
5. weak (used with the main verb)
6. strong (question tag – no main verb)
7. strong (*have* is the main verb here, not an auxiliary)
8. strong (stress for emphasis – marked by italics in writing)
9. strong (short answer)

4
1. know (/əʊ/) (the others are pronounced /aʊ/)
2. pass (/ɑː/) (the others are pronounced /ɔː/)
3. helicopter (/e/) (the others, unstressed, are pronounced /ɪ/)
4. afterwards (/ɑː/) (the others, unstressed, are pronounced /ə/)

GRAMMAR

5
1. To get; pour
2. clean; washing
3. to play; practise
4. to mend
5. was walking; saw
6. shouting; took; jumped; to save
7. are made
8. was written
9. will be announced
10. are being destroyed; do
11. was broken / broke; was being moved
12. to tell
13. to know
14. have been having

6
1. must
2. should
3. must
4. must
5. should

LANGUAGE IN USE

7 (Possible answers – many other answers may be appropriate.)
1. That's all right.
2. Doesn't work? / I am sorry – what's the trouble?
3. What's the trouble/matter?
4. I'm afraid he's not here right now. Can I take a message?
5. Oh, dear, have you called the police?

VOCABULARY

8

bus station
chewing gum
clothes dryer
convector heater
find out
food mixer
ground floor
on fire
personal stereo
political party
post office
vacuum cleaner
washing machine

9

bad line – phone
cabinet – minister
date – go out with
elect – president
helicopter – pilot
hoover – clean
iron – clothes
saucepan – boil
socket – plug
traffic – vehicle

10

1. disagree
2. mend
3. full
4. send a letter
5. solid
6. pull
7. switch off

11

1. by/before
2. to
3. in/with/about
4. of
5. into
6. with
7. over

READING AND WRITING

12

f; b; d; g; e; a; c

13

1. stable
2. abroad
3. project
4. go weak
5. give up
6. bothers
7. career
8. mixed up

14 (Many possible answers; look for a fair degree of fluency, accuracy and appropriateness.)

SPEAKING

15 (Remember that fluency is what counts here.)

Test Book recording
A recording for Test 3 in the Test Book follows this lesson on the Class Cassette.

VOCABULARY

8 Two-word expressions: match the two halves.

bus	cleaner
cassette	dryer
chewing	fire
clothes	floor
convector	gum
find	heater
food	machine
ground	mixer
on	office
personal	out
political	party
post	player
vacuum	station
washing	stereo

9 What goes with what?

bad line	boil
cabinet	clean
check the oil	clothes
date	garage
elect	go out with
helicopter	minister
hoover	phone
iron	pilot
saucepan	plug
socket	president
traffic	vehicle

10 Write the opposites.

1. agree   5. liquid
2. break   6. push
3. empty   7. switch on
4. get a letter

11 Write the missing words.

1. I'm not sure how long I'll be out, but I'll be back .... ten.
2. Kevin is really attracted .... Janice, but he's too shy to ask her out.
3. There's nothing wrong .... asking about it.
4. Congress consists .... the Senate and the House of Representatives.
5. Scotland is divided .... counties.
6. My sister has fallen in love .... a much older man, and my parents are really upset.
7. Look, can we talk this problem ....?

READING AND WRITING

12 Here is a letter from a magazine. Read it and do the task.

How do I choose?

Dear Joyce,

1   I have been going out with Tom for two years now, and we are planning to get married. We share a lot of interests, and have enormous fun together. I know that 5 we would have a good and stable marriage.

    Last autumn, however, we had a few problems. I was working abroad for a month, and shortly after I left Tom wrote to 10 me saying that he had been out with his ex-girlfriend a few times. He said they were just friends, but I was quite upset. About this time I met Alan, who was working on the same project as me. I was 15 very, very attracted to him, and we began going out together. He is obviously very much in love with me, and I am in love with him too, in a way. I have never been so physically attracted to a man as I am to 20 him – the memory of certain moments with him still makes me go weak with pleasure. But it is not only physical: we have all sorts of things in common. He wants me to marry him. We have continued to write,

25 and have seen each other once since then, when he came to England. If I did marry him, I would have to give up my job and go abroad, which bothers me – my career is important to me. And I am 30 worried that our relationship might not last.

    Tom knows that I went out with Alan, but he does not know how powerfully I am attracted to him. Tom and I have talked over the problem of his ex-girlfriend, and I 35 was very impressed with the way that we were able to discuss things. I am still very, very fond of Tom, and I am sure that we would have a good life together. In every way but one, we are probably much better 40 suited to one another than Alan and I are.

    What should I do? I feel so mixed up. Should I marry Alan and give up my job? Should I stay with Tom? If I do, I couldn't 45 tell him the whole truth about Alan; but I hate the idea of keeping a secret from my husband.

    Please help me.

    Linda

Put the events in order.

a. Alan asked Linda to marry him.
b. Linda and Tom began going out together.
c. Linda and Tom talked over their problems.
d. Linda went abroad to work.
e. Linda went out with Alan.
f. Tom had a serious relationship with another woman.
g. Tom went out with his ex-girlfriend.

13 Find words or expressions that mean:

1. strong, lasting (*lines 1–6*)
2. in a foreign country (*lines 7–12*)
3. a big and complicated piece of work (*lines 13–18*)
4. suddenly not feel strong (*lines 18–24*)
5. decide to stop doing (*lines 24–31*)
6. worries (*lines 24–31*)
7. job (over many years) (*lines 24–31*)
8. unsure (*lines 42–47*)

14 Write an answer to Linda's letter.

SPEAKING

15 Work with another student. One of you is a shop manager and the other has come to complain about something he/she bought in the shop. You will have a few minutes to prepare before having a conversation.

D1 Danger – little old ladies!

Reading for gist, for detail; grammar (past conditionals and modals); pronunciation: /iː/ and /ɪ/; speaking practice.

1 Work in pairs. One person in each pair should turn to page 132 and study the newspaper report 'MUGGER MEETS LITTLE OLD LADY'. The other person should prepare questions to find out the information listed below. When both students are ready, they should close their books, and then ask and answer the questions. Finally, both students should look at page 132 and check that the answers were correct.

Find out:
1. the place, day and time of the incident
2. the little old lady's appearance and dress
3. what exactly happened
4. the names of the people involved
5. what the police did
6. how much, if anything, was stolen

2 Now exchange roles and do this in the same way as Exercise 1 (the person who read the text last time should prepare the questions this time, and vice versa). The newspaper report is on page 134, and is entitled 'LITTLE OLD LADY IN KNIFE RAID'. The questioner should find out the same information as in Exercise 1.

Lesson D1

Students work on reading for gist and detail, and practise speaking skills.
Principal structures: Past conditional and modal verb constructions.
Phonology: /iː/ and /ɪ/.

Language notes and possible problems
Past conditionals and modals   Most students will have learnt about past conditionals before (they are taught in Unit 34 of *The New Cambridge English Course 2*). In this lesson Exercises 3 and 4 give further practice of this structure, as well as showing how other modal verbs besides *would* (*might*, *could* and *should*) can be used in the same pattern. Students are likely to need more work on all these points, which will be revised in depth in Lesson D2.

If you are short of time
Get students to do Exercise 4 for homework. If pronunciation is not a priority for your students, or they have no difficulty with the ɪ/i: distinction, drop Exercise 5.

1 Reading: information-gap exercise
• Get students into pairs, and give them about five minutes to prepare.
• You may need to help with the construction of suitable questions ('*Where did it happen?*' etc.).
• When students are ready, get them to ask and answer their questions. Make sure they have their books closed.
• Ask one or two of the questioners what they have found out.
• Finally, let everybody look at the text and see how accurately the information was transmitted from one student to another.
• Answer important questions about vocabulary, but don't spend a long time going through the text.

2 Information-gap (continued)
• This can be done in exactly the same way as Exercise 1.

3 Past conditionals

• Get everybody to write answers to the first two questions.
• Check that they are getting the structure right; if there are any problems, revise the grammar. You may want to use the grammar revision exercises on page 127.
• Get students to do the rest of the exercise either individually or by class discussion, as you prefer.
• Note that *could*, *might* and *should* can be followed by *have* + past participle, in the same way as *would*.

4 Personalisation

• This gives students a chance to use the structure to say something about themselves.
• Encourage them to write things which are really true. Go round checking that the grammar is correct.
• When students are ready, let them show each other their sentences.
• Alternatively, collect up the sentences and read them out (or get other students to read them out), while the class tries to guess who wrote them.

5 Pronunciation: /iː/ and /ɪ/

Part 1

• Give students a chance to look back over the two texts. Their task is to listen to the recording and tell you whether the words they hear are in the texts or not.
• Say the words or play the recording.
• If students find this difficult, spend plenty of time on the rest of this exercise (perhaps coming back to the point several times during the course). If they find it very easy, drop the rest of this exercise.

Tapescript and answers to Exercise 5 Part 1
1. eat (*No*)
2. hit (*Yes*)
3. till (*Yes*)
4. ease (*No*)
5. it (*Yes*)
6. heat (*No*)
7. till (*Yes*)
8. is (*Yes*)
9. eat (*No*)
10. heat (*No*)
11. teal (*No*)
12. is (*Yes*)

Part 2

• Play the recording, pausing between items for students to tell you whether they hear words from column A or column B.
• As a variant, you can ask students to write down what they think they hear.

Tapescript and answers to Exercise 5 Part 2
1. eat (A)
2. did (B)
3. hit (B)
4. ease (A)
5. it (B)
6. did (B)
7. heat (A)
8. is (B)
9. eat (A)
10. deed (A)
11. heat (A)
12. is (B)

Part 3

• Play the recording, and ask students whether the words in each group are the same or different. (Make sure students say *the same* and not *same*.)
• When there are three words in a group, ask which one (if any) is different – the first, second or third.

Tapescript for Exercise 5 Part 3
1. it, it
2. it, eat
3. hit, heat
4. till, till
5. did, deed
6. is, is
7. eat, it, eat
8. hit, hit, heat
9. did, did, deed
10. till, till, till

Part 4

• Now get students to practise saying the words in the two lists. (These are recorded.) Note that the difference between /iː/ and /ɪ/ is not simply one of length – a long /ɪ/ doesn't sound like /iː/, and a short /iː/ is not at all the same as /ɪ/.
• Ask students if they can think of other words containing /iː/ or /ɪ/. You may like to mention *women* (/ˈwɪmɪn/) and *minute* (/ˈmɪnɪt/).
• If students have trouble pronouncing /ɪ/, get them to relax their lip and jaw muscles, and to move their tongues down and back from /iː/ towards /ɪ/, pronouncing the sound without too much energy.
• You may like to get students to try giving each other 'A or B' and 'the same or different' tests.

6 Dramatisations

• Get students to look carefully over the stories again and use their dictionaries and/or ask you about vocabulary.
• Then put them into groups of three or four (four people will be needed for the 'Lady Tucker' sketch) to work on preparing their sketches.
• Walk round while they are working to give any help that is needed.
• Preparation and practice for the dramatisations will probably take between twenty and thirty minutes.
• Discourage students from creating over-ambitious material; sketches should be reasonably short and clear, and should contain plenty of the new language from the lesson.
• If you are going to tape- or video-record performances, warn the students beforehand.

Practice Book exercises
1. Writing a story using past conditionals and modals ('third conditionals').
2. Writing personalised sentences using past conditionals and modals ('third conditionals').
3. Revision of questions beginning with *Who* or *What*.
4. Vocabulary revision: appearances; writing a description of a person.
5. Extended writing: students take the part of one of the old ladies in the Student's Book lesson and write a letter to a grandchild describing what happened.
6. Recreational reading: some popular fiction and a newspaper article.

3 Grammar. Write answers to the following two questions.

1. If you had been the lady in the first report, what would you have done?
   (*If I had been the lady, I would have …*)
2. If you had been the shop assistant in the second report, what would you have done?

Now complete these sentences.

3. If the mugger had known what Lady Tucker was like, he would not have …
4. If Lady Tucker had not hit the mugger, …
5. …, the lorry driver might not have come to help.
6. …, the mugger would have got back on his bicycle.
7. … bicycle, he could have got away.
8. … would not … if she had not kept screaming.
9. If Lady Tucker had been an ordinary old lady, the mugger might have …

If … had (not)	been …, hit …, come, *etc.*	… would (not) have … might (not) have … could (not) have	attacked … been … got … *etc.*

4 Now write three or more sentences about yourself, using the following structures.

If I had (not) … when I was younger, I would have …
If I had …, I might have …
If I had had more money/time last year, I could have …
I should never have …

5 🔲 Pronunciation.

1. Listen to each word, and say whether you think it came in one of the stories in Exercises 1 and 2. Examples: *'eat' 'No.' 'is' 'Yes.' 'till' 'Yes.'*

2. Listen to the recording. Say whether each word is from list A or list B.
   A deed   ease   eat   heat   teal
   B did   is   it   hit   till

3. Listen to the recording and say whether the words are the same or different. Examples: *'hit, hit' 'the same' 'hit, heat' 'different'*

4. Now say these words.

   appealing   easy   Georgina's   police   screams   unbelievable
   assistant   business   sandwich   until   with   witnesses

6 Work in groups of three or four. Prepare and act out either a dramatisation of one of the texts in Exercises 1 and 2, or another scene involving a criminal, a victim and a policeman or policewoman (and someone else if you wish).

Learn/revise: appearance; arm; bicycle; business; coat; dress; handbag; help; knife; lorry driver; luck; mugger; note; owner; policeman; policewoman; prisoner; pub; robbery; scream (*noun and verb*); shop assistant; shoulder; till; umbrella; victim; witness; allow (sbdy to do sth); escape; fight (fought, fought); force (sbdy to do sthg); grab; hit (on + part of body with + object) (hit, hit); hold (held, held); involve; keep (…ing) (kept, kept); push; refuse; steal (stole, stolen); threaten; armed (with); experienced; ordinary; beneath; expensively; in business; at the top of her voice; it's over (= finished).

D2 Focus on systems

GRAMMAR: PAST MODAL STRUCTURES

Structure: modal verb + *have* + past participle

I **could have played** football yesterday (but I didn't).

He **should have stopped** the newspapers (but he forgot).

Why did she go out? It **must have been** because …

Granny **may have had** an accident.

She **can't have gone** to the cinema.

If the mugger had known what she was like, he **would** not **have attacked** her.

If she hadn't screamed, the lorry driver **might** not **have come** to help.

1 Write a sentence to say how you spent last weekend. Then write five sentences to say what you could have done instead. Example:

*I stayed at home and worked. But I **could have played** football. Or I **could have gone** …*

2 Robert went on holiday for two weeks, but he fell in love with the receptionist in his hotel and stayed away for six weeks. When he got back home he found a number of problems. Look at the illustration and say what he should(n't) have done. Example:

'He should have stopped the newspapers.'

ELEC BOARD   Mr Robert Parsons

£ 5,125·65

Dear Mr Parsons,
You're fired.

3 The teacher will give you a paper with a problem or a piece of advice. Find the person whose paper goes with yours. Example:

'I felt really ill yesterday.'   'You should have gone to the doctor.'

Lesson D2

Grammar: modals with perfect infinitives.
Vocabulary: buildings.
Phonology: letter *o* pronounced as /ɒ/ and /ʌ/; word stress.

Language notes and possible problems

1. Modals with perfect infinitives You may need to remind students that most modal verbs (e.g. *should, must, may, might*) do not have normal past forms. However, a special structure is possible in which the modal verb is followed by a perfect infinitive (e.g. *should have gone, might have been*). Students are likely to have come across some of these at least: *would have ...* is common in conditional structures, and there are examples of *would have ...* and *might have ...* in Lesson D1. These forms are used to talk about events and situations (usually past) which did not take place, or which are not known for certain to have happened. Students are likely to have difficulty with the structures, which are idiomatic to English. (The French or German equivalents of *She should have gone*, for example, translate literally into English as **She would have should go*.)

2. Irony The dialogue in Exercise 6 contains several ironic remarks which mean the exact opposite of what the words say (e.g. *Oh, good. Let's buy it at once!*). This rhetorical device is not common to all cultures, and it may be necessary to explain it carefully.

3. Two pronunciations of the letter *o* (Exercise 8) Although the normal 'short' pronunciation of *o* in British English is /ɒ/ (as in *stop*), there are quite a large number of common words in which *o* is pronounced /ʌ/ (like the *u* in *cup*). This may cause problems for some students, especially those (e.g. French-speakers) who tend anyway to confuse the vowels /ɒ/ and /ʌ/. Note that American English does not have the vowel /ɒ/; words which have this vowel in British English are mostly pronounced with either /ɑ/ or /ɔː/ in American.

4. Stress (Exercise 9) Note that some words which are stressed at the end in isolation (e.g. *hotel, weekend*) may change their stress to an earlier syllable in the context of a sentence (e.g. *the hotel staff; a weekend flight*).

Extra materials

You will need to prepare slips of paper for Exercise 3.

1 Introducing past modals: *could have ...*

• Start by talking about your own weekend (or your last holiday, or yesterday evening or whatever), saying what you did and what you could have done instead.
• When students are clear about both the structure and its meaning, get them to write sentences about their own weekend.
• If you want more practice, ask them to suggest things that the class could have done in this lesson instead of studying past modals. Another possibility for adult students: ask them what other things they could have done with their lives instead of taking up their present jobs.

2 *Should have ...*

• Students can discuss this in groups and agree on suitable answers.
• You may need to give some background information (for example, students may not know that newspapers and milk are delivered to people's houses in Britain).

Possible answers to Exercise 2
He should have asked somebody to water his plants.
He should have stopped the newspapers.
He should have stopped the milk.
He should have switched off the electricity.
He should have turned off the water.
He should have told his boss what was happening.

3 *Should have* (continued)

• Prepare slips of paper with problems and replies. There are some suggestions below, but you can probably think of more appropriate examples for your students. You will need as many problems as you have students in the class or in each group (depending on how you organise the exercise), and a reply for each problem.
• If walk-round exercises are possible in your teaching situation, divide the class in half: give problems to the students in one half and the corresponding replies to the others.
• Tell the people with problems to go to the members of the other group in turn, saying their sentences and listening to the replies. Their task is to find the reply that matches their problem.
• When everybody is matched up, repeat the exercise the other way round (give problems to those who had replies, and vice versa).
• If you can't do it as a walk-round activity, divide the class into groups of at least eight and get students to match up problems and replies inside each group.
• If you want more practice, ask students to mention things they should have done last weekend but didn't. Most people will be able to think of something.

Suggestions for Exercise 3
My cat's died.
You should have fed it.
I've lost my bike.
You should have locked it up.
I'm tired.
You shouldn't have gone to bed so late last night.
My legs ache.
You shouldn't have walked so far.
My English isn't good enough.
You should have studied harder.
I've forgotten an important phone number.
You should have written it down.
I've lost all my friends.
You shouldn't have been so unpleasant to them.
The flowers in my garden have died.
You should have watered them.
There's no food in the house.
You should have done some shopping.
The phone has been cut off.
You should have paid the bill.
I missed the train.
You should have got to the station earlier.
I'm hungry.
You should have had breakfast.
I haven't got any money left.
You shouldn't have spent it all on clothes.
The car's broken down.
You should have checked the oil.
I flew to America, but they wouldn't let me into the country.
You should have got a visa.
My sister told all my secrets to her friends.
You shouldn't have told her anything.
I couldn't see anything through my glasses.
You should have cleaned them.
My feet hurt.
You should have put on more comfortable shoes.

4 May/must/can't have ...

• Get students to look at the first three pictures and the example sentences. Point out the symbols in the corners of the pictures: ✓ corresponds to *must*, *?* to *may* and ✗ to *can't*.
• Then tell students to write some or all of the sentences corresponding to the other clues. Suggest that they try to add a sentence with their own explanation for the woman's disappearance.
• Get them to compare notes before discussing the answers with them.

Possible answers to Exercise 4
4. It must have been urgent.
5. She must have taken the car.
6. She can't have gone to the hairdresser.
7. She may have gone to see Joe.
8. She can't have decided to leave home.
9. She may have gone to the dentist.
10. She can't have gone shopping.

5 Vocabulary revision and extension: buildings

• This can be done in groups, with students pooling their knowledge.
• If they use dictionaries, warn them that these may contain words that are no longer common (such as *parlour*).
• Don't let the exercise run on for too long: there is no value in students writing down enormous lists of words that they will never learn.

6 Listening: finding differences

• Let students read through the advertisement. Give whatever help is necessary.
• You may want to point out the typical use of impressive synonyms: *residence* instead of *house*; *cloakroom* instead of *toilet*; *lounge* instead of *sitting/living room*; *mature garden* instead of *garden with plants growing*.
• When students are ready, tell them that they will hear a conversation between John, who has just been to look at the house advertised, and his wife Sally.
• The students' task is to see how many differences they can find between what John says about the house and the advertiser's description.
• You may like to play the recording twice, letting students compare notes after the first hearing.
• Note that they are not expected to understand every word, and neither you nor they should worry if there are passages they cannot understand. This is quite normal at this stage.
• It would be a mistake to spend a lot of time going through the recording explaining low-priority words and structures.

Tapescript for Exercise 6
JOHN: Hi, darling.
SALLY: Hello, John. Well, did you see the 'magnificent town residence'?
JOHN: Yes.
SALLY: So what's it like?
JOHN: Well, first of all it's four miles out of the town centre.
SALLY: Oh, no!
JOHN: And it's not all that big. Three bedrooms: one quite big, one smallish, and one that would be OK for the cat. The luxury bathroom doesn't have a shower, and the downstairs cloakroom is at the end of the garden – at the end of the jungle, I should say. The sitting and dining rooms are both pretty small.
SALLY: What about the kitchen? Is it big enough to have breakfast in?

JOHN: Oh, yes. Easily. If you sit on the fridge and put your feet out of the window there's plenty of room.
SALLY: The garage?
JOHN: Fine for a bicycle. *A* bicycle, mind. Not two bicycles. And there's oil-fired central heating, which doesn't work. And the walls and roof are in a very bad state. Apart from that it's fine.
SALLY: Oh, good. Let's buy it at once!

7 Writing advertisements

• Students can do this individually or in groups, putting their advertisements on the classroom notice board when they are ready.

8 Two pronunciations of the letter o

• Give students a few minutes to make their decisions and compare notes.
• Then play the recording or say the words, while students change their answers if necessary.
• Finally, go over the answers and get the students to practise the words.
• Make sure they realise that /ɒ/ is the *normal* 'short' pronunciation of *o*, and that /ʌ/ is the exception (though it comes in some very common words).
• Ask if students can think of any other common words in which *o* is pronounced /ʌ/. (Some examples: *some*, *other*, *mother*, *brother*, *wonder*, *once*, *come*, *none*.)

Answers to Exercise 8
/ɒ/: gone got holiday lost lot not off often stop
/ʌ/: done love nothing one

9 Word stress

• This can be done in the same way as the last exercise.

Answers to Exercise 9
accident according advertisement advice cinema description difference divide example family happened holiday hotel illustration instead newspaper nothing picture practise problem pronunciation recording sentence weekend yesterday

Practice Book exercises
1. Writing questions for answers.
2. Student's Cassette exercise (Student's Book Lesson D2, Exercise 6). Students try to complete the transcript of the conversation from memory. They check their answers with the recording and then practise the conversation.
3. Completing sentences using past conditionals and modals ('third conditionals').
4. *Since, for* and *ago*.
5. Spelling: single and double letters.
6. Reading and grammar: past modals.
7. Recreational reading: a poem.

4 A woman got a phone call and rushed out of the house, saying nothing to her family. They are wondering what can have happened. Look at the clues and see if you can make some of their sentences. Examples:

'It must have been because of the phone call.'
'Granny may have had an accident.'
'She can't have gone to the cinema.'

1 ✔ 'It must have been because of the phone call.'

2 ? 'Granny may have had an accident.'

3 ✗ 'She can't have gone to the cinema.'

4 ✔ 'It ...'

5 ✔ THE CAR KEYS HAVE GONE! 'She ...'

6 ✗ 'She ...'

7 ? JOE OFTEN RINGS UP WITH A PROBLEM. 'She ...'

8 ✗ HAS SHE DECIDED TO LEAVE HOME? 'She ...'

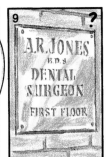

9 ? A.R. JONES B.D.S DENTAL SURGEON FIRST FLOOR 'She ...'

10 ✗ 'She ...'

VOCABULARY: BUILDINGS

5 How many words can you add to these three lists? (Time limit ten minutes.)

Rooms: bedroom, office, cellar, ...
Buildings: house, factory, hotel, ...
Parts of buildings: wall, ceiling, roof, ...

6 📼 Read the advertisement and listen to the recording. How many differences can you find between the two descriptions of the house?

Central York
MAGNIFICENT TOWN RESIDENCE
Four double bedrooms, luxury bathroom, upstairs and downstairs cloakrooms, lounge, dining-room, kitchen/breakfast room, double garage, beautiful mature garden, gas-fired central heating.
In first-class condition.
£150,000

7 Write an advertisement for your home, your school, or some well-known building (The Eiffel Tower, The White House, ...).

PRONUNCIATION: THE LETTER O; WORD STRESS

8 📼 Divide these words into two groups, according to the pronunciation of the letter *o*. Listen to the recording and check your answers, and then practise saying the words.

done gone got holiday lost lot love
not nothing off often one stop

9 📼 Mark the main stress on these words. Listen to the recording and check your answers, and then practise saying the words.

accident according advertisement advice
cinema description difference divide
example family happened holiday hotel
illustration instead newspaper nothing
picture practise problem pronunciation
recording sentence weekend yesterday

Learn/revise: accident; advertisement; (piece of) advice; building; ceiling; cellar; description; difference; factory; office; phone call; problem; receptionist; roof; wall; check; divide; rush; spend time (spent, spent); wonder; well-known; according to; because of; on holiday.

D3 Families

Talking about families; asking about and expressing preferences; writing: connecting sentences; *Would you rather ...?*; listening for gist, for detail; pronouncing words together.

1 Work with a partner. Look at the box and try to fill in the blanks. Do you know what all the words mean?

mother/father/parent
daughter/ .... /child(ren)
grand.............. / .... / grandparents
grand.............. / .... / grandchild
wife/.............. aunt/..............
niece/.............. cousin
..............-in-law (*several possibilities*) relative
single/.............. / .... / .... adopted

Now look at the pictures and talk about what you think the family relationships might be. You can use the words in the box to help you. Example:

'*I think this woman is this boy's mother.*'
'*Perhaps – or perhaps she's his grandmother.*'

2 Listen to the recording and try to match the voices and the pictures.

A

B

C

D

E

F

Lesson D3

Students learn to talk about family relationships, practise asking about and expressing preferences, and learn some ways of connecting sentences in a written text. They listen for gist and for detail.
Principal structures: *Would you rather*; sentence linking.
Phonology: linking with /r/, /j/ and /w/.

Language notes and possible problems

1. Pronunciation: linking Exercise 3 helps students to realise and practise the differences in pronunciation that occur when two vowels are pronounced one after another. Three cases are studied:
– words ending in /iː/, /i/, /eɪ/, /ɔɪ/ and /aɪ/: when these are followed by a vowel, a very slight /j/ is pronounced between the two words.
– words ending in /uː/ (and /əʊ/ and /aʊ/): when these are followed by a vowel, a very slight /w/ is pronounced between the two words.
– words ending in written -r or -re: when these are followed by a vowel, /r/ is pronounced.
You may wish to make these rules explicit for the students; guidance for this is given in the notes for the exercise.

2. *Fewer* and *less* both appear in Exercise 5. You may wish to remind students that, in general, *fewer* is used with countables (e.g. *fewer problems*) and *less* with uncountables (e.g. *less difficulty*). Note, however, that some people also use *less* with countables (e.g. *less problems*).

If you are short of time
You can leave out Exercise 6. Students can do Exercise 4 for homework.

1 Revision of family vocabulary
• Students should work in pairs, trying to complete the sets of words in the box. Once a pair of students have completed as many of the sets as they can, they should compare answers with another pair.
• When you check the answers with them, make sure that they know what all the words mean and can pronounce them.
• Then the pairs should talk about each picture, trying to decide what the family relationships might be.
• Walk round while they are working to give any help that is needed.

Answers to the first part of Exercise 1
mother/father/parent   daughter/*son*/child(ren)
grand*mother*/grand*father*/grandparents
grand*daughter*/grand*son*/grandchild   wife/*husband*
aunt/*uncle*   niece/*nephew*   cousin
mother-in-law/*father*-in-law/*brother*-in-law/
sister-in-law/*daughter*-in-law/*son*-in-law/*parents*-in-law
relative   single/*married*/*divorced*/*separated*   adopted

2 Listening: matching
• Explain to students that they will hear someone from each picture talking about their family. The students' task is to match the voices with the pictures.
• Play the recording twice, pausing after each voice to give students a chance to try and match it with its picture.
• Let students compare their answers. You may then want to play the recording again to give them another chance to confirm their answers.
• Go over the answers with the class.

Tapescript and answers for Exercise 2
1. Don and I are really Kenny's grandparents. Kenny, who's five now, has lived with us since he was a baby, and last year we adopted him as our own child. (*D*)
2. May and I are married, but we have decided not to have children. Although we enjoy playing with our nieces and nephews, we both feel that we don't want to be full-time parents. (*A*)
3. John and I have got three children – Simon, Lucy and Emma. There are a lot of couples with young children in our neighbourhood, so we often help one another out. (*F*)
4. I have got four children. Besides my husband, Surendra, and the children, I also share my home with my mother-in-law, my brother-in-law and his wife. The children get on well with their aunt and uncle, and like listening to their grandmother's stories. (*G*)
5. Claire and I live together. We both work outside the home, and we share the care of Beth, who is my six-year-old daughter. (*C*)
6. Our mum and dad have been divorced for ten years. My sister Ruth and I live with our mum, and see our dad almost every week. (*E*)
7. Because my dad is too ill to live on his own, and I wouldn't want him to live in an old people's home, he lives with me. I am getting married soon, and Dad will continue to live with me and my wife. We hope to give him some grandchildren to play with before long! (*B*)

3 Pronouncing words together

- Play or read the first example to the students.
- Ask them to tell you what the difference is when the words are pronounced together, and then get them to practise saying the example.
- Do the same with the other two examples.
- You may wish to elicit or point out the fact that in the first example, /j/ is the closest consonant to /iː/, which is why it is lightly pronounced to separate the two words; and that in the second example /w/ is lightly pronounced because it is the closest consonant to /uː/.
- Get volunteers to pronounce the next six lines. Get the class to listen; the volunteers should continue trying until the class decides that their pronunciation is acceptable.
- Afterwards, put the students in pairs to practise all twelve lines for a minute or two.

4 Sentence connectors

- Get the students to look at the words in the box and make sure they know what they mean; let them use their dictionaries or ask you for the meanings of any words they do not know.
- All the words are in the tapescript for Exercise 2; you may want to write some of the sentences on the board:

  Besides my husband, Surendra, and the children, I *also* share my home with my mother-in-law, …
  Although we enjoy playing with our nieces and nephews, we both feel that we don't want to be full-time parents.
  Because my dad is too ill to live on his own, *and* I wouldn't want him to live in an old people's home, he lives with me.
  May and I are married, *but* we have decided not to have children.
  There are a lot of couples with young children in our neighbourhood, *so* we often help one another out.

- Then ask them to read the text in Exercise 4, trying to put one of the words from the box into each blank.
- They can use their dictionaries or consult you about difficulties.
- Walk round while they are working to give any help that is needed.
- After working individually, they should compare answers and try to reach a consensus before checking with you.
- Practice Book exercise 2 gives more work on these words.

Answers to Exercise 4
1. Although
2. but
3. besides
4. so
5. also
6. because
7. and

5 Class survey

- Go over the questions with the students, making sure they understand each one.
- You may have to remind or teach students the meaning of *Would you rather*.
- Then tell them they can ask *you* any of the questions they want.
- Try to answer truthfully: it will help them enjoy the exercise more.
- You can take this opportunity to help them with pronunciation, and to point out the reply forms *I'd rather* … and *I'd rather not*.

- Then tell each student to choose one question to ask as many other class members as possible. They should note the answers. (It does not matter if two students choose the same question.)
- Ideally, this will be done as a walk-round activity so everyone can ask everyone else.

6 Reporting the survey

- Go over the example with the students, and then get each student to report the results of his or her survey to the class, or to a group of five or six if the class is large.

7 Listening: native speakers doing the survey

- Ask students to write the numbers 1 to 5 on a piece of paper, and to keep their books open so they can see the questions in Exercise 5.
- Then play the recording, pausing after each item so that students can look at Exercise 5, decide which question the people are answering, and write its letter down.
- Remind the students that it is not necessary to understand every word, but just to decide which question is being answered.
- You may want to play the recording through a second time so that students can check their answers.

Answers to Exercise 7
1c; 2f; 3b; 4g; 5e

Tapescript for Exercise 7: see page 150

8 Song: *So near yet so far*

- Ask the students to close their books.
- Play the recording through once, and then ask the students to tell you any words they remember.
- Let them open their books and read the lyrics, and answer any questions they have about meaning.
- Play the song again so the students can try to hear the missing verbs (mostly irregular past tense forms).
- Let them compare answers with one another before checking with you.
- After going over the answers, the students may want to hear the song one more time.

Answers for Exercise 8
1. lives	11. agreed	21. was
2. 's	12. was	22. climbs
3. works	13. dreams	23. have turned
4. lives	14. will come	24. 's got
5. to earn	15. are joined	25. to get
6. fishes	16. 'll be married	26. heading
7. met	17. was	27. met
8. was	18. met	28. agree
9. held	19. sits	29. is
10. gave	20. 's gone	

Practice Book exercises
1. Reading skills (anaphoric reference).
2. Linking words (*also, although, and, because, besides, but, so*).
3. Quantifiers.
4. Vocabulary revision: members of the family.
5. Student's Cassette exercise (Student's Book Lesson D3, Exercise 8). Students listen to the song and write Maria and Antonio's story in their own words.
6. Students write at least eight sentences about changes in family life in their countries over the last century.

3 🔊 Pronouncing words together. Some words change their pronunciation before vowels. Listen to the differences in pronunciation.

1. we   we adopted him
2. who   who is five now
3. Claire   Claire and I

Now pronounce these.

4. our own child
5. May and I are married
6. we enjoy playing
7. Lucy and Emma
8. we often help one another out
9. their aunt and uncle
10. Beth, who is my six-year-old daughter
11. see their father almost every week
12. too ill to live on his own

4 Make sure you know all the words in the box. Then put one word in each of the blanks in the text.

also	although	and	because	besides	
but	so				

......1...... there are many different kinds of families in the world, there are some things that are the same everywhere. Not all societies have western-type marriage with one wife and one husband, ...2...... some kind of marriage is universal. And when a person marries, ...3...... the new wife or husband, he or she also gets a complete new family of in-laws. Marriages with close relatives do not always produce healthy children, ...4...... all societies have rules about who can marry who. Each society ......5...... has a division of work based on age and sex. In modern western societies, there is a move to change this last rule ......6...... it can be unfair to women, ...7...... it will be interesting to see if this succeeds.

5 Class survey. Make sure you understand the questions. Then choose one question to ask other people in the class.

a. Would you like to live alone part of the time – say, one week a month?
b. Would you rather have more or fewer brothers and sisters than you have?
c. Would you like to have children? How many? OR: Would you like to have more or fewer children than you have?
d. Would you rather live in the same town as your parents or not?
e. Would you rather spend less time working or studying and more time with your family?
f. If you were very rich, would you rather give your parents the money to have a nice holiday on their own, or take them on holiday with you?
g. What's the best age for having children? Is it better to be young or a bit older?

6 Report the results of your survey to the class or to a group. Example:

'Nine people would rather spend less time working or studying and more time with their families, and six people think they see enough of their families.'

7 🔊 Listen to the recording. Some British people are answering questions from the survey. As you hear their answers, write the letters of the questions they are answering.

8 🔊 Listen to the song. Tell the teacher some of the words you remember. Then turn to page 132: can you write down any of the missing verb forms? Listen to the recording again to check your answers.

G

> **Learn/revise:** age; aunt; bride; cousin; division; family; gold; granddaughter/son/child; grandmother/father/parent; groom; husband; in-laws; marriage; mother/father/brother/sister/daughter/son/parents-in-law; neck; nephew; niece; relative; rule; sex; society; uncle; wife (wives); adopt; continue; dream (dreamt, dreamt); enjoy (...ing); get on (with) (got, got); hope; produce; share (sth with sbdy); spend (time) (spent, spent); succeed; alone; close (*adjective*); divorced; full-time; healthy; ill; married; romantic; separated; single; unfair; fewer; less; together; also; although; besides; so; outside (*preposition*).

SKILLS FOCUS
SKILLS FOCUS
SKILLS FOCUS
SKILLS FOCUS
SKILLS FOCUS
SKILLS FOCUS

D4 Having an amazing time

Writing: personal letters (persuasion); reading: main ideas, guessing words from context, inference; vocabulary work.

Introduction to the lesson
Your teacher will put you in **Group A** (young people) or **Group B** (parents).
Group A (*young people*): Start on Exercise 1. When you have written your letter, go to Exercise 3. If you get a reply to your letter, break off and answer it; then go back to Exercise 3.
Group B (*parents*): Start on Exercise 3. When you get a letter, break off, go to Exercise 2, and answer the letter. When you have done that, go back to Exercise 3 until you get another letter.

1 Group A (young people): You are on a hitchhiking and camping holiday abroad. Write a letter to your parents saying that you would like to stay abroad and work at one of the jobs listed in the box. You need money to be able to do this; try and convince your parents to help you. Ask your teacher for help with any words you don't understand.

> bouncer in nightclub   busker   lion tamer
> photographer   pop singer   private detective
> taxi driver   a job of your choice

When you have written your letter, give it to the teacher and go to Exercise 3. Be ready to stop if you receive an answer from your parent.

2 Group B (parents): Read the letter you receive and answer it. You are not happy with your child's choice of job, will not send him/her any money, and want him/her to return home as soon as possible and begin one of the jobs in the box. Try and convince your child that this is the right thing to do. When you have written an answer to your child's letter, go back to Exercise 3 (but be ready to stop if you receive another letter).

> bank clerk   car salesman/woman   nurse
> policeman/woman   postman/woman
> shop assistant   soldier   teacher
> a job of your choice

Lesson D4

Writing skills: writing personal letters (to persuade).
Reading skills: getting the main ideas; guessing meaning from context; making inferences.
Vocabulary work: choosing words and expressions to learn.

Language notes and possible problems

Structure of the lesson This lesson requires careful organisation on your part, as students will not all be doing the same exercise at the same time. The lesson is organised in this way in order to give students more realistic writing practice. When people write something in real life they have an audience in mind, whether it be one person or, for example, all the readers of a particular newspaper. In this lesson students will be given roles, and will know what sort of people they are writing to; their letters will be read for meaning, and answered by the people who read them. This not only helps with motivation and with focus, but also makes for a more natural tone and content in the writing. Here is how the lesson is organised:

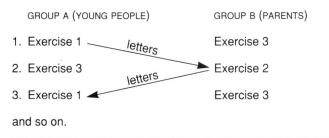

GROUP A (YOUNG PEOPLE)	GROUP B (PARENTS)
1. Exercise 1	Exercise 3
2. Exercise 3	Exercise 2
3. Exercise 1	Exercise 3

and so on.

If you are short of time

If the 'young people' don't have time to answer the letters they get from their 'parents', they can do this for homework.

Introduction

• Ask all the students to keep their books closed. Elicit from the class where you would put the following things in a letter in English: the address of the person writing the letter, the date, the 'Dear ...' line, the signature of the person writing the letter. Write these things on the board as they tell you (whether they are wrong or right).
• Let them open their books and check their answers with the letters in Exercise 3. (You may want to point out that we do not write our address on a letter when we are sure that a family member or friend already knows it: 'Dad' does not write his address on his letter to his son.)
• Divide the class into two equal groups (Group B, the 'parents' group can have one more member than Group A, the 'young people' group).
• Ask Group B to begin reading the two letters in Exercise 3, using their dictionaries, while you help Group A to begin Exercise 1.

1 Young people's letters

• Make sure the students understand the meanings of the words in the box. They will probably need to be told that the job of a *bouncer* is to keep unwelcome people out of, for example, a club or pub; and that a *busker* is a street musician.
• Go over the exercise instructions with them. Discuss what will go into their letters: remind them that they must convince their parents to give them some money. Get them each to choose one of the jobs in the box and begin working on the letters.
• They can look at the letters in Exercise 3 if they wish.

• Once they have started working, go to help Group B with Exercise 3.
• When both groups are working, make yourself available to give any help that is needed.
• Students in Group A should let you know when they have finished their letters. As each student finishes, take her/his letter and deliver it to one of the parents in Group B. The young person should then begin the tasks in Exercise 3.
• If there is time, bring the parent's answer back to the young person and ask them to reply.

2 Parents' letters

• Interrupt one of the parents who is doing Exercise 3 and tell them you've got a letter from their daughter/son for them. (If there are more parents than children, one child's letter can be answered by both 'Mum' and 'Dad'.)
• Ask them to read the instructions to Exercise 2 and make sure they understand them; they should then choose one of the jobs in the box and write an answer to the letter they have received. Remind them that they must convince their child that coming back is the right thing to do.
• Students should let you know when they have finished. As each student finishes, take her/his letter and deliver it to his/her 'child'. The parent should then go back to working on Exercise 3.
• If there is time, bring the young person's answer back to the parent and ask them to reply.

3 Reading

- Group B, the 'parents', should begin by reading the two letters with a dictionary, and doing the tasks in Exercise 3.
- Group A, the 'young people', will begin Exercise 3 once they have finished their first letter from Exercise 1.
- In each case, you will need to explain the first task: there are five points from each letter, and the students must choose which three of the five are the most important points and write them down in the same order as in the letter. Tell them you will be available while they are working to give any help that they need.
- When a member of Group A (young people) gives you a letter to deliver, take it for delivery to a member of Group B, and get the young person to begin Exercise 3. You will need to explain the first task to them.

Answers to Exercise 3

A *Jonathan's letter*: 5, 2, 4
  Dad's letter: 4, 3, 2

B *Jonathan's letter*
  1. amazing
  2. broke up
  3. running
  4. sudden
  5. expand
  6. consider
  7. interest
  Dad's letter
  1. recovering
  2. all set
  3. the other night
  4. been fond of you
  5. school leaver
  6. opportunity

C 1. He thought he would never fall in love again after Angela.
  2. Jonathan and Anastasia plan to travel to England after the tourist season is over.
  3. It is the summer, he is a school leaver, he begins his letter by saying he is having a good time and describing the sea and the weather.
  4. Jonathan's dad speaks of a 'perfect English summer', and they are planning to holiday in Wales.
  5. Peter is able to offer Jonathan a job in his insurance company.
  6. The job that Peter is offering to Jonathan requires somebody with good maths.

Practice Book exercises

1. Grammar and vocabulary revision: prepositions and household objects.
2. *Can, could, will be able to*, and *would be able to*.
3. Vocabulary revision: 'odd word out'.
4. Word stress.
5. Recreational reading: two humorous texts.
6. Extended writing: 'an amazing time'.

3 Here are two letters written on the same day. Read them and answer the questions.

Triton Hotel
Ayia Trias
Greece
28 June 1992

Dear Mum and Dad,

I'm having an amazing time. The sea's lovely, and the weather's been wonderful.

And something else has been wonderful, too: I've met the most marvellous woman. I thought I'd never fall in love again after Angela and I broke up, but this is the real thing. It just knocked me over. Her name's Anastasia, she comes from a family that's lived in the village since time began, and she's beautiful and clever, and, well, just wonderful. She's a year younger than me, but has been running the family grocery business on her own since her parents died four years ago.

I know this is sudden, but I'm sure she's the one for me. I've asked her to marry me, and I hope I'll have your blessing. I'd like to bring her home for you to meet when the tourist season's over, and we'd like to get married here in January.

Meanwhile, I wonder if I could ask you a favour? We'd really like to expand the grocer's shop to meet the growing demand from tourists. Would you consider making us a loan? We could pay you back over five years or so, and pay the same kind of interest as you'd get from a bank account. I hope you'll say yes. And I hope you'll like Anastasia – I can't wait for you to meet her.

Love,

Jonathan

28 June 1992

Dear Jonathan,

We hope you're enjoying yourself. The weather here's lovely at the moment, lots of sun and flowers everywhere – a perfect English summer. Your Mum's recovering well from her operation, and we're all set to go to Wales in the third week of July.

Jonathan, I'm writing to say that I've been talking to my old school friend Peter. You remember him – he's the one who used to bring you chocolates when he came to see us. Well, I've been playing badminton with him from time to time. The other night when we were having a drink after a game he asked how you were doing. He's always been fond of you, you know. Well, when I told him you'd finished school and were a bit undecided about what to do, he offered you a job! You know he works for Scottish Standard, the insurance company. Well, he has a place in his department for a school leaver 'with good maths and an outgoing personality'. You could begin in September, and you'd be in their management trainee programme. So you could end up President of the company, if you kept at it!

I hope you'll consider this seriously. Your mother and I think it's a marvellous opportunity for you.

Much love,

Dad

A. The main ideas. You can work in pairs or small groups, but you may have to stop before the end of the exercise. For each letter: choose the three main points from the list and write them out in the same order as in the letter.

Jonathan's letter
1. The weather has been wonderful.
2. I want to marry her.
3. I would like you to meet Anastasia.
4. Please lend us some money for her business.
5. I am in love with a wonderful woman.

Dad's letter
1. You could begin work in September.
2. Mum and I think you should take the job.
3. My friend Peter has offered you a job.
4. Your Mum is better.
5. You could end up President of the company.

B. Guessing words from context. Find words or expressions in the letters that mean the following (the expressions here are in the same order as the words and expressions in the letters).

Jonathan's letter
1. unbelievably good
2. stopped being together
3. managing, organising
4. fast and surprising
5. make (something) bigger
6. think about
7. money that is earned by letting someone keep your money for a time

Dad's letter
1. getting back to normal health
2. completely ready
3. one night recently
4. liked you
5. someone who's just finished secondary school
6. chance

C. Find things in the text that tell you:

1. Jonathan had probably been very much in love with his girlfriend Angela.
2. The grocer's shop is probably not very busy out of the tourist season.
3. Jonathan is probably on holiday.
4. Jonathan's parents are probably happy being in Britain.
5. Peter probably has quite a good job.
6. Jonathan is probably good at maths.

D. Choose seven or more words or expressions from the letters to learn. If you have time, tell another student why you have chosen those items.

Learn/revise: bank account; business; company; interest; loan; opportunity; personality; policeman/woman (policemen/women); school leaver; break up (with sbdy) (broke, broken); choose (chose, chosen); consider; enjoy; fall in love (with sbdy) (fell, fallen); meet (met, met); pay back (paid, paid); recover (from sth); run (sth) (ran, ran); amazing; clever; fond (of sbdy); marvellous; outgoing; sudden; undecided; wonderful; really; seriously; the other night.

D5 Places

Speaking and listening skills: talking about places; giving directions; hearing unstressed syllables.

1 Look at the picture. Which word goes with which number?

hill   mountain   valley   wood   stream   waterfall   island
river   lake   bridge   path   road

2 How do you get from A to B? Use the words in Exercise 1 with these prepositions: *across, through, along, up, down*. Start: *'You go down the hill ...'.*

3 📼 Look at the map and listen to the recording. Decide whether the sentences are true or false. Example:

There's an island at the south end of Derwent Water.

False.

80

Lesson D5

<table>
<tr><td>

Students practise talking about places: they learn the words for some features of landscape and revise the expressions used for asking and giving directions.
Phonology: perceiving unstressed syllables.

</td></tr>
</table>

Language notes and possible problems

Level   This is a rather easier lesson, which gives students a chance to relax a little with some undemanding fluency practice.
Conditional structures   Note the use of *would* and past tenses with *imagine* in Exercise 5 (*Imagine that somebody asked you ... What would you say?*).

If you are short of time
Exercise 3 or 4 could be dropped; so could Exercise 7 or 8.

1 Vocabulary extension: landscapes
• Practise the pronunciation first of all (make sure students don't make an *s* in *island*).
• Then let students pool their knowledge in groups. When they have done what they can, go over the answers with them.
• Answer any questions they may have about other vocabulary in this area, within reason. (But if a student wants to learn a large number of words, he or she probably ought to work at home with a dictionary.)

Answers to Exercise 1
1. wood   2. waterfall   3. stream   4. island   5. river
6. mountain   7. road   8. lake   9. path   10. bridge
11. hill   12. valley

2 Prepositions
• Get students to write the answer (so that everybody has to try). Then let them compare notes before you check the answer with them.
• If necessary, explain the exact meanings of the prepositions.

Answer to Exercise 2
You go down the hill, along the road, across the bridge, through the wood and up the other hill.

3 Listening   📼
Note The map shows a part of the 'Lake District', a wild and beautiful area of moorland and mountain in north-west England.
• Look at the map with the class. Not all students may be used to reading maps; check that they know the meaning of the main symbols, can identify roads and rivers, and understand the use of colour and contour lines to show height (darker shades of brown mean higher ground).
• Check that students remember the words *north*, *south*, *east* and *west*, and can identify the directions on the map.
• When students are familiar with the map, play the recording and ask them to note their answers. (You will need to stop the recorder after each sentence to give them time to think and write.)
• Play the recording once more if necessary. Then let students compare notes before telling them the answers.

Tapescript and answers to Exercise 3
1. There's an island at the south end of Derwent Water.   (F)
2. There are three big lakes on the map.   (T)
3. Dark colours on the map mean high ground. (T)
4. Cat Bells is a hill just east of Derwent Water. (F)
5. Cat Bells is higher than High Seat. (F)
6. St Herbert's Island is in the middle of Derwent Water. (T)
7. There's a wood to the east of Derwent Water. (T)
8. Buttermere is in a deep valley. (T)
9. The map shows three high waterfalls between Crummock Water and Buttermere. (F)
10. There's a road on the south-west side of Buttermere. (F)

80

4 Perceiving unstressed syllables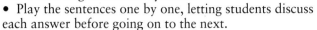

- Play the sentences one by one, letting students discuss each answer before going on to the next.
- Don't play a sentence more times than necessary: students must learn to cope with real-life speech.
- Finish by getting students to pronounce the sentences with a natural rhythm.

Tapescript and answers to Exercise 4
1. There are three big lakes on the map.   (8)
2. There's an island at the south end of the lake.   (11)
3. Go across the bridge and through the wood.   (8)
4. Can you tell me the way to the post office?   (10)
5. You have to turn right after the police station.   (9)
6. It's ten or fifteen minutes' walk from here.   (9)
7. Go straight ahead for about half a mile.   (8)
8. You have to go up a hill and over a bridge.   (11)
9. How far do you think it is to the station?   (10)

5 Giving directions (introduction)

- Give students a minute or two to think about this. You could get them to mask the jumbled sentences and write their own version of the directions; then sort out the jumbled sentences and compare the two versions.
- Discuss the answer and explain any difficulties.

Answer to Exercise 5
Go straight ahead for about 200 metres, then turn right at the big crossroads. Then take the first left. Keep straight on past the station; you'll see it on your left.

6 Giving directions (continued)

- This is a straightforward exercise. You may like to start it off yourself by asking a bright student for directions to one of the places on the map.

7 Speaking practice

- If time allows, you may wish to do both of these activities. Otherwise, get the class to choose, or let students choose individually and put them in groups according to their choice of activity.
- The first activity should be a genuine piece of communication. Students should try to make the others 'see' the place they are describing.
- Students who are doing the second option will speak much better if they stand up and act out the situation.

8 Song: *The Island*

- The song contains a lot of the vocabulary from the first part of the lesson.
- Play it once right through, and ask students what they have understood.
- Then play one section, stopping and repeating if necessary, while students try to work out the words.
- Finally, let students look at the words on page 132 while you play the song once more. Encourage them to sing along with the recording.

Practice Book exercises
1. Rewriting a text to make it more interesting.
2. *If*-sentences (hypothetical, 'second' conditionals).
3. Student's Cassette exercise (Student's Book Lesson D5, Exercise 8). Students listen to the recording and decide which of the words in the box do not appear in the song.
4. Completing a vocabulary network (*street*).
5. Making a vocabulary network (*house*).
6. Recreational reading: humorous autobiography; *Strange but true!* (places).
7. A choice of extended writing tasks: a letter from someone on holiday; a view from a window; a favourite place.

4 [cassette] Pronunciation. Listen to the recording. How many words do you hear in each sentence? What are they? (Contractions like *there's* count as two words.)

5 Look at the town plan. Imagine that somebody asked you how to get from the car park to the post office. What would you say? If you don't know the answer, put these sentences in order.

Then take the first left.
You'll see it on your left.
Then turn right at the big crossroads.
Go straight ahead for about 200 metres.
Keep straight on past the station.

6 Work in groups. Ask and give directions from the car park to other places on the map. Example:

'*Excuse me, can you tell me the way to the Rainbow Theatre?*'
'*Yes. Go straight ahead ...*'

Give directions to the other students, and then ask them where they think they are. Example:

'*You are at the car park. Go straight ahead for two hundred metres, turn left at the crossroads, ..., and take the first right. Where are you?*'

7 Work in groups of three or four.
EITHER: Tell the other students in the group about a place that you like (somewhere in the country, a town, a street, a building, a room, or any other kind of place).
OR: One of you is a stranger visiting the local town. He/she asks the other two for directions. They disagree. Act out the situation.

8 [cassette] Listen to the song and see how much you can understand. Then look at the words on page 132 and listen again. Sing along if you like.

Learn/revise: bridge; hill; island; lake; mountain; path; river; road; stream; valley; waterfall; wood; car park; college; hospital; park; police station; post office; railway station; swimming pool; theatre; town hall; north; south; west; east; true; false; across; through; along; up; down; past; Can you tell me the way to ...?; take the first left / second right / *etc.*; turn left/right at ...; go/keep straight on/ahead.

81

D6 Focus on systems

A choice of exercises: Present Perfect Simple and Progressive; *have to*, *don't have to* and *mustn't*; the vocabulary of games-playing; /ɜː/ and /eə/.

GRAMMAR: PRESENT PERFECT SIMPLE AND PROGRESSIVE

1 Which Present Perfect tense (Simple or Progressive) is used to express ideas of *completion* and *change*?

1. Have you *finished / been finishing* that report yet?
2. He thinks he's a great novelist, but he's never *written / been writing* anything worth reading.
3. What's *happened / been happening* to the little shop that used to be here?
4. The children *have been getting / have got* much bigger since I last saw them.

Which tense is used to say 'x times up to now'?

5. He's *changed / been changing* schools three times this year.
6. 'How are you getting on at tennis?' 'I've *won / been winning* every match this summer.'

Which tense is used to talk about *continuation/ repetition* up to now?

7. I've *thought / been thinking* about you all day.
8. Jane and I have *seen / been seeing* a lot of each other lately.
9. What have you *done / been doing* since I last saw you?
10. 'You look hot.' 'Yes, I've *played / been playing* tennis.'

Which tense is used to talk about *duration* ('how long?') up to now?

11. Sorry I'm late – have you *waited / been waiting* long?
12. We've *tried / been trying* to find a place to live since Christmas.

Which tense do we use for *very long* or *permanent* states? Compare:

13. I've *stayed / been staying* with Jake for the last few days.
14. My family have always *lived / been living* in York.

2 Present Progressive or Present Perfect Progressive? Why?

1. *I'm working / I've been working* in a bookshop just now.
2. *I'm working / I've been working* there for about six weeks.
3. My parents *are travelling / have been travelling* round America at the moment.
4. They *are travelling / have been travelling* since May.

5. How long *are you studying / have you been studying* English?
6. Recently *I'm getting / I've been getting* more and more interested in a boy in my class.

Present or Present Perfect? Why not Progressive?

7. How long *do you know / have you known* Pete?
8. *I have / I've had* a headache since I got up this morning.

3 Choose the right tense (Present Perfect Simple or Progressive).

1. I .... letters all morning. (*write*)
2. I .... sixteen letters. (*write*)
3. And I still .... them all. (*not finish*)
4. One of the people I've written to ....; I don't know her new address. (*move*)
5. I .... to find out where she is for weeks, but nobody seems to know. (*try*)
6. I'd be sorry to lose touch with her; we .... each other since we were babies. (*know*)
7. I'm a bit worried about her, because she .... more and more depressed recently. (*get*)
8. She .... her job twice this year, and I know she's got problems at home. (*change*)
9. I hope she .... anything stupid. (*not do*)

GRAMMAR: *HAVE TO, DON'T HAVE TO AND MUSTN'T*

4 Put the beginnings and ends together.

SOME OF THE RULES OF 'SNAKES AND LADDERS'
In order to move,
Before you can start,
If you come to a snake,
If you come to a ladder,
If you throw a six,
If you land on an occupied square,
If you throw three sixes one after another,

you have to throw a dice.
you have to go down it.
you have to go back four squares.
you have to throw a six.
you have to go up it.
you have to miss a turn.
you can have another throw.

Lesson D6

Grammar: Present Perfect Simple and Progressive; *have to* and modal verbs referring to obligation.
Vocabulary: games-playing.
Phonology: /ɜː/ and /eə/; rhythm and stress.

Language notes and possible problems
1. Present Perfect Simple and Progressive Most students will probably need to revise the use of these tenses. Exercises 1–3 give students a chance to develop a conscious understanding of the rules. Note that the rules given are necessarily somewhat simplified; even so, not all students will find it easy to focus on the rather abstract concepts (completion, duration etc.) that lie behind the choice between simple and progressive forms.

Duration up to the present is expressed by present tenses in many languages (see Exercise 2). Look out for mistakes like *How long are you here already?* or *I know her all my life.*

2. Have to This lesson practises the use of *have to* to talk about rules, laws, and other kinds of permanent obligation. You may also wish to mention that *have got to* is commonly used informally to talk about immediate obligation (compare *If you want to drive you have to take a test* and *I've got to take my driving test tomorrow*).

3. Have to and must Students may ask about the difference between *have to* and *must*. Most often, *have to* refers to an external obligation which already exists, while *must* is often preferred when obligation is imposed by the speaker or hearer. (Compare *I have to be at the office at eight every morning* and *I really must get up early and write some letters tomorrow.*) However, the distinction is not very clear-cut.

4. Mustn't and don't have to Remind students, if necessary, that *mustn't* (obligation not to do something) is very different from *don't have to* (no obligation to do something).

5. Pronunciation of have to: normally /ˈhæftə/.

1 Present Perfect: reasons for choosing Simple or Progressive
• This exercise takes students step by step through the main ideas that are expressed by the choice between Present Perfect Simple and Progressive. It can be done in writing or by group/class discussion, as you prefer. The answers should be obvious to most students in each case.

Answers to Exercise 1
(Simple Present Perfect for completion/change)
1. finished   2. written   3. happened   4. got
(Simple Present Perfect to say 'how many times up to now')
5. changed   6. won
(Present Perfect Progressive to talk about continuation/repetition up to now)
7. been thinking   8. been seeing (seen *also possible*)
9. been doing   10. been playing
(Present Perfect Progressive to talk about duration up to now)
11. been waiting   12. been trying
(Progressive for more temporary states; Simple for more permanent states)
13. been staying   14. lived

2 Present and Present Perfect
• Some students may need to revise this very elementary point (see *Language notes*). It can be done quickly by class discussion unless students are really unclear about the rule (in which case it might be better to get them to write the answers individually).

Answers to Exercise 2
1. I'm working (*focus on present*)
2. I've been working (*focus on duration up to present*)
3. are travelling
4. have been travelling
5. have you been studying
6. I've been getting
7. have you known (*the verb* know *is not normally used in progressive forms*)
8. I've had (*the verb* have *is not used in progressive forms in non-dynamic meanings*)

3 Present Perfect tenses: test
• This small test gives students a chance to see if they have grasped the rules in Exercises 1 and 2.

Answers to Exercise 3
(Contracted forms are also possible.)
1. have been writing
2. have written
3. have not finished
4. has moved
5. have been trying
6. have known
7. has been getting
8. has changed
9. has not done

4 Have to: snakes and ladders
• Explain to students that the complete board has 100 squares, that you move by throwing a dice, and that the first person to get to the top is the winner.
• Don't tell students any more than this: they can work out the rest of the rules by doing the exercise.
• When they are ready, let them compare notes and then give them the answers.
• Discuss the meaning of *have to* if necessary, and clear up any other problems.

Answers to Exercise 4
In order to move, you have to throw a dice.
Before you can start, you have to throw a six.
If you come to a snake, you have to go down it.
If you come to a ladder, you have to go up it.
If you throw a six, you can have another throw.
If you land on an occupied square, you have to go back four squares.
If you throw three sixes one after another, you have to miss a turn.

82

5 *Have to, don't have to* and *mustn't*: games and rules
- The first part of the exercise can be done individually or by class discussion, as you prefer.
- Before moving on, make sure students are clear about the difference between *don't have to* and *mustn't*.
- The second part of the exercise will take rather longer, and can be done for homework (or dropped) if time is short.

Answers to Exercise 5
1. tennis   2. football   3. baseball   4. golf   5. chess
6. hockey

6 Matching exercise: games-playing
- This can be done in groups, with students pooling their knowledge.
- When they are ready, go through the answers, explaining any problems. Note that in British English *dice* is now commonly used as the singular form, rather than *die*.
- If students are interested, they could also try to name the unlabelled playing cards, and/or match the chess pieces with their names.

Answers to Exercise 6
1. dealing   2. tennis racquet   3. baseball bat
4. golf club   5. moving   6. playing cards
7. snooker table   8. ball   9. chess pieces
10. dice   11. kicking   12. serving   13. net
14. goal   15. chess/draughts board

7 Vocabulary extension
- Don't let this take too long – there is no point in students writing down large numbers of words that they are never going to learn. Anybody who wants to do a lot of research can be advised to continue at home.

8 /ɜː/ and /eə/
- Let students try this individually first of all, before comparing notes with other students.
- Play the recording or say the words while students check their answers.
- Tell them the answers (*air* and *square*), and get them to practise the words.
- Students whose language does not contain a vowel similar to /ɜː/ or /ə/ (e.g. Spanish- or Japanese-speakers) may find this difficult. It may help if you start by making the vowel very long, and getting students to relax their mouths as much as possible; point out that the tongue is roughly in the middle of the mouth.
- Ask if students can think of any more words with these two vowels.
- Discuss the most common spellings of the two sounds. (/ɜː/ is most often written *er*, *ir* or *ur*; sometimes *or* after *w*; occasionally *ear*. /eə/ is most often written *air* or *are*; *ere* in *there* and *where*; sometimes in other ways.)
- Get students to practise the words.

Practice Book exercises
1. Choosing the right tense (Present Perfect Simple or Progressive).
2. National laws: *have to*, *don't have to*, *mustn't* and *can*.
3. Jobs: *have to*, *don't have to*.
4. Translation of material from Lessons D1 to D6.
5. Recreational reading: humorous autobiography.
6. Reading skills: linking words.
7. Extended writing: a note modelled on the one in Exercise 6.

5 Match the games and the rules. Then think of a game that the others may not know (or invent a game) and write out the rules for it.

> hockey   chess   football   golf   tennis   baseball

1. You have to hit a ball over a net; it mustn't land outside the white lines.
2. You can kick the ball but you mustn't touch it with your hands.
3. You have to hit a ball and run; you can have three tries.
4. You have to hit a ball into a small hole; you don't have to run.
5. You have to capture a king.
6. You have to hit a ball into a goal with a stick; you mustn't use your hands.

VOCABULARY: PLAYING GAMES

6 Match the words in the box with the pictures.

> ball   baseball bat   chess/draughts board
> chess pieces   dealing   dice   goal   golf club
> kicking   moving   net   playing-cards
> serving   snooker table   tennis racket

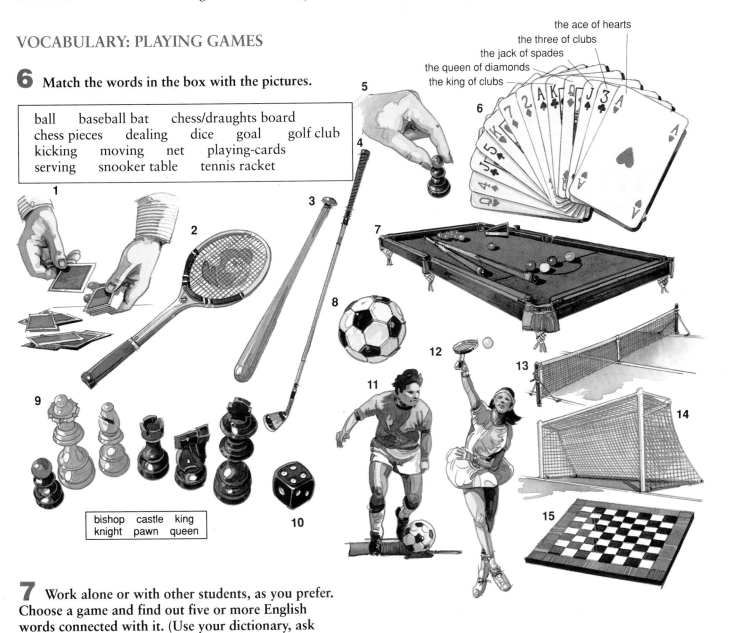

the ace of hearts
the three of clubs
the jack of spades
the queen of diamonds
the king of clubs

bishop   castle   king
knight   pawn   queen

7 Work alone or with other students, as you prefer. Choose a game and find out five or more English words connected with it. (Use your dictionary, ask other students or ask the teacher.)

PRONUNCIATION

8 🔲 Two of these words have a different vowel sound from the others. Which are they? Can you pronounce all the words?

air   dirty   early   learn   prefer   serve
square   turn   word   work

> **Learn/revise:** ball; baseball; chess; game; goal;
> golf; headache; hockey; hole; ladder; match;
> novelist; report; rule; snake; square; stick; tennis;
> change schools/jobs *etc.*; go back; hit (hit, hit);
> kick; miss; move; run (ran, run); stay (with sbdy);
> think about (sbdy/sth); throw (threw, thrown);
> touch; travel (travelling, travelled); try (tried); win
> (won, won); occupied; one after another; all day;
> worth ...ing.

D7 Where does it hurt?

Talking about illness; giving advice; reporting orders and advice; frequency adverbs; reading and listening for detail; listening for gist; pronunciation: connecting words together.

1 Read the dialogues below while you listen to the recording. Listen for the differences. (D = doctor; P = patient)

A

D: Where does it hurt?
P: Just here, doctor.
D: Mm. And is that all the time?
P: No. Only when I walk, or when I'm going downstairs. Sometimes when I carry things.
D: When you carry things. Big things?
P: Yes.
D: I see. Now I want you to stand up ...

B

D: How often do you get them?
P: Oh, three or four times a week.
D: Three or four times a week. I see. Are they very bad?
P: Oh, yes. They stop me driving. Sometimes I can hardly see, you know.
D: Yes. Do you often get colds?

C

P: It's a really bad cough. It's really bad.
D: Does it hurt when you talk?
P: If I talk a lot, yes.
D: I see. Well, I'll just have a look at your chest. Do you drink?

Now listen to these conversations and try to write down the words that go in the blanks.

D

P: It's a really bad pain, doctor. .... here.
D: Which side?
P: .... side.
D: How long has this been going on? When did it start?
P: .... morning, doctor. I thought perhaps it was indigestion, but it's too .... for that.
D: .... Now just .... down here. That's right. Now .... exactly does it hurt? Is it here?
P: Ooh! Yes!

E

D: Good morning, ... Palmer. What's the ....?
P: Well, I've got a .... sore throat, ...
D: .... How long have you had it?
P: Oh, about .... It's .... very painful. It's difficult to ....

F

P: It's every .... about the same time, doctor. Stuffed-up nose, my .... itch, and I feel sort of .... the whole time.
D: Is it .... when you're inside or outside?
P: When I'm in the ....

G

P: I get this .... when I bend ...., doctor. Just here.
D: I see. Take your .... off.

2 Copy this list, and then close your book. Find out what each of the words or expressions means, by using a dictionary or asking your teacher. Then listen to the conversations again. Which patient has which problem?

headaches	bronchitis	back trouble
appendicitis	a pulled muscle	hay fever
tonsilitis		

3 Here are some more things the doctor said:

A Don't carry heavy things for a while.
B I think you should make an appointment at the Eye Hospital.

And here is what the patients told their families:

A He told me not to carry heavy things.
B He advised me to make an appointment at the Eye Hospital.

What do you think the doctor told the other patients? Work in groups to decide, and report to the class. You can use words from the list below, or ask your teacher for help. Begin your sentences like this:

'We think the doctor told/advised patient C ...'

to have:	an operation some physiotherapy
	some tests a rest an injection
to take:	some tablets some medicine
	some syrup some vitamins
to wear:	a bandage
to do:	some exercises

Lesson D7

Students learn to talk about illnesses and to understand what doctors say to them, and to report orders and advice. They practise reading and listening for detail and listening for gist.
Principal structures: frequency adverbs; adverbials of frequency; reporting orders and advice.
Phonology: assimilation of consonants and linking.

If you are short of time
If pronunciation is not a high priority for your students, you can leave out Exercise 4. You can give Exercise 3 for homework.

---

1 In the doctor's surgery: listening   📼
- For the first three dialogues, ask the students to listen to the recording and try and write down the differences between the version in their books and the version on the recording.
- Point out that neither version is more correct than the other.
- You may want to play the recording a second time.
- Let students compare answers before checking the differences with you.
- For the last four dialogues, put the students into pairs and get them to try and guess what might go into the blanks.
- Go over the dialogues with them, asking for their answers; make sure you accept any answer that is appropriate, not just the ones in the recording.
- Then let them listen to the recording to find out what was meant to be in the blanks.
- You may want to play the dialogues more than once.
- Answer any questions students may have about the meaning of words and expressions in the dialogues.

Tapescript and answers to Exercise 1: see page 151

2 Which illness?   📼
- Ask students to close their books. Write the names of the illnesses on the board.
- Let students look them up in their dictionaries, or explain the meanings if you prefer.
- Practise the pronunciation carefully (there are several difficulties). Make sure students know how to say the ending -itis (/aɪtəs/).
- Then play the recording through without stopping, more than once if necessary, while students note down which problem corresponds to each dialogue.
- Let them compare notes before checking with you.

Answers to Exercise 2
A back trouble (*or* a pulled muscle)
B headaches
C bronchitis
D appendicitis
E tonsilitis
F hay fever
G a pulled muscle (*or* back trouble)

3 Reported instructions and advice
- Explain the examples to the students.
- Then put them into groups of three or four students and ask them to do the exercise.
- They should use their dictionaries to find out the meanings of the new words in the box.
- Walk round while they are working to give any help that is needed.
- When they have finished, let them read their sentences to the class. You may want to put a few sentences on the board.
- Practice Book exercise 2 gives more work on this point.

4 Pronunciation: linking and assimilation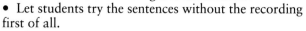

- Let students try the sentences without the recording first of all.
- Then play the recording sentence by sentence, giving the students plenty of practice on each one.
- Pay special attention to the marked links.

Tapescript for Exercise 4
Where does it hurt? (No gap before *it*; the *t* of *it* merges with the *h* of *hurt*.)
Only when I run. (No gap before *I*.)
I want you to stand up.
How often do you get them? (*do you* becomes /djuː/ or /dʒuː/; the final *t* in *get* is 'unexploded'.)
They stop me working. (The *p* in *stop* is unexploded.)
Sometimes I can hardly see.
Do you ever get hay fever?
It's a really bad cough. (Unexploded *d*.)
It's a really bad pain. (Unexploded *d*.)
This side. (One long *s*.)
Just lie down here. (The *t* of *just* merges with the *l* of *lie*.)
It's difficult to eat.
It's every year about the same time.
I get this pain.

5 Students choose language items to learn

- Let the students work individually on this exercise, noting five or more useful expressions to learn from Exercise 1.
- Then they can compare their lists with one another, saying why they have chosen each item.

6 Oral fluency activities and writing

- Put students into pairs and let them choose which of the two exercises they want to do.

A. Lists of questions

- This exercise provides some practice with frequency adverbs.
- Partners should ask one another the questions and note the answers. Walk round while they are working to give any help that is needed.
- The questions are based on some studies that show that certain personality types are more likely to have heart attacks than others, due to the amount of stress they put on themselves. If anyone answered 'Yes' to five or more of the questions, he or she is probably a 'Type A' person and may have a higher risk of a heart attack.
- When students have finished the first part of the exercise, they should get into groups of three or four and imagine that they work for an insurance company. Their job is to produce a list of about ten questions for people who want to buy life insurance.
- They should try to ask questions about people's health, family history, and habits (e.g. dangerous sports) that they think will 'weed out' people who stand a higher than normal risk of dying soon. In some classes you may want to tell them that silly questions are permitted.
- Walk round while they are working to help where needed.
- When the groups have finished, they can compare their lists; in a competitive class, they may want to vote for the best one.

B. Doctor-patient conversations

- One in each pair is a doctor, the other is a patient.
- They should prepare conversations similar to the dialogues in Exercise 1, using as many as possible of the items they noted in Exercise 5 and making sure they include at least two of the frequency adverbs/adverbials from the list.
- Let them know if you are going to tape- or video-record the conversations.
- Go round helping with vocabulary and pronunciation, and correcting mistakes if necessary.
- When students are ready, listen to them practise and then let them perform their conversations for the class.
- Don't correct while they are performing, but note serious mistakes for treatment later.
- Exercises 4 and 5 in the Practice Book give more vocabulary revision on the items from this lesson.

Practice Book exercises

1. Position of frequency adverbials.
2. Reported speech.
3. Student's Cassette exercise (Student's Book Lesson D7, Exercise 1). Students mark and practise sentence stress.
4. Grammar and vocabulary revision: completing a dialogue.
5. Writing one side of a dialogue.
6. Recreational reading: a choice of three texts.
7. Extended writing: a personal experience of being ill or in hospital.

4 🔊 Pronunciation. Say these sentences. Don't separate the words.

Where does it hurt?

Only when I run.

I want you to stand up.

How often do you get them?

They stop me working.

Sometimes I can hardly see.

Do you ever get hay fever?

It's a really bad cough.

It's a really bad pain.

This side.

Just lie down here.

It's difficult to eat.

It's every year about the same time.

I get this pain.

5 Look back at the dialogues in Exercise 1 and note down five or more useful expressions to learn. Compare your list with those of the students sitting near you.

6 Choose one of these activities. Or if you have time, do them both.

A. Are you likely to have a heart attack? Work with a partner: ask each other the questions below, and note down the answers. Then your teacher will tell you how to score the questionnaire.

1. Do you usually eat very quickly?
2. Do you sometimes do more than one thing at a time – for example, work while you're eating?
3. Do you ever have trouble finding time to get your hair cut or styled?
4. Are you often in a hurry?
5. Is success in your work very important to you?
6. Do you get upset if you have to wait in a queue?
7. Is finishing a job you've started very important to you?

Now imagine you are working for an insurance company. Your job is to make up a list of about ten questions, like the one here, for people who want life insurance. You don't want to give insurance to anyone who is likely to die very soon!

B. Work in pairs. Prepare a conversation between a doctor and a patient. Use at least two of these words or expressions in the conversation. You can ask your teacher for help with other words.

often	usually	sometimes	never	always

every year/week/*etc.*   two or three times a ...
all the time   the whole time

"It's a pity you haven't got appendicitis – I'm rather good at that."

"I wish you'd called me sooner, Mrs. Moodie."

Learn/revise: appendicitis; back trouble; bronchitis; chest; (a) cold; cough; hay fever; headache; injection; insurance; muscle; operation; pain; patient; queue; success; tablet; tonsilitis; advise; bend over (bent, bent); boil; breathe; carry; hurt (hurt, hurt); itch; lie down (lay, lain); stand up (stood, stood); tell (told, told); wear (wore, worn); heavy; upset; hardly; inside; outside; always; never; often; sometimes; usually; every year/week/ *etc.*; two or three times a ...; all the time; the whole time; a pulled muscle; a sore throat; in a hurry; How often ...?

D8 ...drove off without stopping

SKILLS FOCUS
SKILLS FOCUS
SKILLS FOCUS
SKILLS FOCUS
SKILLS FOCUS
SKILLS FOCUS

> Reading for detail; guessing meaning from context in written and recorded texts; vocabulary building and consolidation; listening for gist; listening for detail; simple report writing.

1 Read the newspaper report. Then look at the two maps and choose the map which corresponds to the report. Find on the map: a roundabout, a pedestrian crossing, a junction.

Driver forgets crashes

MOTORIST Lesley Aston doesn't remember much about her trip home from work.

But villagers at Studley, Warwicks., will never forget it.

First, her Austin 1300 rammed the back of another car waiting at a junction.

She drove off without stopping, overtook cars waiting at a pedestrian crossing and swung into a roundabout on the wrong side.

Then 20-year-old Lesley crashed head-on into a second car, swerved into a third and careered into a brick wall before coming to rest on a garage forecourt.

She later told police that she had only vague memories of what had happened, magistrates were told yesterday at Alchester, Warwicks.

Lesley, of Hewell Road, Redditch, Worcs., was fined £150 for reckless driving and failing to stop after an accident or report it.

2 Read the article again and try to guess the meaning of the following words and expressions.

trip   rammed   head-on   swerved   vague
fined   reckless   failing to stop

3 Work with another student. You have got five minutes to write down as many words and expressions as you can that have to do with driving. Examples:

Steering wheel, petrol, traffic light, ...

4 Read the following account of an accident and draw what happened.

Car A tried to overtake car B approaching a road junction. Car C, which was coming in the opposite direction, swerved to avoid car A and crashed into a tree on the corner of the junction.

5 Imagine an accident – you were the only witness besides the driver(s). Or remember a real accident you have witnessed or been involved in. Write a very simple report of the accident, like the one in Exercise 4. Read it to another student: he or she must try to draw what happened.

Lesson D8

Reading skills: reading for detail and guessing meaning from context.
Listening skills: listening for gist; listening for detail; guessing meaning from context.
Writing skills: simple reports.
Vocabulary: extension and consolidation of driving vocabulary.

Language notes and possible problems
Into Note the use of *into* after verbs like *crash*, *drive* etc., to talk about impacts.

If you are short of time
Drop Exercise 8.

1 Newspaper report
• This is an authentic report, unedited.
• Students will not understand everything, but they should be able to answer the question if they read carefully.
• Give them a few minutes to read the report (without dictionaries).
• Ask them to decide which map is the right one (it is the first), and let them compare notes.
• See if they can explain their reasons for choosing one or other map.
• Don't explain the difficult words (students have to guess what they mean in Exercise 2).

2 Guessing words
• Make sure students know what they are supposed to do.
• Although they are not very likely to know these words, they should be able to get a good idea of their meanings, without asking questions or looking them up, just by seeing how they are used in the text.
• Some students are not very good at contextual guessing of this kind, while others find it easy.
• When students have decided what they think the words mean, ask them to try to explain their ideas to each other.
• Finally, get volunteers to tell you their interpretations. (Let them explain in any way they like: with gestures, translations, synonyms or whatever.)

3 Vocabulary consolidation and extension
• Put students into pairs. Each pair should try to write down all the words and expressions they can think of that have to do with driving. Give them a five-minute limit.
• Walk round while they are working to give any help that is needed. The students can use their dictionaries or ask you for a few words, but be careful not to let the exercise turn into a dictionary search.
• When the five minutes is up, ask each pair to find another pair to compare answers with, or make up a class list.
• Each student should choose what he or she considers the five most important words in the list and tell one or two other students which words have been chosen and why.

4 Drawing what happened
• Give students five minutes or so to read the text and do their drawings.
• Then get them to work in groups exchanging drawings and discussing their different interpretations.

5 Pair work: accounts and drawings
• Make sure students understand the task.
• They will probably need a quarter of an hour or so to write their accounts.
• Emphasize that they should write simple reports like the one in Exercise 4. Help with vocabulary if necessary, but discourage students from using difficult words which their partners will not understand.
• When they are ready, get them to work in pairs, taking turns to read their descriptions to their partners. They will probably want to read their report two or three times. Partners have to draw the accident without looking at the text, but they can ask questions for clarification.

6 Listening for gist

- Give students a minute to look at the pictures.
- Their only task is to decide which picture goes with which recording. Make sure they understand that there are four pictures but only three recordings.
- Play the recording, and then let them consult in pairs or threes.
- If they want, play the recording once more before giving them the answers.

Answers to Exercise 6
1D; 2A; 3B

Tapescript for Exercise 6: see page 152

7 Listening: meaning from context

- In this exercise students will try to guess the meanings of unfamiliar words from the recordings by listening to their context.
- Let them look over the words and the choices of definitions. Make sure they understand the words in the definitions. (Note that *flung* can mean 'threw' or 'was/were thrown'; but in the context of the recording it is the second meaning that applies.)
- Then play the recording, stopping after each item to give them a chance to write down their answers.
- Let students consult about their answers; you will probably have to play the recording again before checking the answers.
- Make sure that they understand that the definitions given only apply to the context where they appear: they should not try to learn them for productive use.

Answers and tapescript for Exercise 7
1c; 2b; 3a; 4a; 5c; 6a; 7c

1. I got out of the car as usual and went to see the er, night porter, and er, he saw me, recognised me, came to the door, and at that moment the doors flung open, and just like a TV, in a TV series, er, these plainclothes people whipped out their wallets and showed, showed their er, showed their badges and said, ...
2. ... and they took some persuading that someone looking as scruffy as I in a tiny little Mini could possibly live in such a smart block of flats.
3. ... directly behind me, was a police car, and he saw me go through the light on amber/red, I thought, but he thought it was red, so he followed us round the corner onto the bridge, ...
4. ... so he followed us round the corner onto the bridge, overtook, stopped, and I sat tight in my car while Pete leapt out and defended me, ...
5. ... and er, we said that we didn't want to make a noise because the baby was asleep in the back, but er, we didn't get away with it, and I did get my licence endorsed.
6. ... I'd got this hot jazz blasting out of the erm, car cassette player at enormous volume, ...
7. And the policeman wound down his window, I wound down mine, and I was too perturbed to turn off the jazz.

8 Fluency choice: speaking/writing

- Give students a minute to read the two tasks. Each student should choose which task she/he wants to do.
- Group the students into pairs wanting to do the same task. If numbers are uneven, it will work to make a few groups of three.

A. Storytelling

- Students should work in pairs to tell each other their stories, ask any questions they want to, and then find new partners to repeat the process. Make yourself available to help if anyone gets stuck for a word or needs other information on language. When they finish

or you stop them, you might want to ask them to volunteer nominations for the most interesting story/ies and get it/them retold to the class.
- If you are worried about discipline problems in a younger class, you may prefer to get them to work in groups of four to six, telling their stories to the group. Groups can then vote on the one or two best stories to be retold to the class.

B. Writing questions on a text

- (This is based on the tapescripts of the recordings in Exercises 6 and 7.) Put students into pairs. Ask them to turn to page 133 in their books. Give them three minutes for each pair to decide which two stories they will work on, and which of them will work on each story.
- Tell them they can use their dictionaries.
- Give them a time limit, say ten minutes, for each student to write five to seven questions on the chosen text. Make yourself available to give any help that is needed.
- They should then exchange questions and try to write the answers. They can ask one another questions during this time.
- You may want to take up the questions and answers to see if there are recurrent mistakes that you want to treat in a later lesson; or you may want to ask the students if they want you to look at their work or not.

Practice Book exercises

1. Recreational reading: a humorous captioned picture story.
2. Revision of prepositions.
3. Student's Cassette exercise (Student's Book Lesson D8, Exercise 6). Students listen to the three stories and try to find two short sections from the first two stories which have been hidden in the transcript of the third story.
4. Predicting how a car accident is going to happen.
5. Recreational reading: a poem.
6. A choice of writing tasks: stories of motor accidents.
7. Crossword.

6 🔲 Listen, and match each recording to one of the pictures. There is one extra picture.

7 🔲 Listen to parts of the recordings again. Choose a likely meaning for each of the numbered words.

First recording
1. flung
   a. couldn't   b. stayed   c. were thrown
2. scruffy
   a. rich   b. untidy   c. sleepy

Second recording
3. amber
   a. yellow   b. broken   c. fast
4. leapt
   a. jumped   b. kept   c. shouted
5. endorsed
   a. given back   b. taken off the car
   c. marked with a bad point

Third recording
6. blasting
   a. coming very loudly   b. coming very quietly
   c. falling
7. wound
   a. broke   b. thought
   c. turned a handle to move

8 Choose one of the activities.
A. Have you / a family member / a friend ever been involved in a car accident or been stopped by the police? Work in pairs or groups and tell your stories to each other. You can ask questions about your partner's story. If there is time, form new pairs and exchange stories again.
B. Turn to page 133. With a partner, choose two of the three stories. Then each of you should work on one of the stories, writing five to seven questions about it for your partner to answer. You can use dictionaries while you are writing; your partner can ask you what some words mean.

Learn/revise: accident; corner; diagram; flat; garage; jazz; junction; (driving) licence; licence number; memory; motorist; noise; pedestrian; pedestrian crossing; porter; report (*noun and verb*); roundabout; (road) sign; space; speed limit; traffic; traffic lights; trip; university; wall; approach; avoid; crash (into); draw (drew, drawn); drive (drove, driven); fail; follow; overtake (overtook, overtaken); park; realise; crazy; smart; underground (*adjective*); opposite (*adverb*); in the opposite direction; go through a red light.

Summary D

Simple Present Perfect

completion

Have you **finished** that report yet?

change

What **has happened** to that shop that used to be here?

how many times up to now?

I've **played** tennis six times this week.

very long or permanent states

My family **have** always **lived** in York.

Present Perfect Progressive

continuation/repetition up to now

I've **been thinking** about you all day.
Jane and I **have been seeing** a lot of each other lately.

duration ('how long?') up to now

Sorry I'm late – **have** you **been waiting** long?
(... are you waiting long?)

Non-progressive verbs

How long **have** you **known** Pete?
(... have you been knowing Pete?)
I've **had** a headache since I got up.
(I've been having ...)

Modal verbs with perfect infinitives

I stayed at home and worked. But I **could have played** football.
'I felt really ill yesterday.' 'You **should have gone** to the doctor.'
'Why did she go out?' 'It **must have been** because of the phone call.'
She **may have had** an accident.
She **can't have gone** to the cinema.

can, have to, don't have to and *mustn't*

You **can** kick the ball but you **mustn't** touch it.
You **have to** hit a ball over a net.
You **have to** hit a ball and run; you **can** have three tries.
You **have to** hit a ball into a small hole; you **don't have to** run.

Reporting orders and advice

The doctor **advised me to make** an appointment at the Eye Hospital.
She **told me not to carry** heavy things.

Irregular verbs in Lessons D1–D8

INFINITIVE	PAST	PAST PARTICIPLE
bend	bent	bent
break	broke	broken
choose	chose	chosen
draw	drew	drawn
drive	drove	driven
fall	fell	fallen
fight	fought	fought
hit	hit	hit
hold	held	held
hurt	hurt	hurt
keep	kept	kept
lie	lay	lain
meet	met	met
overtake	overtook	overtaken
pay	paid	paid
run	ran	run
spend	spent	spent
stand	stood	stood
steal	stole	stolen
take	took	taken
tell	told	told
throw	threw	thrown
wear	wore	worn
win	won	won

Modal verbs with perfect infinitives in sentences with *if*

If ... had (not) been ..., hit ..., come, *etc.*	... would (not) have ... might (not) have ... could (not) have	attacked ... been ... got ... *etc.*

If I **had** not **been** ill when I was younger, I **would have** studied physics.
If I **had gone** to university, I **might have become** a doctor.
If I **had had** more time last year, I **could have gone** to America.

8 Interviews

• You will need to arrange, or to get students to arrange, for one or more English-speaking visitors to come to your class. (If it's impossible to get outside English-speakers, try to get English-speaking colleagues from your school to come along.) Make sure you choose visitors who don't mind being asked personal questions.

• Ideally, you should have several visitors (all at the same time) and the same number of groups of students, each with a set of questions prepared on a different topic. (For instance, one group will have prepared questions on childhood, one on family, one on social and political attitudes, one on likes and dislikes, one on work.) Then the visitors can rotate, each one going to each group in turn.

• An alternative is to arrange for students to interview English-speaking people outside the school (or to get students to arrange this for themselves).

• Follow up by having students report (in writing or orally) on what they found out and how they reacted to the various people.

Revision and fluency practice D

Students and teacher choose from a range of practice activities.

Teaching notes
Detailed teaching notes are not provided for all exercises in this section, since most of the activities are self-explanatory.

---

1 Mystery conversation
- Go over the instructions and the words in the box.
- Play the first section of the recording (a 'bleep' will tell you when to stop).
- Ask students what they can say about the mystery object. (For instance, it can't be a baby because one of the speakers says it's expensive.)
- Play the next section of the recording and ask students what they can say about the thing now.
- Continue in the same way (there are six sections).
- By the end of the fifth section, students may already have realised that the thing in question is a piano. The sixth section will make this clear.
- Follow up by getting students to make up their own mystery conversations in groups.

Tapescript for Exercise 1
A: It's a good one.
B: Do you think so?
A: Oh, yes.
B: I hope so. It's expensive enough.

A: Where shall we put it?
B: In the living room, I thought.

A: What, by the window?
B: I think it'll look better by the sofa.
A: Yes, maybe you're right. It's big, isn't it?
B: That's why I got this kind. I wanted a really big one. One with eight what-do-you-call-them, things, you know.
A: Yes, I know. They don't usually have eight, do they?
B: No, not usually.

A: I'm surprised you got a white one.
B: Well, I would have liked a red one, actually. But they don't make them in red.

A: It's nice to look at, isn't it?
B: Lots of room on top.
A: You could put flowers on it.
B: I'd be afraid to do that. I mean, if you knocked them over – suppose you knocked them over, and the water went inside, it'd ruin it.
A: Yes, I suppose it would.

A: Are you going to play it?
B: Oh, yes.
A: Can you play?
B: Well, not yet. But I'm going to take lessons. I expect I'll soon pick it up. My family's very musical, you know. Can you play?
A: Yes, a bit ...

(Note: the 'eight what-do-you-call-them' referred to in the third section are octaves – most pianos have seven and a quarter.)

Would you rather ...?

Would you rather have more or fewer brothers and
   sisters than you have?
Would you rather live in the same town as your
   parents or not?

Frequency adverbs; how often

often
usually
sometimes
never
always
ever (*usually in questions*)
every year/week/*etc.*
two or three times a ...
all the time
the whole time

Connecting words

Although there are many different kinds of families in
   the world, there are some things that are the same
   everywhere.
Not all societies have western-type marriage, **but**
   some kind of marriage is universal.
When a person marries, **besides** a new wife or
   husband, he or she gets a complete new family of
   in-laws.
Marriages with close relatives do not always produce
   healthy children, **so** all societies have rules about
   who can marry whom.
Each society **also** has a division of work based on age
   and sex.
There is a move to change this last rule **because** it can
   be unfair to women, **and** it will be interesting to see
   if it succeeds.

Prepositions of movement

down the hill   **along** the path
across the bridge   **up** the mountain
through the wood   **past** the station

Asking for and giving directions

Can you tell me the way to ...?
Take the first left.
You'll see it on your left.
Turn right at the first crossroads.
Go straight ahead for about 200 metres.
Keep straight on past the station.

Talking about illness

I've got a sore throat.
It's very painful.
It's difficult to talk.
It's a very bad cough.
It's really bad.
I get this pain when I bend over.
It's a really bad pain.
The headaches stop me driving.
How often do you get these headaches?
Are they very bad?
Do you drink?
Do you often get colds?
How long has this been going on?
How long have you had it?
When did it start?
Where exactly does it hurt?
I'll just have a look at your chest.

Vocabulary

Look through the 'Learn/revise' boxes at the ends
of Lessons D1–D8.

Revision and fluency practice D

A choice of activities.

1 🔲 Listen to the conversation. It is about one of the things in the box. Each time the conversation stops, say what you think. Examples:

'It might be a baby.'
'It could be a fridge.'
'It can't be a piano.'
'It must be a tree.'

baby	bookcase	canary	car	dog	electric typewriter
flower	fridge	garden	house	piano	piece of beef
statue	table	tree	wardrobe		

Make up similar conversations in groups, and see if the other students can work out what you are talking about.

2 🔲 Listen to the recording two or three times, and then look at the pictures. You must make up a story which explains the sounds in the recording, and which includes the people and things in the pictures. When you are ready, tell the other students.

3 Reading report. Talk to the class about what you have been reading recently in English.

4 Memory test. Work with a partner. Both of you look very carefully at the room (and the people and things in it) for one minute. Then one of you closes his or her eyes, while the other asks questions about the room.

5 Guided tour. Prepare a 'guided tour' for a visitor to your school, your home town or some other place. Then give your talk to a group of the other students.

6 Complete the dialogue and act it out for the class.

ANN: ....
BEN: My God!
ANN: ....
BEN: ....
ANN: ....
BEN: A big red one.
ANN: ....
BEN: ....
ANN: In the car park, I think.
BEN: ....
ANN: ....
BEN: £37.50.
ANN: ....
BEN: ....
ANN: Florida.
BEN: ....
ANN: ....
BEN: As soon as possible.
ANN: ....

7 Person of the year. Work in groups of three or four. In each group, choose the man or woman of the year – the person that you think has done most for the world during the last twelve months. When you have agreed on your choice, tell the rest of the class who you have chosen and why.

8 Interview. Prepare questions for an interview with an English-speaking stranger. You must find out as much as possible about him/her, including details of his/her childhood, education, family, work, interests, and social and political attitudes. Prepare 'follow-up questions' for some of your questions. Examples:

'Do you like music?'
'Yes, I do.'
'What kind?'

'What's your job?'
'I'm a builder.'
'Do you like it?'

When you have prepared your interview, arrange for one or more English-speaking people to visit your class. (Get your teacher to help if necessary.) Interview the person/people, and write a report on what you have found out.

9 Reacting to poetry. Here are three poems about animals. How do you feel about them? (Like / dislike / no reaction / ...?) See if you can find somebody else in the class who shares your reactions.

SOFTLY
Strong and long
The tiger crouches down
Orange and black in
The green grass.
Careful little fawn how
You pass.
(*Peter Sandell*, aged 8)

MEDITATIO
When I carefully consider the curious habits of dogs
I am compelled to conclude
That man is the superior animal.

When I consider the curious habits of man
I confess, my friend, I am puzzled.
(*Ezra Pound*)

CAGED BIRD
Bars are all she knows.
But every night in her dreams
High and free she flies.
(*Evan Stabetsi*)

10 Writing poetry. The last poem in Exercise 9 is a haiku. Haikus have three lines, usually containing five, seven and five syllables respectively (though some are more free than this). See if you can complete one of the following haikus; or write one of your own.

Outside my window
Snow lies on the high branches.

....

As one gets older
People give one more respect.

....

Right at this moment
What I would most like to do

....

In a new country

....

....

When you look at me

....

....

Test D

LISTENING

1 📼 Look at the map and listen to the three sets of directions. Where does each set of directions take you to? Possibilities:

Castle   National Museum
Cathays Station   National Stadium
Cathedral   Queen Street Station
Central Station   St David's Hall
Hospital   University

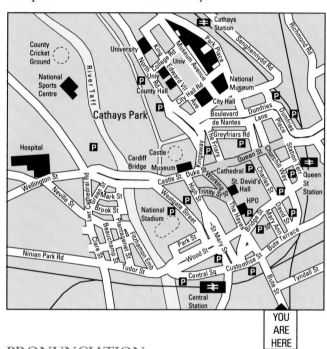

PRONUNCIATION

2 📼 Listen to the recording. Do you hear A or B?

	A	B
1.	deed	did
2.	ease	is
3.	eat	it
4.	feet	fit
5.	green	grin
6.	sheep	ship
7.	feel	fill

3 Look at these words. In each group, the underlined sounds are the same except in one word. Which word is different?

1. d<u>o</u>ne   g<u>o</u>ne   l<u>o</u>ve   s<u>o</u>n
2. g<u>o</u>t   l<u>o</u>st   h<u>o</u>liday   n<u>o</u>thing
3. h<u>air</u>   g<u>ir</u>l   w<u>or</u>k   h<u>ear</u>d
4. th<u>ere</u>   app<u>ear</u>ance   w<u>ear</u>   prep<u>are</u>
5. w<u>or</u>n   s<u>ore</u>   h<u>or</u>se   w<u>or</u>k
6. <u>ear</u>n   r<u>ear</u>   d<u>ir</u>ty   s<u>er</u>vice
7. thunde<u>r</u>sto<u>r</u>m   greengroce<u>r</u>   prefe<u>r</u>   loude<u>r</u>
8. w<u>ear</u>   p<u>ur</u>pose   em<u>er</u>gency   g<u>ir</u>l

4 Mark the main stress on these words.

assistant   condition   direction   experienced
headache   insurance   involve   operation
opposite   pedestrian   personality   police
prisoner   recover   tonsilitis   witness

GRAMMAR

5 Fill in the gaps with a structure using *must, may, should, can, could, can't, will, would, (don't) have to* or *had to*, together with the verb in brackets.

1. I don't think Agnes really wanted to see us – she said she had an appointment, but I'm sure she .... it if she really wanted to. (*change*)
2. 'Someone came to see you – a good-looking red-haired man.' 'Oh, that .... my cousin Isaac.' (*be*)
3. 'Do you know where the car keys are?' 'I'm not sure – I .... them on top of the fridge.' (*leave*)
4. I'm surprised Barbara has left – she .... her work already. (*finish*)
5. I suppose I .... my parents about my problems at school, but I didn't want to worry them. (*tell*)
6. When I was younger you .... twenty-one to vote. (*be*)
7. Americans .... a passport to go from one state of the US to another, but they .... one to go to France. (*have, have*)

6 Rewrite the sentences as in the example. Use *tell* or *advise*.

Ann: 'Take the first left.'

Ann told me to take the first left.

1. Doctor: 'Don't carry heavy things for a while.'
2. Elizabeth: 'You should get more exercise.'
3. Mark: 'I wouldn't go to Greece in August if I were you.'
4. Teacher: 'Learn the irregular verbs as soon as possible.'

LANGUAGE IN USE

7 Use each word in a question.

1. rather (*ask about preferences*)
2. the way (*ask for directions*)
3. hurt
4. problem

8 Write down five things you might say at the doctor's.

92

Test D

This test covers work done in Lessons D1–D8.

Administration of the test

1. General procedure Give students a few minutes to look over the test and make sure they understand what they are to do in each part.

2. Listening (Exercise 1) Give students a few minutes to look at the map, and to look over the list of places. Make sure they understand that they will hear three sets of directions, each to one of the places listed.

Play the recording, twice or three times, pausing after each speaker for the students to note their answers.

3. Pronunciation (Exercise 2) Make sure students understand the instructions. Get them to write the numbers 1 to 7 on their papers, and to look over the two lists of words. Tell them they have only to write *A* when they hear a word from the first column and *B* if they hear a word from the second column.

Play the recording twice, pausing after each item for students to write their answers.

4. Speaking (Exercise 15) You will have to take students aside in pairs for the Speaking part of the test. If you have a large class and a short class period, you may have to drop this part of the test.

Explain to students what they will be doing in the speaking exercise after they have done Exercise 2. Each student should take a few minutes at that time to decide which of the two options he or she wants to choose for the speaking test.

Call each pair of students out of the class, for example to your desk or to the back of the classroom, while the others work on the written part of the test.

Try to make the students feel comfortable. Tell them that the person who is listening can ask for clarification if she/he wants.

Remember that what you are looking for in this Speaking test is fluency, not perfect grammar or pronunciation. What counts is whether the students can make themselves understood.

LISTENING

1

Tapescript and answers
1. Er, yes, quite simple really, you should make it, I think. Go straight on, over the crossroads, and then turn right at Bridge Street. Continue straight on, over two crossroads, and then the street sort of curves around to the left. It's just after that curve, with the car park across the street. (*Queen Street Station*)
2. Yes. Er, go up here to the first set of lights, erm, at the crossroads, you'll see the car park on your left, and turn left. Continue on past the station. Then turn sort of left over the bridge – you can't go wrong, it's the only bridge and you have to cross it. Then go straight on, don't worry about all the little streets on the right, three of them I think, but when you get to a crossroads, then turn right. Take the one, two, third left and it will be at the first crossroads, right across the street from you – you can't miss it, it's a great big building. (*Hospital*)
3. Yes, well, let's see, it's a long walk, what's the best way to tell you? Go straight on here, past the car park, over the crossroads, and then take a right at Bridge Street. Then first left, and go straight on for quite a way – you'll cross the pedestrian precinct at Queen Street, just continue on, over the big double carriageway, Dumfries I think it's called – do be careful there, some people do drive fast on that street – and then take the first left after that, and the second right. Go straight on over one crossroads and you're there. (*University*)

PRONUNCIATION

2

Tapescript and answers
1. did (*B*)
2. is (*B*)
3. eat (*A*)
4. fit (*B*)
5. green (*A*)
6. sheep (*A*)
7. fill (*B*)

3

1. gone /gɒn/ (the others have /ʌ/)
2. nothing /nʌθɪŋ/ (the others have /ɒ/)
3. hair /heə/ (the others have /ɜː/)
4. appearance /ə'pɪərəns/ (the others have /eə/)
5. work /wɜːk/ (the others have /ɔː/)
6. rear /rɪə(r)/ (the others have /ɜː/)
7. prefer /prɪ'fɜː(r)/ (the others have /ə/)
8. wear /weə(r)/ (the others have /ɜː/)

4

assistant	condition	direction	experienced
headache	insurance	involve	operation
opposite	pedestrian	personality	police
prisoner	recover	tonsilitis	witness

GRAMMAR

5

1. could have changed
2. must have been / must be
3. may / might have left
4. can't / must have finished
5. should have told
6. had to be
7. don't have to have; have to have / must have

6

1. The doctor told me not to carry heavy things for a while.
2. Elizabeth advised me to get more exercise.
3. Mark advised me not to go to Greece in August.
4. My/The teacher told me to learn the irregular verbs as soon as possible.

LANGUAGE IN USE

7

(Many possible answers – accept anything appropriate. Examples:)
1. Would you rather go on holiday on your own than go with your family?
2. Can you tell me the way to the Regent Cinema?
3. Where does it hurt?
4. What's the problem?

8

(Many possible answers – see Lesson D7 for possibilities.)

READING AND WRITING

9

1. marched him out
2. at gunpoint
3. whispering
4. nightstand
5. locked
6. astounded
7. complied with his request
8. porch

(Summary: various answers possible. The facts should be corrected as follows:)
A woman woke up to find a man crawling *into her bed*. She made the man leave by threatening him with a *gun*, and *then* she phoned the police. A few minutes later the man knocked on the door to ask *for a light for his cigarette*. The police arrived, saw him running away and *arrested* him.

10
(Many possible answers; look for a fair degree of fluency, accuracy and appropriateness.)

VOCABULARY

11
(Many possible answers: these are taken from Lessons D1–D8.)
1. bathroom, bedroom, breakfast room, cloakroom, dining room, (double) bedroom, (double) garage, downstairs, garden, gas-fired/oil-fired central heating, kitchen, library, living room, lounge, reading room, residence, roof, shower, sitting room, storeroom, toilet, upstairs, wall, window
2. aunt, cousin, family, granddaughter, grandson, grandchild, grandfather, grandparent, husband, in-laws, marriage, mother-in-law, brother-in-law, sister-in-law, daughter-in-law, son-in-law, nephew, niece, relative, uncle, wife, adopt, divorced, married, separated, single
3. bridge, east, island, lake, mountain, north, path, road, south, stream, valley, waterfall, west, wood
4. ball, chess, chess board, chess piece, deal, dice, draughts, draughts board, goal, golf club, kick, move, net, playing-cards, snooker table, tennis racket
5. back trouble, bronchitis, chest, a cold, cough, hay fever, headache, insurance, muscle, operation, pain, patient, tablet, tonsilitis, breathe, hurt, itch, pulled muscle, sore throat
6. corner, junction, driving licence, motorist, pedestrian, pedestrian crossing, road sign, speed limit, traffic, traffic lights, trip, drive, overtake, park, approach, in the opposite direction

12
1. of
2. in
3. from
4. in; with
5. with
6. of
7. with
8. on/over; with
9. with

13
1. to go out
2. trying
3. to lie down
4. learning

14
at once
bank account
car park
full-time
hay fever
lie down
pay back
pulled muscle
railway station
sitting room
town hall

SPEAKING

15
(Remember that fluency is what counts here.)

Test Book recording
A recording for Test 4 in the Test Book follows this lesson on the Class Cassette.

READING AND WRITING

9 Read the newspaper article and do the tasks that follow.

Fag end of the evening

From UPI in Dallas

A 35-YEAR-OLD woman who was awakened by an unknown man crawling into her bed marched him out at gunpoint, only to have him knock on her door a few moments later and ask for a light for his cigarette.

The woman told police she awoke to find a partially dressed man crawling into her bed whispering: "I want you, I love you." She responded by grabbing a small pistol from her nightstand and telling him: "I'll kill you. I want you out of my house."

The woman said she forced the man out of her apartment at gunpoint, locked the door, and called the police. But within seconds, there was a knock on the door. She opened it, its chain still in place, to find her assailant calmly asking her for a light for his cigarette. The astounded woman said she got her lighter, complied with his request, and re-locked the door.

Police arrived to see the man running from the woman's porch carrying a lighted cigarette, and arrested a 20-year-old suspect a short time later.

(from The Guardian)

Find words or expressions that mean:

1. made him walk out (*lines 1–8*)
2. by threatening him with a gun (*lines 1–8*)
3. speaking very quietly (*lines 9–18*)
4. small table next to a bed (*lines 9–18*)
5. closed with a key (*lines 19–24*)
6. surprised (*lines 24–32*)
7. did what he asked (*lines 24–32*)
8. area just outside a front door (*lines 33–38*)

Here is a summary of the article; but there are some things in it that are not true. Rewrite the summary, correcting the mistakes.

A woman woke up to find a man crawling through her window. She phoned the police, and then she made the man leave by threatening him with a knife. A few minutes later the man knocked on the door to ask to use the telephone. The police arrived, saw him running away but did not catch him.

10 Choose one of these tasks. Write 150 words or more.

1. Have you ever been a victim or a witness of a theft, a burglary, a robbery, a mugging? Write about what happened.
2. Imagine you are the woman in the story in Exercise 13. Write a letter to a close friend telling her or him what happened.
3. Have you ever been surprised when someone (or you yourself!) thought and acted quickly in a dangerous situation? Write about what happened.
4. Has anyone in your family, or any of your friends, ever done something you were proud of? Write about it.

VOCABULARY

11 Add some words and/or expressions to each list.

1. central heating, upstairs, ... (*six or more words or expressions*)
2. father-in-law, grandmother, ... (*ten or more*)
3. river, hill, ... (*four or more*)
4. baseball bat, serve, ... (*eight or more*)
5. appendicitis, injection, ... (*five or more*)
6. roundabout, crash, ... (*four or more*)

12 Put the right word in each blank.

1. I'm very fond .... Jill.
2. Are you .... a hurry?
3. Has John recovered .... his operation?
4. Have you ever fallen .... love .... someone who doesn't speak your language?
5. I've heard that Jo is breaking up .... Bob.
6. Veronica's mother is very proud .... her.
7. Would you like to share my lunch .... me?
8. She hit the mugger .... the head .... her briefcase.
9. Do you get on .... Alex?

13 Infinitive or *-ing* ?

1. Do your parents allow you .... with anybody you want? (*go out*)
2. Just keep .... and you'll succeed one day. (*try*)
3. The bank robber forced the customers .... on the floor. (*lie down*)
4. Do you enjoy .... languages? (*learn*)

14 Two-word expressions: match the two halves.

at	account
bank	back
car	down
full-	fever
hay	hall
lie	muscle
pay	once
pulled	park
railway	room
sitting	station
town	time

SPEAKING

15 Choose one of these tasks.

1. Describe a place you know to another student so that she/he can draw a simple sketch of it.
2. Look back at the map in Exercise 1: give another student directions to a place; see if the student can tell you where you have led him/her.

E1 Another good day

Weather vocabulary; *will*-future; reporting with *would*; pronunciation of /h/, *it'll* and *there'll*; listening, speaking and writing practice.

1 📼 Copy the table. Listen to the recording and circle the expressions which you hear.

TODAY	another good day not a good day sunshine rain drought
TOMORROW	it'll cloud over tomorrow evening showers today warm temperatures 36–37 maximum
SUNDAY	rather cloudy a few showers not much cooler
MONDAY	sun very hot normal temperatures

2 Look at these three ways of talking about the weather.

WITH A VERB	WITH A NOUN	WITH AN ADJECTIVE
It often **rains**.	There is often **rain**.	It is often **rainy/wet**.
It often **clouds over**.	There is often **cloud**.	It is often **cloudy**.

Now put these words into the correct columns:
blow   cold   cool   fog   foggy   hot   shine   sunshine
snow (*two places*)   sun   sunny   warm   wind   windy

Can you add the other points of the compass?

3 Read the text about the weather in East Texas. Then complete the text about the weather in Britain, using the words and expressions in the box. Finally, write a short text about the weather in your country (or another country, or an imaginary country).

THE WEATHER IN EAST TEXAS

In East Texas, in the area of the Gulf of Mexico, the climate is generally hot and often very humid. Temperatures in summer range from 30° to 40°C; 25°C is a normal winter temperature. It is sometimes cold, but only for two or three days at a time; it snows perhaps once every twenty years. It quite often rains heavily for two or three days or more, but most of the time the weather is sunny with bright blue skies. Occasionally there are droughts – periods when there is no rain for a long time. It is not usually very windy, but there are hurricanes every few years, with wind speeds reaching over 150 kilometres an hour.

THE WEATHER IN BRITAIN

In Britain, the ......1...... is very ......2......; it ......3...... a lot, but the sun often ......4...... too. ......5...... can be ......6...... cold and damp, with an average ......7...... of 5°C in the south; there is often snow. Summers can be cool or warm, but the temperature ......8...... not usually go above 30°C. It is ......9...... cloudy, and there are ......10...... grey ......11...... for days or weeks ......12....... Days are ......13...... in summer and ......14...... in winter. There is sometimes fog, especially in ......15...... and autumn, ...16...... it is not so common as foreigners think. Thunderstorms (storms with thunder and ......17......) are quite common in mountainous areas. British ......18...... never ......19...... what tomorrow's weather will be ......20.......

at a time	but	changeable	does
fairly	know	lightning	like long
often	people	rains	shines short
skies	sometimes	spring	temperature
weather	winters		

94

Lesson E1

Students revise and expand their knowledge of the language used to talk about weather.
Principal structures: *will*-future; frequency adverbs; reported speech with *would*.
Phonology: /h/; *it'll* and *there'll*.

Language notes and possible problems

1. Will This lesson gives some revision practice in the use of the *will*-future for prediction. Students who are weak on the expression of the future may find it useful to do some of the exercises on pages 122–123.

2. Frequency adverbs For detailed work on the position of words like *sometimes* and *often*, see Lesson E6.

3. Reported speech Exercise 7 gives a little practice in the use of *would* to report direct-speech *will*. For more on this, see Lesson E2.

4. It Students should already be familiar with the use of *it* in sentences about the weather, but it may be worth mentioning it if a similar structure does not occur in their mother tongue(s).

5. Word formation Exercise 2 gets students to take a look at relationships between nouns, verbs and adjectives that have the same form or the same root.

6. Vocabulary problems You may need to explain the differences between *warm* and *hot*, and *cool* and *cold*. Make sure students realise that *humid* is used in English mainly for climate, especially in warm countries; this word is a 'false friend' for speakers of some romance languages, and students may confuse it with *damp*.

If you are short of time
Exercise 2, 5 or 8 could be dropped

1 Listening for specific information

- This is a piece of relatively difficult authentic speech – an extract from a radio weather forecast. The exercise should help students to realise that they can pick out key information from fast difficult unclear material even when they can't understand every word.
- Explain what is going to happen and get students to copy the table. Clear up any difficulties.
- Play each part of the recording once, pausing at the places shown in the tapescript while students circle the words and expressions they identify.
- Play the recording again once or twice.
- Let students compare notes with their neighbours.
- Go through the recording pointing out the expressions which actually occur.
- Discourage students from trying to write down and learn every new word and expression in the recording – this will take time which could probably be used more constructively.

Tapescript and answers to Exercise 1
'What's actually going to happen today, then?'
'Well, today is *another good day*. Much the same as yesterday, with the mist and foggy patches clearing in the next hour or so, and then everywhere should have prolonged *sunshine* throughout the day ... (*Pause*)
Tomorrow morning bright and dry, but *it'll cloud over* gradually during the day, and there is a threat *tomorrow evening* and tomorrow night of some showery outbreaks of rain. I think it'll be mostly small amounts, but one or two of the *showers* could be a bit heavy tomorrow night. *Temperatures* a little bit cooler, but not much, probably about 26–27 maximum tomorrow, with a light southerly wind.'
(*Pause*)

'Briefly, Sunday and Monday?'
'Sunday, a *rather cloudy* day in this area I think, with *a few showers*, not much sunshine, much cooler, maximum 23 ... (*Pause*)
but dry on Monday I think with a fair amount of *sun*, but again rather cool with, well, *normal temperatures* 22 or 23 centigrade.'
'Still, not bad, not bad at all. OK, Harry, thanks very much indeed. Bye now.'
'Bye-bye.'

2 Word formation

- This is probably best done as a whole-class activity.
- Put the three columns on the board with their example sentences.
- Ask students where to put *sunny* and get them to make a sentence.
- Continue in the same way with the other words.
- Students should notice two things:
  - Some words can function as nouns and verbs (e.g. *rain, snow*).
  - Some adjectives are formed by adding *-y* to nouns (e.g. *rainy, windy, cloudy, foggy*).
- If students are interested, you could get them to try to think of more examples of this kind of correspondence.

Answers to Exercise 2

VERB	NOUN	ADJECTIVE
blow	fog	cold
shine	sunshine	cool
snow	snow	foggy
	sun	hot
	wind	sunny
		warm
		windy

3 Climate: reading, text completion and writing

- Give students a minute or two to read through the first text, using dictionaries or asking questions about the vocabulary.
- The text completion can be done as a group or whole-class activity.
- Finally, get students to write individual descriptions of the climate in whatever country they choose. (Descriptions of imaginary countries can be very entertaining.)

Answer to Exercise 3
In Britain, the (1) *weather* is very (2) *changeable*; it (3) *rains* a lot, but the sun often (4) *shines* too. (5) *Winters* can be (6) *fairly* cold and damp, with an average (7) *temperature* of 5°C in the south; there is often snow. Summers can be cool or warm, but the temperature (8) *does* not usually go above 30°C. It is (9) *often* cloudy, and there are (10) *sometimes* grey (11) *skies* for days or weeks (12) *at a time*. Days are (13) *long* in summer and (14) *short* in winter. There is sometimes fog, especially in (15) *spring* and autumn, (16) *but* it is not so common as foreigners think. Thunderstorms (storms with thunder and (17) *lightning*) are quite common in mountainous areas. British (18) *people* never (19) *know* what tomorrow's weather will be (20) *like*.

94

4 Information transfer: weather map
• This can be done in groups, with groups comparing notes when they are ready.
• Various answers are possible.

5 Pronunciation: *h, it'll* and *there'll*
• Not all students will need to practise /h/. Those who do may need to be reminded that the *h* in *hour* is silent.
• The 'laterally exploded' /t/ before /l/ in *it'll* is difficult for some learners, and there is no need to insist on an accurate pronunciation unless students are really anxious to get it right. However, it is important that they recognise the sound as a /t/ when they hear it, and the exercise should help with this.
• It is also important that they learn to recognise the weak pronunciation of *there* in *there'll* and similar combinations, even if they don't learn to pronounce it correctly themselves.
• Let students try the different sections of the exercise before they hear the correct pronunciation. Use the recording as a model if you wish; if not, make sure that you don't produce over-clear variants of *it'll* and *there'll*.

6 Students' weather forecasts
• Give students a few minutes to prepare these.
• Then ask them to give their forecasts (either to the whole class or to groups) as if they were reading them on radio or TV.
• Listeners should make notes of differences, in preparation for the next exercise.

7 Reporting forecasts
• Students should write at least five sentences. Make sure they use reported speech structures with *would*, as in the example.

8 Song: *Thirty degrees*
• Play the song once while students listen. See if they have some idea of what it's about in general, and get them to mention any details that they have understood.
• Then play the song again while students try to write down words related to weather and cars.
• Finally let them turn to page 133 and read through the text. Answer questions and clear up any problems.

Practice Book exercises
1. Vocabulary revision: completing a text.
2. *Can't, might, must, shall, will* (or *'ll*), and *would* (or *'d*).
3. *Will, 'll* and *going to*.
4. Words which can have more than one grammatical function.
5. Student's Cassette exercise (Student's Book Lesson E1, Exercise 8). Students listen to the song and decide which words they hear.
6. Recreational reading: a choice of popular fiction and two newspaper articles.

4 What is the weather forecast for Western Europe? Write five or more sentences using information from the map. Example:

It will be dry and sunny in Spain.

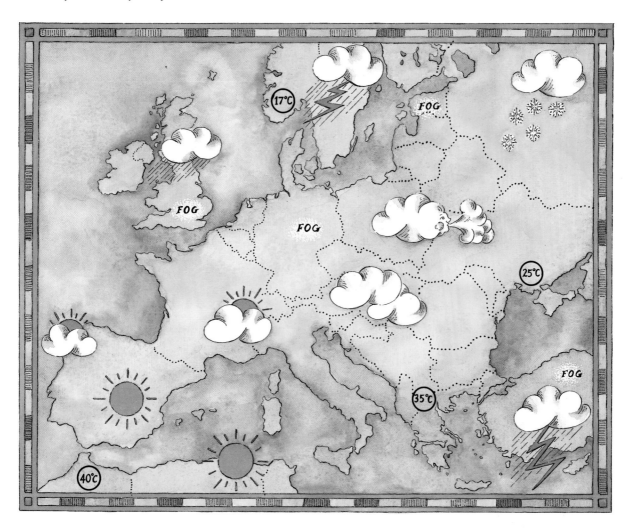

5 🔳 Pronounce these words and expressions.

hot   humid   heavy   hurricane   hour
very hot   very humid   there are hurricanes
heavy rain   it rains heavily   for hours

It'll be very hot.
It'll cloud over.
It'll rain.
It'll snow.

There'll be rain.
There'll be snow.
There'll be sunshine.
There'll be fog on high ground.

6 Prepare and give your own weather forecast for tomorrow (a good or bad one, as you like).

7 Write five sentences comparing different people's forecasts. Example:

Maria said it would be sunny tomorrow, but Paul said it would rain.

8 🔳 Listen to the song without looking at the words and write down five or more words connected with *weather* or *cars*. Then look at the words as you listen a second time. (The text is on page 133.)

Learn/revise: cloud; drought; fog; hurricane; lightning; rain (*noun and verb*); shower; sky; snow (*noun and verb*); speed; sun; sunshine; temperature; thunder; thunderstorm; weather; weather forecast; wind; spring; summer; autumn; winter; north; south; west; east; north-west; north-east; south-west; south-east; blow (blew, blown); cloud over; shine (shone, shone); average; bright; changeable; cloudy; cold; cool; damp; foggy; grey; hot; humid; maximum; normal; rainy; sunny; warm; wet; windy; fairly; heavy rain; high ground; what ... like; at a time.

E2 Focus on systems

A choice of exercises: reported speech with *would* and *had*; names of everyday objects; punctuation; spelling and pronunciation of contractions.

GRAMMAR: REPORTED SPEECH WITH *WOULD* AND *HAD*

'You **will** have a wonderful week.' My horoscope said that I **would** have a wonderful week.	'John **has** gone on a business trip.' Mary knew that John **had** gone on a business trip.

1 Here is your horoscope from the beginning of last week. Say whether it was true or not. Use *would*. Examples:

'My horoscope said I would have a wonderful week, but actually it was a terrible week.'
'My horoscope said I would make new friends, and I did.'
'My horoscope said I would get bad news on Monday, but I didn't.'

YOUR STARS THIS WEEK

ARIES (Mar 21–Apr 20)
You will have a wonderful week. Lots of money will come to you, and you will go on a long journey at the weekend. You will make exciting new friends.

Taurus (Apr 21–May 21)
There will be bad news on Monday. On Tuesday afternoon at 3.45 you will meet a tall dark stranger. This will be a good week for love, but a bad week for money.

Gemini (May 22–June 21)
You will receive an exciting offer in Wednesday's post, and on Thursday you will meet somebody who could change your life. But you will have a lot of trouble with children this week.

Cancer (June 22–July 22)
You will have a terrible week, and something very strange will happen on Thursday. You will fall out of bed on Sunday and hurt your elbow.

Leo (July 23–Aug 23)
You will get a shock on Friday, and something that you value will be stolen from you. A large animal will bring problems. There will be a lot of bills to pay.

Virgo (Aug 24–Sept 23)
You will meet an old friend that you had lost contact with, and you will quarrel violently with a member of your family. On Tuesday you will have to make an important decision.

Libra (Sept 24–Oct 23)
There will be a misunderstanding with somebody you love. If you keep your ears open you will learn an important secret. On Saturday you will break something valuable.

Scorpio (Oct 24–Nov 22)
The first part of the week will be better than the second. This will not be a good time for love, and you will not meet anybody interesting. You will make a big mistake on Thursday, and an even bigger one on Friday.

Sagittarius (Nov 23–Dec 21)
Nobody will fall in love with you this week, and you will be ill on Wednesday. A letter will bring a pleasant surprise. At the weekend, you will do something you have never done before.

Capricorn (Dec 22–Jan 20)
You will make an unexpected journey, and meet an old friend at the end of it. You will lose some money in the middle of the week. On Tuesday evening you will have a small accident – nothing serious.

Aquarius (Jan 21–Feb 18)
At last, people will realise how clever you are. You will be elected President of an important organisation. A machine will bring you unusual problems.

Pisces (Feb 19–Mar 20)
You will be very unhappy this week. You will fall into a river on Wednesday. The end of the week will be especially bad. Perhaps next week will be better. It can't be much worse.

2 🔲 Listen to the recording and try to complete some of the sentences. Example:

'Mary knew that John had gone on a business trip.'

Mary knew ... had ...
Mary wondered if ... had ...
Mary found out ... had ...
The hotel told Mary ... had ...

Mary told her mother ... had ...
John told Joe ... had ...
Joe told Mary ... had ...
Mary asked Joe if ... had ...

96

Lesson E2

Grammar: reported speech using *would*, reported speech using Past Perfect.
Punctuation: revision of basic rules.
Phonology: contractions.
Vocabulary: names of everyday objects.

Language notes and possible problems

1. Reported speech   Students at this level should have a reasonable grasp of the rules for the use of tenses in reported speech. Some may still have problems with less common structures; Exercises 1–3 give practice in the use of *would* and Past Perfect forms in reported speech clauses. Students who still have difficulty with the basic rules should work on the revision exercises on pages 124–125.

2. Punctuation   Speakers of languages which do not use the Roman alphabet may still be shaky on punctuation and capitalisation. Exercise 4 will help you to see where the problems lie. Note that in German and some other Northern European languages, commas are used before noun clauses. Look out for mistakes like *She thought, that he had taken her keys.*

3. Contractions   Some students may find certain contractions difficult to pronounce, especially those ending in *'ll* and those in which *n't* follows a consonant. You may also like to make sure that students are distinguishing adequately between *won't* and *want*.

  Note that students from some cultures may have a resistance to using contractions because they feel that colloquial forms are 'incorrect'. Help them to understand that these forms are correct in English, and that it is in fact often *incorrect* to use full forms in unemphatic informal speech.

---

1 Reported speech with *would*: horoscopes

• Tell students to think about what happened to them last week.
• Then get them to read the horoscopes, imagining that these were printed in a magazine the weekend before last.
• Their task is to make some sentences about whether the horoscopes came true or not. (Note the use of *actually* to signal a correction. This word is a 'false friend' for many speakers of European languages, who may think it means 'now'.)
• When they have done this, ask if anybody else's horoscope was more accurate for them than their own (and if so why).
• As a follow-up exercise, you could get them to write horoscopes for each other for the coming week (and to report back on their accuracy in a week's time).

2 Reported speech with Past Perfect: listening

• Play the recording through once while students listen.
• Then see if they can complete any of the sentences. They do not need to complete them all.
• Play the recording again, and let students compare notes before you discuss the answers.

Possible answers to Exercise 2

(Various other answers are also acceptable.)
Mary knew that John had gone on a business trip.
Mary knew that John had checked out of the hotel.
Mary wondered if he had taken her keys.
Mary found out that John had checked out of his hotel.
The hotel told Mary that John had cancelled his booking.
Mary told her mother that John had gone off with another woman.
John told Joe that he had tried to phone Mary.

John told Joe that he had run into an old friend and was staying with him.
Joe told Mary that John had phoned him and asked him to give her a message.
Mary asked Joe if John had left a phone number.

Tapescript for Exercise 2

MARY: Bye, darling. Have a good trip.
JOHN: Hope so. See you on Thursday. Bye.
MARY: Bye.

PAUL: Hello, John. What are you doing here?
JOHN: Paul! Good heavens! What a surprise. It must be five years. Well, well, well … I'm here on business for a couple of days. What about you?
PAUL: Me? Oh, I live here. Look, why don't you come and stay with us?
JOHN: Oh, no, I couldn't. Really, I –
PAUL: There's plenty of room. We'll phone your hotel and cancel your booking. Come on. My car's just round the corner.
JOHN: Well, if you're really sure. OK, …

MARY: Oh, God. Where are my keys? Where the hell are my keys? I wonder if John's taken them. I'll have to phone his hotel.

RECEP: Royal Hotel.
MARY: Hello. Could I speak to Mr John Develin, please?
RECEP: I'm sorry, madam, Mr Develin isn't staying here.
MARY: But he must be. He's booked in for two nights.
RECEP: He was booked in, madam, but he phoned and cancelled half an hour ago. He said he'd changed his plans.
MARY: I see. All right. Thank you.

MARY: Mother. He's checked out of his hotel. I don't know where he is.
MOTHER: Calm down, Mary, calm down. I'm sure there's some perfectly simple explanation, dear.
MARY: I'm sure there is, and I know exactly what it is. He's gone off with that Smith woman. Oh, when I get my hands on her …

JOE: Parkside 35426.
JOHN: Hello, Joe. This is John. Look, could you do me a favour? I've tried to phone Mary six times and I can't get through. It's engaged all the time. Could you possibly go next door and give her a message?
JOE: Sure. What do you want me to tell her?
JOHN: Could you just say I've run into an old friend and I'm staying with him, and not at the hotel. I'll give her a ring later.
JOE: Sure. I'll go round now.
JOHN: Thanks a lot, Joe.
JOE: OK. Cheers.
JOHN: Bye.

JOE: Hello, Mary.
MARY: Hello, Joe.
JOE: What's the matter?
MARY: It's John. He's run off with some woman.
JOE: No, he hasn't. He's just rung me. He's staying with an old friend; he asked me to tell you.
MARY: Well, why didn't he ring me?
JOE: He couldn't get through.
MARY: Couldn't get through? Hah! Well, did he leave a phone number?
JOE: No, actually, I don't think he did.
MARY: I knew it! Old friend – I know just who that old friend is. When I get my hands on her …
JOE: But Mary. He said …
MARY: You men! You're all in it together!

3 Mixed reported speech: reporting John and Mary's conversation

• Give students a few minutes to suggest some of the things that John and Mary may have said to each other when John phoned later on. Write these on the board.
• Then get them to write brief reports, using past reporting verbs (*said* etc.).
• They should be able to get in some examples of *would* and Past Perfect tenses.
• This exercise could also be done in groups, or as a class composition using the board.

4 Punctuating a letter

• This can be done individually, in groups or by class discussion, as you prefer.
• Punctuation in informal letters is not always very careful, and quite a lot of variation is possible, especially in the divisions between sentences and the use of commas. Accept any reasonable answers.
• Explain any points that students are having trouble with.

Possible answer to Exercise 4

Dear Sue(,)

  How are you these days? I made a real fool of myself last week. It happened like this. John went off on a business trip, and then I thought that he'd taken my keys, so I rang up his hotel. 'I'm sorry,' the girl said, 'but he's not here. He's cancelled.' Well, I was sure he'd gone off with that American woman. (Do you remember me telling you about her last year?) But actually it turned out that he'd met an old school friend and gone to stay with him. He tried to phone me but he couldn't get through, because I was telling mother all my troubles. Then when he got our neighbour to give me a message, I wouldn't listen, and shut the door in his face. So when John finally rang up we had a colossal row, and things are still a bit difficult. Sue, I do feel stupid. Have you ever done anything like that, or am I the only one?

  Give my love to Fred and the kids.
  Mary

5 Changing full forms to contractions; pronouncing contractions

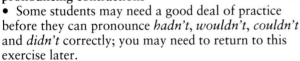

• Some students may need a good deal of practice before they can pronounce *hadn't, wouldn't, couldn't* and *didn't* correctly; you may need to return to this exercise later.
• The recording can be used as a guide if you wish.

6 Vocabulary: names of everyday objects

• This can be done by group discussion, with students pooling their knowledge.

Answers to Exercise 6

1. a coin   2. a bath   3. a brick   4. a screwdriver
5. a corkscrew   6. a ruler   7. a pair of scissors
8. a pillow   9. an umbrella   10. a mug
11. a lampshade   12. a basket   13. a dustbin
14. a towel   15. a briefcase   16. a torch
17. a toothbrush   18. a nail   19. a spade
20. a lipstick   21. a cardboard box   22. a comb
23. a needle   24. a saucepan   25. a button

7 Unorthodox uses of objects

• This gives students a chance to practise passive infinitives.
• It could be done as a competition, with a small prize for the person or group that can think of the craziest uses.

Practice Book exercises

1. Reading skills: separating two mixed-up stories and writing one of them out in full.
2. Reported questions.
3. Vocabulary revision: opposites (*rough, smooth,* etc.).
4. Student's Cassette exercise (Student's Book Lesson E2, Exercise 2). Students mark and practise sentence stress.
5. Reading skills (deducing meaning from context); personalised writing.
6. Recreational reading: prose fiction.
7. Extended writing: a short story about giving or receiving some good or bad news.

3 Imagine the conversation between John and Mary when John phones later on. Then write a report of it using reported speech (including structures with *would* and *had*). Example:

John rang up and said he was staying with an old friend. So Mary asked if ...

PUNCTUATION

4 Write out the letter with capitals and punctuation where necessary.

dear sue how are you these days i made a real fool of myself last week it happened like this john went off on a business trip and then i thought that hed taken my keys so i rang up his hotel im sorry the girl said but hes not here hes cancelled well i was sure hed gone off with that american woman do you remember me telling you about her last year but actually it turned out that hed met an old school friend and gone to stay with him he tried to phone me but he couldnt get through because i was telling mother all my troubles then when he got our neighbour to give me a message i wouldnt listen and shut the door in his face so when john finally rang up we had a colossal row and things are still a bit difficult sue i do feel stupid have you ever done anything like that or am i the only one give my love to fred and the kids mary

PRONUNCIATION AND SPELLING: CONTRACTIONS

5 [cassette] Change the full forms to contractions and practise the pronunciation. Example:

I am	I am tired.
'I'm	*I'm tired.'*

I have	I have forgotten her name.
he had	He had taken my keys.
I will	I will phone you.
it will	It will rain this afternoon.
I would	I would like something to drink.
cannot	I cannot understand him.
will not	He will not be here tomorrow.
is not	The car is not ready yet.
does not	She does not work on Saturdays.
has not	The postman has not come yet.
had not	He had not taken my keys.
would not	I would not like to do her job.
could not	He could not get through.
did not	I did not believe him.

VOCABULARY: EVERYDAY OBJECTS

6 Do you know the names of all these objects?

7 Think of different uses for some of the objects, and write sentences. Examples:

A coin can be used as a screwdriver.
A bath can be used as a bed.
A brick can be used for breaking into a house.

Learn/revise: bad news; business trip; elbow; misunderstanding; organisation; river; secret; shock; stranger; cancel (cancelled); elect; find out (found, found); give sbdy a message (gave, given); have trouble with sth; lose contact with sbdy (lost, lost); make a decision (made, made); make a fool of oneself; make a mistake; make friends (with sbdy); meet (met, met); offer; quarrel (quarrelled); ring sbdy up (rang, rung); stay with sbdy; steal (stole, stolen); wonder; clever; exciting; serious; stupid; terrible; unusual; valuable; wonderful; actually; violently; *words from Exercise 6.*

E3 A dream

Listening for gist; listening for exact comprehension; discussion or writing skills work; Past Progressive tense; vocabulary; pronunciation (weak forms of words).

1 🔲 You are going to hear the first part of a story. Before you listen, look at the words and expressions in the box. (They come in the story in the same order.) If there are any that you don't know, ask about them or look them up in a dictionary. What do you think happens in this part of the story? Listen to the recording and see if you are right.

by myself	moped	tent	camp sites
facilities	safer	convenient	
I camped rough	hidden	hedge	
wood	pleasant	I pitched my tent	
plastic	supper	went to sleep	

2 🔲 Now listen to the second part of the recording twice. When you have done that, work in small groups and try to remember and write down what you heard as exactly as possible. The words and expressions in the box will help you (but three of them shouldn't be there).

unusual	episodes	hard to tell	1930s
World War II	on farms	barn	children
didn't last	scenes	laughing	smiling
puzzled	connect		

3 🔲 Now listen to the end of the story.

98

Lesson E3

Students practise listening skills (listening for gist and for exact words), and discussion or writing skills.
Principal structure: Past Progressive.
Phonology: stress; rhythm; weak forms.

Language notes and possible problems

1. Weak forms   Students may need to be reminded that there are fifty or so words in English that have two different regular pronunciations: the 'strong form', used in cases where the word is stressed, and the 'weak form', used when it is unstressed. The strong form usually has the vowel that is written (e.g. *can* /kæn/); most weak forms are pronounced with the vowel /ə/ or no vowel at all (e.g. *can* /k(ə)n/). Since the words in question are 'grammatical words': auxiliary verbs, conjunctions, prepositions, pronouns and the like (e.g. *was*, *and*, *for*), they are most often unstressed. It is therefore particularly important for students to be able to recognise the weak forms of these words (and failure to do so is a frequent cause of comprehension problems). Students who want a good standard of pronunciation must also be able to produce weak forms when appropriate – a common characteristic of many foreign accents in English is the over-use of strong forms. Exercise 4 should help to consolidate students' command of the point.

2. Choice of writing or speaking activities   Note that students are given a choice between Exercise 5 (a writing skills activity) and Exercise 6 (a speaking fluency activity). You may like to let students vote on which exercise to do; if there are enough students wanting to do each activity, you can let them go on simultaneously.

If you are short of time
Do the shorter alternative version of Exercise 2.

---

1 Predicting and listening

• Give students a few minutes to look at the words and expressions in the box. If there are any that they don't know, let them find out their meanings in any way they like – by looking them up, asking other students, or asking you. You will need to explain that *moped* is a noun meaning a motorised bicycle, pronounced /'məʊped/, not the past of *mope*.
• Tell them to work in pairs or small groups, discussing what they think they are going to be told in the story.
• Ask a few of the groups for their ideas.
• Then play the first part of the recording. Stop at the words *went to sleep*. If students have had difficulty following, you may like to play it again once or twice.
• The speaker has an American (Texan) accent, modified a little by living in Britain.
• Students may ask you to give them the text of the recording and to go through it explaining everything. This would probably be an inefficient use of your time. They will get a chance to see a written version of the story in Exercise 5.

Tapescript for Exercise 1
A few years ago I was travelling in France. I was by myself, and I was travelling on a moped. I usually camped in the evenings, I had a tent. I camped in camp sites whenever I could, both for the facilities of washing and so on, and because it was a bit safer. But when I couldn't find a convenient camp site, I camped rough, trying to find places that were fairly hidden from the road. One evening like this, I found quite a nice place. It was up against a tall hedge in a little wood, it couldn't be seen from the road, and it was quite a pleasant place. So I pitched my tent, and covered my moped up with plastic, and cooked my little supper over my camping gas fire,

and got ready for bed. Read for a little while, and then went to sleep.

2 Listening and recalling

• Look over the words in the box with the students. Make sure they understand them all, and that they know what they have to do.
• Play the next part of the recording twice (up to *it was just very unusual*).
• Give students ten minutes or so to work in groups trying to recall and write down what they heard.
• Then play the recording once more so that they can check their answers.
• (The three items that 'should not be in the box' are *World War II*, *children* and *laughing*.)

Alternative to Exercise 2
• Just play this part of the recording twice, and get students to tell you informally what they have understood.

Tapescript for Exercise 2
And I had the most unusual dream. I've never had another dream like this before or since. It was like short episodes, a few minutes each, it seemed, though it's hard to tell in a dream how long things are. Young men and women that I had never seen and didn't know, all very happy, dressed as if it were the 1930s and 40s. Some of them were on farms, I remember a dance in a barn, walking along the streets in a small town in America – they were all Americans, and each episode had different people in it, and didn't last for very long. It wasn't a frightening dream at all – all the scenes were very happy, smiling people, happy people, and I woke up a bit puzzled, because it didn't seem to connect with anything that had been happening to me, I didn't know anybody that was in the dreams, and it was just very unusual.

3 Listening

• In this exercise, students simply listen to the rest of the story and try to understand it. You may need to explain one or two words, and to play the recording more than once.

Tapescript for Exercise 3
So I got up and fixed breakfast, and packed my tent securely on the back of my moped, and set on my way. This little wood, as I said, was up against a hedge, a very tall hedge that you couldn't see over, and there was a bend in the road just at the hedge, so I hadn't been around the bend in the road. And when I did wheel my Solex up to the road and go around the bend, I saw that just on the other side of this hedge there was a small American war cemetery from World War II, and – full of the graves of young men who could have lived the scenes that I had had in my dream.

4 Weak forms

• Ask students how they normally pronounce the words listed. They will probably give you something close to the strong forms: /wɒz/, /ænd/, /fɔː/, /ɒv/, /tuː/, /ðæt/, /wɜː/, /frɒm/.

• Play the first five sentences of the recording from Exercise 1, up to *fairly hidden from the road*, and ask students to listen carefully for the words in the list. They are all pronounced as weak forms (with the vowel /ə/ or no vowel at all). You may have to play the recording several times, however, before students are ready to accept this: one tends to hear what one expects to hear.

• Get students to say the sentences after you or after the recording, using weak forms where necessary. They should be careful to pronounce the weak forms quickly and quietly, and NOT to give them extra emphasis in an effort to get them right!

• Finally, get students to ask each other what they were doing yesterday at a particular time. In their answers, they should use the weak form of *was* (/wəz/).

• Note that this exercise revises a use of the Past Progressive tense.

Student choice

• Let students choose either Exercise 5 or Exercise 6 (see *Language notes and possible problems*).

5 Drafting and improving written stories

• Give students a minute to choose which story they are going to write about.

• Make sure they understand the instructions for the first part of the exercise. Writing on every second line of the paper is done to make revising easier in the second part of the exercise.

• Walk round while they are working to give any help that is needed.

• Tell them they have ten minutes and let them start writing. (If many people have not finished at the end of the ten minutes, you can always extend the limit.) When the time is up, get the students to exchange stories in pairs, read each other's stories and ask questions.

• Go on to the second part of the exercise. Make sure students understand the instructions; if you think your class needs extra support, turn to pages 133 and 134 and let the students pick out how the different devices are used in the story there.

• Tell students they can just use the blank second lines on their papers to write in any revisions.

• Walk round while they are working to give any help that is needed.

• When you mark the papers, make sure to comment positively on content.

6 Exchanging spoken stories

• Give students a few moments to think about their stories.

• Then put them in groups and get them to tell their stories to the others in the group.

• Finally, each group can choose one or two of the stories to tell another group or the rest of the class. You may find that one or two students have nothing to say. This doesn't matter provided most of the class are able to produce something.

• If students have difficulty in getting started, tell a story of your own to get things moving.

Practice Book exercises

1. Vocabulary revision: different kinds of container.
2. Revision of prepositions.
3. Student's Cassette exercise (Student's Book Lesson E3, Exercise 1 – the first four sentences only). Students listen and write down as much as they can.
4. Reading skills: ordering the paragraphs in a story and integrating extra sentences.
5. A choice of extended writing tasks: an adventure story; a supernatural experience.
6. Recreational reading: a choice of a poem and four prose texts.

4 🔊 Pronunciation. How are these words usually pronounced: *was, and, for, of, to, that, were, from*? Listen to the recording and see if you were right. Practise saying the sentences. Then ask other students what they were doing yesterday at a particular time.

> What were you doing at 10 o'clock yesterday evening?

> I was dancing.

> I was asleep.

> I was eating.

> I can't remember what I was doing.

Tell the class what you have found out.

> Jean was eating.

> Alex says he was asleep.

DO EITHER EXERCISE 5 OR EXERCISE 6.

5 Choose one of these questions.

– Have you ever had an experience of telepathy (knowing or dreaming what is happening to somebody else)?
– Have you ever had a dream which told you what was going to happen in the future?
– Have you ever experienced a strange coincidence?
– Or have any of these things happened to someone you know?

1. Write at least 100 words about the question you have chosen. Write on every second line of your paper. Don't spend more than ten minutes. When you have finished, exchange stories with another student. Read the other student's story and ask two or more questions about what happened.
2. Try and make your story better by doing some of the things in the box. You can look at the written version of the dream story on page 133 if you want.

> Dividing the story into paragraphs
> Using conjunctions like *and, because, but, though, when*
> Using relative pronouns like *that, which, who*
> Not making all the sentences the same length – using a variety of longer and shorter sentences

6 Choose one of the questions from Exercise 5. Work with three or four other students. Tell your story to the group. The group should choose the one or two most interesting stories to tell to another group or to the whole class.

> **Learn/revise:** camp; camp site; coincidence; dream; farm; plastic; scene; story; supper; tent; wood; the future; the 1930s; World War II; connect; go to sleep; happen; hide (hid, hidden); last; smile; travel; convenient; pleasant; safe; strange; unusual; in order; by myself.

E4 Nice woman, 42

Fast reading for specific information; listening for detail; asking for things when you don't know the exact words.

BILLIARD TABLES bought and sold. Mr Villis. (02805) 66 (Bucks).

GIFT CHAMPAGNE. We post a bottle with your message. From £16.50 incl. Orders or details 0642 45733

CHRISTINE'S beauty treatment and body therapy. 402 6499, 0473 4004

SMOKED SALMON 8oz sliced £7.75, 1lb sliced £13, 2lb 4oz side £18.90, 2lb 8oz side £21, 400gms offcuts £6. Prices include UK 1st class postage. Cheques with order. Cornish Smoked Fish Co. Ltd, Charlestown, St. Austell, Cornwall.

CHATEAU LATOUR, 1964. 24 bottles, £75 each. Phone (0227) 9848 evenings.

GOING INTO BUSINESS? Send £7.45 inc p&p for 'The Beginners Guide to Success in Business.' Comquip Ltd, 189 Highview, Meopham, Gravesend, Kent. (0732) 22315.

C-SCOPE METAL DETECTORS The ideal family gift to treasure from £39.99 to £449.50. Tel. Ashford (0233) 2918 today for free colour brochure.

MAKE A GUITAR 12 week courses. Details : Totnes School of Guitarmaking, Collins Rd, Totnes, Devon. 0803 65255.

HAVANA CIGARS And other fine cigars at wholesale prices. Send for list to James Jordan Ltd, Shelley Hall, Shelley, Huddersfield. Tel.: 0484 60227

400-YEAR-OLD thatched cottage between Winchester/Basingstoke: 3 dble beds, sec gdn & extras. £110,000. (0962) 88109

BEAUTIFUL farm estate, total 700 acres. Diplomats 4 bed 1832 house. £220,000 ono. 0639 73082

5 BEDROOMED HOUSE in quiet mid-Wales village. 1 acre of land, fishing and shooting available. £42,000. Tel : 059 787 687 (after 6 p.m.).

W. ANGLESEY. 2 dble beds. S/d bung. Lge with patio drs to ½-acre garden, kit/b'fast room, bathroom. Dble glaz/ins. GCH. Garage & util rm, summer hse, grn hse. Scope for extensions. £29,500 o.n.o., quick sale. Tel 040 741031.

HAVE A very happy birthday Paul.

NICE WOMAN, 42, seeks close, affectionate friendship with independentish man. Non-smoker, sense of fun, creative. Enjoys walks, talks, sensuality. Photo please. London area. Box (50) 2059. N50 3

OLGA: RUSSIAN/FRENCHWOMAN from Lille, seeks an Englishman, tall, 50s, open-minded, with whom she can have a close, but stable relationship. Box (50) 2051. N50 2

OXFORD: lively divorcee, mid forties, bored with solitude and the cat, seeks male, preferably tall, to share local pleasures and pastimes, music, the arts etc. Box (50) 2050.

VERY PERSONABLE, attractive, charming, amusing, considerate graduate, professional – 40 – own lovely coastal home, seeks lady – friendship/marriage – personality more important than age. All nationalities welcome. Box (50) 2052 N50 6

WARM, ATTRACTIVE, humorous woman, 35, lover of music , literature, cinema, theatre and leftish politics, seeks man of similar inclinations, to share it all with. London. Box (46) 1899. N49 8

SENSITIVE, TALL, caring, unattached man, 55, likes people, music, walking, seeks intelligent, helpful n/s woman, mid forties. South Essex. Box (49)2011. N49 13

SILVER CROSS detachable coach Pram (navy), shopping tray, excellent clean condition, £30; Carry Cot, £5; Baby Bath, £2.50; Atari system, joystick and paddle sticks, in good working order, needs a new mains adapter, £40; 5 Atari Cassettes, £10 each, very good condition, ideal Xmas presents. – Apply 34 Kynaston Road, Didcot, Oxon. evenings. 415702

THE TIMES (1814-1985). This Xmas give someone an original issue dated the very day they were born. £12.50 or 2 for £21. Tel 01-486 6305 or 0492 3314

PARTYMANIA, everything for your party in one "funtastic" store. – 179 Kingston Road, Oxford 513397, own parking. 376851

GIVE HER a luxurious Christmas with a special gift set of soothing bath, body and face oils. Send £9.50 to Claydon Aromatherapy, 107 Marine Parade, Worthing BN11 3QG.

LADIES NARROW SHOES. AA and narrower, sizes 2½–11½. Also wide EE. SAE Muriel Hitchcock Shoes, 3b Castle Mews, Arundel BN18 9DG.

1 Fast reading practice. Look at the small ads and see how quickly you can answer the questions.

1. What does the cheapest metal detector cost?
2. A man in South Essex is looking for a friend. How old is he?
3. Will Christine improve your mind or your body?
4. Which costs more – a 400-year-old cottage near Winchester or a 5-bedroom house in Wales?
5. Why is today a special day for Paul?
6. How much will two bottles of Château Latour 1964 cost you?
7. What town do you write to for bath, body and face oils?
8. Where can you buy things for a party?
9. How long will it take you to learn to make a guitar?
10. Does the lady who is bored with the cat prefer tall or short men?
11. How much will it cost you to give somebody a pound (1lb) of smoked salmon and a bottle of champagne (with a message)?
12. You can buy something that was produced on the day you were born. What?
13. Somebody is offering a baby bath for sale. How much for?
14. Does the nice 42-year-old woman smoke?
15. How many nationalities has Olga got?

2 Look again at the 'contact ads' (the ones in which people are advertising for friends). Write a contact ad for yourself or a friend.

3 Do you know the pronunciation, meaning and use of all of these words? Check them in a dictionary if necessary, or ask your teacher.

advertise   an advertisement   a small ad
a poster   a sale   a bargain   a gift
a catalogue   a price   choice   quality   value
free   cheap   expensive   save

Lesson E4

Reading skills: scanning.
Listening skills: listening for detail.
Speaking skills: paraphrase strategies.

Language notes and possible problems

1. Vocabulary   Some students get very worried if they don't understand every word in a spoken or written text, or if they don't know the exact word or phrase needed to express a particular idea. One of the main purposes of this lesson is to encourage students not to be too perfectionist about vocabulary. Exercises 1, 5 and 6 should help them realise that they can achieve some communicative purposes without 'knowing all the words'.

2. Contact ads (Exercise 2)   This could cause trouble with immature or difficult students, or in certain cultures. Leave it out if necessary.

Materials

You may like to prepare additional pictures for Exercise 6.

If you are short of time

Exercise 4 could be dropped.

1 Scanning

• This exercise is intended especially to help the kind of student who tends to read English one word at a time, looking up all unknown words in a dictionary.

• Begin as soon as you can (so that students don't find out half the answers before the exercise starts).

• Give a time-limit of, say, eight minutes, and see how many of the answers students can write down correctly in the time available.

• In order to get a reasonable score, students will need to 'scan' the text – searching very quickly for the items they need, without spending time on other irrelevant points.

• After the exercise, point out to students that different kinds of reading are needed for different purposes, and that one does not always need to read and understand every word in a text.

Answers to Exercise 1
1. £39.99.
2. 55.
3. Your body.
4. The cottage.
5. It's his birthday.
6. £150.
7. Worthing.
8. At Partymania.
9. 12 weeks.
10. Tall.
11. £29.50.
12. An issue of *The Times*.
13. £2.50.
14. No.
15. Two.

2 Contact ads

• This is not a very important exercise, but it can provide quite a lot of amusement.

• It can be done individually or in groups, with students writing ads for themselves, for other students, or both.

• One approach is to get students to hand in their ads to the teacher, who mixes them up and then reads them out. The class has to guess who wrote the ad and who it refers to (if this is not the person who wrote it).

3 Vocabulary study

• These are some common words that relate to selling and advertising. (Some of them will be needed for Exercise 4.) Get students to go through them; deal with any difficulties, and make sure the pronunciation is learnt.

• This is another opportunity to check that students are using dictionaries efficiently.

• Students may wish to ask about other words and expressions that belong in the same lexical field. Answer a reasonable number of questions, but don't let this kind of activity get out of control – there is no value in students writing down more words than they can learn, and the main aim of this lesson is skills practice, not vocabulary building.

4 Listening practice

- These are extracts from some advertisements on a British commercial radio programme, broadcast just before Christmas. Warn students that the advertisements are authentic, fast and difficult: they must not expect to understand every word.
- First of all, look through the printed text and clear up any difficulties. (A 'cash-and-carry' is a wholesale warehouse open to the public, where goods can be bought at very low prices.)
- Students may like to try to guess what words come in some of the blanks.
- Then play the first extract once without stopping, and see whether students can fill in any of the blanks (working in groups or as a whole class, as you prefer).
- Play the extract once or twice more. When students have done as well as they are going to, give them the answers.
- Move on to the next extract.

Answers and tapescript for Exercise 4

Hickman's aren't (1) *as* (2) *expensive* (3) *as* you think. A Panasonic VHS video is only (4) *£399.95*. If you add up the extras at other (5) *places*, it's (6) *cheaper* by far (7) *at* Hickman's.

McIlroy's (8) *is* first for choice, (9) *quality* and value, so make us first (10) *for* (11) *your* Christmas shopping. (12) *Our* new-look store means an even better choice of gifts for the (13) *whole* (14) *family*. Make shopping part (15) *of* (16) *the* pleasure (17) *of* Christmas. Experience the new-look McIlroy's.

(18) *Save*, (19) *save*, (20) *save* on Christmas shopping (21) *at* Scat's Cash-and-Carry (22) *at* Devizes and Salisbury. There are thousands of (23) *bargains* for (24) *everyone* at cash-and-carry prices all the year round.

5 Preparation for paraphrasing

- This gives students further practice in asking for things in a roundabout way, when they don't know the exact words.
- Look through the words and structures illustrated. Clear up any difficulties.
- Help students to see how these words and structures can often be used to identify a thing or substance even if the exact word is not known.
- Ask if students can think of any other words or structures which might be added to the list.
- Look at the two examples and get students to try to write similar descriptions of some of the other things listed.
- Both the structures illustrated are likely to be difficult for students. Make sure they can use them confidently before going on.

6 Paraphrasing

- Get one or two students to stand in front of the class in turn and (pretending to be in a shop) to ask for one of the things illustrated, without mentioning its name and without using gesture. If the class can identify the object being asked for, the student has communicated successfully.
- Then let students continue the exercise in groups.
- Don't insist on correct grammar in this exercise.
- You may like to supplement the illustration with pictures of your own.
- For your reference, the objects illustrated are:
  1. a coffee pot
  2. a sparking plug
  3. a plug
  4. a wellington boot
  5. a spanner
  6. a paper clip
  7. a clothes peg
  8. a wheelbarrow
  9. a hair-dryer
  10. a violin
  11. a crutch
  12. a candle
  13. a pair of shears
  14. a light bulb
  15. a mallet
  16. a supermarket trolley
  17. a chessboard
  18. a ladle
  19. a tin/can opener
  20. a bicycle saddle
  21. a globe
  22. a cardboard box
  23. a clothes hanger
  24. a tyre

Practice Book exercises

1. Reading skills: global comprehension; text completion.
2. Revision of the Present Progressive.
3. Choosing the right tense (Simple Present and Present Progressive).
4. Modal verbs.
5. Drawing conclusions (*must, might*).
6. Recreational reading: amusing advertisements.
7. A choice of writing tasks: opinions of advertising; an advertisement.

4 🔊 Listen to the recording and see how many of the missing words you can fill in.

Hickman's aren't ......1...... ......2...... ......3...... you think. A Panasonic VHS video is only £......4....... If you add up the extras at other ......5......, it's ......6...... by far ......7...... Hickman's.

McIlroy's ......8...... first for choice, ...9...... and value, so make us first ......10...... ......11...... Christmas shopping. ......12...... new-look store means an even better choice of gifts for the ......13...... ......14....... Make shopping part ......15...... ......16...... pleasure ......17...... Christmas. Experience the new-look McIlroy's.

......18......, ...19......, ...20...... on Christmas shopping ......21...... Scat's Cash-and-Carry ......22...... Devizes and Salisbury. There are thousands of ......23...... for ......24...... at cash-and-carry prices all the year round.

5 Can you ask for things when you don't know the exact word? Here are some useful words and expressions.

a thing   a machine   a tool

stuff   liquid   powder   material

square   round   pointed   sharp

a point   an end   a hole   a handle

a thing with a (hole, handle, *etc.*)

a thing/tool/machine for (making ..., cutting ..., *etc.*)

a thing that you ... with/in/on/*etc.*

a thing that goes on top of / under / ...

material/liquid/powder/stuff for ...ing

How could you ask for these things if you didn't know their names?

fly-spray
'liquid for killing flies'

a typewriter
'a machine that you write with'

a fork   an umbrella   a hat   a bath   a car
beer   soap   glasses   tea   string   a hammer
shoe-polish

6 Now look at the pictures and ask for one of the things illustrated. Don't use its name (if you know it), and don't use your hands. See if the other students can say what you are asking for.

E5 This is great

Formal and informal language; asking, offering and answering; grammar (verbs with two objects); reading and listening for detail; speaking practice.

1 🔲 Formal and informal language. Read the dialogue and listen to the recording. Can you write down some of the differences?

HE: That's really a beautiful dress.
SHE: Thank you. I'm glad you like it.
HE: Would you like some more wine?
SHE: I beg your pardon?
HE: Would you like some more wine?
SHE: Oh, er, no thank you. But perhaps you could bring me a little orange juice?
HE: Yes, of course.
            *   *   *
HE: Here you are.
SHE: Thank you.
HE: Would you like to dance?
SHE: Well, I'd love to, but I'm afraid I don't know how to tango.
HE: Actually, I think this is a waltz.
SHE: I see. I'm afraid I don't know how to waltz, either.
HE: Oh, do let me teach you. It's very easy.

2 Now can you rewrite this dialogue to make it more formal?

ALAN: This is great, Sue.
SUE: Glad you like it. It's dead easy to make. Have some more potatoes?
ALAN: Er, no, thanks. But I'd like a bit more beef.
SUE: Yes, sure. Here you are.
ALAN: Thanks.
SUE: Sauce?
ALAN: Yes, please.
SUE: And have some more wine.
ALAN: Oh, yeah. Great. Thanks. Say, how's Barry?

3 Ways of asking and offering. Match the questions and answers.

1. Excuse me. Could you help me for a minute?
2. Have you got the time?
3. Have you got a light?
4. Shall I give you a hand with the cooking?
5. Can you lend me some stamps?
6. Sprechen Sie Deutsch?
7. Could I borrow your car for half an hour?
8. Have you got change for £5?
9. Would you like to come and have a drink this evening?
10. Could I use your phone?

a. Sorry, I don't smoke.
b. I'm afraid I haven't got any.
c. Sorry, I'm using it.
d. Sorry, I'm not free. My sister's coming round.
e. Just after five.
f. I'll have a look. Just a moment.
g. Sorry, I don't understand.
h. Well, I'm in a bit of a hurry.
i. Of course. It's over there on the table.
j. That's very kind of you.

Lesson E5

Students revise ways of offering, asking for things, asking people to do things, inviting, and replying to offers, requests and invitations. They study differences between formal and informal usage. They practise the skills of reading and listening for detail.
Principal structure: verbs with two objects.

Optional extra materials
For the second suggested treatment of Exercise 3: the questions and replies, copied and cut into strips with a question or a reply on each strip.

---

1 Listening (degrees of formality)

• Let students look over the dialogue for a few minutes. Give whatever explanations are necessary.
• Play the recording through once without stopping. Ask students to tell you any differences that they have noticed. Play the recording again without stopping, and see if students can give you some more of the differences.
• Play it a third time.
• Put students in groups of three or four, and get them to work together to try to write down the exact text of the recorded dialogue.
• When they are ready, play the recording once more and put the text on the board.
• Finally, discuss the differences in formality between the two texts. Help students to see how the written text contains a number of formal, polite forms suitable for conversation between (for example) people who don't know each other very well, while the recorded text contains more casual informal expressions typical of conversation between friends or relations.

Tapescript for Exercise 1
HE: Great dress!
SHE: Oh, thanks. Glad you like it.
HE: Have some more wine.
SHE: What?
HE: Have some more wine.
SHE: No, thanks. But I wouldn't mind a drop of beer.
HE: OK.
SHE: And I'd like a bit of that bread and cheese, if you can get me some.
HE: Sure. Don't go away.

      *   *   *

HE: Here you are.
SHE: Thanks. Do you want to dance?
HE: Well, actually, believe it or not, I can't dance.
SHE: Aw, come on – I'll teach you. It's dead easy.

2 Writing (degrees of formality)
• This can either be done in groups, or as a whole-class blackboard composition.
• As an alternative to this exercise, students can make up their own dialogues in two versions (formal and informal).
• If students have worked in groups and you have got the time, you may want to let groups perform their dialogues for one another.

Possible answer to Exercise 2
(Obviously there are various possible formal versions of almost every phrase. The following is not the 'right answer', but simply one possible solution which may be useful for reference.)

ALAN: This is delicious, Sue.
SUE: I'm glad you like it. It's very easy to make. Would you like some more potatoes?
ALAN: Er, no, thank you. But could I have a little more beef?
SUE: Yes, of course. Here you are.
ALAN: Thank you.
SUE: Would you like some more sauce?
ALAN: Yes, please.
SUE: And do have some more wine.
ALAN: That would be very nice. Thank you. Tell me, how's Barry?

3 Matching questions and answers
• This exercise revises a number of useful conversational formulae used in making and replying to requests, offers etc.
• Give students a few minutes to work alone, and then let them compare notes with their neighbours before checking with you.
• When you are checking the answers, give students a chance to practise saying the sentences, concentrating on rhythm and stress.

Alternative approach to Exercise 3
• Copy the questions and replies and cut them up so that there is one question or one reply on each piece of paper.
• Give each student at least one piece of paper. Students must memorise what is on their piece(s) of paper and then walk round trying to find people with matching lines.
• Offer to give help with stress, rhythm and linking while they are memorising their lines: walk round while' they are working so that you will be available for this.
• Continue walking round while they are searching for their partners, so that you can give any help that is needed.

Answers to Exercise 3
1h; 2e; 3a (or f); 4j; 5b (or f); 6g; 7c; 8f; 9d (or j); 10i

4 Verbs with two objects

- Let students look over the examples and explanations. Give whatever help is necessary.
- Tell or remind them that the words whose main syllables take the stress in a sentence are usually content words, and not form words: so we would say *Could you **bring** me some **water**?* Make sure they understand by asking them to give you some examples of form words (pronouns, auxiliary verbs, determiners, articles).
- You may like to mention that *explain* is not one of the verbs that take two objects (**Can you explain me ...?* is a common mistake).
- You may want to give students a chance to write some sentences down before volunteering to say them for you.

5 Verbs with two objects (further practice)

- Give students a minute or two to prepare their requests. Tell them to look back at the replies in Exercise 3. Give them a chance to ask you about sentence stress.
- Then each student should talk to as many others as possible in three or four minutes, making and replying to requests. Ideally this will be done by getting up from desks and walking round the classroom, but this may not be practical in some classes.
- Let them carry their books with them in case they need to look up replies from Exercise 3.

6 Making up dialogues

- Students learn new material best if they can use it creatively. This exercise gives them a chance to re-use and memorise words and expressions from the lesson.
- Get students to work in pairs preparing their conversations. Tell them that they should use plenty of the language from the lesson, especially words and expressions that they want to remember.
- Give them a time-limit – say 15 minutes.
- Go round helping where necessary.
- When a pair of students are ready, listen to their conversation. Don't make too many corrections: this can damage students' confidence.
- If time allows, let students learn their conversations by heart and act them out for the others. (If the standard is good, you may like to tape- or video-record them. Warn them in advance.)

Practice Book exercises

1. Verbs with two objects.
2. Grammar and vocabulary revision: completing sentences.
3. Vocabulary: recognising words from their descriptions.
4. Writing descriptions like those in Exercise 3.
5. Student's Cassette exercise (Student's Book Lesson E5, Exercise 1). Students try to complete the transcript of the conversation from memory. They check their answers with the recording and then practise the conversation.
6. Recreational reading: prose fiction.
7. Extended writing: a story about having difficulty saying something in a foreign language.

4 Grammar: verbs with two objects. Look at these sentences from the lesson.

Perhaps you could bring me a little orange juice?
I'd like a bit of that bread and cheese, if you can get me some.
Shall I give you a hand?
Can you lend me some stamps?

Bring, get, give and *lend* can be used with two objects – an indirect object (*me* and *you* in the examples), and a direct object (*a little orange juice, some,* etc.).

A lot of other verbs can be used with two objects; for example, *buy, teach, tell, order, send, write, offer, make, do, pass, show.*

See if you can make some examples from the table.

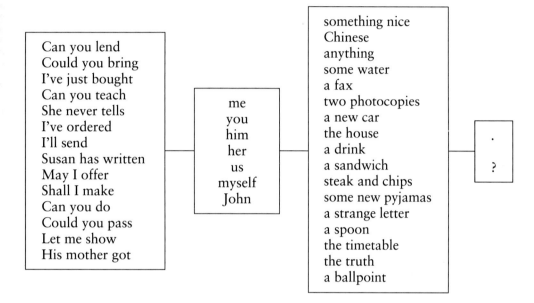

| Can you lend
Could you bring
I've just bought
Can you teach
She never tells
I've ordered
I'll send
Susan has written
May I offer
Shall I make
Can you do
Could you pass
Let me show
His mother got | me
you
him
her
us
myself
John | something nice
Chinese
anything
some water
a fax
two photocopies
a new car
the house
a drink
a sandwich
steak and chips
some new pyjamas
a strange letter
a spoon
the timetable
the truth
a ballpoint | .

? |

5 Now work with as many other students as possible, making and replying to requests. Use at least four of the following beginnings: *Could you lend/tell/get/make/teach/give/show me ...?* See Exercise 3 for possible replies.

6 Work in pairs. Make up and practise a conversation including some or all of the following: a request; an offer; an invitation; a question; a disagreement; a misunderstanding. Possible situations: borrowing a car; borrowing clothes; looking for a room to rent; in a restaurant; trying to buy a computer; looking for somewhere to camp; first day in an English-speaking country. Ask the teacher for help if necessary.

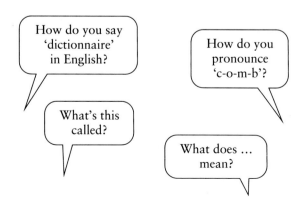

Learn/revise: beef; change; chips; computer; country; disagreement; dress; invitation; (a) light (for a cigarette *etc.*); misunderstanding; offer; orange juice; photocopy; pyjamas; request; restaurant; sandwich; sauce; spoon; steak; fax; timetable; (the) truth; water; borrow; bring (brought, brought); buy (bought, bought); call; camp; come round (came, come); get (got, got); help; lend (lent, lent); make (made, made); mean (meant, meant); offer; order; pass; pronounce; rent; say (said, said); send (sent, sent); show (showed, shown); teach (taught, taught); understand (understood, understood); use; write (wrote, written); glad; actually; for a minute; in a bit of a hurry; over there; How do you pronounce ...?; How do you say ... in English?; What does ... mean?; What's this called? *Formal:* Do let me (teach you) ...; I beg your pardon; I'm afraid ...; I'm glad you like it; Perhaps you could bring me ...?; That's very kind of you; Yes, of course. *Informal:* great; thanks; give sbdy a hand; Don't go away; Glad you like it; I wouldn't mind ... (*request*); OK; believe it or not; Say, ... (*for change of subject*); What?; Yes, sure.

> A choice of exercises: position of adverbs; clothes and parts of the body; typical pronunciations of vowel letters.

GRAMMAR: POSITION OF ADVERBS

1 Look at the examples. Study the position of the words *always, usually, often, sometimes, occasionally, hardly ever, never*. Can you work out the rules?

She **is always** late.
Ann and Phil **are usually** at home at the weekend.
We **were very often** hungry when I was a child.
I **am never** sure what he thinks.

It **often rains** in England in summer.
My mother **sometimes loses** her temper for no reason.
I **occasionally go** to the cinema, if there's a really good film.
We **hardly ever have** lunch on Sundays.

I've **never been** to India.
You **can always ask** me for help.
She says she **will never leave** me.
I'm **quite often invited** to have dinner with the boss.
I **would never have known** if you hadn't told me.

2 Talk about the personality of somebody you know.

… is	always usually (very/quite) often sometimes occasionally hardly ever never	friendly. cheerful. happy. unhappy. depressed. bad-tempered. worried about something. *etc.*

"The postman's in one of his moods again, Fred."

3 Make sentences using *always, usually, (very/quite) often, sometimes, occasionally, hardly ever* or *never*. Example:

'*I never play the piano after midnight.*'

BEGINNINGS
I think about life
I go to sleep
I sing in a loud voice
I play cards
I write poetry
I eat toast
I read letters
I speak English
I play the piano
I worry about money
I smoke cigars
I drink coffee
I boil eggs
I play football
I cry
I forget my name
I wash my hands
I laugh

ENDS
in the bath.
during lessons.
on the bus.
at breakfast.
on the roof.
outside.
while I'm working.
in the toilet.
in New York.
in bed.
in restaurants.
in shops.
after midnight.
in the police station.
in the river.
at Christmas.
when I'm tired.

4 Complete some of these sentences, and put in *very often, quite often, sometimes, occasionally, hardly ever* or *never*. Examples:

'*I have very often wanted to change my job.*'
'*I have never eaten snake.*'

1. I have … wanted …
2. I have … eaten …
3. I have … played …
4. I have … thought …
5. I have … understood …
6. I have … studied …
7. I have … made …
8. I have … read …

5 Look at these examples. Can you find another rule about word order?

She speaks English well.
   (She speaks well English.)

I like cross-country skiing very much.
   (I like very much cross-country skiing.)

You must cook the meat slowly.
   (You must cook slowly the meat.)

He probably has a lot of friends.
   (He has probably a lot of friends.)

She carefully opened the letter.
OR She opened the letter carefully.
   (She opened carefully the letter.)

104

Lesson E6

Grammar: mid- and end-position of adverbs.
Vocabulary: clothes, accessories and parts of the body.
Pronunciation: spelling and pronunciation (single vowel letters).

Language notes and possible problems

1. Adverb position is a very complicated area of English grammar. This lesson gives a simplified treatment of two points which often cause difficulty; for fuller details, see a good grammar.

2. Frequency adverbs (Exercises 1–4)   Adverbs of indefinite frequency (*always, often* etc.) most often go in 'mid-position' – that is to say, with the verb. The exact position depends on the kind of verb phrase; for more detailed rules, see the instructions for Exercise 1. Some other kinds of adverb also go in mid-position (for instance, adverbs of degree like *quite, very much*, and adverbs referring to certainty like *certainly, definitely*); *all* and *both* can also go in mid-position. Look out for mistakes like *She often is late*; *I always have loved you*. Note that the rules given here are only valid for non-emphatic British usage; mid-verb adverbs may be placed earlier for emphasis, and they can also come earlier in non-emphatic American usage.

3. Verb and object (Exercise 5)   It is unusual in English to separate the verb from its object. Look out for mistakes like *I like very much skiing*; *She opened carefully the letter.*

4. Pronunciation and spelling (Exercise 8)   Students should by now have a sense of the 'typical' pronunciations corresponding to various letters. Despite the irregularity of English spelling, the single vowel letters *a, e, i, o* and *u* each have two normal pronunciations in stressed syllables: a 'short' one, and a 'long' one. The 'short' pronunciation (/æ/, /e/, /ɪ/, /ɒ/, /ʌ/) is common when there is no following syllable, or when the next syllable is 'closed off' by two consonants. The 'long' pronunciation (/eɪ/, /iː/, /aɪ/, /əʊ/, /(j)uː/) is common before one consonant which is followed by another syllable or by silent *e*. (There are of course exceptions.) A following *r* or *re* also makes a difference, giving a total of four typical sounds for each letter.

Students are likely to vary in their reactions to Exercise 8: some people like systematic tabular presentations of language facts, while others are put off by this kind of approach.

Optional extra materials
Slips with half-sentences for Exercise 3.

1 Mid-verb adverbs: working out rules
• Let students discuss this in groups. They ought to come up with something close to the following set of rules:
– These adverbs come after *am, are, is, was* and *were*.
– They come before other one-part verbs.
– They come after the first part of longer verb phrases.

2 Mid-verb adverbs with *be*: personality
• This can be done as a whole-class exercise with students volunteering answers. They will probably be able to think of other adjectives besides the ones suggested.

3 Other one-word verbs: split sentences
• A nice way to do this is to write out the half-sentences in advance on separate slips of paper, and let students in turn take a 'beginning' and an 'end' without seeing what is written on the slips (as if they were drawing playing cards from a pack). They then read the slips and put them together with a frequency adverb of their choice.

4 Two-word verbs: experiences
• This can be done in writing or orally as you wish.

5 Adverbs with verb and object: working out the rules
• This can be done by group discussion. If students get stuck, tell them to begin their rule *Don't put adverbs …*

6 Test

• This gives students a chance to see if they have grasped the rules presented in Exercises 1–5. It is probably best to do it in writing, so as to check on everybody in the class.

Answers to Exercise 6
1. My father plays the piano very badly.
2. I have often thought of becoming a student again.
3. My sister is always happy.
4. Small children usually say what they think.
5. We'd better clean the kitchen quickly before your mother gets here.
6. I can never understand the words of songs.
7. She likes sport very much. OR She very much likes sport.
8. He often loses his keys.
9. I will always love you.
10. I never forget people's faces.
11. You must never tell me lies.
12. He would probably like money for his birthday.

7 Matching

(This exercise is adapted from an activity in A Way With Words 1, *by Stuart Redman and Robert Ellis, Cambridge University Press 1989. We are grateful to the authors of this excellent vocabulary practice book for allowing us to use their idea.)*

• The exercise can be done by class or group discussion, with students pooling their knowledge. Let them use dictionaries or ask other people about words if necessary.

• As a follow-up, give students one minute to observe each other in pairs; then get them to stand back to back and describe each other's appearance and clothing from memory.

8 Rules and exceptions

• Give students a few minutes to look over the table.

• Practise the pronunciation of the various words (using the recording as a guide if you wish).

• Then ask students to see if they can find exceptions to any of the groups. They shouldn't find that many (which may persuade them that English spelling is not quite as unpredictable as they thought). Some common categories of exception:
– *a* pronounced /ɑː/ (e.g. *father, ask*).
– *a* pronounced /ɒ/ or /ɔː/ after *w* (e.g. *watch, water*).
– *al* pronounced /ɔː(l)/ (e.g. in *walk, all*).
– *o* pronounced /ʌ/ (e.g. *come, love*).

• You could continue, if students are interested, by discussing common pronunciations of two-vowel combinations like *ea, ee, ie, oa, oo, ou* and *ow*. Note however that some of these are less predictable.

Practice Book exercises
1. Position of frequency adverbials.
2. Word order.
3. Revision of irregular verbs.
4. Pronunciation and vocabulary revision.
5. Recreational reading: magazine texts.
6. Extended writing: how a person's physical appearance can affect their lives.

6 Put the adverbs in the right places in the sentences.

1. My father plays the piano. (*very badly*)
2. I have thought of becoming a student again. (*often*)
3. My sister is happy. (*always*)
4. Small children say what they think. (*usually*)
5. We'd better clean the kitchen before your mother gets here. (*quickly*)
6. I can understand the words of songs. (*never*)
7. She likes sport. (*very much*)
8. He loses his keys. (*often*)
9. I will love you. (*always*)
10. I forget people's faces. (*never*)
11. You must tell me lies. (*never*)
12. He would like money for his birthday. (*probably*)

VOCABULARY: CLOTHES AND PARTS OF THE BODY

7 What goes where? Match the clothes and accessories with the parts of the body.

belt	blouse	boots	bracelet	brooch
contact lenses	ear-rings	glasses		glove
handbag	hat	jacket	necklace	ring
scarf	shirt	shoes	skirt	socks
T-shirt	tie	tights	trousers	watch

arm	chest	ears	eyes	face	feet
finger	hand	head	legs and feet		
lower body	neck	neck and shoulders			
upper body	waist	wrist			

PRONUNCIATION: TYPICAL PRONUNCIATIONS OF VOWEL LETTERS

8 🔲 Look at the table. It shows the most typical pronunciations of the letters *a, e, i, o* and *u* when they are stressed. Note that a following *e* usually gives the letter a 'long' pronunciation (compare *hat* and *hate*), and that a following *r* also changes the pronunciation. Can you find more examples for each group? Can you find any common exceptions?

	short	long	before *r*	before *re*
a	/æ/ hat, matter	/eɪ/ hate, name	/ɑː/ car, start	/eə/ share, care
e	/e/ when, letter	/iː/ scene, complete	/ɜː/ serve, perfect	/ɪə/, /eə/ here, there
i	/ɪ/ sit, village	/aɪ/ fine, bite	/ɜː/ first, shirt	/aɪə/ fire, tired
o	/ɒ/ on, officer	/əʊ/ no, home	/ɔː/ sort, born	/ɔː/ more, store
u	/ʌ/ up, number	/juː/, /uː/ tune, blue	/ɜː/ turn, hurt	/jʊə/ cure, pure

Learn/revise: bad-tempered; cheerful; depressed; friendly; worried; hardly ever; occasionally; usually; *vocabulary from Exercise 7.*

E7 Every hour

1 What is your attitude to hunting animals 1) for sport 2) for their fur 3) for food?

2 Read the text and answer the questions.

Every hour, two or three kinds of animals, plants or insects die out for ever. If nothing is done about it, one million species that are alive today will have become extinct twenty years from now.

QUESTION: What is your reaction to this information?
1. You already knew.
2. You are surprised and shocked.
3. You don't believe it.
4. You are not very interested.
5. Other.

The seas are in danger. They are being filled with poison: industrial and nuclear waste, chemical fertilisers and pesticides, sewage. The Mediterranean is already nearly dead; the North Sea is following. If nothing is done about it, one day soon nothing will be able to live in the seas.

QUESTION: Which of these sources of poison is not mentioned in the text?
1. factories
2. lavatories
3. atomic power stations
4. oil tankers
5. farms

The tropical rain forests, which are the home of half the earth's living things (including many rare animals and plants), are being destroyed. If nothing is done about it, they will have nearly disappeared in twenty years. The effect on the world's climate – and on our agriculture, wood, food supplies and medicine – will be disastrous.

QUESTIONS:
1. Do you know any places where rain forests are being destroyed?
2. Do you know why the world's climate will be affected?

Fortunately, somebody is trying to do something about it. In 1961, the World Wildlife Fund was founded – a small group of people who wanted to raise money to save animals and plants from extinction. Now called the World Wide Fund for Nature, WWF is a large international organisation working to stop the destruction of the earth's natural resources. It has raised over 230 million pounds for conservation projects over the last ten years, and has created or given support to National Parks in five continents. It has helped 30 mammals and birds – including the tiger – to survive. Perhaps this is not much, but it is a start. If more people give more money – and if more governments wake up to what is happening – perhaps the World Wide Fund for Nature will be able to help us to avoid the disaster that threatens the natural world, and all of us with it.

QUESTION: Does the text say where the WWF gets its money from?

106

Lesson E7

Students practise reading, oral fluency and writing, and explore vocabulary in the field of conservation and ecology.

Possible problems
Text study
This lesson focuses on reading skills, and students start by working on two substantial texts. Don't let the lesson turn into a session of intensive vocabulary-explanation – this will slow things down and is unlikely to be very valuable. In Exercise 2, in particular, students should ask for, look up or guess only the vocabulary they need in order to understand the general meaning and answer the questions. Other difficult words can be left for self-study or ignored.

If you are short of time
If time is tight, or if your students have very limited vocabulary, you may wish to drop Exercise 2 or give it for homework. In that case, tell students briefly about the World Wide Fund for Nature before starting Exercise 3.

You may want to drop the written part of Exercise 5, and just get students to report their decisions to the class.

1 Warm-up discussion
- This can be done with books closed.
- Explain *hunting* if necessary.
- Get brief reactions from as many people as possible to the three parts of the question. Alternatively, get three students to go round the class (one asking about hunting for sport, one about hunting for fur and one about hunting for food).
- You may like to tabulate the results on the board, showing how many people are in favour of or against hunting in each case.
- The exercise may grow into a small-scale discussion, especially if some students hunt or fish.

2 Reading
- The questions are intended to help the students read more actively, digesting and reacting to each part of the text.
- Give students a minute or two to read each part.
- Let them ask about or look up key vocabulary, but don't slow the exercise down by spending time on less important words.
- You can vary the way you deal with the questions. (For example: the first can be discussed round the class; students can write their answers to the second and then compare notes with their neighbours; and so on.)

Answers to Exercise 2
Question on second section: oil tankers.
Questions on third section:
1. For example the Amazon, South-East Asia, tropical Africa, New Guinea.
2. Large forests hold water and evaporate it back into the atmosphere, so they are important for soil conservation and rainfall. Cutting down forests can cause both flooding and drought. Also, trees 'breathe out' oxygen, helping to maintain the correct balance of gases in the atmosphere; and they remove carbon dioxide (CO_2) from the atmosphere, lessening the Greenhouse Effect.
Question on fourth section: Not directly.

3 Reading and vocabulary

• This exercise helps students to focus selectively on some of the vocabulary of the subject.

• It can be done in groups. Give each group one or more sections, and get them to read their completed texts to the rest of the class.

Answers to Exercise 3

OPERATION TIGER

Seventy years ago there were 100,000 tigers in the wild. Today there are not more than 8,000 *left*. In 1972 the World Wildlife Fund launched 'Operation Tiger' to *save* the tigers that *remained*. Eighteen tiger reserves have been *created* in India and three in Nepal.

THE LAST THIRTY ORYX

By the 1970s, *hunters* had killed *almost* all of the Arabian oryx. The WWF helped to capture the last thirty *surviving* oryx and send them to Phoenix *Zoo* in Arizona, where a herd of these *rare* animals has been built up. Other *zoos* and *wildlife* parks have helped, and the oryx has been reintroduced into its *natural* surroundings in Oman, Jordan and Saudi Arabia.

THE LAST THOUSAND POLAR BEARS

Thirty years ago *fewer* than 1,000 polar bears were left *alive* in the wild in Norway, Greenland and the USSR. WWF persuaded the five *Arctic* nations of Canada, the USA, Denmark (Greenland), the USSR and Norway, to agree to control *hunting* and promote scientific study. Now the 'ice bears' are *living* and breeding *successfully* once again, and those 1,000 bears have *increased* their numbers to about 5,000.

THE TROPICAL FORESTS

Tropical forests have *supplied* us with very many sorts of plants for food, *medicine* and industry. They could probably supply many more. They also reduce *floods* and droughts, keep water clean, and slow down the Greenhouse Effect. But the tropical forests are being *destroyed* to make room for things like farms, ranches, mines and hydroelectric *dams*. About 20 million hectares are lost each year – an area more than twice the size of Austria. WWF is working to *protect* and save the forests that are *in danger*; to plant new trees for fuel wood and to slow down the Greenhouse Effect; and to *encourage* governments to think about the forests and their importance when giving *international* aid.

4 Student-directed vocabulary learning

• Give students a few minutes to choose words and expressions to learn.

• If you have not already talked about this, you may want to discuss *how many* words it is useful for them to list, and *how* they actually intend to learn them (see *Introduction* page x). Point out that one of the best ways of learning vocabulary is to use it to express one's own ideas in speech or writing. Students should try to bring their new words into Exercise 5 and the Practice Book exercises.

5 Role play discussion and writing

• The decision part of the exercise can be done in three stages.

• First of all, give students a few minutes to work individually, drawing up their own lists.

• Then get them to work in groups. Each group must produce an agreed list of priorities, with reasons for their choices. Give them a time limit, say ten minutes, for this part of the exercise.

• One member of each group should act as secretary, noting down the group's decisions. It may be useful also to appoint a group chairperson, who is responsible for seeing that everybody in the group talks. (This can be a good role for fluent or over-confident students who talk too much.)

• Give them a minute to decide whether they are going to design a poster or write a letter.

• Then walk round while they are working, giving any help that is needed.

• When they have finished, they should exchange posters/letters with other groups; or you can post the posters and letters up on the class notice board for everyone to read.

Practice Book exercises

1. Vocabulary revision: animals and animal products.
2. Word stress.
3. Punctuation and paragraphing.
4. Expressing opinions.
5. Recreational reading: *Strange but true!* (animals).
6. Extended writing: expressing an opinion in greater detail.

3 Read the texts and put in the words from the boxes. You may have to make some small changes.

OPERATION TIGER

create	left	remain	save

Seventy years ago there were 100,000 tigers in the wild. Today there are not more than 8,000 .... In 1972 the World Wildlife Fund launched 'Operation Tiger' to .... the tigers that .... Eighteen tiger reserves have been .... in India and three in Nepal.

THE LAST THIRTY ORYX

almost	hunter	natural	rare	survive
wildlife	zoo (*twice*)			

By the 1970s, ... had killed .... all of the Arabian oryx. The WWF helped to capture the last thirty .... oryx and send them to Phoenix .... in Arizona, where a herd of these .... animals has been built up. Other .... and .... parks have helped, and the oryx has been reintroduced into its .... surroundings in Oman, Jordan and Saudi Arabia.

THE LAST THOUSAND POLAR BEARS

Arctic	alive	fewer	hunting	increase
live	successfully			

Thirty years ago .... than 1,000 polar bears were left .... in the wild in Norway, Greenland and the USSR. WWF persuaded the five .... nations of Canada, the USA, Denmark (Greenland), the USSR and Norway, to agree to control .... and promote scientific study. Now the 'ice bears' are .... and breeding .... once again, and those 1,000 bears have .... their numbers to about 5,000.

THE TROPICAL FORESTS

dam	destroy	encourage	flood
in danger	international	medicine	
protect	supply		

Tropical forests have .... us with very many sorts of plants for food, ... and industry. They could probably supply many more. They also reduce .... and droughts, keep water clean, and slow down the Greenhouse Effect. But the tropical forests are being .... to make room for things like farms, ranches, mines and hydroelectric .... About 20 million hectares are lost each year – an area more than twice the size of Austria. WWF is working to .... and save the forests that are .... ; to plant new trees for fuel wood and to slow down the Greenhouse Effect; and to .... governments to think about the forests and their importance when giving .... aid.

(information supplied by WWF)

4 Choose some vocabulary to learn from the texts in Exercises 2 and 3. Compare notes with other students, and talk about the reasons for your choices.

5 Work in groups of three or four. Imagine that you are the executive committee of a wildlife conservation organisation in the year 2500.

You have enough money to save several, but not all, of the following from extinction: the lion, the rabbit, the sheep, the cat, the dog, the horse, the golden eagle, the bee, the cobra, the rose. Draw up a list of priorities: three things that you will certainly save, three more that you will save if you have enough money left over, and four that you will not try to save.

Design a poster, or write a letter to be sent to all the members of your organisation, persuading people that your three priority species must be saved.

Learn/revise: animal; Arctic; climate; continent; disaster; extinct; flood; food; fur; hunter; industry; insect; lavatory; medicine; Mediterranean; organisation; place; plant; poison; tropical forest; reaction; sea; zoo; create; destroy; disappear; hunt; increase; live; remain; save; supply (sth; sbdy with sth); survive; threaten; alive; chemical; dead; international; left; living; natural; nuclear; rare; shocked; almost; fortunately; successfully; in danger.

E8 'A shock'

Speaking practice.

Work in groups of four, five or six.

Each group is to prepare, practise and perform a dramatic sketch lasting about five minutes.

The subject of the sketch is 'a shock'.

It is up to you to decide what sort of shock this is, what you do about it, what sort of person each of you is, *etc*.

Besides the shock, you must also bring into your sketch three or more of the following:

– a story
– travel
– illness
– a song
– electricity
– a suggestion
– an offer
– a meal
– a bet
– money
– love
– a little old lady
– a quick thinker
– a favour
– something very big
– something very small

Sketch

• You should allow plenty of time for this sketch. Its purpose is to give students an opportunity to re-use a lot of the language that they have learnt during the course, and to gain confidence from realising how much more fluent they have become.

• Detailed instructions are unnecessary: students should be familiar with the technique of preparing and performing sketches by this time.

• You may need to put a little pressure on groups that find it difficult to make decisions at the beginning. If necessary, make up their minds for them.

• Stress that this is a *revision* sketch. Students should be looking back through their books to remind themselves of useful language for the topics they have chosen. Discourage them from incorporating too much new language.

• If possible, get students to learn their parts by heart before they perform.

• Warn them in advance if you are going to tape- or video-record them. This will give them an incentive to reach a high standard.

Practice Book exercises
1. Imaginative response to one of two photographs.
2. Grammar and vocabulary revision: completing a short story.
3. Translation of material from Lessons D7 to E7.
4. Recreational reading: two articles.
5. Extended writing: a 'shock' story.
6. Crossword.

Summary E

will-future

It **will be** dry and sunny.
It**'ll be** very hot.
It**'ll cloud** over.

it'll and *there'll*

It'll + verb

It**'ll be** very hot.
It**'ll cloud** over.
It**'ll rain**.

There'll be + noun

There'll be rain. (~~It'll be rain.~~)
There'll be snow. (~~It'll be snow.~~)
There'll be sunshine. (~~It'll be sunshine.~~)

Past Progressive tense: use and pronunciation

What **were** /wə/ you **doing** at ten o'clock last night?
I **was** /wəz/ **reading**.

Passive infinitives after modal verbs

A coin **can be used** as a screwdriver.
A bath **can be used** as a bed.

Irregular verbs in Lessons E1–E8

INFINITIVE	PAST	PAST PARTICIPLE
blow	blew	blown
bring	brought	brought
buy	bought	bought
come	came	come
cost	cost	cost
find	found	found
give	gave	given
hide	hid	hidden
lend	lent	lent
lose	lost	lost
make	made	made
mean	meant	meant
meet	met	met
ring	rang	rung
say	said	said
send	sent	sent
shine	shone	shone
show	showed	shown
steal	stole	stolen
teach	taught	taught
understand	understood	understood
write	wrote	written

Reported speech with *would* and *had*

- 'It **will** be sunny tomorrow.' 'No, it won't. It'll rain.'
  Maria **said** it **would** be sunny tomorrow, but Paul **said** it **would** rain.
- You **will** have a wonderful week.
  My horoscope **said** I **would** have a wonderful week.
- I know John **has gone** on a business trip.
  Mary **knew** John **had gone** on a business trip.
- **Has** John **gone** off with that American woman?
  Mary **wondered** if John **had gone** off …

Position of frequency adverbs

Adverbs of frequency (*always, usually, often, sometimes, occasionally, hardly ever, never*) usually go with the verb.

1. They go after *am/are/is/was/were*.

She **is always** late.
Ann and Phil **are usually** at home at the weekend.
We **were** very **often** hungry when I was a child.
I **am never** sure what he thinks.

2. They go before other one-part verbs.

It **often rains** in England in summer.
My mother **sometimes loses** her temper for no reason.
I **occasionally go** to the cinema, if there's a really good film.
We **hardly ever have** lunch on Sundays.

3. They go after the first part of two- or three-word verbs.

I've **never been** to India.
You **can always ask** me for help.
She says she **will never leave** me.
I'm quite **often invited** to have dinner with the boss.
I **would never have known** if you hadn't told me.

Expressing the same idea in different ways

WITH A VERB

It often **rains**. It's **snowing**. The sun **shone**.

WITH A NOUN

There is often **rain**. There will be **snow**. There was **sun(shine)**.

WITH AN ADJECTIVE

It is often **rainy/wet**. It was **sunny**.

Summary E

Summary of language taught in Lessons E1–E8.

This section displays most of the more important systematic language points that students should have learnt or revised in the last eight lessons. Spend a short time going over the material with the students, answering questions and clearing up any difficulties. Get them also to look over the vocabulary from Lessons E1–E8 (in the *Learn/revise* panels at the end of each lesson), making sure they know at least the more important new words and expressions. They may need to spend time at home consolidating their learning before moving on.

Word order: verb, object and adverb

We do not usually put adverbs between the verb and the object.

She speaks English well.
   (She speaks well English.)
I like cross-country skiing very much.
   (I like very much cross-country skiing.)
You must cook the meat slowly.
   (You must cook slowly the meat.)
He probably has a lot of friends.
   (He has probably a lot of friends.)
She carefully opened the letter.
OR She opened the letter carefully.
   (She opened carefully the letter.)

Verbs with two objects

Many verbs can be followed by two objects. Common examples: *bring, buy, get, give, lend, make, offer, order, pass, send, show, teach, tell, write.*

Perhaps you could **bring me a little orange juice?**
Shall I **give you a hand?**
Can you **lend me some stamps?**
She wants me to **teach her French.**

Punctuation

Capital letters are used at the beginning of sentences.

It happened like this. (it happened like this)

Capital letters are used for names.

Dear Sue (Dear sue)

Capital letters are used for nationality words, including adjectives.

that American woman (that american woman)

'I' is always capitalised.

I made a real fool of myself (i made ...)

Full stops separate one sentence from another.

I made a real fool of myself last week. It happened like this.
   (I made a real fool of myself last week it happened like this)

Question marks are used instead of full stops after direct questions.

... am I the only one?

Commas are used between clauses to break up longer sentences.

Have you ever done anything like that, or am I the only one?

Commas are used to separate 'discourse markers' like *Well.*

Well, I was sure he'd gone off with that American woman.
   (Well I was sure ...)

Commas are used to separate phrases that 'interrupt' a clause.

'I'm sorry,' the girl said, 'but ...'

Commas are not used before *that.*

It turned out that he'd met an old school friend.
   (It turned out, that ...)

Brackets are used to separate less important points that interrupt the main ideas.

Well, I was sure he'd gone off with that American woman (do you remember me telling you about her last year?). But actually ...

Quotation marks are used to show that we are quoting somebody's actual words.

'I'm sorry,' the girl said ...
   (I'm sorry, the girl said ...)

Apostrophes are used in contractions.

I'm   he'd   he's   couldn't
   (Im   hed   hes   couldnt)

Examples of common contractions

I'm   I've   he's (= *he is* or *he has*)
she'd (= *she had* or *she would*)   I'll   it'll
can't   won't   isn't   doesn't   hasn't
hadn't   wouldn't   couldn't   didn't

Asking for things when you don't know the exact words

a thing   a machine   a tool
stuff   liquid   powder   material

square   round   pointed   sharp

a point   an end   a hole   a handle

a thing with a (hole, handle, *etc.*)

a thing/tool/machine for (making ..., cutting ..., *etc.*)

a thing that you ... with/in/on/*etc.*

a thing that goes on top of / under / ...

material/liquid/powder/stuff for ...ing

Vocabulary

Look through the 'Learn/revise' boxes at the ends of Lessons E1–E8.

Revision and fluency practice E

A choice of activities.

1 🔲 Read the text and listen to the recording. There are a large number of differences. How many can you find?

And now yesterday's weather. There may be some cloud and rain in the south-east at first tomorrow, but most of France, Belgium and northern Switzerland will have sunny periods. There may be storms, especially in the south and east, and snow is probable on low ground in northern and eastern Scotland. It will not be much colder or windier tomorrow, with temperatures ranging from 3° Celsius (27° Fahrenheit) in northern France to 9°C (48°F) in south-west England. Outlook for the weekend: it will be mainly very dry, with exceptional showers in western districts. Temperatures will be lower. There could be strong winds in southern England and Ireland, reaching gale force in some land areas.

2 🔲 Listen to the recording. It is the background music from an imaginary film. Work in groups and decide what is happening in the film as the music plays.

3 Strange presents. On three separate pieces of paper, write the names of three things that would make strange birthday presents. (Examples: a baby crocodile; a chocolate clock; a bottle of sea water.) The teacher will collect the papers in, mix them up and give them out again. As soon as you get your paper, explain why the thing written on it would make a really good present for you.

4 Talk for a minute or two (to your group or the whole class) about your childhood or your family. Put in three lies, and at least one thing that is strange but true. The others have to decide which are the lies.

5 Here is the script of a game of 'Twenty Questions'. One person is thinking of a common object, and the others are trying to guess what it is. What do you think the object is?

'Is it useful?'
'Yes.'
'Can you eat it?'
'No.'
'Is it manufactured?'
'Yes.'
'Does it cost more than £5?'
'Yes.'
'Does it cost more than £100?'
'No.'
'Is it made of metal?'
'Yes, partly.'
'Is it used in an office?'
'No.'
'In a kitchen?'
'No.'
'Outside?'
'Yes.'
'Is the metal part made of iron?'
'No.'
'Steel?'
'Yes.'
'Is it a means of transport?'
'No.'
'Can you hold it in your hand?'
'Yes.'
'Has it got a point?'
'Yes.'
'Is it bigger than a lighter?'
'Yes.'
'Is part of it made of string?'
'No.'
'Is part of it made of wire?'
'No.'
'Is it used at a particular time of day?'
'No.'
'Is it waterproof?'
'Yes.'
'Is it an ...?'
'Yes.'

6 Play 'Twenty Questions' yourselves in groups of four or five. Try to use words and expressions from Exercise 5.

Revision and fluency practice E

Students and teacher choose from a range of practice activities.

Teaching notes
Detailed teaching notes are not provided for all exercises in this section, since most of the activities are self-explanatory.

---

1 Finding differences
- One way to do this is as a dictation.
- Give students a few minutes to look over the text and try to memorise it.
- Then tell them to close their books. Play the recording, pausing while students write down what they hear.
- Then ask them how many differences they think there are between this version and the one in the book.
- When they have found all they can, let them open their books and check.

Tapescript and answers to Exercise 1
And now *tomorrow's* weather. There *will* be some cloud and rain in the south-*west* at first tomorrow, but most of *England*, *Wales* and Northern *Ireland* will have sunny periods. There may be *showers*, especially in the *north* and east, and snow is *possible* on *high* ground in northern and eastern Scotland. *It will be* much colder *and* windier tomorrow, with temperatures ranging from 3°Celsius (*37°Fahrenheit*) in northern *Scotland* to 9°C (*48°F*) in south-west England. Outlook for the weekend: it will be mainly *dry*, with *occasional* showers in western districts. Temperatures will be *higher*. There *will* be strong winds in *northern* England and *Scotland*, reaching gale force in some *sea* areas.

2 Background music
- There is not of course a 'right answer' to this.

5 Twenty questions
- The object is an umbrella.

7 Family decision

• One way to do this is to prepare role-cards for the family members. Use your own judgement as to how many to prepare, and what to put on them. Suggestions:

Father: This new job would be much better paid than your present one. It also offers more responsibility and better career prospects. You think you would be quite happy to live abroad: you enjoy travel and like learning foreign languages.

Mother: You have a good job which you enjoy; you have good career prospects with your present company. If you go abroad you will lose this, and you may not have much chance of finding a good job in the new country. You like travel, but you don't think you would like to live abroad permanently. You are worried about being cut off from your friends and relations.

Son/Daughter 1: You have got important exams coming up next year, and moving abroad would make it impossible for you to study for these. Also, you dislike travel and hate learning foreign languages, and you think that your own country is the only really civilised place in the world.

Son/Daughter 2: You like the idea of living abroad for a time, making new friends and learning about a new culture. But you are worried about losing touch with your friends in your own country; especially one particular friend …

Son/Daughter 3: You hate your school, your home town, the people in it, the political system, the weather and the food. You would love to start life again in a new country.

Grandmother: You have lived in the same town all your life. The thought of moving to another country horrifies you.

7 Work in groups of four, five or six. Prepare and practise a sketch for the following situation. When you are ready, perform your sketch for the class.

The group is a family. (Each student in the group should play the part of one of the family members.) Father has been offered a very well-paid job abroad; he wants to accept it and take the family with him. The rest of the family disagree about whether to go or not (each person should have a good reason for staying or going). In the middle of their discussion, the postman comes with a letter for one of the family (not Father).

8 Work in pairs. Make up a conversation, lasting a maximum of 90 seconds, in which you use as many as possible of the following words.

asleep	centimetre	end	go away		haircut
menu	pen	purse	quick	rock	second
sex	taste	tie	towel	zero	

9 Mime a machine. See if the other students can write down the name of your machine.

10 Read the story, and list the people in order, according to whose behaviour you think was worst, whose was next worst, *etc.* Discuss your lists in groups. Useful structure: *he/she should(n't) have ...ed.*

ANNETTE AND CLIVE

Annette's boyfriend Clive went to the Far East for six months on business. Annette loved Clive desperately, and couldn't stand being away from him for so long. She wanted to go and see him, but she couldn't afford the air fare. So she telephoned Clive, asking him to come over to London for a few days to see her, but he said that he couldn't because of pressure of work. So then she went to see Ian, an old boyfriend of hers, and asked if he would lend her the money. He said he would, but only if she would go away for the weekend with him. Annette refused, and went to her father Jake. (Jake had plenty of money but didn't like Clive at all.) Jake said no. So Annette went back to Ian and agreed to his terms. They spent the weekend together, Ian lent Annette the money for the plane ticket, and on Monday she flew to see Clive.

When Clive asked Annette how she had got the money, she told him the truth. Clive was furious and broke off their relationship. Annette flew back to London in despair. When she got home, she went to see her father and told him what had happened. Her father did not take it well. He phoned a friend of his, and the two of them went round to Ian's place and beat him up.

11 Look at the cartoons and talk about your reactions. Which ones do you find funny? Which ones don't make you laugh? Are there any that you don't understand? Discuss your reactions with other students.

"Good morning, Mr Dolby! It's 5.15 am and this is radio station WJRM. If you name the next tune you will win a ride on an elephant and two tickets to a rock concert!"

"The committee on women's rights will now come to order."

Test E

LISTENING

1 📼 Listen and match: what will the weather be like when?

1. this morning
2. this afternoon
3. tonight
4. tomorrow morning
5. tomorrow evening

a. cloudy, rain
b. dry, nice
c. the occasional shower
d. showers, cloud, rain
e. sunny

GRAMMAR

2 Choose the right verb forms.

1. Temperatures .... a bit cooler tomorrow. (*be*)
2. There .... any rain today, but there is a possibility of some light rain tomorrow. (*not be*)
3. My horoscope said that I .... a very interesting person on Wednesday, but I didn't meet anyone at all. (*meet*)
4. I didn't know that you .... Martin. (*already meet*)
5. I tried to phone you at the office this afternoon, but they said you .... (*leave*)

3 Put each sentence into the right order.

1. a ballpoint can for lend me minute you your ?
2. and bring chips could fish some us you ?
3. he her never tells the truth .
4. holiday let me my photographs show you .
5. could me pass salt the you ?

4 Copy each sentence, adding the word or expression in brackets in the right place.

1. Jonathan is on time. (*always*)
2. Children are afraid of the dark. (*very often*)
3. I forget where I put things. (*sometimes*)
4. We invite friends to lunch on Sunday. (*hardly ever*)
5. I've been to Moscow. (*never*)
6. I can remember her husband's name. (*never*)
7. She is asked to talk to school children about being blind. (*quite often*)
8. She plays tennis. (*well*)
9. I like Josie. (*very much*)
10. You should open it. (*very carefully*)
11. You left your keys in the car. (*probably*)
12. You should tell your parents the truth. (*usually*)

LANGUAGE IN USE

5 Here is a dialogue where A (Anne) is speaking formally and B (Barry) is speaking informally. Rewrite the dialogue, so that both people speak *either* formally *or* informally.

A: That's a lovely tie.
B: Thanks.
A: Would you like another drink?
B: What?
A: Would you like another drink?
B: No, thanks. But how about some more pizza?
A: Yes, of course.
      *   *   *
A: Here you are.
B: Thanks.

VOCABULARY

6 Write the names of these.

Test E

This test covers work done in Lessons E1–E8.

Administration of the test

1. General procedure   Give students a few minutes to look over the test and make sure they understand what they are to do in each part.

2. Listening (Exercise 1)   Give students a few minutes to look at the two lists.

Then play the recording twice, pausing after each time for the students to note their answers.

3. Speaking (Exercise 12)   You will have to take students aside in pairs for the Speaking part of the test. If you have a large class and a short class period, you may have to drop this part of the test.

Explain to students what they will be doing in the speaking exercise after they have done Exercise 1. The students should take a few minutes at that time to decide what objects they are going to describe – each person should think of three objects, though they will probably only need two.

Call each pair of students out of the class, for example to your desk or to the back of the classroom, while the others work on the written part of the test.

Try to make the students feel comfortable. Tell them that the person who is listening can ask for clarification if she/he wants.

Remember that what you are looking for in this Speaking test is fluency, not perfect grammar or pronunciation. What counts is whether the students can make themselves understood.

LISTENING

1

Answers

1a; 2c; 3b; 4e; 5d

Tapescript

Let's have a quick update on that weather check from the Bristol Met. Office. Cloudy and misty this morning, little bit of rain, fairly heavy at times. Should be a br-, a little bit brighter this afternoon with just the occasional shower. 14 degrees the high, down to about 8 Celsius overnight, that's er, mostly dry, clear spells, so fairly nice night actually. Bright, sunny tomorrow morning, so go shopping then. Scattered showers and cloud and rain by the evening is the picture for tomorrow. Looks like it could be a damp weekend.

GRAMMAR

2

1. will be / are going to be
2. won't be / will not be
3. would meet / was going to meet
4. had already met
5. had left

3

1. Can you lend me your ballpoint for a minute?
2. Could you bring us some fish and chips?
3. He never tells her the truth.
4. Let me show you my holiday photographs.
5. Could you pass me the salt?

4

1. Jonathan is *always* on time.
2. Children are *very often* afraid of the dark.
3. I *sometimes* forget where I put things.
4. We *hardly ever* invite friends to lunch on Sunday.
5. I've *never* been to Moscow.

6. I can *never* remember her husband's name.
7. She is *quite often* asked to talk to school children about being blind.
8. She plays tennis *well*.
9. I like Josie *very much*.
10. You should open it *very carefully*.
11. You *probably* left your keys in the car.
12. You should *usually* tell your parents the truth.

LANGUAGE IN USE

5   (Many possible answers. Two possibilities are given here.)

A: That's a lovely tie.
B: Oh, thank you very much. I'm glad you like it.
A: Would you like another drink?
B: I beg your pardon?
A: Would you like another drink?
B: Oh, no, thank you. But perhaps you could bring me a little pizza?
A: Yes, of course.
   * * *
A: Here you are.
B: Thank you.

A: Great tie.
B: Thanks.
A: Have another drink?
B: What?
A: Do you want another drink?
B: No, thanks. But how about some more pizza?
A: Sure.
   * * *
A: Here you are.
B: Thanks.

VOCABULARY

6

Answers

1. a basket
2. a brick
3. a computer
4. a coin
5. a toothbrush
6. the sun
7. a cloud
8. a mug
9. an ear-ring
10. a pair of scissors
11. lightning
12. rain
13. ear
14. shoulder
15. waist
16. wrist
17. finger
18. foot
19. blouse
20. dress
21. belt
22. socks
23. towel

READING

7

1. Treeport 7162
2. £175
3. Westport 56655
4. Westport 56655
5. Yes
6. £129

WRITING

8

1. haven't	7. she's
2. won't	8. it'll
3. can't	9. they're
4. aren't	10. wouldn't
5. don't	11. I'd
6. she's	12. I'd

9 (Some variation is possible.)

Dear Alice,

Thank you very much for a lovely time on Saturday. We enjoyed meeting your friends Susan and Carol, and the food was delicious.

I have asked about the book you wanted, but I don't think you can get it in this country; however, if you want, I can write to my friend Nadine in Paris, and I am sure she will be happy to get it for you. You must meet Nadine sometime anyway – I am sure you two would get on really well.

Well, I am writing this while having my breakfast, and if I don't stop now I will miss my bus. Thanks once again for Saturday evening.

Love to you both,
Sarah

10 (Many possible answers; look for a fair degree of fluency, accuracy and appropriateness.)

PRONUNCIATION

11

1. That's a lovely tie.
2. Would you like to dance?
3. The first thing that I do when I get up is make a cup of tea.
4. I find it very difficult to get to sleep at night and to wake up in the morning.
5. Fifty years ago there were a hundred thousand tigers in the wild.

SPEAKING

12 (Remember that fluency is what counts here.)

Test Book recording
A recording for Test 5 in the Test Book follows this lesson on the Class Cassette.

READING

7 Answer the questions by looking at the small ads. *Don't* read all the words in all the ads.

MISCELLANEOUS FOR SALE `401`

ANTIQUES, jewellery, collectables for £5 upwards, gifts for every occasion at Hardy's Antiques, 55 Oswin Road, Treeport. Open Saturdays and Sundays 11am to 4pm, weekdays 10am to 2pm except Mondays. — Tel (0235) 4182.
NEW solid pine furniture, free delivery. — Tel (0235) 8510.
SCAFFOLDING towers £120, industrial £190, immediate delivery. — Tel Lower Harborne 332.
SECTIONAL timber buildings, e.g. 12'x8' Acme with floor, £420, free catalogue. — Tel Bognor Regis 5772.
SHEDS half price, free catalogue. — Tel Bognor Regis 5772.
SWIMMING POOL, 12ft across, 3ft deep, new, guaranteed, £175. — Tel Chichester 6464.
LARGE tea chests with lids, delivered free. — Tel 317625

MISCELLANEOUS WANTED `402`

OLD postcards bought and sold, Yewbarrow Postcards. — Tel Hinton Gurney 2123.
PHOTOGRAPHIC enlarger needed urgently. Prefer Apollo type but any considered. — Tel 623529.
PIANOS wanted, anything considered. — Tel Westport 56655 or Chichester 3111.
WANTED, old furniture, bric a brac, china, curios, postcards. Houses and garages cleared. — Tel Bognor Regis 5633.

TV, VIDEO AND AUDIO `404`

12" FERGUSON portable colour TV with remote control, excellent condition, £150 ono. — Tel (0235) 8869.

MUSICAL INSTRUMENTS `406`

PIANOS from £350 guaranteed. Clavinovas and other digital pianos, Yamaha Keyboards, organs, guitars, sheet music and accessories. 0% interest free credit. The Music Supermarket, 71/72 Bygrave Street, Westport. — Tel 56655.

FARM & GARDEN `413`

DECORATIVE bark, ideal for borders, 30 litre bags £2.50 or loose at £35 per metre, also wood chips, 60 litre bags £2.75 inc VAT, can deliver. — Tel Chesterton 683 6071.

PAVING slabs, crazy paving, sand, ballast, quick delivery. — Tel 0235 6522/7635.
TIMBER cut to your own measurements; also NPC Tagrip treatment; new sawmill operating at Irish Common, Chesterton. — Tel Chesterton 589 0766.
200 garden gnomes, free to good home. — Tel Bognor Regis 5639.
DINGWALL Supreme edge and featheredge boards for sheds. Tel Chesterton 589 0766.

PETS `415`

DOG grooming, clipping, bathing and stripping of all breeds, also Cashmere baby and full-grown rabbits. — Tel Treeport 7162.
HANDSOME grey tabby cat and her ginger brother need loving home after death of owner, other cats also looking for good homes. — Tel South Coast Animal Rescue 0235 83441.
TERRIER puppies, show or pet, ready now, £120. — Tel Water Harborne 623.
COLLIE puppy, home reared, KC registered, pedigree ensured. — Tel Chesterton 776 7742.

LIVESTOCK `416`

WANTED, child's first pony for eight-year-old girl, sale or hire, must be 100%, about 13/14hh, excellent and experienced home. — Tel Bognor 8858.

FURNITURE `419`

ANTIQUES warehouse at Worsden, near Stowfield, 10 miles from Westport, over 1000 items of furniture. Tel (0235) 9677.
OLD and antique furniture wanted, best prices. House clearances. — Tel Bognor Regis 8080 or call at 91 Upper Parade.

SPORTING GOODS `410`

GOLF CLUBS, new, complete set, 9 irons and three metal woods, one year guarantee, £129. — Tel Undersley 763.

---

1. What number should I phone to get my terrier bathed?
2. How much can I buy a swimming pool for?
3. What Westport number do I phone to sell a piano?
4. What Westport number do I phone to buy a piano?
5. Can you have sand delivered or do you have to go and get it?
6. How much do twelve golf clubs cost?

WRITING

8 Write the contractions for these expressions.

1. have not
2. will not
3. cannot
4. are not
5. do not
6. she is
7. she has
8. it will
9. they are
10. would not
11. I had
12. I would

9 Write this letter with correct punctuation and capital letters.

dear alice
thank you very much for a lovely time on saturday we enjoyed meeting your friends susan and carol and the food was delicious

i have asked about the book you wanted but i dont think you can get it in this country however if you want i can write to my friend nadine in paris and i am sure she will be happy to get it for you you must meet nadine sometime anyway i am sure you two would get on really well

well i am writing this while having my breakfast and if i dont stop now i will miss my bus thanks once again for saturday evening
love to you both
sarah

10 Write two horoscopes for tomorrow: a really good one for yourself and a really bad one for someone you don't like.

PRONUNCIATION

11 Copy the sentences and underline the stressed syllables.

1. That's a lovely tie.
2. Would you like to dance?
3. The first thing that I do when I get up is make a cup of tea.
4. I find it very difficult to get to sleep at night and to wake up in the morning.
5. Fifty years ago there were a hundred thousand tigers in the wild.

SPEAKING

12 Work with another student. Each of you must describe one or two objects in English without saying their names and without using your hands. The other must try and guess what they are.

Grammar revision section

Simple Present and Present Progressive

1 Look at the examples and think about how each tense is used.

SIMPLE PRESENT TENSE
Jan often talks to herself.
I never drink anything with my meals.
The days get longer from January to June.
We go out a lot in the summer.

PRESENT PROGRESSIVE TENSE
Look – Jan's talking to herself.
'What are you drinking?' 'Tonic water.'
The days are getting longer now.
We're going out with Annie on Tuesday.

Which tenses do we use to talk about the following?
A things that are happening now, these days
B things that are always true
C things that happen often, usually, always, never *etc.*
D things that are changing
E plans for the future

2 Write the correct verb forms.

1. 'What's that terrible noise?' 'Katy .... the violin.' (*practise*)
2. Do you know anyone who .... Russian? (*speak*)
3. I wonder if Wayne is ill – he .... thinner and thinner. (*get*)
4. Oak trees .... much more slowly than pine trees. (*grow*)
5. She can't come to the phone right now – she .... a bath. (*have*)
6. She .... to church with her brother on Sundays. (*usually go*)
7. Unemployment .... at an alarming rate. (*rise*)
8. .... you .... to the meeting next Tuesday? (*go*)
9. .... your brother ever .... at the weekends? (*work*)

3 Work in groups of four or five. One person should choose *either* a job (plumber, doctor, …) *or* an animal to say two sentences about. The others should ask *Yes/No* questions to find out what the person or animal is. Examples:

'This person works with people. Most people don't like to visit this person.' 'Is it a doctor?' 'No.' 'A nurse?' 'No.' 'Does this person sometimes work at night?' 'Not usually.' …

'This is an animal with a long tail. It eats meat.' 'Is it a big animal?' 'Not very big.' 'Does it live with people?' 'Yes.' …

4 Work with a partner. Choose one of the people in the picture and say what he/she is wearing and doing. Your partner must try to guess which person you are talking about. Example:

'I'm looking at a woman. She's wearing a blue dress, and she's drinking something.' 'Is she sitting down?' …

5 Who are these people and what are they doing? Can you write a 'riddle' like this yourself?

1. This person usually sits down and uses a machine with a screen all day. But right now she is sliding down a mountainside on two pieces of plastic. (*Answer: a computer operator who is skiing*)
2. In his job this person usually stands up, talks, listens and writes on a board. But right now he is sitting down hitting some black and white keys with his fingers.
3. On most days this person walks from house to house putting things into boxes or through holes. At the moment, though, she is standing inside a box and water is falling on her.
4. This person usually works with paints, brushes, pens, inks, paper and canvas. But right now he is pushing two wheels around by moving his legs.

Simple Present and Present Progressive

1 Deducing the rules
• Make sure students understand what they are to do, and then ask them to work individually looking at the tables and the examples, and choosing the best rules for each tense.
• Walk round while they are working to give any help that is needed, but encourage the students to try and work things out for themselves.
• When most of them have finished, get them to compare answers before checking with you.
• Answer any questions that come up.

Answers to Exercise 1
Present Progressive: A; D; E
Simple Present: B; C

2 Structured practice
• Give students a few minutes to work individually writing the answers.
• Go through the answers with the class, getting them to tell you which rule applies for each item.

Answers to Exercise 2
1. is practising (*Rule A*)
2. speaks (*Rule B or C*)
3. is getting (*Rule D*)
4. grow (*Rule B or C*)
5. is having (*Rule A*)
6. usually goes (*Rule C*)
7. is rising (*Rule A or D*)
8. Are ... going (*Rule E*)
9. Does ... work (*Rule C*)

3 Guessing professions/animals: Simple Present
• Put the students into groups of four or five, and go over the examples with them to make sure they understand what they are to do.
• In each group, students should take turns being the person who gives the description.
• Point out that the other students can only ask questions that can be answered with *Yes* or *No*.
• Walk round while they are working to give any help that is needed, and to check their use of the verb forms.

4 'Which person?': Present Progressive
• Put students into pairs, and make sure they understand the instructions.
• Point out that each student should try and give a description that forces his/her partner to ask questions to find the right answer.
• Walk round while they are working to give any help that is needed, and to check their use of the verb forms.

5 Riddles: contrasting the two tenses
• The first item is done as an example. Go over it with the students and then ask them to work individually to do the other three riddles.
• Get the students to compare answers among themselves before checking with you.
• After you have checked the answers, ask each student to try writing a riddle like the ones in the book. When they have finished they should exchange papers with as many other students as possible, trying to guess each other's riddles.

For work on possible confusions between present tenses and the Present Perfect, see page 119.

For more about the use of present tenses to talk about the future, see pages 122–123.

Simple Past and Past Progressive

1 **Thinking about the rules**
• Make sure students understand what they are to do –
they are expected to think about *when* the Past
Progressive is *used*, not just how it is formed.
• Then ask them to work individually looking at the
tables and the examples.
• Walk round while they are working to give any help
that is needed, but encourage students to try and work
things out for themselves.

2 **Focusing on the rules**
• Stronger students can do this by group discussion.
With weaker students, you may prefer to talk through
the exercise with the whole class.

Answers to Exercise 2
Simple Past: A; B; C; D; G
Past Progressive: E; F

3 **Structured practice: gap-filling**
• Give students a few minutes to work individually
writing the answers.
• Go through the answers with the class, getting them
to tell you which of the rules from Exercise 2 apply in
each case.

Answers to Exercise 3
1. phoned; was trying (*Rules C and E*)
2. did ... get (*Rule A*)
3. saw; was walking (*Rules C and E*)
4. was getting; heard (*Rules E and C*)
5. spent (*Rule G*)
6. was talking; went (*Rules E and D*)
7. was reading; came (*Rules E and C*)
8. left; got (*Rule B*)
9. Were ... playing (*Rule F*)
10. worked; left (*Rules G and B*)
11. started; ran (*Rule B*)

4 **Personalisation**
• This can be done informally, with students
volunteering answers – perhaps after writing the first
one or two individually. Make sure they use the Past
Progressive appropriately.

5 **Class survey**
• Make sure the students understand the task, and then
let them work individually to write their questions.
• Walk round to check that they are getting the forms
right and to give any help that they ask for.
• This is best done as a walk-round, with each student
asking her/his question of all the others; but if this is
impractical in your classroom, each student can simply
ask as many others as possible without standing up.
Remind students that they should note the answers they
get.
• When the students have finished asking and
answering, get them to report their results either to the
class or in small groups.

6 **Looking out of the window**
• If it is dark outside, or if it is not practicable to get
students looking out of a window, ask them to imagine
that they are doing so.
• An alternative approach is to tell them to shut their
eyes, and then tell them five times to open their eyes for
a moment and close them again. Each time you are
doing something different (e.g. standing on a chair;
looking at the ceiling; lying down; writing; reading;
throwing a pen in the air; dancing; running; walking).
When you have finished, ask them to write from
memory what you were doing the first/second/etc. time
they opened their eyes.

7 **Cartoon**
• This can be done by group or class discussion.
• See if students can work out the reason for the Past
Progressive in the correct caption ('... *We were just
talking about you.*'). Help them to see that the talking
was a 'background' to Ferguson's entrance, which
interrupted it.

Simple Past and Past Progressive

1 Look at the tables and examples and try to see how each tense is used. Can you make a rule for the Past Progressive?

SIMPLE PAST TENSE

> I left, you left, he/she left *etc.*
> did I leave? *etc.*
> I did not leave *etc.*

PAST PROGRESSIVE TENSE

> I was leaving, you were leaving *etc.*
> was I leaving? *etc.*
> I was not leaving *etc.*

Examples:
1. While I was driving to work, I heard an old friend on the radio.
2. I was trying to explain something to Mark and the phone rang.
3. When she heard the noise, she turned to see what it was.
4. What were you doing at ten o'clock last night?
5. What did you do last weekend?
6. I got a letter from Phil this morning.
7. We lived in a very small town when I was a girl.

2 Which of the two tenses do we use for these?

A a short past event
B a short event that happened before or after another event
C a shorter event which came in the middle of a longer, 'background' event
D a shorter event which interrupted a longer, 'background' event
E the 'background' situation at the moment when something happened
F the situation at a particular past moment
G a long past situation, with nothing else happening in the middle of it

3 Write the correct verb forms.

1. As usual, Roger .... while I .... to get some work done. (*phone; try*)
2. What time .... you .... up this morning? (*get*)
3. I .... Jenny while I .... up Blake Street. (*see; walk*)
4. I .... undressed when I .... a strange sound in the kitchen. (*get; hear*)
5. He .... the last twenty years of his life in Tahiti. (*spend*)
6. I .... to Chris on the phone this morning and the line suddenly .... dead. (*talk; go*)
7. Anna .... the newspaper when I .... into the office this morning. (*read; come*)

8. We .... as soon as Tom .... the tickets. (*leave; get*)
9. .... you .... the violin at about nine last night? (*play*)
10. I .... in a bank after I .... school. (*work; leave*)
11. When it .... raining we all .... into the tent. (*start; run*)

4 Say what you were doing, or what was happening, at three or more of these moments.

1. The last time your phone rang.
2. The last time you were really frightened.
3. The last time you felt very happy.
4. The last time you got really angry.
5. The last time you got very bored.

5 Write questions using two of the expressions below, or write your own question(s) with Past Progressive and Simple Past verbs. Ask some other students your questions and report the answers.

1. when you first met your best friend
2. at 11 o'clock last night
3. when you fell asleep last night
4. at 5.30 this morning
5. when you got home yesterday

6 Go and look out of the nearest window for five seconds. Then sit down and write at least three things that were happening when you looked out of the window.

7 Choose the correct caption for the cartoon.

'Come in, Ferguson. We just talked about you.'
'Come in, Ferguson. We were just talking about you.'

117

Present Perfect and Simple Past with time expressions

1 Look at the tables and examples. When do we use the Present Perfect with time expressions, and when do we use the Simple Past?

SIMPLE PRESENT PERFECT TENSE

> I have seen, you have seen *etc.*
> have I seen? *etc.*   I have not seen *etc.*

SIMPLE PAST TENSE

> I saw, you saw, he/she saw *etc.*
> did I see? *etc.*   I did not see *etc.*

Examples:
1. 'Have you seen Joan today?' 'Yes, I saw her at about nine, but I haven't seen her since then.'
2. I've always wanted to go to New Zealand, but I've never managed to get there.
3. I wanted to be a doctor until I was fifteen.
4. I haven't seen much of Al lately – have you?
5. We went to church every Sunday when I was a child.
6. Hannah's worked with horses all her life.
7. Benjamin's been to Africa several times this year.
8. Somebody broke into our house last night.
9. Janice went to France on holiday fifteen years ago, and she has lived there ever since.
10. I've climbed quite a lot of mountains, but I've never been up Mont Blanc.

2 Only one of these rules is true. Which one?

When we give the time of a past event:
A the Present Perfect is used when the time is finished; the Simple Past is used when it is not finished
B the Present Perfect is used when the time is not finished; the Simple Past is used when it is finished
C the Present Perfect is used for longer periods of time; the Simple Past is used for shorter periods
D the Present Perfect is used for repeated actions; the Simple Past is used for actions that are not repeated

3 Finished or unfinished time?

today	since I got up
yesterday	three years ago
this morning	for the last three years
ever	this year
never	last year
always	for the last year
when I was nine	in 1991
until I was nine	since 1991
since I was nine	recently/lately
after I got up	up to now

4 Write the correct verb forms.

1. '............... Ken .... to school at all this week?' 'He .... on Tuesday morning – that's all, I think.' (*be; come*)
2. Bridget .... in Dublin. (*always live*)
3. I .... a lovely day today – the telephone .... working at about ten, and it .... so peaceful ever since! (*have; stop; be*)
4. I .... to write to Judy yesterday. (*not manage*)
5. It certainly .... cold this winter! (*be*)
6. Karen .... an enormous amount of work last week. (*do*)
7. Isaac and Martin .... about ten years ago. (*first meet*)
8. My grandmother .... in Louisiana until she was twenty. (*live*)
9. .... you ever .... a musical instrument? (*study*)
10. I .... ill a lot last year. (*be*)
11. I .... ill for the last year. (*be*)
12. We .... each other all our lives. (*know*)
13. 'How's your new job?' 'Everything .... all right up to now.' (*be*)
14. I .... Mary recently – have you? (*not see*)

5 Work in groups and discuss the answers to these questions.

1. A woman says 'I've been in Africa for six years.' Is she in Africa when she says this?
2. A man says 'I was in Canada for three years.' Is he in Canada when he says this?
3. Somebody says 'I've worked with Sue for ten years, and I worked with Jake for twelve years.' Which one does he or she still work with?
4. Somebody says 'I did seven years' French at school.' Is he or she still doing French at school?
5. You are in America. Somebody says 'How long are you here for?' Does the person want to know when your visit started, or when it will end? How would he or she express the other meaning?

6 Write two questions: use an expression from each group. Ask other students your questions and report the answers.

First group:
When did you first ...?
How long ago ...?
When you were a child, ...?
Last year, ...?

Second group:
Have you ever ...?
Have you ... today?
What/Who ... lately?
Have you ... since ...?

7 Complete this rule:

DON'T USE THE PRESENT PERFECT WITH EXPRESSIONS OF .... TIME.

Present Perfect and Simple Past with time expressions

Language notes and possible problems
Present Perfect   The differences between the Simple Present Perfect and the Simple Past are complicated and sometimes difficult to analyse. This section deals with the most basic difficulty – the correct choice of tense with expressions of time. In some languages of European origin, there is a tense which is constructed like the English Simple Present Perfect, but which may be used (like the English Simple Past) with expressions referring to past moments and finished time periods. This can lead students to make mistakes like *I have seen him yesterday*. The following exercises are intended to clear up this problem.

The key point is whether the reference is to a finished time (e.g. *yesterday*) or to a period continuing up to the present. It is very rare in English to use the Present Perfect with a finished time reference.

Some grammars use the term 'definite time' instead of 'finished time'. This is misleading and best avoided.

---

1 Deducing the rules
• Make sure students understand what they are to do, and then ask them to work individually looking at the tables and the examples, and trying to work out or remember a rule for each tense.
• Walk round while they are working to give any help that is needed, but encourage the students to try and work things out for themselves.
• When most of them have finished, get them to compare answers before telling you their rules.
• Don't tell them at this stage whether their rules are valid or not.

2 Choosing between rules
• Students' personal versions of grammar rules may be very different from the rules followed by native speakers of English. This exercise will help students to focus on a valid rule and compare it with their own intuitions.
• Make sure students understand the four rules. Ask them which they think is correct. When they have made their choice, ask them to look back at Exercise 1 and see whether their chosen rule works.
• Most of them should see that rule B is the only correct one.
• Clear up any remaining confusions. Make sure students realise that the choice of tense in these cases depends on whether we are talking about a finished or unfinished *time period*, not a finished or unfinished action. (The Present Perfect often refers to finished *actions* – see examples 1, 7 and 10.)

3 Finished or unfinished time?
• If students are still not clear what is meant by 'finished' and 'unfinished' time in this context, this exercise should help.
• Note that we can use *recently* and *lately* to mean 'at any recent time up to now', so that they are often used with the Present Perfect.
• *Ever*, *never* and *always* are put in the 'unfinished time' category here, but they can of course also refer to finished periods in certain contexts.
• You may need to explain the difference between *after* and *since*, and between *last* and *the last* in, for instance, *last year* and *the last year*.

• There are separate exercises on *for* and *since* on page 120.
• The exercise can be done by group discussion.

Answers to Exercise 3
Finished time: yesterday; when I was nine; until I was nine; after I got up; three years ago; last year; in 1991
Unfinished time: today; ever; never; always; since I was nine; since I got up; for the last three years; this year; for the last year; since 1991; recently/lately; up to now
Either (depending on time of day): this morning

4 Choice of tenses: gap-filling
• Give students a few minutes to work individually writing the answers.
• Let them compare answers before checking with you.

Answers to Exercise 4
(Alternative answers with contracted or uncontracted forms are also possible in some cases.)
1. 'Has Ken *been* to school at all this week?' 'He *came* on Tuesday morning – that's all, I think.'
2. Bridget *has* always *lived* in Dublin.
3. I *have had* a lovely day today – the telephone *stopped* working at about ten, and it *has been* so peaceful ever since!
4. I *didn't manage* to write to Judy yesterday.
5. It certainly *has been* cold this winter!
6. Karen *did* an enormous amount of work last week.
7. Isaac and Martin *first met* about ten years ago.
8. My grandmother *lived* in Louisiana until she was twenty.
9. *Have* you ever *studied* a musical instrument?
10. I *was* ill a lot last year.
11. I *have been* ill for the last year.
12. We *have known* each other all our lives.
13. 'How's your new job?' 'Everything *has been* all right up to now.'
14. I *haven't seen* Mary recently – have you?

5 Choice of tenses: situations
• Give students enough time to discuss the questions, and then get them to give their answers and the reasons for them.

Answers to Exercise 5
1. Yes 2. No 3. Sue 4. No 5. When the visit will end. The other meaning might be expressed as 'How long have you been here (for)?'

6 Class survey
• Make sure the students understand the task, and then let them work individually to write their questions.
• Walk round to check that they are getting the forms right and to give any help that they ask for.
• The exercise is best done as a walk-round, with each student asking her/his question of all the others; but if this is impracticable in your classroom, each student can simply ask as many others as possible without standing up. Remind students that they should note the answers they get.
• When the students have finished asking and answering, get them to report their results either to the class or in small groups.

7 'Golden rule'
• Get students to try this individually in writing first of all. Most of them should complete the rule with the word 'finished'.

Present Perfect Progressive

Language notes and possible problems
1. Ongoing states   The Present Perfect Progressive is used to refer to temporary events or states which began in the past and are still continuing. This happens especially when the focus is on the length of time involved; in other cases the Present Progressive is more normal. (Compare: *I've been learning English since February; I'm also learning French.*) In many languages, a present tense would be used to talk about the duration of such states and events: look out for mistakes like *I'm learning English since February.*
2. Causes   The Present Perfect Progressive is also often used to refer to a recent continuing event or state which accounts for a present situation (e.g. *'You look hot.' 'Yes, I've been running.'*).
3. Non-progressive verbs   With some common verbs such as *be, have, know, love,* simple tenses are used instead of progressive forms to express these meanings (e.g. *I've had a headache all day,* NOT *I've been having a headache all day.*). See Exercises on page 120.

---

1 Examples
• Tell students to look at the examples; explain anything that is not clear.
• When they have done this, get them to close their books and try to write at least three of the examples from memory.
• If they have difficulty with this, give them more time to study the examples and let them try again.

2 Practising the forms: gap-filling
• This simple exercise helps students to get a feel for the formation and use of the structure. If you want to provide maximum practice, get students to do it individually in writing.

Answers to Exercise 2
(Contracted forms are also possible.)
1. I *have been learning* English for three years.
2. She *has been working* in the same job since 1988.
3. It *has been snowing* for the last two days.
4. Prices *have been going up* very fast recently.
5. How long *have* you *been staying* in this hotel?
6. 'What *have* you *been doing* all morning?' 'I *have been writing* letters.'
7. 'You look tired.' 'Yes, I *have been working*.'

3 Finding a rule
• Give students plenty of time to think about this and discuss it among themselves. They will probably see that the tense is used to refer to longer actions that have continued up to the present or have just stopped. You may wish to say something about the relevance of the ideas of *duration* and *cause* (see *Language notes*).

4 Personalisation: drawings
• If students are slow to start, you may like to give them a few examples of your own to help them get the idea.
• Instead of showing their drawings to other individuals, students might draw them on the board for the whole class to interpret.

5 Recent causes of present situations: pictures
• This can be done individually or by group discussion, as you wish.

Answers to Exercise 5
The people have been
 1. writing letters
 2. playing football
 3. painting
 4. eating
 5. phoning
 6. driving
 7. playing the piano
 8. swimming
 9. cycling
10. dancing

6 Non-progressive verbs
• This helps to remind students, if necessary, that some common verbs are not used in progressive forms.

Answers to Exercise 6
1. How long have you *known* Alex?
2. How long have you *been learning* French?
3. How long have you *had* your car?
4. Since we first met yesterday morning, I have *loved* you passionately.
5. I've *been trying* to phone him all day.

7 Present Perfect or Present?
• Some students may be inclined to use present tenses instead of Present Perfect tenses when talking about *duration* (see *Language notes*). This short exercise will help them to focus on the point.

Answers to Exercise 7
1. I *have been writing* letters for the last two hours.
2. I *am training* for a ski competition at the moment.
3. How long *have you been working* as a driver?
4. At last! *I've been waiting* for you since ten o'clock.
5. *I've known* her for years.
6. Why *are you looking* at me like that?
7. *He's been* ill for a long time.
8. How long *have you had* that car?

Present Perfect Progressive

1 Look at the examples. Then close your book and try to write down three of them from memory.

*Where have you been? I **have been waiting** for you since six o'clock.*
*It **has been raining** all day.*
*'You look hot.' 'Yes, I've **been running**.'*
*How long **have** you **been learning** English?*
*Who's **been sleeping** in my bed?*

2 Complete the sentences with Present Perfect Progressive verbs.

1. I .... English for three years. (*learn*)
2. She .... in the same job since 1988. (*work*)
3. It .... for the last two days. (*snow*)
4. Prices .... very fast recently. (*go up*)
5. How long .... you .... in this hotel? (*stay*)
6. 'What .... you .... all morning?' 'I .... letters.' (*do; write*)
7. 'You look tired.' 'Yes, I ....' (*work*)

3 When do we use the Present Perfect Progressive? Can you find a rule?

4 Do a small drawing to show something that you do regularly, and how long you have been doing it. Show it to another student and see if he/she can interpret your drawing. Example:

You've been playing tennis for seven years.

6 Some verbs are not used in progressive forms. Choose the correct tense (Present Perfect Simple or Progressive).

1. How long have you *known / been knowing* Alex?
2. How long have you *learnt / been learning* French?
3. How long have you *had / been having* your car?
4. Since we first met yesterday morning, I have *loved / been loving* you passionately.
5. I've *tried / been trying* to phone him all day.

7 Present Perfect or Present? Choose the right tense.

1. I *am writing / have been writing* letters for the last two hours.
2. I *am training / have been training* for a ski competition at the moment.
3. How long *are you working / have you been working* as a driver?
4. At last! *I'm waiting / I've been waiting* for you since ten o'clock.
5. *I know / I've known* her for years.
6. Why *are you looking / have you been looking* at me like that?
7. *He's / He's been* ill for a long time.
8. How long *do you have / have you had* that car?

5 Look at the pictures. What has the person been doing in each one?

He has been writing letters.

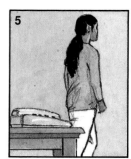

119

Non-progressive verbs

1 Here are some pieces of conversation recorded at a party. Put in the right present-tense verb forms.

1. 'I .... you. You're Bill's cousin. What ....
   Bill .... now?' 'He .... in a circus.'
   (*remember; do; work*)
2. 'I .... your dress.' 'Thanks. I .... your
   shirt.' (*like; not like*)
3. 'Why .... you .... football boots?'
   'They're not mine.' (*wear*)
4. 'It's a good party, but I .... the music.' 'I
   .... it's beautiful.' (*hate; think*)
5. 'You say you .... me now, but will you still
   love me in the morning?' 'Of course I will.' 'I
   .... you.' (*love; not believe*)
6. 'You have beautiful eyes.' 'You .... on my
   foot.' (*stand*)
7. '............... you .... some more wine?' 'No, it
   .... like furniture polish.' 'How .... you
   .... ?' (*want; taste; know*)
8. 'Everything is nothing, baby. Everything is
   nothing.' 'I .... what you ....' 'It
   ....' (*not understand; mean; not matter*)
9. 'What's your name?' 'I ....' (*forget*)
10. 'I .... tired. Let's go home.' 'I .... to stay
    here all night.' (*get; want*)
11. 'Who .... this glass .... to?' 'I...............'
    'Well, it's mine now.' (*belong; not know*)
12. 'Let me give you some advice.' 'I .... your
    stupid advice.' (*not need*)
13. 'I .... you're crazy.' 'I ....' 'That's
    because you're crazy.' 'I ....' (*think; not
    agree; see*)
14. 'Why .... you .... to yourself?' 'I
    .... my conversation more interesting than
    yours.' (*talk; find*)

2 Look again at Exercise 1. Make a list of the verbs that are not usually used in progressive forms.

3 Put together some of the beginnings and ends to make sensible sentences.

BEGINNINGS	ENDS
I think	'Welcome' in Welsh.
I know	any more.
I don't like	beer.
I hate	I'm right.
I don't want	in Father Christmas.
We don't need	it's Tuesday.
I remember	my first day at school.
I forget	to me.
I don't understand	washing-up liquid.
I don't believe	what you mean.
It tastes like	with everything you say.
Croeso means	you're right.
This bag doesn't belong	you.
I agree	your face.
	your name.

Since and *for*

1 Look at the examples. We use different kinds of expression after *since* and *for*. Can you make a rule?

I've lived here since 1984.
It's been raining since early this morning.
She's been ill since she came back from holiday.
I've lived here for ten years.
It's been raining for hours.
She's been ill for three months.

2 Fill in the gaps.

since yesterday = for 24 hours
for 400 years = since the 16th century
since 1977 = for ...   for ten years = since ...
since last July = ...   for the last five days = ...
since last Tuesday = ...   for the last three hours = ...
since nine o'clock = ...
since my birthday = ... the last ... days/months
all my life = ... I was born

3 Put in *since* or *for*.

1. I haven't seen Joe .... Saturday.
2. My father's worked here .... 40 years.
3. We've had the same government .... twelve
   years.
4. I've been looking for a job .... Easter.
5. I've had a headache .... I woke up.
6. It's been raining .... a week.
7. They've been playing cards .... 24 hours.
8. We've been painting our house .... months.

4 Write sentences with *since* and *for* for these situations.

1. Carlos works for his mother. He began doing this
   seven years ago.
2. Claudia began working for the World Health
   Organisation in 1990.
3. Jack plays the violin. He began when he was three.
4. Yasuko is taking riding lessons. She started on her
   last birthday.
5. Ali has a house in Marrakesh. He bought it five
   years ago.
6. Sergei is staying with friends in Moscow. He
   arrived last week.
7. Sigrid lives in Munich. She started living there five
   years ago.

5 Make questions beginning *How long have you lived/been/had/known* ... and ask another student. Answer questions using *since* or *for*.

Non-progressive verbs

Language notes and possible problems
'Non-progressive' verbs   This is a complicated area of grammar. Quite a number of verbs are either not generally used in progressive forms (even when the meaning makes a progressive form appropriate), or are only generally used in progressive forms in certain of their meanings. Many of these verbs refer to mental/emotional states or sense-perceptions, but not all verbs in these areas are non-progressive (compare *I **don't like** this party* and *I'm **not enjoying** this party*). Verbs which are only non-progressive in certain meanings include *see* (compare *I **see** what you mean* and *I'm **seeing** him tomorrow*), *think* (compare *I **think** she's lovely* and *What **are** you **thinking** about?*) and *taste* (compare *It **tastes** awful* and *I'm just **tasting** the soup to see if there's enough salt in it*). Other non-progressive verbs may have occasional progressive uses in particular contexts. For more detailed information, see a good grammar.

The exercises here deal only with the most common and basic non-progressive verbs and uses. They focus on present-tense instances, but you should point out that these verbs are non-progressive in other tenses such as past or Present Perfect (e.g. *How long have you **known** her?* NOT ** ... have you **been knowing** her?*).

---

1 Sensitisation exercise
• This exercise tests students' command of a number of very common non-progressive verb uses. Most students should get most of the questions right even without having any conscious awareness of the rules involved.
• The exercise can be done individually or by group/class discussion, as you prefer.

Answers to Exercise 1
1. remember; 's ... doing; 's working
2. like; don't like
3. are ... wearing
4. hate; think
5. love; don't believe
6. 're standing
7. Do ... want; tastes; do ... know
8. don't understand; mean; doesn't matter
9. forget
10. 'm getting; want
11. does ... belong; don't know
12. don't need
13. think; don't agree; see
14. are ... talking; find

2 Listing non-progressive verbs
• Point out that some of the verbs in Exercise 1 are not used in progressive forms, even though they refer to things that are going on at the moment of speaking. Students will probably recognise that it would be odd to say, for example, **I'm remembering you* or **I'm liking your dress*.
• Get students to go through the exercise listing verbs of this kind.
• Let them compare notes in pairs or groups, and then check their lists.

Answer to Exercise 2
remember; like; hate; think; love; believe; want; taste; know; understand; matter; forget; belong; need; agree; see; find.

3 Putting together beginnings and ends
• This can be done informally, with students saying their answers as they think of them. Various combinations are possible.

Since and *for*

Language notes and possible problems
1. Common mistakes   These exercises are intended for students who confuse *since* and *for*. The most common error is to use *since* with a reference to a period (e.g. **since six weeks*).
2. Tenses   Students may need to be reminded that we use Present Perfect tenses, not present tenses, to say how long present situations have been going on.
3. Other tenses with *for*   *For* can of course be used with various other tenses besides the Present Perfect, to refer to past, present or future periods.
4. *Since* as a conjunction   Students who have grasped that *since* is used 'with the Present Perfect' may be confused by sentences like *I've had a headache since I woke up*, in which *since* introduces a clause with a past-tense verb. You may need to explain that, although the main verb is Present Perfect, the time-reference **after** *since* can contain a past-tense verb.

---

1 Deducing the rules
• Get students to discuss this in small groups. They should be able to see that *since* is followed by a reference to a 'starting point', and *for* by a reference to a period.

2 Equivalences
• If necessary, get students to do this individually in writing in order to get maximum practice.

3 Choosing between *since* and *for*
• This can also be done individually in writing. Get students to compare notes when they have finished.

Answers to Exercise 3
1. since   2. for   3. for   4. since
5. since   6. for   7. for   8. for

4 Writing sentences for situations
• Ask students to work individually to try and write sentences. Point out that in some cases more than one correct answer is possible.
• Walk round while students are working to give any help that is needed.
• Get students to compare notes before checking with you.

Answers to Exercise 4
(Alternative answers may be possible in some cases.)
1. Carlos has worked / been working for his mother for seven years.
2. Claudia has worked / been working for the World Health Organisation for ... years / since ...
3. Jack has played / been playing the violin since he was three.
4. Yasuko has been taking riding lessons since her last birthday.
5. Ali has had a house in Marrakesh for five years.
6. Sergei has been staying with friends in Moscow since last week / for a week / for the last week.
7. Sigrid has lived / been living in Munich for five years.

5 Questions and answers
• As the students do the exercise, go round checking on their use of *since* and *for*.
• When they have finished, ask each student to write down one of the things he/she found out about the person he/she worked with.

Past Perfect

Language notes and possible problems

Past Perfect   Here, students simply revise the most basic rules. These do not cover all cases: it is difficult to give complete rules for all uses of the Past Perfect tenses, or to explain why in some situations a Past Perfect is necessary, while in other situations a similar meaning can be expressed with a Simple Past tense.

Note that in some languages the equivalent of the Past Perfect can be used to refer to past events which account for present situations. This is not normally possible in standard British English. Look out for mistakes like *I had left some photos to be developed. Are they ready yet?*

---

1   **Trying to see the rule**
• If necessary, make sure students realise that the Past Perfect verbs in the examples are the ones in **bold type**.
• Give students time to think about the question and to try to formulate some kind of rule. Do not comment on their rules at the moment, but move on to Exercise 2.

2   **Choosing between rules**
• Look through the five rules, explaining any difficulties.
• Get students to choose one of the rules, and then encourage them to look back at the examples to see if their rule works.
• Most students should come to see that rule C works best.

3   **Choosing between Simple Past and Past Perfect**
• For maximum practice, this is best done individually in writing.

Answers to Exercise 3
(Contracted/uncontracted alternatives are possible.)
1. When he *started* telling the joke I realised that I *had heard* it before.
2. When I *looked* at the car I could see that somebody *had driven* into the back of it.
3. When we *got* to the restaurant we *realised* that nobody *had remembered* to reserve a table.
4. The doctor *examined* her and found that she *had broken* her arm.
5. I *had not been* abroad before, so I *enjoyed* every moment of my first visit to Germany.
6. We were a few minutes late, so the film *had started* when we *arrived* at the cinema.
7. When she came to England, she found that the language was quite different from the English that she *had learnt* at school.
8. 'Good afternoon. Can I help you?' 'Yes, I *brought* my watch to you for repair three weeks ago. Is it ready yet?'
9. I *told* him twice that I *didn't know* who *had broken* the window, but he *did not believe* me.

4   **Past Perfect Progressive: working out the rule**
• If students are familiar with the Present Perfect Progressive, they should find it easy to see that the Past Perfect Progressive has a parallel use (to refer to extended temporary events continuing up to the past moment that is being focused on). It does not of course matter if they can't put this into words in English, provided they have a reasonably clear understanding of the idea.

5   **Making sentences: situations and reasons**
• Get students to make at least five sentences. Various combinations are possible.
• An alternative way to do the exercise is to give out beginnings and ends on separate pieces of paper and get students to try to find their 'other halves'.

6   **Personalisation**
• You may be able to suggest other appropriate reference points besides *last weekend* etc.

7   **Cartoon**
• This can be done by group or class discussion.
• Help students to see the reason why the first caption ('... *We thought you'd brought him.*') is the correct one.

Past Perfect

1
Look at the examples and try to see when we use the Past Perfect tense.

*I woke up late this morning because I **had forgotten** to set my alarm clock.*
*When I saw her I knew that we **had met** before.*
*After she **had finished** breakfast she made some phone calls.*
*I wondered why Chris **hadn't written** for so long.*
*He told me he **had** never **been** to India.*

2
Choose the best rule.

We use the Past Perfect:
A to talk about the reason why something happened
B to talk about something that happened a long time ago
C when we are already talking about the past, to go back for a moment to an earlier past time
D mainly in reported speech
E to show that a past action was completed

3
Choose the correct tense (Simple Past or Past Perfect).

1. When he .... telling the joke I realised that I .... it before. (*start; hear*)
2. When I .... at the car I could see that somebody .... into the back of it. (*look; drive*)
3. When we .... to the restaurant we .... that nobody .... to reserve a table. (*get; realise; remember*)
4. The doctor .... her and found that she .... her arm. (*examine; break*)
5. I .... abroad before, so I .... every moment of my first visit to Germany. (*not be; enjoy*)
6. We were a few minutes late, so the film .... when we .... at the cinema. (*start; arrive*)
7. When she came to England, she found that the language was quite different from the English that she .... at school. (*learn*)
8. 'Good afternoon. Can I help you?' 'Yes, I .... my watch to you for repair three weeks ago. Is it ready yet?' (*bring*)
9. I .... him twice that I .... who .... the window, but he .... me. (*tell; not know; break; not believe*)

4
Look at the examples and try to see when we use the Past Perfect Progressive. Can you make a rule?

*He was tired because he **had been looking** after the children all day.*
*When I looked out of the window I could see that it **had been raining**.*
*I suddenly realised that I **had been thinking** about Peter all afternoon.*
*When she got home she found that the children **had been playing** with her computer.*

5
Make sentences by putting together situations and reasons. Example:

'*I was very hungry because I hadn't eaten for two days.*'

SITUATIONS
I couldn't get a job
I couldn't get into the house
I couldn't write
I decided to have a sandwich
I didn't know what to do
I felt really stupid
I had to walk
I kept singing
I smiled at everybody in the street
I was angry
I was frightened
I was tired
I was very hungry
I was worried

REASONS
I had failed all my exams.
I had fallen in love again.
I had just won £1 million.
I had lost all my money.
I hadn't eaten for two days.
I hadn't filled in a form.
I'd been working all day.
I'd broken my pen.
I'd forgotten the name of my hotel.
I'd lost my keys.
my boss had just been very rude to me.
somebody had stolen my bike.
the last bus had gone.
the police had come for my sister.

6
Think of three things that you had never done before last weekend / your last birthday / you started school.

7
Choose the correct caption for the cartoon.

'No, he's not ours! We thought you'd brought him.'
'No, he's not ours! We had thought you brought him.'
'No, he's not ours! We thought you've brought him.'

Talking about the future

1 Write sentences to say what you are doing this evening / tomorrow / tomorrow evening / on Saturday / on Sunday / next weekend. Examples:

I'm washing my hair this evening. (I wash my hair ...)
We're seeing my parents at the weekend. (We see ...)

2 Plan what you are going to do, and when, next Saturday and Sunday. Include at least eight of the following activities (and any others that you want to add), but leave yourself some free time. Note the time of each activity.

wash your hair   play tennis   write letters
shop for clothes   see a film   go to a party
see a friend   clean the kitchen   mend clothes
practise the guitar   study English grammar
do your ironing   make a cake   wash your car
go to church   see your sister   do some gardening

3 'Telephone' another student. Try to arrange to do something together at the weekend. (Look back at your answer to Exercise 2 to see when you are free.) Use some of the expressions in the box. Example:

> Hello, Ann. This is Sue.
> Are you doing anything on Sunday morning?

>> It depends. What time?

> About ten o'clock. Would you like to play tennis?

>> Could we make it later? I'm seeing my sister at ten.

> OK. How about eleven?

>> That would be very nice. See you then.

Are you doing anything on ... morning?
Would you like to ...?
It depends.
What time?
That would be very nice.
Sorry, I'm not free. I'm ...ing.
Could we make it earlier/later? I'm ...ing
   at/until ... o'clock.
OK. See you then.

---

4 Write sentences to say what you are going to do on two or more of these occasions: next time you have a few days free; when you have finished learning English; when you leave school; during your next summer holiday; when you retire. Have you got any plans for the next year or so? Are you going to make any changes in your life? Think of something that you are never going to do again in your life.

5 Look at the pictures. What is going to happen?

6 What presents do you think people will give you next Christmas, or on your next birthday? Use *I (don't) think, I'm sure, perhaps, probably*. Examples:

I think my father will give me money.
Perhaps somebody will give me perfume.
I don't think anybody will give me a car.
Alice will give me a book. She always does.
If I'm lucky, I'll get jewellery.

122

Talking about the future

Language notes and possible problems

1. Structures referring to the future   English has no single 'future tense'; there are several common ways of talking about the future, and the differences between them are not always easy to analyse. The exercises here concentrate mainly on three structures: the use of the Present Progressive to talk about the future, the *going to* structure, and *will* + infinitive. There is also an exercise on the use of present tenses with future reference in subordinate clauses. Some simple rules are given, but they do not of course cover all possible cases; note also that distinctions in this area are not always very clear-cut, and it is possible in some situations to use either of two structures with little difference of meaning.

2. 'Present-future' and pure future   When future events have some 'present reality' – for example when they are already planned, or we can see them coming – we tend to use present tenses to refer to them: either the Present Progressive of the relevant verb, or *be going* + infinitive. When what is predicted has less 'present reality', we are more likely to use *will* + infinitive. For more detailed rules and examples, see the notes on the exercises.

3. *Shall* and *will*   You may wish to tell students that *shall* can be used as a first-person alternative to *will* in most cases. This is not practised here; nor is the use of *shall* in requests for instructions.

4. Simple Present   Although the Simple Present can be used in main clauses with future reference, this is limited to certain kinds of context such as 'timetabled' events (e.g. *What time **does** the film **start**?*). Look out for mistakes like **Do you work late tomorrow?* **I give it you back, I promise*.

5. Subordinate clauses (Exercise 10)   However, the Simple Present is very common with future reference in subordinate clauses. This is because, if the main clause already has future reference, it is not usually necessary to specify this again. Simple Present tenses with future reference are very common after *if* and conjunctions of time such as *when, before, after,* but they come in many other kinds of subordinate clause as well.

---

1 Present Progressive: students' plans
- Get students to write at least three sentences each.
- Explain the use of the Present Progressive to talk about fixed arrangements for the future, especially when the time and/or place are specified.
- Make sure students understand that it is not normally correct to use the Simple Present in this context.

2 and **3** Simulation: making plans and fitting in appointments
- This gives students a further chance to practise realistic uses of the Present Progressive to talk about plans.
- Make students 'telephone' others who are some distance away from them in the room, if possible.

4 *Going to:* students' plans
- This could be done partly in writing and partly with students volunteering sentences.
- Explain the use of the *going to* structure to talk about plans and intentions for the future; unlike the Present Progressive, *going to* is common even when the time and/or place are not specified.

5 Predictions with *going to:* pictures
- This could be done in groups with students discussing possible answers.
- Explain the use of *going to* to predict events when we can 'see them coming'.

Possible answers to Exercise 5
(Variations in the wording are of course possible.)
1. It's going to rain.
2. She's going to win.
3. She's going to have a baby.
4. The car's going to crash.
5. He's going to fall.
6. They're going to kiss.
7. He's going to play tennis.
8. The ball's going to break the window.
9. She's going to open the door.
10. He's going to sit down.
11. They're going to see a film.
12. She's going to drive.

6 Predictions with *will:* presents
- This is easily done orally.
- You may of course need to change the situation if the reference to Christmas and/or birthday presents is culturally inappropriate.
- Talk about the use of *will* for predictions which depend more on people's knowledge or opinions than on outside evidence.

122

7 Predictions with *will*: life in the year 3,000
• Some of the sentences might generate small discussions, especially if students do the exercise in groups.

8 Revising the rules
• This should help students to pull together their understanding of the rules for the use of the three future forms.

Answers to Exercise 8
(These are the most likely forms for each situation, but not necessarily the only possibilities.)
1. *will* + infinitive
2. *going to* + infinitive
3. Present Progressive
4. *going to* + infinitive

9 Choosing the correct forms
• This is probably best done in writing individually, with students discussing their answers in groups when they have finished.
• When they have done this, go through the answers clearing up any problems.

Answers to Exercise 9
(The answers given here are the most natural in normal contexts, and the ones that follow the rules the students have been given. However, in one or two cases both forms may be possible.)
1. *I'm doing* my exams next week.
2. Have you heard? Mary *is going to have* a baby.
3. I expect *I'll get* perfume for Christmas.
4. *Are you doing* anything on Sunday?
5. People probably *won't be* very different in the year 3,000.
6. Look at those clouds. *It's going to rain* soon.
7. John and Sally *are going to get* married.
8. Look! That police car *is going to stop* outside our house.

10 Tenses after *if, when* etc.
• If necessary, explain the point of grammar involved before students start the exercise.
• If you want maximum practice, get students to write the answers individually.

Answers to Exercise 10
1. If you *come* round this evening I *will show* you the new clothes I've bought.
2. Perhaps I *will become* an interpreter when I *finish* studying English.
3. Wars *will stop* when people *get* more sensible.
4. If you *go* to China next year you *will need* a visa.
5. I expect Jane *will tell* us when she *finds* a job.
6. It *will rain* before we *get* home.
7. The meeting *will start* when everybody *has* arrived.

Infinitives with and without *to*

1 Infinitives after auxiliary verbs
• Some students may still make the mistake of using a *to*-infinitive after *do* or a modal auxiliary. This exercise should help to clarify the point of grammar for them.
• Not all students may realise that *ought* is followed by a *to*-infinitive.

2 Infinitives after ordinary verbs
• Learners often make mistakes with the verbs listed.
• Get them to decide first of all what kind of infinitive is used after *want*. Then get them to work through the list, discussing their ideas in pairs or small groups.
• Some students may be surprised to learn that *all* the verbs are followed by *to*-infinitives. (*Need* can also be followed by an infinitive without *to* in certain structures – for more details, see a good grammar.)

3 Discrimination exercise
• Encourage students to try this first without looking back at Exercises 1 and 2.

Answers to Exercise 3
1. I would like *to go* out tonight.
2. I hope *to see* you again soon.
3. 'That's the doorbell.' 'I'll *go*.'
4. Can you *lend* me some money?
5. What time do you expect *to be* home?
6. Shall I *carry* that bag for you?
7. We may *be* going to Australia.
8. I didn't manage *to do* all the shopping.
9. Suddenly it started *to rain*.
10. You mustn't *believe* her.
11. I really ought *to phone* my mother.
12. I don't *have* a secretary.
13. Everybody should *learn* maths.
14. We need *to talk* to Andy.
15. She seems *to be* very happy.

4 Special structures
• Some of these, at least, are likely to cause confusion.
• Get students to write the answers individually before they compare notes.

Answers to Exercise 4
1. She doesn't even know how *to boil* an egg.
2. 'Let's drive.' 'I would rather *walk*.'
3. 'I don't know what *to do* this weekend.' 'Why not *come* out with us?'
4. His parents never make him *study*.
5. Let me *help* you.
6. You had better *tell* me.
7. Do you have *to work* very long hours?

5 Personalisation
• Encourage students to write genuine sentences which communicate something real.

7 What do you think life will be like in the year 3,000? Put *perhaps, probably (not), certainly (not)* or *not* into the sentences. Add one or more sentences of your own.

1. People will wear clothes.
2. Cars will still exist.
3. There will be a war somewhere in the world.
4. People will travel to the planets for holidays.
5. People will believe in God.
6. There will be a world government.
7. People will live longer than now.
8. Food will be very different from now.
9. Money will still exist.

PRESENT PROGRESSIVE, *GOING TO* OR *WILL*?

8 Which form would you use to talk about the following?

1. Something in the future that you think is probable.
2. Something in the future that is obviously on the way.
3. A plan to meet somebody at a particular time.
4. Your intentions for your next holiday.

9 Choose the correct forms.

1. *I'm doing / I'll do* my exams next week.
2. Have you heard? Mary *is going to have / will have* a baby.
3. I expect *I'm getting / I'll get* perfume for Christmas.
4. *Are you doing / Will you do* anything on Sunday?
5. People probably *aren't going to be / won't be* very different in the year 3,000.
6. Look at those clouds. *It's raining / It's going to rain* soon.
7. John and Sally *are going to / will* get married.
8. Look! That police car *is going to stop / will stop* outside our house.

TENSES AFTER *IF, WHEN* ETC.

10 Choose the correct forms.

1. If you (*come / will come*) round this evening I (*show / will show*) you the new clothes I've bought.
2. Perhaps I (*become / will become*) an interpreter when I (*finish / will finish*) studying English.
3. Wars (*stop / will stop*) when people (*get / will get*) more sensible.
4. If you (*go / will go*) to China next year you (*need / will need*) a visa.
5. I expect Jane (*tells / will tell*) us when she (*finds / will find*) a job.
6. It (*rains / will rain*) before we (*get / will get*) home.
7. The meeting (*starts / will start*) when everybody (*has / will have*) arrived.

Infinitives with and without *to*

1 Infinitives after auxiliary verbs. Which is correct?

1. I **will write** soon.   2. I **will to write** soon.

These verbs are followed by the infinitive without *to*, with one exception. Which is the exception?

can   could   do   may   might   must   ought
shall   should   would

2 Infinitives after ordinary verbs. Which is correct?

1. I **want go** home.   2. I **want to go** home.

What kind of infinitive comes after these?

expect   hope   manage   need   prefer   seem
start   would like

3 Put in the correct kind of infinitive.

1. I would like (*to go / go*) out tonight.
2. I hope (*to see / see*) you again soon.
3. 'That's the doorbell.' 'I'll (*to go / go*).'
4. Can you (*to lend / lend*) me some money?
5. What time do you expect (*to be / be*) home?
6. Shall I (*to carry / carry*) that bag for you?
7. We may (*to be / be*) going to Australia.
8. I didn't manage (*to do / do*) all the shopping.
9. Suddenly it started (*to rain / rain*).
10. You mustn't (*to believe / believe*) her.
11. I really ought (*to phone / phone*) my mother.
12. I don't (*to have / have*) a secretary.
13. Everybody should (*to learn / learn*) maths.
14. We need (*to talk / talk*) to Andy.
15. She seems (*to be / be*) very happy.

4 Special structures. Which is correct?

1. She doesn't even know how (*to boil / boil*) an egg.
2. 'Let's drive.' 'I would rather (*to walk / walk*).'
3. 'I don't know what (*to do / do*) this weekend.' 'Why not (*to come / come*) out with us?'
4. His parents never make him (*to study / study*).
5. Let me (*to help / help*) you.
6. You had better (*to tell / tell*) me.
7. Do you have (*to work / work*) very long hours?

5 Complete three sentences using infinitives.

1. I don't know what …
2. If you're free next weekend, why not …?
3. My parents used to make me …
4. My parents never let me …
5. In my work, I have …
6. I don't know how …
7. I don't want to learn English. I'd rather …
8. If the government want my support, they had better …

Reported speech

1 Tenses in statements and questions. Look at the examples. If the reporting verb is not past, what happens to the other verb(s)? If the reporting verb is past, what happens to the other verb(s)?

She thinks 'He's boring.'
She thinks that he's boring.

He will probably say 'I'm sure I've seen you somewhere before.'
He will probably say that he **is** sure he **has** seen her somewhere before.

He said 'I'm sure I've seen you somewhere before.'
He said (that) he **was** sure (that) he **had** seen her somewhere before.

'I **don't** remember ever meeting you,' she said.
She said (that) she **didn't** remember ever meeting him.

'I **think** we **met** on holiday,' he said.
He said he **thought** they **had met** on holiday.

He said 'I'll buy you a drink.'
He said he **would** buy her a drink.

2 Reported statements and thoughts. What did they say?

1. She said 'I'm tired.'
2. He said 'We've only just started talking.'
3. She thought 'He's really boring.'
4. She said 'It's getting late.'
5. He said 'It's still early.'
6. She said 'I started work at six o'clock.'
7. He said 'It's time to relax.'
8. She said 'I have a very busy week.'
9 He thought 'She'll be much nicer after a drink.'
10. She thought 'I made a mistake accepting his invitation.'
11. He said 'You'll feel much better after a drink.'
12. She thought 'One drink will be all right.'
13. She said 'I'll just have one before I go.'

3 Reported questions. Look at the examples. Can you make a rule about word order? When is *if/whether* used?

He said 'Where **do you live**?'
He asked her where she **lived**. (... where did she live.)

'**Have you** always **lived** in London?' he asked.
He asked her if/whether **she had** always **lived** in London.

He said 'What's **your name**?'
He asked what **her name was**.
   (... what was her name.)

He asked '**Do you like** dancing?'
He asked her if/whether **she liked** dancing.

He said 'Where **did you go** to school?'
He asked her where **she had gone** to school.

4 Reported question-word questions. What did they ask?

1. He said 'What are you going to drink?'
2. She asked 'What is there?'
3. He said 'Which do you prefer – white wine, red wine or beer?'
4. She said 'What else is there?'
5. He said 'How do you feel about a small whisky?'
6. She asked 'What did you say?'
7. He said 'What do you want in your whisky?'
8. 'Why does he think I want whisky?' she wondered.

5 Reported *yes/no* questions. What did they say?

1. She said 'Can you just get me some orange juice?'
2. He said 'Can I get you a gin and tonic instead?'
3. She said 'Do you know where my coat is?'
4. He said 'Do you really want to go?'
5. She said 'Are you as stupid as you look?'
6. He said 'Did I say something to annoy you?'
7. 'Am I dreaming? Is he real?' she wondered.
8. She said 'Have you finished?'

6 Reported instructions and requests. Look at the examples. Can you make a rule?

He said 'Do have another drink.'
He invited her **to have** another drink.

She said 'Stop saying that.'
She told him **to stop** saying that.

She said 'Please don't forget my coat.'
She asked him **not to forget** her coat.

7 Reported instructions and requests. What did they say?

1. He said 'Do stay.'
2. She said 'Go and jump in the river.'
3. He said 'Don't go away.'
4. She said 'Get lost.'
5. He said 'Please give me your address.'
6. She said 'Drop dead.'
7. He said 'Don't say that.'
8. She said 'Give me my coat before I kick your teeth in.'

124

Reported speech

Language notes and possible problems

1. 'Reported speech' is a misleading name: the structure is used not only to report speech, but also to say what people think, believe, hope etc. In this group of exercises, basic structures are revised: typical problems involve tense and word order.

2. Tenses   After past reporting verbs, we generally use different tenses in reported speech from those that were used in direct speech. This 'backshift' is natural: what was present for the original speaker is likely to be past for somebody who reports the speaker's words on a later occasion. However, in some languages the original 'unshifted' tenses are used in reported speech after past reporting verbs, leading to mistakes in English like *She said she is thirsty.*

3. Word order   English does not usually use interrogative word order in reported questions. Look out for mistakes like *She asked where was the bathroom.*

4. *If* and *whether*   Students at this level do not need to worry about the rather unimportant differences between *if* and *whether* in reported speech.

---

1   Tenses: working out the rules

• Give students a few minutes to look over the examples and think about their answers. You may like to let them compare notes in groups.

• They should come to see that, after past reporting verbs, the original speaker's tenses become 'more past' (Simple Present changes to Simple Past, Simple Past and Present Perfect change to Past Perfect, *will* changes to *would*, etc.). After present or future reporting verbs, this does not of course happen.

• You may need to keep an eye on the pronunciation of *said*.

2   Practice: reported statements and thoughts

• This can be done in writing or orally as you prefer. However, students will get more individual practice if at least some of the exercise is done in writing.

Answers to Exercise 2
1. She said (that) she was tired.
2. He said (that) they had only just started talking.
3. She thought (that) he was really boring.
4. She said (that) it was getting late.
5. He said (that) it was still early.
6. She said (that) she had started work at six o'clock.
7. He said (that) it was time to relax.
8. She said (that) she had a very busy week.
9. He thought (that) she would be much nicer after a drink.
10. She thought (that) she had made a mistake accepting his invitation.
11. He said (that) she would feel much better after a drink.
12. She thought (that) one drink would be all right.
13. She said (that) she would just have one before she went.

3   Reported questions: working out the rules

• Give students a few minutes to look over the examples and think about their answers. You may like to let them compare notes in groups.

• They should come to see that reported questions do not have interrogative word order, and that *if* or *whether* is used to report *yes/no* questions (where there is no question word to act as a conjunction).

• Keep an eye on the pronunciation of *asked* (/ɑːskt/ or /ɑːst/, not /ˈɑːskɪd/ or /ˈɑːsked/).

4 and 5   Practice: question-word questions and *yes/no* questions

• In these exercises, too, students will get more practice if at least some of the questions are answered in writing.

Answers to Exercise 4
1. He asked (her) what she was going to drink.
2. She asked (him) what there was.
3. He asked (her) which she preferred – white wine, red wine or beer.
4. She asked (him) what else there was.
5. He asked (her) how she felt about a small whisky.
6. She asked (him) what he had said.
7. He asked (her) what she wanted in her whisky.
8. She wondered why he thought she wanted whisky.

Answers to Exercise 5
(Slight differences of wording are possible in some cases.)
1. She asked (him) if he could just get her some orange juice.
2. He asked (her) if he could get her a gin and tonic instead.
3. She asked (him) if he knew where her coat was.
4. He asked (her) if she really wanted to go.
5. She asked (him) if he was really as stupid as he looked.
6. He asked (her) if he had said something to annoy her.
7. She wondered if she was dreaming, or if he was real.
8. She asked (him) if he had finished.

6   Reported instructions and requests: working out the rules

• Students should easily see that instructions and requests are reported with infinitives. Make sure they are clear about the structure of negative infinitives (*She asked him not to forget* her coat, NOT *... to not forget ...*).

• If necessary, point out that *tell* and *ask* (but not *say*) are commonly used to report instructions and requests. Make sure students are clear about the differences.

7   Practice: instructions and requests

• This can be done in the same way as the earlier exercises.

Answers to Exercise 7
(Slight differences of wording are possible in some cases.)
1. He asked her to stay.
2. She told him to go and jump in the river.
3. He asked her not to go away.
4. She told him to get lost.
5. He asked her to give him her address.
6. She told him to drop dead.
7. He asked/told her not to say that.
8. She told him to give her her coat before she kicked his teeth in.

8 Further practice: interpreting drawings

• Get students to look at the pictures. Tell them to write some of the answers and compare notes in groups. Other answers can be given orally.

Answers to Exercise 8

(The answers can of course be expressed in various different ways. Possible versions:)

2. He asked her what her phone number was. She said that she was not on the phone.
3. He asked her what sign she was. She said that she was Libra.
4. He asked her if she would like to dance. She told him to go and jump in the river.
5. He asked her if she would like a drink. She said that she didn't drink.
6. He asked her if she would like a cigarette. She said that she didn't smoke.
7. He asked her if she would like to go to Miami with him. She said that she didn't like flying.
8. He asked her if she would marry him (or :... to marry him). She said that she would rather shoot herself.

Optional activity

• Students continue Exercise 8 by making their own drawings and asking each other to guess the words.

9 *Say* and *tell*: working out the rules

• Start by getting students to look at the first three examples. Help them to see: 1) that *say* (but not *tell*) is used when reporting direct speech; 2) that both verbs can be used in the 'reported speech' construction; 3) that *tell* is normally followed by an object (without *to*) saying who is told; while *say* can be followed by an object (with *to*), but doesn't have to be.
• The second pair of examples should show them that *tell* (but not *say*) is used for reporting instructions and requests.

10 *Say* and *tell*: practice

• Students should produce sentences beginning *She told him …* and *He told her …*

Articles

Language notes and possible problems

1. Generalisations (Exercises 1–2) In some languages with article systems, a noun that is used in a general sense may have a definite article. In English, a 'general' meaning is signalled by 'zero article' with uncountable and plural nouns. Look out for mistakes like *The food is getting very expensive* or *The life is hard*.

2. Classifying (Exercises 3–4) In some languages, nouns may be used without articles to say what category a person or thing belongs to – for example, when giving somebody's profession. Look out for mistakes like *My sister is bank manager* or *I used my shoe as hammer*.

3. Countable/uncountable (Exercises 5–6) Some English uncountable nouns have countable equivalents in certain other languages. Look out for mistakes like *an advice* or *an information*.

---

1 Generalisations: thinking about the rule

• Let students think about this individually first of all, and then get them to compare notes in groups.
• Point out that the nouns without *the* have a more general meaning, whereas the nouns with *the* refer to particular examples.

2 Generalisations: applying the rule

• This is probably best done individually in writing.

Answers to Exercise 2

1. (–) policemen
2. (–) wine
3. *the* music
4. (–) snow
5. *the* rain
6. (–) computers
7. (–) money
8. *the* money
9. *the* cats
10. (–) dogs; (–) cats

3 Classifying: thinking about the rule

• This exercise should reveal any uncertainty students have about article use in this context. Students may be surprised to learn that none of the sentences is possible without an article.
• Note that it is generally wrong to use a singular countable noun in English with no article.

4 Classifying: applying the rule

• As students write their sentences, go round helping and checking that they are all using articles correctly.

5 Identifying uncountable words

• Students may find this difficult. Let them discuss the question in groups, and then go through the list of words clearing up difficulties.

Answers to Exercise 5

The following words are either always uncountable or do not have singular countable uses, and therefore cannot normally be used with *a/an*: *advice*; *English*; *furniture*; *information*; *luggage*; *news*; *travel*; *weather*. The other words are countable (*headache*, *problem*, *table*) or have countable uses (*cold*, *glass*, *ice*, *light*, *room*) and can therefore be used with *a/an*.

6 Using uncountable words in sentences

• This is a straightforward exercise to help students get used to using these words without articles.
• Get students to do it individually first of all and then compare notes.

8 Look at the pictures. Can you suggest what the questions and answers were? Example:

Q   A

1. *'He asked her what her address was.'*   *'She said that she lived in Paris.'*

9 *Say* and *tell*. Look at the first three examples. Can you make a rule? What about the last two?

She **said** 'I want to go home.'
   (She ~~told 'I want to go home.'~~)
She **said** (to him) **that** she wanted to go home.
   (She ~~told (to him) that~~ she wanted ...)
She **told him that** she wanted to go home.
   (She ~~said him that she wanted to go home.~~)

She **said** 'Go and jump in the river.'
She **told him to go** and jump in the river.
   (She ~~said him to go ...~~)

10 Change three of the sentences in Exercise 2, using *told* instead of *said*.

Articles

1 Look at the examples. Why is *the* used in the first three and not in the last three?

*Could you turn down **the music**? It's too loud.*
*Would you mind passing **the bread**?*
*I couldn't find **the books** you wanted.*
*Do you study **music** at school?*
*We never eat white **bread** at home.*
***Books** are very expensive.*

2 Put in *the* or – (= 'no article').

1. Why don't you like .... policemen?
2. I don't drink .... wine.
3. It's a good party, but .... music's terrible.
4. I think .... snow is the most beautiful thing in the world.
5. We couldn't play tennis yesterday because of .... rain.
6. I'll never understand .... computers.
7. Is .... money important to you?
8. I couldn't study without .... money I get from my parents.
9. Have you fed .... cats this evening?
10. People say that .... dogs are more intelligent than .... cats.

3 Look at the examples. Would any of the sentences be correct without the article *a/an*?

*My father's **a teacher**.*
*I'd like to become **an engineer**.*
*The witch turned the prince into **a frog**.*
*We converted the bedroom into **a bathroom**.*
*I used my shoe as **a hammer**.*

4 Complete some of these sentences using nouns.

1. I'd like to work as ....
2. .... is studying to become ....
3. It would be nice if I could turn myself into ....
4. I can't imagine what it would feel like to be ....
5. We ought to convert the school into ....
6. You can use a .... as a ....

5 Look at the words in the box. Eight of them cannot normally be used with *a/an*. Which are they?

> advice cold English furniture glass
> headache ice information light luggage
> news problem room table travel
> weather

6 Make three sentences with words from the box in Exercise 5.

If

1 Look at the examples and choose the correct form of the rule. Then close your book and write down the examples and the rule from memory.

*We're going swimming today **if it doesn't rain**.*
***If I have enough time tomorrow**, I'll go and see Jack.*

Rule: In *if*-clauses, we use a (*future/present/past*) tense to talk about the (*future/present/past*).

2 Put the beginnings and ends together.

BEGINNINGS
If I have enough money next year
If she passes her exams
If you don't invite Pete to the party
If we get up early enough
If you keep eating chocolate
If you don't put the meat in the fridge

ENDS
he'll be furious.
I'll travel round the world.
it will make you ill.
she's going to study medicine.
it will go bad.
we'll be able to catch the first train.

3 Put in a present tense or a *will*-future.

1. If you .... that button, a bell .... (*press; ring*)
2. If I .... time, I .... you. (*have; visit*)
3. If it ...., we .... at home. (*rain; stay*)
4. I .... you if I .... help. (*tell; need*)
5. I .... you if I .... in town. (*phone; be*)
6. If you .... that door, you .... something strange. (*open; see*)
7. I .... surprised if she .... before seven o'clock. (*be; arrive*)
8. If you .... fast, we .... time to play a game of tennis. (*eat; have*)
9. If you .... up early tomorrow, I .... you swimming. (*get; take*)
10. I .... my car if I .... to London. (*sell; move*)

4 Complete these sentences.

1. If you don't eat, you'll get ...
2. If you eat too much, you ...
3. If you don't have something to drink, ...
4. If you drink any more beer, you'll ...
5. If you don't go to bed, ...
6. If you go out in the rain without an umbrella, ...
7. If you go out without a coat, ...
8. If you hurry, we'll be able to ...

5 Look at the examples and complete the rule. Then close your book and write down one of the examples, and the rule, from memory.

*If I ever **became** rich, I **would try** to help homeless people.*
*It **would be** amazing if I **passed** my exams.*
*If I **were** you, I **would get** a haircut.*
*Everything **would be** all right if I **had** a little more money.*

Rule: When we talk about an unreal or improbable situation, we use (*a present tense / a past tense / would*) in the *if*-clause, and (*a present tense / a past tense / would*) in the rest of the sentence.

6 Choose the correct forms to complete the sentences.

1. If John (*were / would be*) here, he (*knew / would know*) what to do.
2. Do you think it (*were / would be*) a good idea if I (*phoned / would phone*) the police?
3. What (*did / would*) you do if you (*won / would win*) a million pounds?
4. If I (*had / would have*) time I (*learnt / would learn*) the piano.
5. What (*did / would*) you say if I (*asked / would ask*) you to marry me?
6. If you (*changed / would change*) your job, what (*did / would*) you do instead?
7. If today (*were / would be*) Sunday I (*were / would be*) in bed.
8. I (*went / would go*) and see Jake tomorrow if I (*knew / would know*) his address.

7 Read the sentences, and then write a similar 'if-chain' yourself. Start: '*If I won a million dollars ...*'

If I won a million dollars, I would buy a fast car.
If I bought a fast car, I would probably drive it too fast.
If I drove it too fast, perhaps I would have an accident.
If I had an accident, I would go to hospital.
If I went to hospital, perhaps I would meet a beautiful nurse and fall in love with her.
If she fell in love with me, we would get married.
If we got married, we would be very happy at the beginning.
But then perhaps I would meet somebody else.
If I met somebody else ...

If

Language notes and possible problems

'Conditionals' 'Conditional' is a confusing term: people use it both for a verb form (*would* + infinitive) and for a set of sentence structures involving *if*-clauses.

Textbooks often talk about the 'first', 'second' and 'third' kinds of conditional sentence. This is rather misleading. A more realistic analysis is as follows:

A. Open conditions
In one kind of sentence with *if* (which we can call 'open conditions') we use the tenses which are normal for the situation, whatever they are. Examples:

*If Mary **came** yesterday, she **won't come** again today.*
*If you **love** me, why **did** you **call** me a fool?*

The only restriction is that it is unusual to have *will* in the *if*-clause; after *if*, a present tense is usually used to express a future idea (as in many other kinds of subordinate clause).

*If you **come** tomorrow, I'll see what I can do.*

B. Hypothetical conditions
In the other kind of sentence with *if*, we use special verb forms to stress that we are talking about something that might not happen, or might not be true. In the *if*-clause we use a past tense to talk about the present or future; in the main clause we use a modal auxiliary (usually *would*). This is the so-called 'second conditional'.

*If I **knew**, I **would tell** you.*
*If you **came** tomorrow, I **might be able** to help you.*

To talk about the past (the so-called 'third conditional') we use a past perfect tense and **would have** + **past participle**, or a similar structure with another modal verb (e.g. **might have** + **past participle**).

*If you **had been** on time, we **would have won**.*

---

1 If-clauses in open conditions: working out the rule
• Give students a few minutes to look over the examples and think about their answers. You may like to let them compare notes in groups.
• Then get them to close their books and try to write at least one of the examples from memory, together with the rule if possible. If they don't manage to memorise the rule it doesn't really matter, but the attempt should make them focus more closely on the details of the structure.

Answer to Exercise 1
Rule: In *if*-clauses, we use a *present* tense to talk about the *future*.

2 Beginnings and ends
• One way of doing this is to put the beginnings and ends on slips of paper, and get students to walk round finding their 'other halves'.

Answers to Exercise 2
(Alternatives may be possible in some cases.)
If I have enough money next year, I'll travel round the world.
If she passes her exams, she's going to study medicine.
If you don't invite Pete to the party, he'll be furious.
If we get up early enough, we'll be able to catch the first train.
If you keep eating chocolate, it will make you ill.
If you don't put the meat in the fridge, it will go bad.

3 Gap-filling: present tense or *will*?
• This can be done in writing or orally as you prefer. However, students will get more individual practice if at least some of the exercise is done in writing.

Answers to Exercise 3
(Contracted forms are also possible in many cases.)
1. If you *press* that button, a bell *will ring*.
2. If I *have* time, I *will visit* you.
3. If it *rains*, we *will stay* at home.
4. I *will tell* you if I *need* help.
5. I *will phone* you if I *am* in town.
6. If you *open* that door, you *will see* something strange.
7. I *will be* surprised if she *arrives* before seven o'clock.
8. If you *eat* fast, we *will have* time to play a game of tennis.
9. If you *get* up early tomorrow, I *will take* you swimming.
10. I *will sell* my car if I *move* to London.

4 Sentence completion
• This can be done individually or by group/class discussion as you prefer. If at least some of the sentences are done in writing, students will of course get more individual practice.

Possible answers to Exercise 4
(Various other answers are of course possible.)
1. thin/ill
2. 'll get fat
3. you'll be thirsty later
4. get drunk
5. you'll be tired in the morning
6. you'll get wet
7. you'll get cold
8. catch the train

5 Unreal and improbable situations: working out the rule
• This is similar to Exercise 1.
• Point out that *were* is often used instead of *was* after *if*; but that *was* is also correct, and is possibly more common in an informal style.
• Make sure students understand clearly that the past tense in these examples expresses unreality, and does **not** refer to the past.

Answer to Exercise 5
Rule: When we talk about an unreal or improbable situation, we use *a past tense* in the *if*-clause, and *would* in the rest of the sentence.

6 Gap-filling: past tense or *would*
• Students should probably write the answers to at least some of these.

Answers to Exercise 6
1. If John *were* here, he *would know* what to do.
2. Do you think it *would be* a good idea if I *phoned* the police?
3. What *would* you do if you *won* a million pounds?
4. If I *had* more time I *would learn* the piano.
5. What *would* you say if I *asked* you to marry me?
6. If you *changed* your job, what *would* you do instead?
7. If today *were* Sunday I *would be* in bed.
8. I *would go* and see Jake tomorrow if I *knew* his address.

7 If-chain
• Look through the example with the students. Explain any difficulties, and make sure they see how the 'chain' works (the end of one sentence gives the start of the next).
• Ask students to close their books and see if they can remember the chain. (This could be done in pairs or groups if you wish.)
• Then get students to make their own chains individually or in groups. Alternatively, have the chains go round the class: each student writes the first sentence and then passes his/her paper on to another student, who writes the next sentence and passes it on, and so on.

8 Interpreting pictures

• Give students a minute or two to think about each situation (and perhaps write a sentence down) before discussing the answer.

Possible answers to Exercise 8
(Various other answers are of course possible in each case.)
2. If I had plenty of money I would buy a nice house.
3. If I spoke Japanese I would go to Japan.
4. If I had plenty of time I'd go round the world.
5. If I didn't have any children I'd spend all day lying on the beach.
6. If I were more intelligent I would go to university.

9 What would *you* do ...?

• This can be done in groups of four to six.

Optional activity: changing things
• A rather silly game involves getting students to 'change' one thing into another by using *if*. For example: *If a car had two wheels and pedals, it would be a bicycle. If an elephant was black and white and laid eggs, it would be a penguin.*
• Suggest things for students to change; leave it to them to decide what to change them into.

10 Open or unreal conditions?

• This can be done by class discussion. In some cases, answers will depend on individual circumstances.

Answers to Exercise 10
3. b
4. b
5. answer depends on students' views
6. answer depends on local weather conditions
7. b in most cases
8. b in most cases
9. answer depends on students' circumstances
10. b

11 Unreal past situations: working out the rule

• This is similar to Exercises 1 and 5. The most important thing is that students try to memorise an example sentence; the rule is probably too complicated for most people to learn by heart.

Answer to Exercise 11
Rule: When we talk about an unreal past situation, we use *a past perfect tense* in the *if*-clause, and *would have* ... in the rest of the sentence.

12 Would or *had*?

• Point out that 'd can be a contraction of either *would* or *had*.
• The exercise can be done individually or by class/group discussion as you prefer.
• If you ask for written answers to some of the questions you can check on whether everybody has understood how the structure works.

Answers to Exercise 12
1. If she *had* studied harder she *would* have passed her exams.
2. I *would* have come to see you yesterday if I *had* had time.
3. She *would* have married him if he *had* asked her.
4. If I *had* been to university, perhaps I *would* have found a better job.
5. If you *had* asked me, I *would* have helped you.

13 Making sentences for situations

• Various forms of words are possible in each case. Alternative answers can be discussed round the class.

Possible answers to Exercise 13
1. If she had locked her flat, perhaps burglars wouldn't have broken in.
2. If he hadn't driven so fast, he probably wouldn't have crashed.
3. If she had not been alone, she wouldn't have been frightened.
4. If he had spoken French, he would have understood the film.
5. She would have had time for breakfast if she had got up earlier.
6. If he had lived with somebody, he wouldn't have been lonely.
7. He wouldn't have been cold if he had worn / been wearing a coat.
8. If she had had enough money, she would have gone on holiday.
9. She would have got the job if her English had been better.

14 Sentence completion

• Get students to do this individually, orally or in writing.

8 Some people were asked 'What would you do if you had plenty of time and money?' Here are pictures of some of their answers. Try to suggest what they said. Example:

1

'If I were twenty years younger, I would spend all my time skiing.'

2

£ £ £

3

日本語

4

5

6

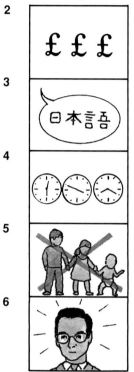

9 What would *you* do if you had plenty of money, or if you had plenty of time, or if ...? Draw a pair of pictures and see if other students can put your answer into words.

10 Ordinary tenses or past + *would*? Which sentence-beginning is better?

1. a. If I become President, I will ...
   b. If I became President, I would ...
   Answer: *b* (because you probably won't become President)
2. a. If I feel tired tomorrow ...
   b. If I felt tired tomorrow ...
   Answer: *b* (you may feel tired tomorrow)
3. a. If I live to be 130, I'll ...
   b. If I lived to be 130, I'd ...
4. a. If I break my leg next week, I'll ...
   b. If I broke my leg next week, I'd ...
5. a. If wars stop, the world will be ...
   b. If wars stopped, the world would be ...
6. a. If it snows tomorrow, I'll ...
   b. If it snowed tomorrow, I'd ...
7. a. If I become rich and famous, will you ...?
   b. If I became rich and famous, would you ...?

8. a. If I learn to speak English perfectly, I'll ...
   b. If I learnt to speak English perfectly, I'd ...
9. a. If I buy a really fast car, I'll ...
   b. If I bought a really fast car, I'd ...
10. a. If the world ends tomorrow, I won't ...
    b. If the world ended tomorrow, I wouldn't ...

TALKING ABOUT THE PAST

11 Look at the examples and complete the rule. Then close your book and write down one of the examples, and the rule, from memory.

*She **would** probably **have married** John if she **had met** him earlier.*
*If you **hadn't driven** me to the station this morning I **would have missed** my train.*

Rule: When we talk about an unreal past situation, we use (*a past tense / a past perfect tense / would have ...*) in the *if*-clause, and (*a past tense / a past perfect tense / would have ...*) in the rest of the sentence.

12 *Would* or *had*?

1. If she'**d** studied harder she'**d** have passed her exams.
2. I'**d** have come to see you yesterday if I'**d** had time.
3. She'**d** have married him if he'**d** asked her.
4. If I'**d** been to university, perhaps I'**d** have found a better job.
5. If you'**d** asked me, I'**d** have helped you.

13 Make sentences with *if* for these situations.

1. A woman didn't lock her flat; burglars broke in.
   'If she had locked her flat, perhaps ...'
2. A man drove too fast and crashed.
   'If he hadn't ...'
3. A child was frightened because she was alone.
4. A man didn't understand a French film.
5. A woman didn't have time for breakfast because she got up too late.
6. A man lived by himself, and was lonely.
7. A child was cold because he wasn't wearing a coat.
8. A woman didn't go on holiday because she didn't have enough money.
9. A woman didn't get a job because her English wasn't very good.

14 Complete one or more of these sentences.

If I hadn't ... yesterday, ...
If Columbus hadn't ...
I would have ... you if ...
It would have been funny if ... yesterday.
If I had been able to do what I wanted when I was younger, I would(n't) have ...

Passives

1 Look at the examples and try to fill in the blanks. Can you choose the right words to complete the rule correctly?

Active: I think somebody **will steal** their car.
Passive: I think their car **will be stolen**.

Active: Somebody **is going to steal** their car.
Passive: Their car **is going to be stolen**.

Active: Somebody **is stealing** their car.
Passive: Their car **is being stolen**.

Active: I'll be surprised if anybody **steals** their car.
Passive: I'll be surprised if their car **is stolen**.

Active: Somebody **has stolen** their car.
Passive: Their car ....

Active: Somebody .... their car.
Passive: Their car **was stolen**.

Active: When I came round the corner, somebody **was stealing** their car.
Passive: When I came round the corner, their car ....

Active: They found that somebody .... their car.
Passive: They found that their car **had been stolen**.

Rule for making passive verb forms:
1. Decide what tense you want to use.
2. Put the auxiliary verb (*be/have/do*) in that tense.
3. Add the (*infinitive / past tense / -ing form / past participle*) of the verb that you want to use.

2 Change these sentences from passive to active. Example:

*'Hamlet' **was written** by Shakespeare.* ➜ *Shakespeare **wrote** 'Hamlet'.*

1. This house was built by my father.
2. The cooking is usually done by Ralph.
3. The club is used by teenagers.
4. The French class will be taught by Mr Simmonds.
5. When I last saw him he was being chased by a large dog.
6. I'm being picked up by a taxi at six o'clock.

3 Change these sentences from active to passive. Example:

*Somebody **has broken** my pen.* ➜ *My **pen has been broken**.*

1. Somebody has invited Jane to a party.
2. Mrs Pettifer will do the cooking for us.
3. When I last saw him, a policeman was questioning him.
4. They've discovered gold in Eastern Canada.
5. Nobody ever cleans that car.
6. I could see that somebody had opened my letters.

4 Put in passive verbs.

1. Our house (*build*) in the 15th century.
2. Paper (*make*) from wood.
3. Paper (*invent*) by the Chinese.
4. German (*speak*) in several different countries.
5. This article (*write*) by a friend of mine.
6. Have you heard the news? Oil (*discover*) under the White House.
7. Your tickets (*send*) to you next week.
8. My sister's very excited: she (*invite*) to a party in New York.
9. Be careful what you say – this conversation (*record*).
10. Her new book (*publish*) next month.

5 Make five or more sentences about where things are manufactured, or where languages are spoken. Examples:

*Cars **are manufactured** in Japan.*
*German **is spoken** in Switzerland.*

6 Make two or more sentences to say where things of yours were made or bought. Examples:

*This sweater **was made** in Scotland. It **was bought** in London.*

7 Put the *-ing* form (e.g. *listening*) or the past participle (e.g. *listened*).

1. 'What is she doing?' 'She's (*listen*) to the radio.'
2. Radio 2 is (*listen*) to all over Britain.
3. When was your house (*build*)?
4. My father is (*build*) an extension at the back of his house.
5. Why are you (*watch*) that bus?
6. Last night's TV news was (*watch*) by about eight million people.
7. Storms have been (*blow*) down trees and (*damage*) people's homes in Jamaica.
8. A big tree was (*blow*) down in our garden last night.
9. The police are (*question*) some people about the damage to the shop.
10. My brother was (*question*) by the police this morning.

Passives

Language notes and possible problems
1. Active and passive structures   Note that these are not simply interchangeable. For some of the reasons affecting the choice between active and passive structures, see Lesson C6 (which also gives practice in more difficult passive structures).

2. Construction of passive verb forms   In real-life use of language, passive verb forms are not of course constructed by transforming active verb forms. However, comparing active and passive forms can help students to understand how passives are put together.

3. 'Present' and 'past' participles   Some students may confuse pairs like *interesting/interested*, *boring/bored*, *breaking/broken* etc. Exercise 7 will help with this.

1 Active-passive correspondences: working out the rule
• Students may need some time to analyse the correspondences and come up with the correct form of the rule.
• When they have done their best, discuss their rules.
• Make sure they finish up by seeing clearly how passive verb forms are constructed.

Answers to Exercise 1
has been stolen; stole; was being stolen; had stolen

Rule for making passive verb forms:
1. Decide what tense you want to use.
2. Put the auxiliary verb *be* in that tense.
3. Add the *past participle* of the verb that you want to use.

2 and 3 Changing passive to active and active to passive
• These exercises can be done in writing or orally as you prefer. However, students will get more individual practice if at least some of the sentences are done in writing.

Answers to Exercise 2
1. My father built this house.
2. Ralph usually does the cooking.
3. Teenagers use the club.
4. Mr Simmonds will teach the French class.
5. When I last saw him a large dog was chasing him.
6. A taxi is picking me up at six o'clock.

Answers to Exercise 3
1. Jane has been invited to a party.
2. The cooking will be done for us by Mrs Pettifer.
3. When I last saw him, he was being questioned by a policeman.
4. Gold has been discovered in Eastern Canada.
5. That car is never cleaned.
6. I could see that my letters had been opened.

4 Constructing passive verb forms
• This can be done in the same way as Exercises 2 and 3.

Answers to Exercise 4
1. Our house *was built* in the 15th century.
2. Paper *is made* from wood.
3. Paper *was invented* by the Chinese.
4. German *is spoken* in several different countries.
5. This article *was written* by a friend of mine.
6. Have you heard the news? Oil *has been discovered* under the White House.
7. Your tickets *will be sent* to you next week.

8. My sister's very excited: she *has been invited* to a party in New York.
9. Be careful what you say – this conversation *is being recorded.*
10. Her new book *is being published / will be published* next month.

5 and 6 Further practice: products, languages, personal possessions
• Get students to volunteer sentences, perhaps writing down one or two of them to consolidate their learning of the structure.

7 Present and past participles
• This exercise is worth doing if students tend to make mistakes like *German is speaking in Switzerland* (see *Language notes*).

Answers to Exercise 7
1. 'What is she doing?' 'She's *listening* to the radio.'
2. Radio 2 is *listened* to all over Britain.
3. When was your house *built*?
4. My father is *building* an extension at the back of his house.
5. Why are you *watching* that bus?
6. Last night's TV news was *watched* by about eight million people.
7. Storms have been *blowing* down trees and *damaging* people's homes in Jamaica.
8. A big tree was *blown* down in our garden last night.
9. The police are *questioning* some people about the damage to the shop.
10. My brother was *questioned* by the police this morning.

Comparatives and superlatives

Language notes and possible problems

1. Formation of comparatives and superlatives
A simple rule which covers most cases is:
– One-syllable adjectives add *-er, -est*; those ending in *-e* have *-r, -st*.
– Two-syllable adjectives ending in *-y* have comparatives in *-ier, -iest*. Others generally have *more, most*.
– Adjectives with three or more syllables have *more, most*.

2. Spelling
You may wish to say a word about the double letters in forms like *bigger, fattest*. Remind students that this happens in the comparatives and superlatives of one-syllable words ending in one vowel letter + one consonant letter (with a few exceptions).

3. The difference between comparatives and superlatives
Some students may confuse the two forms; look out for mistakes like **I'm the taller person in my family*. In general, we use comparatives when we simply compare one thing or group of things with another thing or group of things; we use superlatives to compare something with a group in which it is included. Compare:

*She's **taller than** the others in her family.* (She's not one of 'the others in her family'.)

*She's **the tallest** in her family.* (She is one of 'her family'.)

Many people use comparatives instead of superlatives when talking about membership of a group of two (e.g. *She's **the older** of the two girls*.); however, superlatives are also correct and are probably more natural in an informal style.

---

1 Formation of comparatives and superlatives: working out the rules
• Give students a few minutes to look over the examples and think about their answers. You may like to let them compare notes in groups.
• They will probably have no difficulty in seeing that longer adjectives form their comparatives and superlatives with *more* and *most*, while shorter adjectives have *-er* and *-est*. However, they may find it less easy to work out where the dividing line comes (see *Language notes*).
• You may like to say a word about spelling (see *Language notes*).

2 Irregular comparatives and superlatives
• Get students to write down the three irregular comparatives and superlatives. *Worse* and *worst* are often confused. Note that in British English both *farther* and *further* are used to refer to distance; in American English, only *farther* is used in this sense.

3 Applying the rules
• This can be done individually, with students comparing notes when they are ready.

Answers to Exercise 3
cheap	cheaper	cheapest
cheerful	more cheerful	most cheerful
cold	colder	coldest
correct	more correct	most correct
dangerous	more dangerous	most dangerous
difficult	more difficult	most difficult
funny	funnier	funniest
hot	hotter	hottest
large	larger	largest
late	later	latest
noisy	noisier	noisiest
pretty	prettier	prettiest

red	redder	reddest
rude	ruder	rudest
sleepy	sleepier	sleepiest
small	smaller	smallest
talkative	more talkative	most talkative
terrible	more terrible	most terrible
thin	thinner	thinnest
warm	warmer	warmest
worried	more worried	most worried

4 Comparative or superlative
• You will probably have to help students to formulate the rule here (see *Language notes*).
• Point out the preposition in *in the class/world*; some students will be inclined to use *of* in cases where English prefers *in* to refer to a group or place after a superlative.

5 Gap-filling
• This can be done in writing or orally as you prefer. However, students will get more individual practice if at least some of the exercise is done in writing.
• Students are told what words to use in the first four sentences; after that they are free to complete the sentences as they like.

Answers to Exercise 5
1. Your TV is a lot *better* than ours.
2. This is the *worst* film I've ever seen.
3. Her accent is *more correct* than mine.
4. Policemen seem to get *younger* every year.
5–12. Various possible answers.

6 Superlatives
• One way of doing this is to try to find a superlative for everybody in the class. However, this should obviously be avoided if it might lead to embarrassment (if, for instance, there is a student who is very much fatter or shorter than the others).

7 As ... as
• Some students may need to revise this point. Look out for mistakes like *as ... that* or *as ... than*.
• Get students to do at least some of the sentences individually in writing.

Answers to Exercise 7
1. I'm not *as old as* her.
2. My English is not *as good as* hers.
3. My car is not *as expensive as* hers.
4. My feet are not *as big as* hers.
5. My hair is not *as long as* hers.
6. My flat's not *as big as* hers.
7. I'm not *as mean as* her.
8. My skin is not *as light/fair as* hers.

8 Comparing people
• This can be done orally if you prefer.

9 Cartoons
• This can be done by group or class discussion.
• Most students should be able to see that the version with *best* is the correct one in each case.

Comparatives and superlatives

1 Look at the following comparative adjectives. Some of them are made with *-er*, and some are made with *more*. Can you make a rule? Is the rule the same for superlatives (*oldest, most beautiful* etc.)?

more afraid   more beautiful   bigger   more boring
more careful   easier   more exact   more expensive
fatter   friendlier   happier   more intelligent
more interesting   longer   nicer   older   purer
more stupid   taller   younger

2 Do you know the comparatives and superlatives of the following words?

good   bad   far

3 Write the comparative and superlative of:

cheap   cheerful   cold   correct   dangerous
difficult   funny   hot   large   late   noisy   pretty
red   rude   sleepy   small   talkative   terrible
thin   warm   worried

4 Comparative or superlative? Look at the examples and try to make a rule.

*She's **taller** than her two sisters.*
*She's **the tallest** of the three sisters.*
*I'm **younger** than everybody else in the class.*
*I'm **the youngest** person in the class.*
*I wish we had a **faster** car – this won't go over 60 mph.*
*What's **the fastest** car in the world?*

5 Put in suitable words to complete the sentences.

1. Your TV is a lot .... than ours. (*good*)
2. This is the .... film I've ever seen. (*bad*)
3. Her accent is .... than mine. (*correct*)
4. Policemen seem to get .... every year. (*young*)
5. I'm the .... person in my family.
6. This is the .... meal I've ever eaten.
7. I have a friend who's much .... than me.
8. A friend of mine married a man who is much .... than her.
9. A friend of mine married a woman who is much .... than him.
10. Everest is the .... mountain in the world.
11. I think .... was the .... man/woman who ever lived.
12. The worst thing in the world is ....

6 Think of three people in your family or in the class. Write a sentence about each one using a superlative.

7 *As ... as.* Change the sentences as in the example.

*I'm **shorter than** her.* → *I'm **not as tall as** her.*

1. I'm younger than her.
2. My English is worse than hers.
3. My car's cheaper than hers.
4. My feet are smaller than hers.
5. My hair's shorter than hers.
6. My flat's smaller than hers.
7. I'm more generous than her.
8. My skin is darker than hers.

8 Think of somebody you know well. Can you think of five differences between you? Write sentences using comparatives or (*not*) *as ... as.* Think of two singers, actors, writers or sports personalities. Write two or more sentences about differences between them.

9 Choose the correct captions for the cartoons.

'You were the World's Better Baby.'
'You were the World's Best Baby.'

'The better thing about working here is going home.'
'The best thing about working here is going home.'

Additional material

Lesson A1, Exercise 6

PRIVATE DETECTIVE

He's a very small man
And his face is very thin
He wears a long grey jacket
And he's got whiskers on his chin
He keeps looking back – I keep diving into doorways
Watching every move – I still don't know his name …

He's a dangerous villain
And he's creeping like a fox
There's something in his suitcase
And now he's stepping in a phone box
He keeps looking back – I keep diving into doorways
Watching every move – but I still don't know his
    game …

Private Detective – now he's running free
Private Detective – he'll never get away from me

She's sitting in a café
And she's reaching in her bag
She's looking at a photo
And her face is very sad
She keeps looking up – I dive behind my paper
Something's gonna happen – sooner or later

Private Detective – now she's running free
Private Detective – she'll never get away from me, no,
    no, no!

She's a very smart lady
And her nails are very long
And she's talking to a stranger
And I think she's got a gun
She keeps looking up – I dive behind my paper
Something's gonna happen – sooner or later

Private Detective – now she's running free
Private Detective – she'll never get away – oh no!

Private Detective – now he's running free, no, no
Private Detective – he'll never, never, never get away
    from me!

(Steve Hall)

Lesson B1, Exercise 1

1. .... some aspirins.
2. .... corridor, ... floor.
3. .... off in the bathroom. .... covered with
   water.
4. .... accident. .... hurt. She's bleeding.
5. .... screaming .... upstairs.
6. .... burglary.
7. .... gas ....

Lesson B4, Exercises 1 and 2

Last week my next-door neighbour Steve went to a department store to buy a new suit. He chose two suits to try on and went to the changing rooms. While he was putting the first pair of trousers on, he saw a hand reach in and snatch his own trousers! He shouted, got the new trousers on and ran after the man, but didn't catch him. Now he was stuck in the department store with no trousers, no money, no credit cards and no keys. So he phoned me and I went and rescued him. We left his name, address and phone number with the department store security department.

Later that afternoon, after we managed to get a new house key made for him, he got a phone call.

'This is Mr Daley at Foley's department store,' the man said. 'We've found your wallet, and we think we've got your keys as well. Would you like to come and get them?' So I drove him back to the store.

When we got to the store nobody knew who Mr Daley was. Wondering what was happening, we drove back home. When we got there, we found that the thieves had used Steve's keys to get into his house and burgle it.

Lesson B5, Exercise 1, Dialogue 1

(The doorbell rings.)
PETER: I'll go.
ANN: OK.
        (Peter opens the door.)
PETER: Hello, hello. Nice to see you.
SUE: Hello, Peter. Are we late?
PETER: No, not at all. You're the first, actually.
JOHN: Oh, good. Who else is coming?
PETER: Come in and have a drink. Well, there's Don
        and Emma, Jo and Stephen, and my sister
        Lucy and her new boyfriend. Can't remember
        his name. Let me take your coat. You know
        Lucy, don't you?
SUE: I think we've met her once.
ANN: Hello, Sue. Hello, John. Lovely to see you. I'm
        so glad you could come. Now, what can I get
        you to drink?
SUE: What have you got?
ANN: Oh, the usual things. Sherry; gin and tonic – I
        think; vodka; I think there's some beer; a glass
        of wine …?
SUE: I'll have a gin and tonic, Ann, please.
JOHN: So will I.
SUE: Doesn't the room look nice, John? You've
        changed it round since we were here last,
        haven't you? The piano was, let me see, yes,
        the piano was over by the window, wasn't it?
PETER: That's right. And we've moved the sofa over
        there and …

Lesson B5, Exercise 5, Dialogue 2

JOHN: So you work in a pub?
LUCY: Yes, that's right.
JOHN: What's it like?
LUCY: It's nice. I like it. You meet a lot of interesting people. A lot of boring ones, too, mind you.
JOHN: I beg your pardon?
LUCY: I said, a lot of boring ones too.
JOHN: Oh, yes. I can imagine. A pub – I should think that's hard work, isn't it?
LUCY: Yes and no. It depends.
JOHN: How do you mean?
LUCY: Well, it's hard at weekends. I mean, last Saturday night, with both bars full and one barman away ill – well, my feet didn't touch the ground. But on weekdays it's usually very quiet. What about you? What do you do? You're an accountant or something, aren't you?
JOHN: I work in a bank.
LUCY: Oh yes, that's right. Ann said. That must be nice.
JOHN: It's all right.
LUCY: But you have to move round from one place to another, don't you? I mean, if you get a better job – if they make you manager or something – it'll probably be in another town, won't it?
JOHN: Yes, probably.
LUCY: I wouldn't like that. I mean, I've got lots of friends here. I wouldn't like to move somewhere else.
JOHN: Oh, we like it. We've lived here for, what, six years now. We're ready for a change.

Lesson B5, Exercise 9, Dialogue 3

DON: Have you got the salt down your end, Steve?
STEVE: What are you looking for?
DON: The salt.
STEVE: Salt. Salt. Oh, yes. Here it is. And could you pass me the mustard in exchange? This is delicious beef, Ann. Who's your butcher?
ANN: Not telling you. What are John and Lucy talking about?
JOHN: Work, I'm afraid.
SUE: I thought so. It's all John ever talks about. Work and food.
JOHN: Well, there are worse things in life. Especially if the food's like this.
ANN: Thank you, John. Would you like some more? Have another potato. Some more meat? Some beans? A carrot? A piece of bread?
JOHN: No, thanks. That was lovely, but I've had enough. Really. I'll have another glass of wine, perhaps.
EMMA: Here you are, John.
(*Crash!*)
Oh, damn! I *am* sorry, Ann. How stupid of me.
ANN: That's all right. It doesn't matter at all. Really. They're very cheap glasses.

Lesson B8, Exercise 5

DO YOU KNOW

I will snap you if you don't watch out
When you're alone or if you're in a crowd
See the action if you close one eye
Push my button when the sun is in the sky.

Do you know what it is – what it is?
Can you say what it is?
Do you know what it is – what it is?
Can you say what it is?
Tell me what it is.

Just twist my handle and flick your toe
Wind on your face just see you go
Here comes a corner so you['d] better watch out
You're feeling nervous and you['ve] gotta slow down.

Do you know …

I've got the power to save you from danger
I decide if you live or die
Pull my pin, then grip my lever
Aim me straight at the source of the fire.

Do you know …

Just punch your number, then wait for the tone
I'll take you anywhere you wanna go
I can whisper words of love in your ear
Just hold me close – I can be so sincere.

Do you know …

(Steve Hall)

Lesson C4, Exercise 1: answers

Quick-thinking van driver
A quick-thinking van driver saved 11 people trapped in a blazing house in Birkenhead early today. Mrs Anne Redman of Newbury was driving past a house in Beaufort Road when she saw the ground floor on fire. Four adults and seven children were trapped in the bedroom above. Mrs Redman backed her van across the pavement, smashed through the front fence, and drove up to the front of the house. The trapped occupants were able to jump to safety via the roof of the van.

Firemen catch a man in mid-air
Three firemen caught a man in mid-air yesterday as he leapt from a blazing house. After shouting for help, the man jumped from a top-floor window with his clothes on fire. Firemen who were fighting the fire on a balcony below heard his shouts and realised what was happening. They leaned out and grabbed him by the legs as he hurtled past. Last night 22-year-old Mr Luke Savage, of Moreton Grove, Chester, was recovering in hospital.

Policeman saves boy on motorway
Little John Parker faced death when he fell from a car as it sped down a busy motorway. He was seriously injured and lay helpless in the fast lane with traffic hurtling towards him. But a policeman had seen him

fall. Police Constable Peter O'Donnell, careless of his own life, leapt from a moving patrol car. He dashed across the motorway and grabbed the five-year-old to safety from under the wheels of a vehicle that was almost upon them. Yesterday John, of The Close, Newleigh, Herts, was in hospital with head and leg injuries, but was described as 'satisfactory'.

Helicopter pilot saves swimmers

A quick-thinking helicopter pilot saved three swimmers from shark attacks yesterday. While he was flying off the Australian coast near Sydney, the pilot saw sharks approaching the swimmers. He brought his helicopter down until he was just over the water, and hovered above the sharks. After a few minutes they were frightened away, and the swimmers were able to get back safely to the beach. Swimmer Marion Jacobs said afterwards, 'He saved our lives. If he hadn't come when he did, the sharks would have had us.'

Lesson C5, Exercise 1

ASSISTANT: Good afternoon, madam. Can I help you?
CUSTOMER: Yes, I'd like to see the manager, please.
ASSISTANT: Furniture, madam? Second floor.
CUSTOMER: No, the *manager*. Ma-na-ger.
ASSISTANT: Oh, I *am* sorry. I thought you said furniture.
CUSTOMER: That's all right. But can I see the manager, please?
ASSISTANT: Well, I'm afraid she's *very* busy just now. Have you an appointment?
CUSTOMER: No, I haven't. I want to make a complaint.
ASSISTANT: A complaint. Oh, I see. Well, I'll just see if she's free.

Lesson D1, Exercise 1

Mugger meets little old lady

Jose Ramos is an experienced mugger, but he didn't know about little old English ladies. Now he does.

87-year-old Lady Vera Tucker was walking down New York's East 66th Street. She looked like an easy prey – small, grey-haired and expensively dressed, carrying a handbag over her shoulder.

Ramos came up on his bicycle and grabbed the handbag. Lady Tucker hit him on the head with her umbrella, knocking him off his bicycle, and started screaming at the top of her voice.

The unfortunate mugger tried to get back onto his bicycle and escape, but Lady Tucker kept hitting him. A lorry driver, hearing her screams, came and joined in the fight.

Holding his head, Ramos pushed the handbag at the driver and said, 'Here it is. It's over, it's over.' 'The hell it's over,' said the driver. They went on fighting, and Lady Tucker went on screaming, until a policeman arrived and took Ramos prisoner.

Lady Tucker refused medical help, saying that she felt fine. But she did allow the policeman to take her arm and escort her home.

(from *The South-Western Herald*, 28 May 1986)

Lesson D3, Exercise 8

SO NEAR YET SO FAR

Maria ......1...... on a mountainside with her mother
    and her father – she ......2...... an only child
She ......3...... so hard – in the old vineyard

Antonio ......4...... at the harbour's edge with his uncle
    and aunt ... and ......5...... his bread,
He ......6...... all day – in a rough black sea

They ......7...... at a dance in the market square
A romantic night – there ......8...... love in the air
They ......9...... each other close and he ......10.... her a ring
Both families ......11...... it ......12...... the very best thing

Maria ......13.... that the day ......14...... when she and
    Antonio ......15...... as one
They ......16...... soon – happy bride and groom

One hot summer's day on the mountainside
Maria stared as a stranger came by
In a shiny car and gold round his neck
She ......17...... the prettiest girl he'd ever ......18......

Maria ......19...... alone on the mountainside in a brand
    new dress and tears in her eyes
Now the stranger ......20.... – he ......21.... a handsome one

Antonio ......22...... on an out-of-town bus 'cause now
    his dreams ......23...... to dust
He ......24.... ......25.... away – he's just ......26.... for the city

They ......27...... at a dance in the market square
A romantic night – magic in the air
Both families ......28...... the wedding ......29...... off
So near yet so far from a perfect love.

(Steve Hall)

Lesson D5, Exercise 8

THE ISLAND

Each night I dream of a beautiful island
Surrounded by beaches and covered in flowers.
Butterflies dance through the sweet-smelling meadows
And birds sing their love songs for hours.

Crystal clear water runs down from the mountains
And flows through deep valleys as a sparkling stream.
Gentle sea breezes blow over my island
While sunshine pours over my dream.

Each night I visit the island of my dreams,
Each night I visit the island of my dreams,
I leave the real world behind,
It's somewhere deep in my mind,
Not too easy to find,
The island.

Bright orange squirrels play games in the tree tops
And chase through the branches where nightingales
    sing.
It looks so peaceful I wish I could take you
To where each night's the first day of spring.

Each night I visit the island of my dreams ...

(Jonathan Dykes – lyrics   Robert Campbell –music)

Lesson D8, Exercise 6

1

The time that I recall that was, er, gave me a bit of a *frisson* if you like was er, I was, er, I think I was up at university, and I was down in London at my parents' flat, and I'd been out er, moderately late, and drove er, a little Mini car back to the flat, which was in a rather smart part of London, and er, you had to park the car under the block of flats in an underground car park. And I did this one night and I noticed out of the corner of my eye that there was a car parked opposite, sort of in a right-angled road, er, facing the, the opening of the basement er, car park. And er, but I didn't pay any attention to it, I got out of the car as usual and went to see the er, night porter, and er, he saw me, recognised me, came to the door, and at that moment the doors flung open, and just like a TV, you know, TV series, er, these plainclothes people whipped out their wallets and showed, showed their er, showed their badges and said, 'Just a moment,' you know, you know, and all that sort of stuff, and you had to sort of, in there, and you thought, 'This is, this is ridiculous,' you know, 'this is r-, this is, I mean, this, this can't be serious,' but they were very serious, and they sort of almost frog-marched me to the car and asked me all these usual details, about did I know what licence number it was, how many miles I'd gone, and they took some persuading that someone looking as scruffy as I in a tiny little Mini could possibly live in such a smart block of flats.

2

The time I remember was when Piers was quite tiny and for some long-forgotten reason Peter and I were over to some friends in Burton-on-Trent, and we were in separate cars. And I was trying to follow quite closely to, behind Peter, but er, he always says I leave too much space, and so I did when he went through some traffic lights on green, and I thought, 'If I speed up a little bit I'll just get through.' And I didn't, and what I hadn't noticed was that the only other car on the road, directly behind me, was a police car, and he saw me go through the light on amber/red, I thought, but he thought it was red, so he followed us round the corner onto the bridge, overtook, stopped, and I sat tight in my car while Pete leapt out and defended me, and er, we said that we didn't want to make a noise because the baby was asleep in the back, but er, we didn't get away with it, and I did get my licence endorsed.

3

Yeah, I was driving back from France erm, years ago, and it had been a long drive, and I had had a fairly depressing experience in France, and I was driving as fast as I could through the west London suburbs to get home, and erm, I'd got this hot jazz blasting out of the erm, car cassette player at enormous volume, and erm, as I pulled up at a traffic light I saw this large white car pull up beside me, and I played back things in my mind and I realised that I had just overtaken a police car at 50 miles an hour in a 30 limit. And the policeman wound down his window, I wound down mine, and I was too perturbed to turn off the jazz. And he looked at me, and he listened to this noise coming out of the car, and he looked at me again, and he said, 'You must be bloody crazy!' And the lights changed to green and he drove off.

Lesson E1, Exercise 8

THIRTY DEGREES

It's thirty degrees in the shade
My girlfriend's spent my last dollar
I haven't seen a cloud all day
And she's run back to Minnesota.

My limousine's run clean out of gas
My radiator's dry and my tyres are flat
I'm sitting here in my ten-gallon hat
Wishing it would rain – what d'ya think of that?

It's thirty degrees in the shade
The dust is dirty where the wind blows
We're heading for a heatwave. Uh, huh
And I'm stuck here in Colorado.

My limousine's run clean out of gas
My radiator's dry and my tyres are flat
I'm sitting here in my ten-gallon hat
Wishing it would rain – what d'ya think of that?

It's hot – thirty degrees …
Thirty degrees …

Well, it's thirty degrees in the shade
My girlfriend's spent my last dollar
I haven't seen a cloud all day
And she's run back to Minnesota.

Sleep under a tree when the sun is high
It's better to walk in the desert at night.
I'll wave at the trucks and I'll hitch a ride
Got nothing to lose and I'm travelling light.

It's hot …

(Steve Hall)

Lesson E3, Exercise 5, Writing option

A few years ago I was travelling in France by myself, on a moped. I had a tent, and usually camped in the evenings: in camp sites whenever I could, both for the facilities like washing, shopping, *etc.*, and because it was a bit safer. But when I couldn't find a convenient camp site, I camped rough, trying to find places that were fairly hidden from the road. One evening like this, I found quite a nice place. It was up against a tall hedge in a little wood and couldn't be seen from the road; it was quite a pleasant spot. So I pitched my tent, covered my moped up with plastic, cooked my little supper over a camping gas fire, and got ready for bed. I read for a little while, and then went to sleep.

And I had a very unusual dream. I've never had another one like it before or since. It was in short episodes of a few minutes each, it seemed, though it's hard to tell in a dream how long things are. The people in the dream were young men and women that I had never seen and didn't know, all very happy, dressed as if it were the 1930s and 40s. Some of them were on farms; I remember a dance in a barn; some of them were walking along the streets in a small town in America. They were all Americans. Each episode had different people in it, and none of them lasted for very long. It wasn't a frightening dream at all – all the scenes were of very happy, smiling people. I woke up a bit puzzled, because it didn't seem to connect with anything that had been happening to me, and I didn't know anybody that was in the dream. It was very unusual.

I got up and fixed breakfast, packed my tent securely on the back of my moped, and set on my way. The little wood where I had slept, as I said, was up against a hedge, a very tall hedge that you couldn't see over. There was a bend in the road just at the hedge, which I hadn't been around. And when I did wheel my moped up to the road and go around the bend, I saw that just on the other side of the hedge there was a small American war cemetery from World War II – full of the graves of young men who could have lived the scenes that I had seen in my dream.

Lesson B7, Exercise 1, Dialogue 4

ANDY: I didn't like it at all.

EMMA: Oh, I thought it was lovely.

JOHN: It was rubbish. Complete rubbish. Absolute nonsense.

ANN: I didn't think much of it, I must say.

LUCY: I liked it. At the end, when she was dying, I cried. I couldn't help it. I cried and cried.

STEVE: Jo said it made her laugh.

JO: No, I didn't. Oh Steve, you are awful! Really! No, it's just that – I don't know – it didn't say anything to me.

JOHN: I'm afraid I must be very old-fashioned, but I like things to have a beginning, a middle and an end.

STEVE: Yes, so do I.

JOHN: And I don't like a lot of sex and violence.

EMMA: Oh, I love sex and violence!

ANN: More coffee, anybody?

ANDY: I don't like violence.

EMMA: But listen. Why didn't you like it? I thought it was great. Really.

ANN: So wordy. It was really really boring. They just talked and talked and talked all the time.

STEVE: I can't stand –

EMMA: No, look –

LUCY: I don't think –

DON: Three old women sitting around talking for two and a half hours. If that's what you want, you might as well go and spend the evening in the old people's home.

LUCY: It wasn't like that at all.

ANDY: Yes, it was.

LUCY: No, it wasn't.

ANDY: Yes, it was.

ANN: Who wrote it anyway?

JO: Don't know. What's his name? Fred Walker, something like that.

ANDY: Who's he?

DON: Never heard of him.

STEVE: Didn't he write …

Lesson B7, Exercise 6, Dialogue 5

DON: Well, I'm afraid it's getting late, and we've got a long way to go.

SUE: So have we. We ought to be on our way, I suppose.

JO: Yes, we'd better be going, too. Thank you so much, Ann. We really enjoyed ourselves. Lovely food, nice people, good talk …

ANN: Well, thank you for coming.

EMMA: You must come over to us soon. When we've finished moving. I'll give you a ring.

JOHN: Now, where's my coat?

PETER: Here it is, John.

JOHN: No, that's not mine. This is mine.

PETER: Oh, sorry. Well, whose is this, then?

ANN: Andy's, I think.

ANDY: Is it old and dirty? Yes, that's mine.

LUCY: Well, bye, Ann, bye, Peter. See you next week.

ALL: Bye, bye.

Lesson D1, Exercise 2

Little old lady in knife raid

A little grey-haired woman armed with a knife robbed an Oxfordshire shop after threatening the assistant.

The untidily dressed woman walked into The Sandwich Man shop in Parsons Street, Banbury at 9.30 at night and pulled out the bread knife from beneath her coat.

She threatened the young girl assistant and forced her to open the till before grabbing the entire day's takings.

The robbery happened on Saturday night, and police at Banbury are appealing for witnesses.

The shop owner, Mr Ken Woodd of Deddington, who also runs George's Café and Georgina's in the Covered Market, Oxford, said: 'It is unbelievable. It has never happened before in the 38 years I have been in business.'

Police took the assistant around pubs in the town after the robbery to try to find the woman, but with no luck.

Mr Woodd said the day's takings were snatched. He said it might have been as much as £180.

(from *The Oxford Mail*, 25 March 1986)

Vocabulary index

Irregular verbs: Verbs marked with an asterisk(*) are irregular. There is a complete list of the irregular verbs in *The New Cambridge English Course* at the back of the book.

Stress: In longer single words, only the main stress is normally shown (e.g. *appendicitis* /əpendɪ'saɪtəs/). This is also usually the case with fixed two-word expressions like *bank account* /'bæŋk əkaʊnt/. However, some words and expressions have variable stress; in these cases two stresses are shown (e.g. *inside* /ɪn'saɪd/; *bad-tempered* /'bæd 'tempəd/; *lie down* /'laɪ 'daʊn/).

135

call: What's this called? /kɔːld/ E5
camel /ˈkæml/ A2
camp (noun) /kæmp/ E3
camp (verb) /kæmp/ E5
camp site /ˈkæmp saɪt/ E3
camping /ˈkæmpɪŋ/ A6
Can I use ... /ˈkæn aɪ ˈjuːz/ A7
Can you explain this word/
  expression/sentence? /ɪkˈspleɪn/ A5
Can you remind me: why ...?
  /rɪˈmaɪnd/ A1
Can you tell me the way to ...?
  /ðə' weɪ tə/ D5
cancel /ˈkænsl/ E2
capital /ˈkæpɪtl/ C8
car park /ˈkɑː pɑːk/ D5
card: credit card /ˈkredɪt kɑːd/ B4
cardboard box /ˈkɑːdbɔːd ˈbɒks/ E2
careful /ˈkeəfl/ C1
carrot /ˈkærət/ A2, B5
carry /ˈkæri/ D7
cassette player /kæˈset pleɪə(r)/ C2
cassette recorder /kæˈset rɪˈkɔːdə(r)/ C2
catalogue /ˈkætəlɒg/ E4
catch* /kætʃ/ B4, B6
CD player /ˈsiː ˈdiː ˈpleɪə(r)/ C2
ceiling /ˈsiːlɪŋ/ D2
cellar /ˈselə(r)/ D2
centre /ˈsentə(r)/ C8
champion /ˈtʃæmpɪən/ A8
chance /tʃɑːns/ A3
change (for £5) /tʃeɪndʒ/ E5
change: a change /tʃeɪndʒ/ B5
change jobs/schools etc. /tʃeɪndʒ/ D6
change one's mind /maɪnd/ A3
changeable /ˈtʃeɪndʒəbl/ E1
cheap /tʃiːp/ B5, E4
cheat /tʃiːt/ B3
check /tʃek/ B3, C6, D2
cheek /tʃiːk/ A2
cheerful /ˈtʃɪəfl/ E6
chemical /ˈkemɪkl/ E7
cheque /tʃek/ E2
chess /tʃes/ A6, D6
chest /tʃest/ D7, E6
chewing gum /ˈtʃuːɪŋ gʌm/ C3
chin /tʃɪn/ A2
chips (food) /tʃɪps/ E5
choice /tʃɔɪs/ E4
choose* /tʃuːz/ A5, B4, D4
chop (food) /tʃɒp/ A2
city /ˈsɪti/ A8
clean (verb) /kliːn/ C3, C6
clever /ˈklevə(r)/ D4, E2
climate /ˈklaɪmət/ E7
climbing /ˈklaɪmɪŋ/ A6
close (adjective) /kləʊs/ D3
close down /ˈkləʊz ˈdaʊn/ C6
clothes dryer /ˈkləʊðz draɪə(r)/ C2
cloud /klaʊd/ A2, E1
cloud over /ˈklaʊd ˈəʊvə(r)/ E1
cloudy /ˈklaʊdi/ E1
coal miner /ˈkəʊl maɪnə(r)/ A4
coat /kəʊt/ B5, D1
coffee /ˈkɒfi/ B7
coin /kɔɪn/ E2
coincidence /kəʊˈɪnsɪdəns/ E3
cold /kəʊld/ E1
cold: a cold /ə ˈkəʊld/ D7
collecting: stamp collecting
  /ˈstæmp kəˈlektɪŋ/ A6
college /ˈkɒlɪdʒ/ D5

comb /kəʊm/ E2
Come in and have a drink /ˈkʌm ɪn/ B5
come* round /ˈkʌm ˈraʊnd/ E5
comfortable /ˈkʌmftəbl/ C3
compact disc (CD) player
  /ˈkɒmpækt ˈdɪsk ˈpleɪə(r)/ C2
company /ˈkʌmpəni/ D4
compete /kəmˈpiːt/ A8
competent /ˈkɒmpɪtənt/ A8
competition /kɒmpəˈtɪʃn/ A8
competitive /kəmˈpetətɪv/ A8
complain /kəmˈpleɪn/ C5
complaint /kəmˈpleɪnt/ C5
computer /kəmˈpjuːtə(r)/ C2, E5
concert /ˈkɒnsət/ A4
confidential /kɒnfɪˈdentʃl/ C7
Congress /ˈkɒngres/ C8
connect /kəˈnekt/ E3
Conservatives /kənˈsɜːvətɪvz/ C8
consider /kənˈsɪdə(r)/ D4
consist (of) /kənˈsɪst əv/ C8
contact (noun) /ˈkɒntækt/ A5
contact lenses /ˈkɒntækt ˈlenzɪz/ E6
contact: lose contact with sbdy
  /ˈluːz ˈkɒntækt/ E2
contain /kənˈteɪn/ B3
continent /ˈkɒntɪnənt/ E7
continue /kənˈtɪnjuː/ D3
convector heater /kənˈvektə ˈhiːtə(r)/ C2
convenient /kənˈviːnɪənt/ E3
conversation /kɒnvəˈseɪʃn/ A5, C5
cook (verb) /kʊk/ C6
cooker /ˈkʊkə(r)/ C2
cooking /ˈkʊkɪŋ/ C1
cool /kuːl/ B8, E1
corkscrew /ˈkɔːkskruː/ E2
corner /ˈkɔːnə(r)/ D8
correct /kəˈrekt/ A5
correct: Is this correct: ...? /kəˈrekt/ A5
corridor /ˈkɒrɪdɔː(r)/ B1
cost* /kɒst/ B8, E4
cough (noun) /kɒf/ D7
Could I/you (possibly) ...?
  /ˈkʊd ... ˈpɒsəbli/ A7
Could you do me a favour? /feɪvə(r)/ A7
Could you lend me £10? /lend/ A7
Could you pass me ... /pɑːs/ B5
country /ˈkʌntri/ A3, C8, E5
county /ˈkaʊnti/ C8
cousin /ˈkʌzn/ D3
cover (verb) /ˈkʌvə(r)/ C3
crash (into) /kræʃ/ D8
crazy /ˈkreɪzi/ D8
create /kriːˈeɪt/ E7
credit card /ˈkredɪt kɑːd/ B4
crossing: pedestrian crossing
  /pəˈdestrɪən ˈkrɒsɪŋ/ D8
cultural /ˈkʌltʃərʊl/ C7
culture /ˈkʌltʃə(r)/ C7
cup: make a cup of tea /ˈkʌp əv ˈtiː/ C1
curly /ˈkɜːli/ A1
customer /ˈkʌstəmə(r)/ C5
cut* /kʌt/ B6
cut* up /ˈkʌt ˈʌp/ C6
cycle (verb) /ˈsaɪkl/ A7
cycling /ˈsaɪklɪŋ/ A6
damp /dæmp/ E1
dancing /ˈdɑːnsɪŋ/ A6
dash (verb) /dæʃ/ C4
daughter-in-law /ˈdɔːtər ɪn lɔː/ D3
dead /ded/ E7
death /deθ/ C4

decision /dɪˈsɪʒn/ C7
decision: make a decision
  /ˈmeɪk ə dɪˈsɪʒn/ E2
deep /diːp/ B8
delicious /dɪˈlɪʃəs/ B5
Democrats /ˈdeməkræts/ C8
demonstration /demənˈstreɪʃn/ A5
dentist /ˈdentɪst/ A3
department /dɪˈpɑːtmənt/ B4
department store /dɪˈpɑːtmənt stɔː(r)/ B4
depend: It depends /ɪt dɪˈpendz/ B5
depressed /dɪˈprest/ E6
description /dɪˈskrɪpʃən/ D2
describe /dɪˈskraɪb/ B8
desk /desk/ B8
destroy /dɪˈstrɔɪ/ C7, E7
diagram /ˈdaɪəgræm/ D8
die /daɪ/ B8
difference /ˈdɪfrəns/ D2
difficult /ˈdɪfɪkʊlt/ A5
dirty /ˈdɜːti/ B7, C3
disabled /ˈdɪseɪbld/ A8
disagree /ˈdɪsəˈgriː/ C7
disagreement /ˈdɪsəˈgriːmənt/ E5
disappear /ˈdɪsəˈpɪə(r)/ E7
disaster /dɪˈzɑːstə(r)/ E7
discover /dɪsˈkʌvə(r)/ C6
discuss /dɪsˈkʌs/ A5
dishwasher /ˈdɪʃwɒʃə(r)/ C2
divide /dɪˈvaɪd/ C8, D2
divide into /dɪˈvaɪd ɪntə/ C8
division /dɪˈvɪʒn/ D3
divorced /dɪˈvɔːst/ D3
Do let me (teach you) ... /ˈduː ˈlet miː/ E5
Do you want to ...? /djə ˈwɒnt tə/ A7
Don't go away /ˈdəʊnt ˈgəʊ əˈweɪ/ E5
door: next door /ˈnekst ˈdɔː(r)/ B4
double /ˈdʌbl/ A4
down (preposition) /daʊn/ D5
draw* /drɔː/ D8
dream (noun) /driːm/ A4, E3
dream* /driːm/ D3
dress /dres/ E5
dress (= how someone is dressed)
  /dres/ D1
dressed: get* dressed /ˈget ˈdrest/ C1
drink: Have a drink /ˈhæv ə ˈdrɪŋk/ B5
drink: What can I get you to drink?
  /tə ˈdrɪŋk/ B5
drive* /draɪv/ B1, B4, D8
driver /ˈdraɪvə(r)/ A3
driving licence /ˈdraɪvɪŋ laɪsəns/ B4, D8
driving: rally driving /ˈræli draɪvɪŋ/ A6
drop /drɒp/ B3, B6
drought /draʊt/ E1
dry /draɪ/ C5
dryer: clothes dryer /ˈkləʊðz draɪə(r)/ C2
dryer: tumble dryer /ˈtʌmbl draɪə(r)/ C2
dust (noun) /dʌst/ C3
dustbin /ˈdʌstbɪn/ E2
dustman /ˈdʌstmən/ A4
each /iːtʃ/ C8
ear /ɪə(r)/ E6
earn* /ɜːn/ A4
ear-ring /ˈɪərɪŋ/ E6
east /iːst/ D5, E1
either: You can either ... or ...
  /ˈaɪðə(r), ˈiːðə(r)/ C7
elbow /ˈelbəʊ/ E2
elect /ɪˈlekt/ C8, E2
electric kettle /ɪˈlektrɪk ˈketl/ C2
electric(al) /ɪˈlektrɪk(l)/ C2

136

elephant /'elɪfənt/ A2
else /els/ B5
emergency /ɪ'mɜːdʒənsi/ B1
empty (verb, adjective) /'empti/ C3
end (noun) /end/ B7, E4
enjoy /ɪn'dʒɔɪ/ A8, D3, D4
enjoy ...ing /ɪn'dʒɔɪ/ D3
enjoy (your)self /ɪn'dʒɔɪ jɔː'self/ B7
enough: I've had enough
/aɪv 'hæd ɪ'nʌf/ B5
envelope /'envələup/ B8
Er, that's not quite right
/'nɒt 'kwaɪt 'raɪt/ A1
escape /ɪ'skeɪp/ D1
especially /ɪ'speʃəli/ A5
essay /'eseɪ/ A5
eventually /ɪ'ventʃəli/ C7
ever: hardly ever /'haːdli 'evə(r)/ E6
every year/week/etc. /'evri 'jɪə(r)/ D7
every (5 years) /'evri/ C8
everyday /'evrideɪ/ C3
exact /ɪg'zækt/ A5
exactly: Well, I didn't exactly ...
/ɪg'zæktli/ A1
examination /ɪgzæmɪ'neɪʃən/ A5, C3
exception /ɪk'sepʃən/ A3
exciting /ɪk'saɪtɪŋ/ E2
Excuse me /ɪk'skjuːz miː/ A7
Excuse me, I didn't mean... /miːn/ A1
expect /ɪk'spekt/ A3
expenses /ɪk'spensɪz/ A4
expensive /ɪk'spensɪv/ A7, B3, E4
expensively /ɪk'spensɪvli/ D1
experienced /ɪk'spɪərɪənst/ D1
expert /'ekspɜːt/ A8
explain: Can you explain this word
/expression/sentence? /ɪk'spleɪn/ A5
expression: Can you explain this
expression? /ɪk'spreʃn/ A5
extinct /ɪk'stɪŋkt/ E7
extra /'ekstrə/ A4
extremely /ɪk'striːmli/ A5, C1
eye /aɪ/ A1, E6
face (noun) /feɪs/ E4, E6
factory /'fæktri/ A4, C1, D2
fail /feɪl/ D8
fair (hair) /feə(r)/ A1
fairly /'feəli/ E1
fall* /fɔːl/ B1
fall* in love (with sbdy)
/'fɔːl ɪn 'lʌv/ C7, D4
false /fɔːls/ D5
family /'fæməli/ D3
famous /'feɪməs/ A3
fancy (verb) /'fænsi/ C7
farm /faːm/ E3
farmer /'faːmə(r)/ A3
father-in-law /'faːðər ɪn lɔː/ D3
favour /'feɪvə(r)/ A7
fax /fæks/ E5
federal /'fedərʊl/ C8
federation /'fedə'reɪʃn/ C8
feed* /fiːd/ B8
feel* /fiːl/ A8
fetch /fetʃ/ C1
fever: hay fever /'heɪ fiːvə(r)/ D7
fewer /'fjuːə(r)/ D3
fight* /faɪt/ D1
fill /fɪl/ C3
find* /faɪnd/ B3, B4
find* out /'faɪnd 'aut/ C7, E2
finger /'fɪŋgə(r)/ E6

fire (noun) /faɪə(r)/ B1
fire: on fire /ɒn 'faɪə(r)/ C4
first floor /'fɜːst 'flɔː(r)/ C1
first of all /'fɜːst əv 'ɔːl/ C5
fishing /'fɪʃɪŋ/ A6
fit (adjective) /fɪt/ A8
flashlight /'flæʃlaɪt/ C2
flat (noun) /flæt/ B1, D8
flight /flaɪt/ C3
flood /flʌd/ E7
floor: first floor /'fɜːst 'flɔː(r)/ C1
floor: ground floor /'graund 'flɔː(r)/ C4
flour /'flauə(r)/ A2
fog /fɒg/ A2, E1
foggy /'fɒgi/ E1
follow /'fɒləu/ D8
fond (of sbdy) /'fɒnd əv/ D4
food /fuːd/ B5, E7
food mixer /'fuːd 'mɪksə(r)/ C2
fool: make a fool of oneself
/'meɪk ə 'fuːl əv/ E2
foot (feet) /fut, fiːt/ E6
football /'futbɔːl/ A6
for ... reason /fə(r) ... 'riːzn/ A5
for a minute /fər ə 'mɪnɪt/ E5
for sale /fə 'seɪl/ B3, E4
force (sbdy to do sth) /fɔːs/ D1
forecast: weather forecast
/'weðə 'fɔːkaːst/ E1
fortunately /'fɔːtʃənətli/ E7
free (= not busy) /friː/ C5
free (= not for sale) /friː/ E4
free time /'friː 'taɪm/ A3
fridge /frɪdʒ/ C2
friend: make friends (with sbdy)
/'meɪk 'frendz wɪð/ E2
friendly /'frendli/ E6
frighten /'fraɪtn/ C4
fry /fraɪ/ C6
full /ful/ A4
full-time /'ful 'taɪm/ D3
funny (= strange) /'fʌni/ C5
fur /fɜː(r)/ E7
furniture (uncountable) /'fɜːnɪtʃə(r)/ C5
future: the future /ðə 'fjuːtʃə(r)/ E3
game /geɪm/ D6
garage /'gæraːʒ, 'gærɪdʒ/ D8
gardener /'gaːdnə(r)/ A4
gas /gæs/ B1
general (adjective) /'dʒenrʊl/ A1
generous /'dʒenərəs/ A4, B3
German measles /'dʒɜːmən 'miːzlz/ C3
get* (for changes) /get/ C5
get* (= arrive, receive) /get/ B4
get* (= acquire) /get/ E5
get* dressed /'get 'drest/ C1
get* into trouble /'get ɪntə 'trʌbl/ C1
get* on with sbdy /'get ɒn wɪð/ C1, D3
get* rid of sbdy/sth /'get 'rɪd əv/ C1
get* up /'get 'ʌp/ C1
gift /gɪft/ E4
Give me ... /'gɪv miː/ A7
give* sbdy a hand /gɪv ... ə 'hænd/ E5
give* sbdy a message
/gɪv ... ə 'mesɪdʒ/ E2
Glad you like it E5
glad /glæd/ E5
glad: (I'm) glad you like it
/'glæd juː/ E5
glad: (I'm) so glad you could come
/'səu 'glæd/ B5
glasses /'glaːsɪz/ E6

glove /glʌv/ E6
go* straight ahead /'gəu 'streɪt ə'hed/ D5
go* straight on /'gəu 'streɪt ɒn/ D5
go* (for sounds) /gəu/ C5
go* back /gəu 'bæk/ D6
go* out with sbdy /'gəu 'aut wɪð/ C7
go* through a red light /'gəu 'θruː/ D8
go* to sleep /gəu tə 'sliːp/ E3
goal /gəul/ D6
gold /gəuld/ D3
golf /gɒlf/ D6
good-looking /'gud 'lukɪŋ/ A1
govern /'gʌvən/ C6, C8
government /'gʌvəmənt/ C8
grab /græb/ D1
grammar /'græmə(r)/ A5
granddaughter /'grændɔːtə(r)/ D3
grandson /'grænsʌn/ D3
grandchild (-children)
/'græntʃaɪld, tʃɪldrən/ D3
grandmother /'grænmʌðə(r)/ D3
grandfather /'grænfaːðə(r)/ D3
grandparent /'grænpeərənt/ D3
great /greɪt/ E5
green /griːn/ A1
grey /greɪ/ A1
grey (weather) /greɪ/ E1
groom /gruːm/ D3
ground /graund/ B5
ground floor /'graund 'flɔː(r)/ C4
ground: high ground /'haɪ 'graund/ E1
grow* up /'grəu 'ʌp/ A3, C1
guess (verb) /ges/ A4, C7
guitar /gɪ'taː(r)/ C3
gum: chewing gum /'tʃuːɪŋ gʌm/ C3
hail (noun) /heɪl/ A2
hair /heə(r)/ A1
hair-dryer /'heə draɪə(r)/ C5
hairbrush /'heəbrʌʃ/ B8
hand /hænd/ B4, B8, E6
hand: give sbdy a hand
/'gɪv ... ə 'hænd/ E5
handbag /'hændbæg/ D1, E6
handle (noun) /'hændl/ E4
handsome /'hændsəm/ A1
happen /'hæpn/ B4, E3
hard work /'haːd 'wɜːk/ B5
hard-working /'haːd 'wɜːkɪŋ/ B3
hardly /'haːdli/ D7
hardly ever /'haːdli 'evə(r)/ E6
hat /hæt/ E6
Have a drink /'hæv ə 'drɪŋk/ B5
Have some ... /'hæv səm/ A7
have* trouble with sth
/'hæv 'trʌbl wɪð/ E2
hay fever /'heɪ fiːvə(r)/ D7
head /hed/ E6
head (= boss) /hed/ A4, C8
head of state /'hed əv 'steɪt/ C8
headache /'hedeɪk/ D6, D7
health care /'helθ keə(r)/ C8
healthy /'helθi/ A4, D3
hear* of /'hɪər əv/ B7
heater /'hiːtə(r)/ C2
heavy /'hevi/ D7
heavy rain /'hevi 'reɪn/ E1
height /haɪt/ A1
height: of medium height
/əv 'miːdɪəm 'haɪt/ A1
helicopter /'helɪkɒptə(r)/ C4
help (noun) /help/ B1, D1
help (verb) /help/ E5

love: I'd love to /aɪd 'lʌv tu:/ — A7
lovely /'lʌvli/ — B5, B7
Lovely to see you /'lʌvli tə 'si: ju:/ — B5
lower body /'ləʊə 'bɒdi/ — E6
luck /lʌk/ — D1
machine /mə'ʃi:n/ — E4
machine: washing machine /'wɒʃɪŋ mə'ʃi:n/ — C2
magazine /'mægə'zi:n/ — A3, C7
main /meɪn/ — A5
majority /mə'dʒɒrəti/ — C8
make* /meɪk/ — E5
make* (a cup of) tea /'ti:/ — C1
make* a decision /'dɪ'sɪʒən/ — E2
make* a fool of oneself /ə 'fu:l əv/ — E2
make* a mistake /ə mɪ'steɪk/ — E2
make* friends (with sbdy) /'frendz wɪð/ — E2
manage (to) /'mænɪdʒ/ — B4
manager /'mænədʒə(r)/ — B5, C5
manual: technical manual /'teknɪkl 'mænjuːəl/ — A5
marriage /'mærɪdʒ/ — D3
married /'mærɪd/ — C1, D3
marvellous /'mɑːvələs/ — D4
match (= game) /mætʃ/ — D6
material /mə'tɪərɪəl/ — E4
matter: It doesn't matter (at all) /ɪt 'dʌznt 'mætə(r)/ — B5
matter: What's the matter /'wɒts ðə 'mætə/ — A7
maximum /'mæksɪməm/ — E1
meal /mi:l/ — B3
mean* /mi:n/ — E5
mean*: How do you mean? /'haʊ djə 'mi:n/ — B5
mean*: What does ... mean? /'wɒt dəz ... 'mi:n/ — E5
measles: German measles /'dʒɜːmən 'mi:zlz/ — C3
meat /mi:t/ — B5
medicine /'medsən/ — E7
Mediterranean /medɪtə'reɪnɪən/ — E7
medium: of medium height /əv 'mi:dɪəm 'haɪt/ — A1
meet* /mi:t/ — D4, E2
meeting /'mi:tɪŋ/ — A5
member /'membə(r)/ — C8
Member of Parliament (MP) /'membər əv 'pɑːlɪmənt/ — C8
memory /'meməri/ — D8
mend /mend/ — B6, C3
message /'mesɪdʒ/ — E2, E4
metal /'metl/ — B8, E4
microphone /'maɪkrəfəʊn/ — B8
middle /'mɪdl/ — B4, B7
mind: change one's mind /'tʃeɪndʒ wʌnz 'maɪnd/ — A3
mind: don't mind /'dəʊnt 'maɪnd/ — A3, A7
mind: I wouldn't mind ... (request) /aɪ 'wʊdnt 'maɪnd/ — E5
mind: Would you mind ...ing? /'wʊd ju: 'maɪnd/ — A7
mine (pronoun) /maɪn/ — B7
miner /maɪnə(r)/ — A4
minister /'mɪnɪstə(r)/ — A4, C8
minority /maɪ'nɒrəti/ — C8
minute: for a minute /fər ə 'mɪnɪt/ — E5
mirror /'mɪrə(r)/ — C3
miss (verb) /mɪs/ — D6
mistake: make a mistake /'meɪk ə 'mɪsteɪk/ — E2

misunderstanding /'mɪsʌndə'stændɪŋ/ — E2, E5
mix up /'mɪks 'ʌp/ — C3
mixer /'mɪksə(r)/ — C2
modernise /'mɒdənaɪz/ — C6
money /'mʌni/ — B4
More (bread)? (offer) /'mɔː 'bred/ — A7
mostly /'məʊstli/ — A5
mother-in-law /'mʌðər ɪn lɔː/ — D3
motorbike /'məʊtəbaɪk/ — A3
motorist /'məʊtərɪst/ — D8
motorway /'məʊtəweɪ/ — C4
mountain /'maʊntɪn/ — D5
mouse /maʊs/ — A2
moustache /mə'stɑːʃ/ — A2
move (general) /mu:v/ — B1, D6
move (house) /mu:v/ — B5, B7
MP /'em 'pi:/ — C8
mug /mʌg/ — E2
mugger /'mʌgə(r)/ — D1
muscle /'mʌsl/ — D7
muscle: a pulled muscle /'pʊld 'mʌsl/ — D7
music: listening to music /'lɪsənɪŋ tə 'mju:zɪk/ — A6
mustard /'mʌstəd/ — B5
myself: by myself /baɪ maɪ'self/ — E3
nail /neɪl/ — E2
national /'næʃənl/ — C8
nationality /'næʃə'næləti/ — E4
natural /'nætʃərəl/ — A5, E7
nearly /'nɪəli/ — B3
neck /nek/ — D3, E6
necklace /'nekləs/ — E6
need (verb) /ni:d/ — B3
needle /'ni:dl/ — E2
neighbour /'neɪbə(r)/ — B4, C4
nephew /'nevju:/ — D3
never /'nevə(r)/ — D7
news: bad news /'bæd 'nju:z/ — E2
newspaper /'nju:speɪpə(r)/ — C3
next door /'nekst 'dɔː(r)/ — B4
Nice to see you /'naɪs tə 'si: ju:/ — B5
nice: That would be very nice /'veri 'naɪs/ — A7
nice: That's very nice of you /'ðæts 'veri 'naɪs/ — A7
niece /ni:s/ — D3
nobody /'nəʊbədi/ — B4
noise /nɔɪz/ — D8
nonsense /'nɒnsəns/ — B7
normal /'nɔːml/ — E1
north /nɔːθ/ — D5, E1
north-east /'nɔːθ 'i:st/ — E1
north-west /'nɔːθ 'west/ — E1
Not at all (answer to thanks) /'nɒt ət 'ɒl/ — A7
note (noun) /nəʊt/ — D1
novel /'nɒvl/ — A5
novelist /'nɒvəlɪst/ — D6
nuclear /'njuklɪə(r)/ — E7
number: wrong number /'rɒŋ 'nʌmbə(r)/ — C6
nurse /nɜːs/ — A3, A4
object (verb) /əb'dʒekt/ — C7
occasionally /ə'keɪʒənli/ — E6
occupied /'ɒkju:paɪd/ — D6
of course /əv 'kɔːs/ — A7
of course: Yes, of course /'jes əv 'kɔːs/ — E5
of medium height /əv 'mi:dɪəm 'haɪt/ — A1
offer (noun) /'ɒfə(r)/ — E5
offer (verb) /'ɒfə(r)/ — A7, B3, E2, E5

office /'ɒfɪs/ — B8, D2
officer /'ɒfɪsə(r)/ — B1
often /'ɒfn/ — D7
often: How often ...? /'haʊ 'ɒfn/ — D7
Oh, thank you. Here you are. /'hɪə ju: 'ɑː/ — A7
Oh, yes? /'əʊ 'jes/ — A7
oil /ɔɪl/ — E4
OK /'əʊ 'keɪ/ — A7, E5
old /əʊld/ — B7
old-fashioned /'əʊld 'fæʃənd/ — B7
on business /ɒn 'bɪznɪs/ — C1
on fire /ɒn 'faɪə(r)/ — C4
on holiday /ɒn 'hɒlədi/ — D2
on my own /ɒn maɪ 'əʊn/ — C1
on top of /ɒn 'tɒp əv/ — C1
one after another /'wʌn 'ɑːftər ə'nʌðə(r)/ — D6
operation /ɒpə'reɪʃn/ — D7
operator (telephone) /'ɒpəreɪtə(r)/ — B1
opinion /ə'pɪnjən/ — C7
opportunity /'ɒpə'tju:nəti/ — D4
opposite (adverb) /'ɒpəzɪt/ — D8
opposite: in the opposite direction /də'rekʃən/ — D8
orange juice /'ɒrɪndʒ 'dʒu:s/ — A2, E5
order (verb) /'ɔːdə(r)/ — C5, E5
order: in order /ɪn 'ɔːdə(r)/ — E3
ordinary /'ɔːdənri/ — D1
organisation /'ɔːgənaɪ'zeɪʃn/ — E2, E7
organise /'ɔːgənaɪz/ — C1
out: ask sbdy out /'ɑːsk ... 'aʊt/ — C7
out: go out with sbdy /'gəʊ 'aʊt wɪð/ — C7
outdoors /'aʊt'dɔːz/ — C1
outgoing /'aʊtgəʊɪŋ/ — D4
outside (adverb) /'aʊt'saɪd/ — A8, D7
outside (preposition) /'aʊt'saɪd/ — D3
over (preposition) /'əʊvə(r)/ — C4
over (= finished) /'əʊvə(r)/ — D1
over there /'əʊvə 'ðeə(r)/ — B5, E5
over: talk sth over /'tɔːk ... 'əʊvə/ — C7
overnight /'əʊvə'naɪt/ — C3
overtake* /'əʊvə'teɪk/ — D8
overweight /'əʊvə'weɪt/ — A1
own (determiner) /əʊn/ — C8
own (verb) /əʊn/ — A3
own: on my own /'ɒn maɪ 'əʊn/ — C1
owner /'əʊnə(r)/ — D1
pack /pæk/ — C3
pain /peɪn/ — D7
painting /'peɪntɪŋ/ — A6
pair /peə/ — B4
pair of scissors /'peər əv 'sɪzəz/ — E2
pardon: I beg your pardon /aɪ 'beg jɔː 'pɑːdn/ — B5, E5
parents /'peərənts/ — A3, C7
parents-in-law /'peərənts ɪn lɔː/ — D3
park (noun) /pɑːk/ — D5
park (verb) /pɑːk/ — D8
park: car park /'kɑː pɑːk/ — D5
parliament /'pɑːlɪmənt/ — C8
partly /'pɑːtli/ — C8
party (political) /'pɑːti/ — C8
party (with friends) /'pɑːti/ — E4
pass (= give) /pɑːs/ — E5
Pass the ... /'pɑːs ðə/ — A7
pass: Could you pass me ... /'kʊd ju: 'pɑːs/ — B5
past (preposition) /pɑːst/ — D5
path /pɑːθ/ — D5
patience /'peɪʃəns/ — A3
patient (noun) /'peɪʃənt/ — D7

pay* /peɪ/ C6
pay* back /'peɪ 'bæk/ D4
peace /piːs/ A4
pedestrian /pə'destrɪən/ D8
pedestrian crossing
  /pə'destrɪən 'krɒsɪŋ/ D8
peel /piːl/ C3
perfume /'pɜːfjuːm/ B8
Perhaps you could bring me …?
  /pə'hæps … 'brɪŋ miː/ E5
personal stereo /'pɜːsənl 'sterɪəʊ/ C2
personality /pɜːsə'næləti/ D4
phone (verb) /fəʊn/ B4
phone call /'fəʊn kɔːl/ B4, D2
photocopy (noun) /'fəʊtəʊkɒpi/ E5
piano: playing the piano
  /'pleɪŋ ðə pi'ænəʊ/ A6
pick up /'pɪk 'ʌp/ B6, C2
picnic /'pɪknɪk/ C3
piece /piːs/ B5
piece of advice /'piːs əv əd'vaɪs/ D2
piece of string /'piːs əv 'strɪŋ/ E2
pillow /'pɪləʊ/ E2
pilot /'paɪlət/ C4
pineapple /'paɪnæpl/ A2
place /pleɪs/ E7
plain /pleɪn/ A1
plan /plæn/ A5
plant /plɑːnt/ E7
plastic /'plæstɪk/ E3
play cards /'pleɪ 'kɑːdz/ B3
playing the piano /'pleɪŋ ðə pi'ænəʊ/ A6
pleasant /'pleznt/ E3
plug (noun) /plʌg/ C2
plug in /'plʌg 'ɪn/ C2
PM (= Prime Minister) /'piː 'em/ C8
pocket /'pɒkɪt/ B3
point (on an object) /pɔɪnt/ E4
pointed /'pɔɪntɪd/ E4
poison /'pɔɪzn/ E7
police (plural) /pə'liːs/ C8
police station /pə'liːs steɪʃn/ D5
policeman (policemen)
  /pə'liːsmən/ A4, D1, D4
policewoman (policewomen)
  /pə'liːswʊmən, wɪmɪn/ D1, D4
polish (verb) /'pɒlɪʃ/ B6
political /pə'lɪtɪkl/ C8
political party /pə'lɪtɪkl 'pɑːti/ C8
pool: swimming pool /'swɪmɪŋ 'puːl/ D5
porter /'pɔːtə(r)/ D8
possible: as … as possible
  /əz … əz 'pɒsəbl/ C1
possibly: Could I/you possibly …?
  /'kʊd … 'pɒsəbli/ A7
post office /'pəʊst ɒfɪs/ D5
poster /'pəʊstə(r)/ E4
potato /pə'teɪtəʊ/ B5
pour /pɔː(r)/ B6
powder /'paʊdə(r)/ E4
power /'paʊə(r)/ A3, A4, C8
practical /'præktɪkl/ C3
precise /prɪ'saɪs/ A8
prefer: I'd prefer … /aɪd prɪ'fɜː(r)/ A7
prefer: if you prefer /ɪf ju: prɪ'fɜː/ C5
preferably /'prefrəbli/ A8
pregnant /'pregnənt/ C3
prepare /prɪ'peə/ A7, C6
President /'prezɪdənt/ C8
pretty /'prɪti/ A1
price /praɪs/ B3, E4
primary school /'praɪməri skuːl/ A3, A4

Prime Minister /'praɪm 'mɪnɪstə(r)/ C8
prisoner /'prɪznə(r)/ D1
probably /'prɒbəbli/ B5, C5
problem /'prɒbləm/ A7, C5, C7, D2
produce /prə'djuːs/ D3, E4
professional /prə'feʃənl/ A5
pronounce /prə'naʊns/ E5
pronounce: How do you pronounce …?
  /'haʊ djə prə'naʊns/ A5, E5
pub /pʌb/ B5, D1
public transport /'pʌblɪk 'trɑːnspɔːt/ B3
publish /'pʌblɪʃ/ C6
pull /pʊl/ B6, C4
pull down /'pʊl 'daʊn/ C6
pulled muscle /'pʊld 'mʌsl/ D7
purpose /'pɜːpəs/ A5
push /pʊʃ/ B6, D1
put* down /'pʊt 'daʊn/ B6
put* off …ing /'pʊt 'ɒf/ C1
put* on /'pʊt 'ɒn/ B8
pyjamas /pə'dʒɑːməz/ E5
quality /'kwɒləti/ E4
quarrel (verb) /'kwɒrəl/ E2
queen /kwiːn/ C8
queue (noun) /kjuː/ D7
quick /kwɪk/ C4
quiet /'kwaɪət/ B3
quite (= rather) /kwaɪt/ B7
rabbit /'ræbɪt/ A2, B8, C3
race (human type) /reɪs/ C7
railway station /'reɪlweɪ steɪʃn/ D5
rain (noun and verb) /reɪn/ E1
rainy /'reɪni/ E1
rare /reə(r)/ E7
rat /ræt/ A2
rather /'rɑːðə(r)/ A3
reach /riːtʃ/ B4
reaction /riː'ækʃən/ E7
ready /'redi/ B5
real /riːl/ C8
realise /'rɪəlaɪz/ D8
really /'rɪəli/ D4
reason (for sth) /'riːzn fə/ A5
reasonable /'riːznəbl/ A4
rebuild* /'riː'bɪld/ C6
receptionist /rɪ'sepʃənɪst/ D2
record (verb) /rɪ'kɔːd/ C6
recover /rɪ'kʌvə(r)/ C4
recover (from sth) /rɪ'kʌvə frəm/ D4
red (hair) /red/ A1
refrigerator /rɪ'frɪdʒəreɪtə(r)/ C2
refund (noun) /'riːfʌnd/ C5
refuse /rɪ'fjuːz/ D1
regional /'riːdʒənl/ C8
relationship /rɪ'leɪʃənʃɪp/ C1
relative /'relətɪv/ D3
religion /rɪ'lɪdʒən/ C7
religious /rɪ'lɪdʒəs/ C7
remain /rɪ'meɪn/ E7
remember /rɪ'membə(r)/ A1
remind /rɪ'maɪnd/ A1
rent (verb) /rent/ E5
repair (verb) /rɪ'peə(r)/ C5, C6
replace /rɪ'pleɪs/ C5
reply (noun) /rɪ'plaɪ/ C7
report (verb) /rɪ'pɔːt/ D8
report (noun) /rɪ'pɔːt/ A5, D6, D8
Representative /'reprɪ'zentətɪv/ C8
Republicans /rɪ'pʌblɪkənz/ C8
request (noun) /rɪ'kwest/ E5
rescue /'reskjuː/ A8, B4
respect (verb) /rɪ'spekt/ C7

responsible /rɪ'spɒnsəbl/ C8
restaurant /'restrɒnt/ E5
retire /rɪ'taɪə(r)/ A3
rice /raɪs/ C3
rid: get* rid of sbdy/sth /'get 'rɪd əv/ C1
ride* /raɪd/ A8
riding: horse riding /'hɔːs 'raɪdɪŋ/ A6
right there /'raɪt 'ðeə(r)/ B1
right-wing /'raɪt 'wɪŋ/ C8
right: That's right /'ðæts 'raɪt/ B5
right: the right to do sth /ðə 'raɪt tə/ C7
ring (for finger) /rɪŋ/ C3, E6
ring (= phone call) /rɪŋ/ B7
ring* sbdy up /'rɪŋ … 'ʌp/ E2
river /'rɪvə(r)/ D5, E2
road /rəʊd/ C8, D5
roast (verb) /rəʊst/ C6
robbery /'rɒbəri/ D1
roll (verb) /rəʊl/ B6
romantic /rəʊ'mæntɪk/ D3
roof /ruːf/ D2
round (adjective) /raʊnd/ E4
round: come round /'kʌm 'raʊnd/ E5
roundabout (road) /'raʊndəbaʊt/ D8
rub /rʌb/ C3
rubbish /'rʌbɪʃ/ B7
rugby football /'rʌgbi 'fʊtbɔːl/ A6
rule (noun) /ruːl/ A8, C7, D3, D6
ruler /ruːlə(r)/ E2
run* /rʌn/ D6
run* (sth) /rʌn/ D4
run* after /'rʌn 'ɑːftə(r)/ B4
running (sport) /'rʌnɪŋ/ A6
rush /rʌʃ/ D2
safe (adjective) /seɪf/ C3, E3
safety /'seɪfti/ C4
salary /'sæləri/ A4, C1
sale /seɪl/ E4
sale: for sale /fə 'seɪl/ E4
salt /sɔːlt, sɒlt/ B5
sandwich /'sæmwɪdʒ/ E5
sauce /sɔːs/ E5
saucepan /'sɔːspən/ C3, E2
save (from extinction) /seɪv/ E7
save (money) /seɪv/ E4
save (people) /seɪv/ C4
say* /seɪ/ E5
Say, … (to change subject) /seɪ/ E5
say*: How do you say … in English?
  /'haʊ djə 'seɪ/ A5, E5
say*: What do you say when …?
  /'wɒt djə seɪ/ A5
scarf /skɑːf/ E6
scene /siːn/ E3
school leaver /'skuːl 'liːvə(r)/ D4
school: leave* school /'liːv 'skuːl/ A3
school: primary school
  /'praɪməri skuːl/ A3, A4
scissors /'sɪzəz/ E2
score /skɔː(r)/ B3
scratch /skrætʃ/ B6
scream (noun) /skriːm/ D1
scream (verb) /skriːm/ B1, D1
screwdriver /'skruːdraɪvə(r)/ E2
sea /siː/ E7
secondly /'sekəndli/ C5
secret /'siːkrɪt/ E2
security /sɪ'kjuːrəti/ B4
see*: I see /'aɪ 'siː/ A7
see*: Lovely/Nice to see you
  /'lʌvli tə 'siː juː/ B5

140

see*: Well, you see, it's like this /'wel, ju: 'si:/ A7

Senate /'senət/ C8

Senator /'senətə(r)/ C8

send* /send/ C6, E5

sentence /'sentəns/ A5

sentence: Can you explain this sentence? /'kæn ju: ɪk'spleɪn/ A5

separated /'sepəreɪtɪd/ D3

separately /'seprətli/ C8

serious /'sɪərɪəs/ B3, E2

seriously /'sɪərɪəsli/ C4, D4

serve /sɜːv/ C6

service (e.g. fire service) /'sɜːvɪs/ B1

sex (= male or female) /seks/ D3

sex (= act of sex) /seks/ B7

shake* /ʃeɪk/ C3

Shall I ...? /'ʃæl aɪ/ A7

share /ʃeə(r)/ C1

share (sth with sbdy) /'ʃeə(r) ... wɪð/ D3

sharp /ʃɑːp/ E4

sharpen /'ʃɑːpn/ B6

shine* /ʃaɪn/ E1

shirt /ʃɜːt/ E6

shock /ʃɒk/ E2

shocked /ʃɒkt/ E7

shoe /ʃuː/ E6

shop assistant /'ʃɒp ə'sɪstənt/ D1

shoplifting /'ʃɒplɪftɪŋ/ B3

shopping /'ʃɒpɪŋ/ C1

short (hair) /ʃɔːt/ A1

short (person) /ʃɔːt/ A1

short of money /'ʃɔːt əv 'mʌni/ A7

shoulder /'ʃəʊldə(r)/ D1, E6

shout (verb) /ʃaʊt/ B4

show* /ʃəʊ/ E5

shower /'ʃaʊə(r)/ E1

sign (noun) /saɪn/ D8

sign (verb) /saɪn/ B3

singing /'sɪŋɪŋ/ A6

single /'sɪŋgl/ D3

sister-in-law /'sɪstər ɪn lɔː/ D3

site: camp site /'kæmp saɪt/ E3

skating /'skeɪtɪŋ/ A8

skiing /'skiːɪŋ/ A6

skirt /skɜːt/ E6

sky /skaɪ/ E1

slice /slaɪs/ B6

slightly /'slaɪtli/ C8

slim /slɪm/ A1

small /smɔːl/ A1

small ad /'smɔːl æd/ E4

smart /smɑːt/ D8

smell* /smel/ B8

smile (verb) /smaɪl/ E3

smoke (noun) /sməʊk/ B1

snake /sneɪk/ D6

snow (noun) /snəʊ/ A2, E1

snow (verb) /snəʊ/ E1

so /səʊ/ D3

sociable /'səʊʃəbl/ B3

social /'səʊʃl/ A5

society /sə'saɪəti/ A4, D3

sock /sɒk/ E6

socket /'sɒkɪt/ C2

soldier /'səʊldʒə(r)/ A4

sometimes /'sʌmtaɪmz/ D7

somewhere else /'sʌmweər 'els/ B5

son-in-law /'sʌn ɪn lɔː/ D3

song /sɒŋ/ A5

sore throat /'sɔː 'θrəʊt/ D7

sorry: I'm sorry to trouble you /'sɒri ... 'trʌbl/ A7

sorry: I really am very sorry /'rɪəli 'æm ... 'sɒri/ C5

sort /sɔːt/ B8

sort out /'sɔːt 'aʊt/ C3

south /saʊθ/ D5, E1

south-east /'saʊθ 'iːst/ E1

south-west /'saʊθ 'west/ E1

space /speɪs/ D8

spade /speɪd/ E2

speak* /spiːk/ C6

special /'speʃl/ E4

special: somewhere special /'sʌmweə 'speʃl/ A1

specialist /'speʃəlɪst/ A5

speed /spiːd/ A5, E1

speed limit /'spiːd lɪmɪt/ D8

spell: How do you spell ...? /'haʊ djə 'spel/ A5

spelling /'spelɪŋ/ A5

spend* time /'spend 'taɪm/ D2, D3

spoil /spɔɪl/ B8

spoon /spuːn/ E5

spring (season) /sprɪŋ/ E1

square (noun) /skweə(r)/ D6

square (adjective) /skweə(r)/ E4

squirrel /'skwɪrəl/ A2

stain (noun) /steɪn/ C3

stand* up /'stænd 'ʌp/ D7

start: it won't start /ɪt 'wəʊnt 'stɑːt/ C5

state /steɪt/ C8

station: police station /pə'liːs steɪʃn/ D5

station: railway station /'reɪlweɪ steɪʃn/ D5

stay (with sbdy) /'steɪ wɪð/ D6, E2

steak /steɪk/ E5

steal* /stiːl/ B1, B3, D1, E2

stereo: personal stereo /'pɜːsənl 'sterɪəʊ/ C2

stick (noun) /stɪk/ D6

stomach /'stʌmək/ A2

store: department store /dɪ'pɑːtmənt stɔː(r)/ B4

story /'stɔːri/ B4, E3

straight /streɪt/ A1

straight ahead: go*/keep* straight ahead /'streɪt ə'hed/ D5

straight on: go*/keep* straight on /'streɪt 'ɒn/ D5

strange /streɪndʒ/ B3, E3

stranger /'streɪndʒə(r)/ E2

stream /striːm/ D5

string /strɪŋ/ E2

stuck /stʌk/ B4, C5

stuff /stʌf/ B8, E4

stupid /'stjuːpɪd/ B5, E2

stupid: How stupid of me! /'haʊ 'stjuːpɪd/ B5

subject /'sʌbdʒɪkt/ A5

succeed /sək'siːd/ D3

success /sək'ses/ D7

successfully /sək'sesfʊli/ A8, E7

sudden /'sʌdn/ D4

suggestion /sə'dʒestʃən/ A5

suit (noun) /suːt/ B4

suitable /'suːtəbl/ A5

suitcase /'suːtkeɪs/ B8

summer /'sʌmə(r)/ E1

sun /sʌn/ E1

sunny /'sʌni/ E1

sunshine /'sʌnʃaɪn/ A2, E1

supper /'sʌpə(r)/ E3

supply (sth; sbdy with sth) /sə'plaɪ/ E7

sure /ʃɔː(r)/ B3

Sure (informal agreement) /ʃɔː(r)/ A7

surprise: I'd be surprised if ... /sə'praɪzd/ C7

surprised /sə'praɪzd/ C7

survive /sə'vaɪv/ E7

swimming /'swɪmɪŋ/ A6

swimming pool /'swɪmɪŋ puːl/ D5

swing* (verb) /swɪŋ/ B6

switch (noun) /swɪtʃ/ C2

switch (verb) /swɪtʃ/ A8

switch off /'swɪtʃ 'ɒf/ B6, C2

switch on /'swɪtʃ 'ɒn/ B6, C2

T-shirt /'tiː ʃɜːt/ E6

tablet /'tæblɪt/ D7

take* the first left / second right / etc. /teɪk/ D5

take* (sth) up /'teɪk ... 'ʌp/ A8

take* part in /'teɪk 'pɑːt ɪn/ A8

talk (sth) over /'tɔːk ... 'əʊvə(r)/ C7

tall /tɔːl/ A1

taste (verb) /teɪst/ B8

tax /tæks/ B3

tea: make (a cup of) tea /'meɪk 'tiː/ C1

teach* /tiːtʃ/ E5

tear* /teə(r)/ B6

technical manual /'teknɪkl 'mænjuːʊl/ A5

tell* /tel/ D7

tell* lies /'tel 'laɪz/ B3

tell*: Can you tell me the way to ...? /'kæn ju: 'tel miː/ D5

temperature /'temprɪtʃə(r)/ E1

tend /tend/ A4

tennis /'tenɪs/ A6, D6

tent /tent/ E3

terrible /'terəbl/ B1, E2

Thank you for coming /'θæŋk juː/ B7

Thanks /θæŋks/ A7, E5

thanks: Yeah, thanks /'jeə 'θæŋks/ A7

That would be very nice /naɪs/ A7

That's all right /'ðæts 'ɔːl 'raɪt/ A7, C5

That's right /'ðæts 'raɪt/ B5

That's very kind of you /kaɪnd/ A7, E5

That's very nice of you /naɪs/ A7

That's very strange /streɪndʒ/ C5

the (1930)s /'naɪntiːn 'θɜːtɪz/ E3

the other night /ði 'ʌðə 'naɪt/ D4

the thing is /ðe 'θɪŋ 'ɪz/ A7

the whole time /ðə 'həʊl 'taɪm/ D7

theatre /'θɪətə(r)/ D5

There's nothing wrong in ...ing /'nʌθɪŋ 'rɒŋ/ C7

thief (thieves) /θiːf, θiːvz/ B4

thin /θɪn/ A1

thing /θɪŋ/ B8

think* about sbdy/sth /'θɪŋk ə'baʊt/ D6

thirdly /'θɜːdli/ C5

this way (instruction) /'ðɪs 'weɪ/ A7

threaten /'θretn/ D1, E7

throat: a sore throat /'sɔː 'θrəʊt/ D7

through (preposition) /θruː/ D5

through: go through a red light /'gəʊ 'θruː/ D8

throw* /θrəʊ/ B6, D6

thumb /θʌm/ A2

thunder /'θʌndə(r)/ A2, E1

thunderstorm /'θʌndəstɔːm/ C3, E1

ticket /'tɪkɪt/ B3

tidy (adjective) /'taɪdi/ C1

tidy (verb) /'taɪdi/ B8

141

142

Acknowledgements

The authors and publishers are grateful to the following copyright owners for permission to reproduce photographs, illustrations, text and music. Every endeavour has been made to contact copyright owners and apologies are expressed for any omissions.

page 20: from the *Longman Active Study Dictionary of English* edited by Della Summers. Longman 1983. page 24: Exercise 5 from *Discussions that Work* by Penny Ur, Cambridge University Press 1981. page 24: 'Buckets of Money' advertisement reproduced by permission of Glo-Leisure Ltd. page 25: "Now if the passengers ..." from *Weekend Book of Jokes 22*, reprinted by permission of Harmsworth Publications. "How to eat while reading" and "Your bath's ready, dear" reproduced by permission of *Punch*. page 27: William Davis' article reproduced by permission of *Punch*. page 29: SOS Emergency calls panel reproduced by permission of BT. page 33: "Souvenirs" and "Don't lie to me" reproduced by permission of *Punch*. page 43: 'Elephants are Different to Different People' from *The Complete Poems of Carl Sandburg*, Revised and Expanded Edition, copyright 1950 by Carl Sandburg and renewed 1978 by Margaret Sandburg, Helga Sandburg Crile and Janet Sandburg, reprinted by permission of Harcourt Brace Jovanovich, Inc. page 47: Exercise 9 from *Discussions that Work* by Penny Ur, Cambridge University Press 1981. page 49: The extract from *Family News*, by Joan Barfoot, reprinted by arrangement with The Women's Press, Macmillan of Canada and Bella Pomer Agency Inc. page 60: cartoon reproduced by permission of *Punch*. page 65: from the *Longman Active Study Dictionary of English* edited by Della Summers, Longman 1983. page 69: cartoons reproduced by permission of *Punch*. page 85: "It's a pity ..." by Gax from *Weekend Book of Jokes 21* reprinted by permission of Harmsworth Publications. "I wish you'd called me sooner" reproduced by permission of *Punch*. page 91: 'Meditatio', taken from *Collected Shorter Poems* by Ezra Pound, published by Faber & Faber Ltd; and from *Personae*, copyright 1926 by Ezra Pound. Reprinted by permission of New Directions Publishing Corporation. page 93: 'Fag end of the evening' article reproduced by permission of United Press International Ltd. page 100: magazine covers reprinted by permission of IPC Magazines Ltd. page 101: recording for Exercise 4 and page 114: recording for Exercise 1 by permission of GWR-FM Radio, a commercial radio station covering part of the South West of England. Weather report (Exercise 1) also by permission of the Met. Office, Bristol Weather Centre. page 104: "The postman's in one of his moods again" reprinted by permission of Harmsworth Publications. page 105: Exercise 7 from *A Way with Words 1* by Stuart Redman and Robert Ellis, Cambridge University Press 1989. page 114: "Today's Special", "Good morning, Mr Dolby!" and "The committee on women's rights" reproduced by permission of *Punch*. page 117: "Come in, Ferguson" reproduced by permission of *Punch*. page 121: "No, he's not ours!" reproduced by permission of *Punch*. page 129: "You were the World's Best Baby" and "The best thing about working here" reproduced by permission of *Punch*. page 134: 'Little old lady in knife raid' report from the *Oxford Mail*, by permission.

Steve Hall (music and lyrics) for *Private Detective* (Lesson A1, Exercise 6, page 7); *Do you know* (Lesson B8, Exercise 5, page 43); *So near yet so far* (Lesson D3, Exercise 8, page 77); *Thirty degrees* (Lesson E1, Exercise 8, page 95). Jonathan Dykes (lyrics) and Robert Campbell (music) for *The Island* (Lesson D5, Exercise 8, page 81).

The authors and publishers are grateful to the following illustrators and photographic sources:

Kathy Baxendale, pages 6, 31*t*, 47, 53, 86, 92. Peter Byatt, pages 42 and 43, 74, 80*t*, 83, 101. Celia Chester, pages 31*b*, 52, 59, 97. Anthony Colbert, page 54. Tony Coles (*John Hodgson*), pages 17, 28, 35, 50, 51, 75, 87. Katherine Dickinson, pages 34 and 35. David Downton, pages 39, 72 and 73, 76 and 77. Andrew Harris, page 96. Lorraine Harrison, pages 81, 94, 95. Sue Hillwood Harris, pages 62, 78. Nigel Hawtin, page 106. Kiki Lewis (*Meiklejohn*), pages 8 and 9. Edward McLachlan, pages 14, 55, 80*c*. Michael Ogden, pages 19, 61, 114. Caroline Porter, pages 108 and 109. Felicity Roma Bowers, pages 12 and 13. Chris Ryley, pages 7, 116, 119, 122, 125, 127. Peter Sutton, pages 98 and 99. Peter Tucker, page 57. Kathy Ward, pages 16, 36 and 37, 40 and 41, 102 and 103. Jack Wood, page 80*b*.

Allsport UK Ltd, page 90*l*. Animal Photography, page 90*b*. The Bettman Archive, page 64*t*. John Birdsall, page 56*tr*. Kevin Burton, page 21*b*. Andrew Campbell, page 20*c*. Central Office of Information: page 64*b*. Garrard and Co. Ltd, page 10*t*, 90*r*. Susan Griggs Agency, pages 20 and 21. The Image Bank, page 11, 56*tl*. The Image Bank / Stockphotos, page 10*b*, 90*c*. Peter Jordan / Network, page 56*br*. The Photographer's Library, page 107. Pictor International, pages 64 and 65, 106. Picturepoint-London, page 86. Popperfoto, page 56*bl*. Graham Portlock, pages 6 and 7, 15, 69, 82, 100 and 101, 108 and 109. John Ridley, pages 18, 55, 58, 59, 105. Rolls-Royce Motor Cars Ltd, page 10*c*.

Picture research by Sandie Huskinson-Rolfe (PHOTO-SEEKERS)
Photographs on pages 6 and 7, 15, 108 and 109 taken on location at the Bell School of Languages, Cambridge.

(*t* = top   *b* = bottom   *c* = centre   *r* = right   *l* = left)

Phonetic symbols

Vowels

symbol	example
/iː/	eat /iːt/
/i/	happy /ˈhæpi/
/ɪ/	it /ɪt/
/e/	when /wen/
/æ/	cat /kæt/
/ɑː/	hard /hɑːd/
/ɒ/	not /nɒt/
/ɔː/	sort /sɔːt/; all /ɔːl/
/ʊ/	look /lʊk/
/uː/	too /tuː/
/ʌ/	cup /kʌp/
/ɜː/	first /fɜːst/; burn /bɜːn/
/ə/	about /əˈbaʊt/; mother /ˈmʌðə(r)/
/eɪ/	day /deɪ/
/aɪ/	my /maɪ/
/ɔɪ/	boy /bɔɪ/
/aʊ/	now /naʊ/
/əʊ/	go /gəʊ/
/ɪə/	here /hɪə(r)/
/eə/	chair /tʃeə(r)/
/ʊə/	tourist /ˈtʊərɪst/

Consonants

symbol	example
/p/	pen /pen/
/b/	big /bɪg/
/t/	two /tuː/
/d/	day /deɪ/
/k/	keep /kiːp/; cup /kʌp/
/g/	get /get/
/tʃ/	choose /tʃuːz/
/dʒ/	job /dʒɒb/; average /ˈævrɪdʒ/
/f/	fall /fɔːl/
/v/	very /ˈveri/
/θ/	think /θɪŋk/
/ð/	then /ðen/
/s/	see /siː/
/z/	zoo /zuː/; is /ɪz/
/ʃ/	shop /ʃɒp/; directions /dəˈrekʃənz/
/ʒ/	pleasure /ˈpleʒə(r)/; occasionally /əˈkeɪʒənli/
/h/	who /huː/; how /haʊ/
/m/	meet /miːt/
/n/	no /nəʊ/
/ŋ/	sing /sɪŋ/; drink /drɪŋk/
/l/	long /lɒŋ/
/r/	right /raɪt/
/j/	yes /jes/
/w/	will /wɪl/

Stress

Stress is shown by a mark (ˈ) in front of the stressed syllable.

mother /ˈmʌðə(r)/   **average** /ˈævrɪdʒ/

about /əˈbaʊt/   **tonight** /təˈnaɪt/

Irregular verbs

Infinitive	Simple Past	Participle
be /biː/	was /wəz, wɒz/, were /wə(r), wɜː(r)/	been /bɪn, biːn/
become /bɪˈkʌm/	became /bɪˈkeɪm/	become /bɪˈkʌm/
begin /bɪˈgɪn/	began /bɪˈgæn/	begun /bɪˈgʌn/
bend /bend/	bent /bent/	bent /bent/
bet /bet/	bet /bet/	bet /bet/
bite /baɪt/	bit /bɪt/	bitten /ˈbɪtn/
bleed /bliːd/	bled /bled/	bled /bled/
blow /bləʊ/	blew /bluː/	blown /bləʊn/
break /breɪk/	broke /brəʊk/	broken /ˈbrəʊkn/
bring /brɪŋ/	brought /brɔːt/	brought /brɔːt/
build /bɪld/	built /bɪlt/	built /bɪlt/
burn /bɜːn/	burnt /bɜːnt/	burnt /bɜːnt/
buy /baɪ/	bought /bɔːt/	bought /bɔːt/
can /k(ə)n, kæn/	could /kʊd/	been able /bɪn ˈeɪbl/
catch /kætʃ/	caught /kɔːt/	caught /kɔːt/
choose /tʃuːz/	chose /tʃəʊz/	chosen /ˈtʃəʊzn/
come /kʌm/	came /keɪm/	come /kʌm/
cost /kɒst/	cost /kɒst/	cost /kɒst/
cut /kʌt/	cut /kʌt/	cut /kʌt/
do /dʊ, də, duː/	did /dɪd/	done /dʌn/
draw /drɔː/	drew /druː/	drawn /drɔːn/
dream /driːm/	dreamt /dremt/	dreamt /dremt/
drink /drɪŋk/	drank /dræŋk/	drunk /drʌŋk/
drive /draɪv/	drove /drəʊv/	driven /ˈdrɪvn/
eat /iːt/	ate /et/	eaten /ˈiːtn/
earn /ɜːn/	earnt /ɜːnt/	earnt /ɜːnt/
fall /fɔːl/	fell /fel/	fallen /ˈfɔːlən/
feed /fiːd/	fed /fed/	fed /fed/
feel /fiːl/	felt /felt/	felt /felt/
fight /faɪt/	fought /fɔːt/	fought /fɔːt/
find /faɪnd/	found /faʊnd/	found /faʊnd/
fly /flaɪ/	flew /fluː/	flown /fləʊn/
forget /fəˈget/	forgot /fəˈgɒt/	forgotten /fəˈgɒtn/
get /get/	got /gɒt/	got /gɒt/
give /gɪv/	gave /geɪv/	given /ˈgɪvn/
go /gəʊ/	went /went/	gone /gɒn/, been /bɪn, biːn/
grow /grəʊ/	grew /gruː/	grown /grəʊn/
hang up /ˈhæŋ ˈʌp/	hung up /ˈhʌŋ ˈʌp/	hung up /ˈhʌŋ ˈʌp/
have /(h)əv, hæv/	had /(h)əd, hæd/	had /hæd/
hear /hɪə(r)/	heard /hɜːd/	heard /hɜːd/
hide /haɪd/	hid /hɪd/	hidden /ˈhɪdn/
hit /hɪt/	hit /hɪt/	hit /hɪt/
hold /həʊld/	held /held/	held /held/
hurt /hɜːt/	hurt /hɜːt/	hurt /hɜːt/
keep /kiːp/	kept /kept/	kept /kept/
know /nəʊ/	knew /njuː/	known /nəʊn/
lead /liːd/	led /led/	led /led/
learn /lɜːn/	learnt /lɜːnt/	learnt /lɜːnt/
leave /liːv/	left /left/	left /left/
lend /lend/	lent /lent/	lent /lent/
lie /laɪ/	lay /leɪ/	lain /leɪn/
lose /luːz/	lost /lɒst/	lost /lɒst/
make /meɪk/	made /meɪd/	made /meɪd/
mean /miːn/	meant /ment/	meant /ment/
meet /miːt/	met /met/	met /met/
must /məst, mʌst/	had to /ˈhæd tə/	had to /ˈhæd tə/
overtake /ˈəʊvəˈteɪk/	overtook /ˈəʊvəˈtʊk/	overtaken /ˈəʊvəˈteɪkn/
pay /peɪ/	paid /peɪd/	paid /peɪd/
put /pʊt/	put /pʊt/	put /pʊt/
read /riːd/	read /red/	read /red/
rebuild /ˈriːˈbɪld/	rebuilt /ˈriːˈbɪlt/	rebuilt /ˈriːˈbɪlt/

Infinitive	Simple Past	Participle
ride /raɪd/	rode /rəʊd/	ridden /'rɪdn/
ring /rɪŋ/	rang /ræŋ/	rung /rʌŋ/
rise /raɪz/	rose /rəʊz/	risen /'rɪzn/
run /rʌn/	ran /ræn/	run /rʌn/
say /seɪ/	said /sed/	said /sed/
see /siː/	saw /sɔː/	seen /siːn/
sell /sel/	sold /səʊld/	sold /səʊld/
send /send/	sent /sent/	sent /sent/
shake /ʃeɪk/	shook /ʃʊk/	shaken /'ʃeɪkn/
shine /ʃaɪn/	shone /ʃɒn/	shone /ʃɒn/
show /ʃəʊ/	showed /ʃəʊd/	shown /ʃəʊn/
shut /ʃʌt/	shut /ʃʌt/	shut /ʃʌt/
sing /sɪŋ/	sang /sæŋ/	sung /sʌŋ/
sit /sɪt/	sat /sæt/	sat /sæt/
sleep /sliːp/	slept /slept/	slept /slept/
smell /smel/	smelt /smelt/	smelt /smelt/
speak /spiːk/	spoke /spəʊk/	spoken /'spəʊkn/
spell /spel/	spelt /spelt/	spelt /spelt/
spend /spend/	spent /spent/	spent /spent/
stand /stænd/	stood /stʊd/	stood /stʊd/
steal /stiːl/	stole /stəʊl/	stolen /'stəʊlən/
swim /swɪm/	swam /swæm/	swum /swʌm/
swing /swɪŋ/	swung /swʌŋ/	swung /swʌŋ/
take /teɪk/	took /tʊk/	taken /'teɪkn/
teach /tiːtʃ/	taught /tɔːt/	taught /tɔːt/
tear /teə(r)/	tore /tɔː(r)/	torn /tɔːn/
tell /tel/	told /təʊld/	told /təʊld/
think /θɪŋk/	thought /θɔːt/	thought /θɔːt/
throw /θrəʊ/	threw /θruː/	thrown /θrəʊn/
understand /ʌndə'stænd/	understood /ʌndə'stʊd/	understood /ʌndə'stʊd/
wake up /'weɪk 'ʌp/	woke up /'wəʊk 'ʌp/	woken up /'wəʊkn 'ʌp/
wear /weə(r)/	wore /wɔː(r)/	worn /wɔːn/
will /wɪl/	would /wʊd/	–
win /wɪn/	won /wʌn/	won /wʌn/
write /raɪt/	wrote /rəʊt/	written /'rɪtn/

Tapescripts and answers

Lesson A8, Exercise 6

INTERVIEWER: I wonder if you could tell me – what is dressage exactly?

MRS BURTON: Dressage is erm, movements on a horse that are very precise, erm, the set movements erm, that you would do in a particular pattern. Erm, without actually seeing a horse doing dressage it's, it's quite difficult but it is in the … it's the way that the horse moves front legs and back legs together, it's nothing like walking, trotting or cantering, it's erm, sort of turning circles and walking backwards, and a bit like free skating on a horse.

INTERVIEWER: What first attracted you to this sport?

MRS BURTON: Erm, I was more attracted to cross country on horseback rather than dressage, but erm, there's no competitions for erm, disabled riders in erm, horse riding anything other than dressage and so, being naturally a competitive sort of person, erm, I turned to dressage.

INTERVIEWER: And you've been in quite a few competitions?

MRS BURTON: Yeah. I've never, never got anywhere be-, because all the disabled are together, so you've got people with perhaps a club foot or one hand competing against erm, mentally handicapped and blind and deaf; and so all the advantages and disadvantages are, are so varied, and (clears throat) I'm afraid that the blind never do very well in the competitions.

INTERVIEWER: How often do you work with your horse?

MRS BURTON: I've just started riding again after about eighteen months of not riding at all and I only ride once a week. I don't have my own horse any more erm, because that was just too much like hard work really. Erm, I'd always got to rely on somebody else to be there to take me or to ride out with me, so I find it much easier now to go to the erm, Riding for the Disabled and ride there once a week.

INTERVIEWER: Erm, wh-, what do you think has been your most exciting moment in, in … dressage?

MRS BURTON: Riding at Olympia. Erm (Oh!), in front of, I think it was about 40,000 people. It was a massive crowd and it was at the International Horse Show. And the disabled had erm, a sort of ten minutes' spot right at the end and I was given the pleasure of riding the dressage and that was absolutely amazing, it really was, … er, sent tingles all the way down me spine, it was wonderful, and the horse was just brilliant. I rode erm, an intermediate dressage horse and she was absolutely fantastic.

INTERVIEWER: What, what do you enjoy most about the dressage?

MRS BURTON: Erm …

MR BURTON: Competition.

MRS BURTON: The compe-, yeah, it's got to be the competing. Erm, it would be nice if I could see to do it properly but, erm, dressing up, being all smart and the horse being plaited up and being out there and just looking nice and trying to get it right.

INTERVIEWER: Hmm. What do you, what, what's the most difficult thing, then, about dressage, do you think, for you?

MRS BURTON: Erm … It's the preciseness of the movements just … Erm, because I can't see, everything has to be done by feel and the feel that I would get is from the seat, so it's feeling through me legs and me hips and me back and it's very difficult to analyse the feel until it's too late to do anything about it if the horse's done something wrong. So you've got to be very quiet and concentrate a lot on what you do.

INTERVIEWER: And so how did you learn that? I mean initially you didn't, you didn't know what you were feeling for. How did, how, how did you learn to, to feel that?

MRS BURTON: Through practice. Erm … before you can start to do dressage you've got to be a competent rider, you've got to understand the feel of the horse and riding is, … position is all done by feel, erm, you only really use your eyes when you're looking for direction. So the actual stopping on the horse is all done with feel through the body.

Lesson C8, Exercises 1 and 6

	Britain	The USA
consists of	4 countries; each is divided into counties	50 states; each is divided into counties
is governed from	London	*Washington, D.C.*
Laws are made by	*Parliament*	*Congress*
which consists of	House of Commons and House of Lords	*House of Representatives and Senate*
Members are called	*Members of Parliament ('MPs') (Commons)*	*Representatives or Congressmen/women; Senators*
They are elected	every 5 years or less (Commons)	*Representatives: every 2 years; Senators: every six years*
Head of government is called	*Prime Minister ('PM')*	*President*
Is head of government separately elected?	No; leader of majority party in House of Commons becomes PM	*Yes, every 4 years*
Real power is held by	PM and his/her ministers ('cabinet')	*both Congress and the President*
Do local or regional government bodies have any power?	partly responsible for education, health care, police, roads	*states have a lot of power and independence, including making laws*
How many large political parties are there?	three: Labour (*left*-wing), Conservatives (right-wing) and Liberal Democrats (centre)	*two: Democrats (rather left-wing) and Republicans (right-wing)*
Ceremonial head of state?	King or *Queen*	*no*

Lesson C8, Exercises 3 to 5

The USA – the United States of America – is a federation of fifty states. Forty-eight of these states are in the same general area, between Canada in the north and Mexico in the south. The other two states are geographically separate: Alaska is in the extreme north-west of the American continent, and Hawaii is in the middle of the Pacific Ocean. The federal capital is Washington, D.C., south of New York near the east coast.

Washington is the centre of federal government, but each state has its own capital and its own government. State governments have a large amount of power and independence: they make their own laws, and they're also responsible for education, for the state police force, for the prison system, for road-building and many other things.

Federal laws are made by Congress, which is the equivalent of the British Parliament. There are two 'houses': the House of Representatives and the Senate. Each state sends representatives and senators to Congress. Elections to the House of Representatives are held every two years, while Senators are elected for a six-year period.

The President is elected separately, together with the Vice-President. They serve for a term of four years. The President chooses the people who will form the cabinet. These do not have to be elected members of Congress – they can be brought in from outside Congress – but the Senate must approve their appointment. Power is shared between the President and Congress, and if the President belongs to the minority party in Congress, it can cause problems.

There are two main political parties in the United States: the Democrats and the Republicans. The Democrats are slightly more to the left than the Republicans, but the differences between their policies are not usually very great.

The United States does not have a separate ceremonial Head of State.

Test C, Exercise 1

The Republic of Ireland – Éire in Irish – consists of four provinces; / each province is divided into counties. / Ireland is located in the Atlantic Ocean, to the west of Great Britain. / The national language is Irish, and English is recognised as a second official language. / The central government in Dublin is powerful, but local authorities are partly responsible for education, health care, roads, housing, and so on. /

Laws are made by the National Parliament, which consists of two houses, a House of Representatives and a Senate. / Representatives are elected every five years; some Senators are elected as well, and some are appointed by the Prime Minister (who is elected by the House of Representatives). / The President is mainly a ceremonial head of state, but has some political power; he or she is elected separately for a term of seven years. / Real power is held by the Prime Minister, who chooses the members of the cabinet – but the House of Representatives must approve their appointment. /

There are four main political parties, Fianna Fáil, Fine Gael, the Progressive Democrats and the Labour Party. / Fianna Fáil and Fine Gael are much bigger than the other parties, but not usually big enough to have a majority in Parliament; so one of them must usually join with one of the other parties to form a government. / Fianna Fáil and Fine Gael are both fairly right-wing; / Fianna Fáil is more religious and has more voters in the country while Fine Gael is not religious and has more voters in the cities. /

Lesson D3, Exercise 7

1

JOHN: No, I wou-, I wouldn't like to have more. I got two and I think two is, er, just right.

KEITH: I find occasionally I've earn, well, yearnings, should I say, not earnings, (*laughter*) to erm, have, it would be nice to have another baby, (*Hm-hm*) and, but there are occasions again when it's... would be better without any children at all.

SUE: I, I have no yearnings to have more children at all; I'm quite happy with the two. But like you, there are times when I could do without them. (*laughter*) Very much.

2

JANE: Send them on their own! (*laughter*)

JOHN: Yeah, I think it'd be a great idea to give them the money and let them have a holiday on their own. (*Mm*)

KEITH: As my parents live separately, it could work out quite expensive. (*laughter*)

SUE: I'd rather give them the money, I think, to have a holiday on their own.

JANE: I don't think my parents would go! (*laughter*)

3

SUE: I'm quite happy with what I've got. (*Hm-hm*)

JANE: I always rather fancied an elder brother, but I couldn't arrange it. I thought (*laughter*)

JOHN: Yeah, I think... Yeah, I think our family's about right, but, er, I mean, I hardly ever see them anyway, you know, so ... (*Mm*) I would think if I was living up there, and seeing them every day, every night or whatever, might get a bit put out, you know, with being three brothers and two sisters. But I don't know, ah, it's all right as it is.

MIKE: Can I have the same number but change them? (*laughter*)

4

JOHN: Oh, have them when you're young. Get it over with. (*laughter*)

SUE: I think late twenties is a good age.

ALEX: Yeah. (*Mm-hm*) About twenty-seven, twenty-eight (*Mm*), and then that's, you've had your youth and y, and your enjoyment of everything and met lots of young people, and then, (*laughter*), and then settle down.

KEITH: I think it's reasonably nice to have them youngish. (*Yeah*)

JANE: I think you've got to have a bit of experience of life (*Mm*) beforehand. I wouldn't want, I wouldn't have wanted to go straight from school to having children.

MIKE: I had my first children in my mid-twenties and I think I was, I was too young really, wasn't mature enough. And er, now with Mark erm, I feel fine, just, just about the right age to have a child.

SUE: The answer is, I think, not to, well, if there is an answer, is not to have children until you feel you're ready, no matter what anybody says to you.

5

KEITH: I think I'd prefer to have more time at home. My, my day tends to be a twelve-hour day. And part – after that it's sleeping. It seems to be throughout the week it's getting up, going to work, going to bed; getting up, going to work, you know... (*Mm*) I'd rather see more, I think.

JANE: I think I probably see enough of them.

MIKE: Well, I work at home so I, I already see plenty of my family. I'd certainly like to work less.

Lesson D7, Exercise 1

(Answers are in *italics*.)

A

D: Where does it hurt?
P: Just here, doctor.
D: *I see. Does it hurt* all the time?
P: No. Only when I *run,* or when I'm going *up*stairs. Sometimes when I carry things.
D: When you carry things. *Heavy* things?
P: Yes.
D: *Right.* Now I want you to stand up ...

B

D: How often do you get them?
P: Oh, *two* or *three* times a week.
D: *Two* or *three* times a week. I see. Are they very bad?
P: Oh, yes. They stop me *working.* Sometimes I can hardly see, you know.
D: Yes. Do you *ever* get *hay fever?*

C

P: It's a really bad cough. It *hurts.*
D: Does it hurt when you *breathe?*
P: If I *breathe deeply*, yes.
D: I see. Well, I'll just have a *listen* to your chest. Do you *smoke?*

D

P: It's a really bad pain, doctor. *Down* here.
D: Which side?
P: *This* side.
D: How long has this been going on? When did it start?
P: *Yesterday* morning, doctor. I thought perhaps it was indigestion, but it's too *bad* for that.
D: *All right.* Now just *lie* down here. That's right. Now *where* exactly does it hurt? Is it here?
P: Ooh! Yes!

E

D: Good morning, *Mrs* Palmer. What's the *problem?*
P: Well, I've got a *bad* sore throat, *doctor.*
D: *Oh, dear.* How long have you had it?
P: Oh, about *a week.* It's *getting* very painful. It's difficult to *eat.*

F

P: It's every *year* about the same time, doctor. Stuffed-up nose, my *eyes* itch, and I feel sort of *funny* the whole time.
D: Is it *worse* when you're inside or outside?
P: When I'm in the *garden.*

G

P: I get this *pain* when I bend *over,* doctor. Just here.
D: I see. Take your *shirt* off.

151

Lesson D8, Exercise 6

1. The time that I recall that was, er, gave me a bit of a *frisson* if you like was er, I was, er, I think I was up at university, and I was down in London at my parents' flat, and I'd been out er, moderately late, and drove er, a little Mini car back er, to the flat, which was in a rather smart part of London, and er, you had to park the car under the block of flats in an underground car park. And I did this one night and I noticed out of the corner of my eye that there was a car parked opposite, sort of in a right-angled road, er, facing the, the opening of the basement er, car park. And er, but I didn't pay any attention to it, I got out of the car as usual and went to see the er, night porter, and er, he saw me, recognised me, came to the door, and at that moment the doors flung open, and just like a TV, in a TV series, er, these plainclothes people whipped out their wallets and showed, showed their er, showed their badges and said, 'Just a moment,' you know, you know, and all that sort of stuff, and you had to sort of, in there, and you thought, 'This is, this is ridiculous,' you know, 'this is r-, this is, I mean, this, this can't be serious,' but they were very serious, and they sort of almost frog-marched me to the car and asked me all these usual details, about did I know what licence number it was, how many miles I'd gone, and they took some persuading that someone looking as scruffy as I in a tiny little Mini could possibly live in such a smart block of flats.

2. The time I remember was when Piers was quite tiny and for some long-forgotten reason Peter and I were over to some friends in Burton-on-Trent, and we were in separate cars. And I was trying to follow quite closely to, behind Peter, but er, he always says I leave too much space, and so I did when he went through some traffic lights on green, and I thought, 'If I speed up a little bit I'll just get through.' And I didn't, and what I hadn't noticed was that the only other car on the road, directly behind me, was a police car, and he saw me go through the light on amber/red, I thought, but he thought it was red, so he followed us round the corner onto the bridge, overtook, stopped, and I sat tight in my car while Pete leapt out and defended me, and er, we said that we didn't want to make a noise because the baby was asleep in the back, but er, we didn't get away with it, and I did get my licence endorsed.

3. Yeah, I was driving back from France erm, years ago, and it had been a long drive, and I'd had a fairly depressing experience in France, and I was driving as fast as I could through the west London suburbs to get home, and erm, I'd got this hot jazz blasting out of the erm, car cassette player at enormous volume, and erm, as I pulled up at a traffic light I saw this large white car pull up beside me, and I played back things in my mind and I realised that I had just overtaken a police car at 50 miles an hour in a 30 limit. And the policeman wound down his window, I wound down mine, and I was too perturbed to turn off the jazz. And he looked at me, and he listened to this noise coming out of the car, and he looked at me again, and he said, 'You must be bloody crazy!' And the lights changed to green and he drove off.

Index of structures, notions and functional/situational language

(References are to lessons; GR = Grammar Revision Section.)

154

DATE DUE